AF449149

Immigration and Labor Market Mobility in Israel, 1990 to 2009

Immigration and Labor Market Mobility in Israel, 1990 to 2009

Sarit Cohen Goldner, Zvi Eckstein, and Yoram Weiss

The MIT Press
Cambridge, Massachusetts
London, England

MIT Press books may be purchased at special quantity discounts for business or sales promotional use. For information, please email special_sales@mitpress.mit.edu or write to Special Sales Department, The MIT Press, 55 Hayward Street, Cambridge, MA 02142.

Related material for this book, including tables, figures, data, and programs, can be found at http://www.tau.ac.il/~eckstein/immigrants.html.

This book was set in Times Roman by Toppan Best-set Premedia Limited. Printed and bound in the United States of America.

Library of Congress Cataloging-in-Publication Data

Cohen Goldner, Sarit.
Immigration and labor market mobility in Israel, 1990 to 2009 / Sarit Cohen Goldner, Zvi Eckstein, and Yoram Weiss.
    p. cm.
Includes bibliographical references and index.
ISBN 978-0-262-01767-1 (hardcover : alk. paper)
1. Labor market—Israel. 2. Foreign workers, Russian—Israel. 3. Israel—Emigration and immigration—Economic conditions. 4. Immigrants—Israel—Economic conditions. I. Eckstein, Zvi. II. Weiss, Yoram. III. Title.
HD5812.2.A6C64   2012
331.12′909569409049—dc23
2011048965

10 9 8 7 6 5 4 3 2 1

Contents

Related material for this book, including tables, figures, data, and programs, can be found at http://www.tau.ac.il/~eckstein/immigrants.html.

List of Figures

Acknowledgments

This book is the outcome of fifteen years of data gathering and research led by Zvi Eckstein and Yoram Weiss. The project includes several research papers and the PhD dissertations of Chemi Gotlibovski (1997) and Sarit Cohen Goldner (2002), most of which are included in this book. The data and original papers are available on request.

Financial support for the project came from a number of sources: the US National Institute of Child Health and Human Development grants 1 R01 HD34716-01 and 5 R01 HD34671-03; the German–Israeli Foundation for Scientific Research and Development grant I-084-118.02/95; and the Israel Science Foundation grant 884/01. Smaller grants were received from: the John M. Olin Foundation through a grant to the George J. Stigler Center for the Study of the Economy and State at the University of Chicago; the Pinhas Sapir Center for Development at Tel Aviv University; the Maurice Falk Institute for Economic Research in Israel; the Ministry of Immigrant Absorption; and the Manpower Planning Authority of the Ministry of Industry, Trade, and Labor.

The research would not have been possible without the assistance and data provided by the Myers–JDC–Brookdale Institute and their help in carrying out the additional survey in 2000 and 2001. Data from the CBS Labor Force Survey and Income Survey was provided by the Israel Social Science Data Center (ISDC) at the Hebrew University of Jerusalem.

We would also like to acknowledge the invaluable contribution of the research assistants who have been involved in the project over the years: Marina Agranov, Evgeny Agronin, Chemi Gotlibovski, Tali Larom, Osnat Lifshitz, Giovanni Oppenheim, Maria Tripolski, and Adi Zaidman. Special thanks to Tali Larom who also assisted in writing chapters 6 and 7 and organizing the text, data, and tables. David Simmer provided editing services for the book.

1 Introduction

1.1 Introduction

The unexpected collapse of the Soviet regime in 1989 led to a dramatic change in the country's emigration policy, which now permitted its citizens to emigrate freely. In particular, Jews in the former Soviet Union (FSU) were now able to immigrate to Israel without restriction. On arrival, they automatically became Israeli citizens with access to a generous package of benefits, including subsidized mortgages or rental assistance, language courses, and vocational training. They also gained access to a labor market characterized by much higher wages than those in the FSU. Over the next ten years, Israel absorbed approximately 900,000 immigrants from the FSU (which constituted about 20 percent of the Israeli population), with about 40 percent of them arriving during the first three years. The change in emigration policy was exogenous to the economic conditions in Israel and to the pre-emigration accumulation of human capital by the immigrants. As such, it provides a unique platform for evaluating basic issues in the economics of immigration.

The economic analysis of immigration (see Borjas 1999) starts with two simple questions: Why do some people immigrate? And what happens when they do? The answer to the first question is relatively clear in the case of Israel: the opportunity for higher income and the social and emotional ties of FSU Jews to Israel. The answer to the second question is more complicated and constitutes the main focus of the book. The book's main methodological innovation is the use of empirical stochastic dynamic micro models that combine search with investment in human capital. The focus of the research is on the labor market performance of immigrants in Israel. We also discuss their impact on the wages and employment of native Israelis.

The chapter begins by providing a description of the massive wave of immigration to Israel in the 1990s, which is followed by a summary of the analysis and the findings of each chapter. We conclude with some general lessons for immigration policy and research.

1.2 Background

Israel's population stood at 4.56 million at the end of 1989 and had grown at annual rates of between 1.4 and 1.8 percent during the previous ten years. The wave of immigration in 1990–91 increased the population by 7.6 percent. The most notable characteristic of this wave of FSU immigrants was the high level of education they brought with them. About 60 percent of the working-age immigrants were college educated, compared with only 30 percent of native Israeli Jews in 1990. This is also reflected in the high proportion of immigrants who had worked in scientific, academic, or white-collar occupations in the FSU (table 2.1).

Upon arrival, immigrants were entitled to a package of benefits that included a rental subsidy for a limited period and eligibility to attend a six-month Hebrew course (called an "Ulpan"). During these six months, they also received a stipend to cover living expenses, which enabled them to attend the Ulpan. At the end of the six months, immigrants could take advantage of the welfare and unemployment benefits available to natives, including access to government-sponsored vocational training programs. These programs were in part designed to modify immigrants' skills so as to more closely match those demanded by the Israeli labor market.

In general, there was minimal intervention by the government in the immigrants' choices in Israel. Thus residential location and whether to participate in the Ulpan and in government-provided vocational training courses were left to the discretion of the immigrant with minimal restrictions imposed by the government.

The fact that the option of immigrating to Israel was not readily available to FSU Jews prior to 1989 is important to our analysis since it allows us to treat the immigrant's human capital investment decision in the FSU as exogenous. In other words, an immigrant's human capital on arrival was determined in the FSU before the option of moving to Israel was even considered to be a possibility and is therefore appropriate to the labor market there. As a result there was a complete mismatch between the skill distribution of immigrants and the demand for skills in the Israeli labor market. Therefore it is not surprising that, on arrival, there was a substantial occupational downgrading of immigrants and the local labor market provided a low return on imported skills. It is only over time that immigrants were able to climb the occupational ladder and to improve their wages. We construct and estimate several dynamic models that explain the gradual adaptation of immigrants to the Israeli labor market.

The initial mismatch between the occupational distribution of immigrants and the local labor market distribution of jobs created a difficult dilemma for both the immigrants and policy makers. Should the government intervene in the labor market in order to improve outcomes for both immigrants and natives and if so how is this to be accomplished? The answer to this question depends on the speed of immigrants' adaptation to the Israeli labor market, as a result of which they became closer substitutes for comparable Israeli workers (i.e., those with the same level of schooling and work experience). The substitution between immigrants and native workers and its impact is one of the first issues we analyze in the book. We then shift our focus to the immigrants' employment and wage dynamics during their first decade in Israel.

1.3 Description of the Chapters

Chapter 2 begins with a macroeconomic analysis of the consequences of immigration based on aggregate time series data. Israel provides an interesting case study for exploring the correlation between population growth and economic growth since its population arrived for the most part in concentrated waves of immigration. According to the conventional wisdom, an increase in labor supply leads to a decline in the capital–labor ratio, the marginal productivity of labor, and per capita GDP. In contrast, this chapter presents evidence of a positive link between immigration and growth in per capita income and consumption in Israel. It is of particular interest that per capita GNP increased during every period of rapid population growth.

In this chapter we address the question of why this large wave of immigration had only a small and transitory effect on the employment and wages of native Israelis. We assume a constant returns to scale aggregate production function and consider two different types of frictions: search and costs of adjustment. Search frictions imply that immigrants are not as productive as native workers upon arrival and are only gradually sorted into jobs more suited to their skills. Their wages and productivity rose as a result of the sorting process. To account for the difference in productivity between immigrants and natives, we construct a quality-adjusted labor aggregate and calculate an adjusted capital–labor ratio. The second approach introduces a fixed cost of adjusting labor and capital into a neoclassical growth model, which is characterized by a CRS production function. By calibrating the model, we show that it provides a good fit to the observed changes in Israel's macroeconomic variables. The two approaches differ in the endogeneity of the response of capital and only according to the second method are the changes in capital and labor jointly determined. Nonetheless, the two approaches complement each other and yield similar results.

Based on the empirical evidence on wages and employment and using the two modeling approaches, we are able to conclude that the Israeli economy can be approximated by a competitive economy with a CRS production function. In this framework the wage is proportional to the marginal productivity of labor in the long run, and, hence, the impact of immigrants on natives' wages is expected to be negligible and transitory. The main focus of the following chapters is on a micro-analysis of the wage and employment dynamics among immigrants, which are associated with their investment in local human capital in the form of training, language acquisition, work experience and search strategy.

In **chapter 3** we turn to exploring the dynamics of wage growth for immigrants and the potential convergence of wages between immigrants and natives based on repeated cross-sectional data. The analysis contributes to the existing literature in several ways: First, we extend the standard human capital model by assuming that an immigrant's return on his imported human capital is an increasing function of time in the country. This assumption is based on the casual observation that upon arrival immigrants earn similar wages, regardless of their (imported) schooling level. However, as their time in the new country increases, the distribution of wages according to level of schooling becomes increasingly unequal. Second, we add occupational dynamics to the theoretical framework and the empirical analysis. Third, we formulate and estimate a nonlinear wage function that includes interactions between imported skills and local wage growth using data on native and immigrant males.

The novel aspect of the estimated model is the attempt to identify the sources of wage growth for immigrants. We distinguish between three different sources: (1) the increase in the return on imported human capital, (2) the impact of accumulated experience in the host country, and (3) the mobility up the occupational ladder in the host country. We find that the increase in the return on imported skills accounts for about half of the unconditional annual growth in wages during the first ten years in the country. Occupational transitions are important primarily for high-skilled immigrants who arrived in Israel with academic degrees and for immigrants who arrived at a young age.

The prices that immigrants receive for their imported schooling and experience are initially zero or negative. These prices rise with time spent in the host country but never reach the levels obtained by natives. As immigrants spend more time in the host country, the rate of increase in their return on imported skills declines and the contribution of occupational transitions become more important. Initially there is a substantial occupational downgrading and about half of the male immigrants with more than sixteen years of schooling work in low-skilled occupations during the first three years in Israel. However, immigrants who arrived at a relatively young age are able to move up the occupational ladder.

We compare our findings to those presented in the literature and provide some new results concerning skilled immigrants. First, we show that upon arrival immigrants receive no return on imported skills. During the ten years following arrival, the wages of high-skilled immigrants grow rapidly, which is due primarily to the rising return they receive on their imported skills. In addition there is some downgrading in the occupational distribution of immigrants relative to that of natives during this period. Moreover, the average wages of immigrants approach those of comparable natives, though they do not converge due to the low return on imported skills. The substantial gap in the return on schooling may reflect either an inherent difference in quality of schooling or frictions in the labor market that lead qualified immigrants to "give up" their search for more suitable jobs.

Immigrants who eventually find jobs in high-skilled occupations earn substantially more than those who remain in low-skilled occupations. Thus, occupational mobility is an important determinant of wage growth. This observation leads to the dynamic analysis in the next three chapters, which is based on panel data.

In **chapter 4** we discuss the following questions: (1) What generates the transition from blue-collar to white-collar jobs: the immigrants' investment in local skills via training and work experience or the availability of jobs in white-collar occupations? (2) How important are imported skills (schooling and pre-migration occupation and experience)? and (3) What is the gain from immigration?

The use of a unique panel provides novel insights into the labor market dynamics of immigrants. The panel data makes it possible to design a dynamic model of wage growth and occupational mobility that can separately identify the effects of imported and local human capital on labor mobility and earnings. We formulate dynamic discrete choice models of labor supply and investment in local skills for male and female immigrants separately. The models are based on Ben-Porath's classical model of investment in human capital and follow the specifications of Keane and Wolpin (1997) and Eckstein and Wolpin (1999). The models include two main determinants of occupational transition: (1) investment in local human capital in the form of experience, training and language, and (2) employment opportunities in two broadly defined occupation categories: white-collar and blue-collar. Within this framework we measure the individual and social benefits of government-sponsored classroom training (CT) programs.

Separate models are estimated for males and females, using quarterly panel data on immigrant employment for the five years following arrival in Israel. The main transition patterns of immigrants between different labor market states are as follows: after two quarters, during which the immigrants learn the local language, employment in blue-collar jobs increases rapidly and nonemployment drops sharply; however, employment in white-collar jobs increases at only a slow rate. Participation in training programs begins after learning the language and peaks at the end of the first year in the host country; it then slowly declines to zero. These transitions reach steady state levels after about five years in the host country and the patterns are similar for both males and females.

We find that both the qualitative and quantitative results are similar for female and male immigrants. According to the main result, the availability of white-collar job offers is relatively low and participation in a training program significantly increases white-collar job-offer probability. Hence the impact of training on job search friction is an important channel through which human capital affects labor mobility. In addition we find that training has no impact on wages in blue-collar jobs, while it has a significant impact on white-collar wages. Another important result is that conditional on the investment in local skills, the wage return on imported skills for both male and female immigrants is close to zero.

In order to measure the importance of training, we analyze several alternatives to the estimated policy of government-provided training programs. The individual benefit of each alternative policy is measured by the change in the immigrant's expected present value of utility while the social benefits are measured using simple social cost–benefit calculations. We find that providing higher availability of training to female immigrants is beneficial both for the immigrant and for society, while the same policy for males produces no benefit for society. This difference is primarily due to differences in the opportunity cost of training between males and females. For females, training is a substitute for nonemployment; that is, if she is not in a training program, she is less likely to be employed. In contrast, for males, training is a substitute for work; that is, if he is not in a training program, he is more likely to be employed (in a blue-collar job). Thus a counterfactual policy in which no training is available has the following results: (1) in the case of females, government expenditure will increase due to higher payments for unemployment benefits (since more females are now nonemployed), and (2) in the case of males, the same policy implies lower government expenditure since nonemployment (including training) decreases and the net impact is slightly negative.

In addition, the model's five-year-ahead predictions are evaluated using additional survey data that was not used in the estimation. The results show that the model's predictions of labor market employment and training patterns are consistent with the out-of-sample data, which provides strong support for the interpretation of the data provided by the model.

Finally, we compare the present value of earnings in the FSU to the present value of earnings or utility under various scenarios of integration in Israel. The results show large economic gains for FSU Jews who immigrated to Israel in 1989 to 1992, for both males and females (the expected present value of earnings in Israel is 1.5 to 2.3 times higher than that in the FSU).

Chapter 5 investigates the observed short-run adjustment process in occupational choices and wages among immigrants in order to make some long-run inferences on the loss of human capital. The chapter focuses on the potential loss of imported human capital due to the mismatch between imported skills and the skills demanded by the local market. To this end, a model of on-the-job search is constructed and then estimated using a panel of male immigrants during their first five years following arrival.

The model focuses on the process of matching between immigrants and jobs when workers differ in skills and jobs vary in their skill requirements and are considered to be arranged in a "job hierarchy" (Reder 1957). Finding a suitable job that maximizes the immigrant's output (and wages) given his schooling endowment requires job search. An immigrant who meets a particular employer will be qualified for the job only if his schooling exceeds the job's minimal schooling requirement. A high-skilled immigrant may accept job offers in a low-skilled occupation since offers in high-skilled occupations are rarer, and he can always continue to search while on the job. Generally, workers will select occupations and job acceptance rules that do not fully exploit their formal schooling. However, over time, immigrants find better matches and their wages rise.

Based on the estimates, the loss of human capital is computed, where loss is defined as the difference between expected actual lifetime earnings and expected potential lifetime earnings had the immigrant been employed in the same jobs and earned the same wages as comparable Israelis. The difference between actual earnings and potential earnings is estimated to be 57 percent of the present value of potential earnings over the immigrant's remaining working life. Nearly 75 percent of this estimated loss can be attributed to the fact that in each job, an immigrant's initial wage is only about one-third of a comparable native's. Wages of immigrants rise sharply with time in Israel but do not fully catch up with those of natives. The remaining 25 percent of the loss can be attributed to frictions associated with nonemployment and job distribution mismatch. The estimated loss is probably an upper bound estimate of the social loss associated with the transfer of human capital since an immigrant's potential earnings may fall short of a comparable native's due to differences in the quality of schooling and macro effects.

Chapter 6 assesses the effect of place of residence on immigrants' labor market outcomes. Upon arrival, immigrants choose their location of residence as well as their first job. Location can either be in the Center or on the Periphery, where the Center consists of towns in a given close radius of the three major metropolitan centers in Israel and the Periphery includes the rest. Needless to say, these two decisions are interrelated. According to Israeli immigration policy, each FSU immigrant household is free to choose his place of residence and is provided with a package of benefits that includes a rent subsidy. The analysis in this chapter focuses on the effect of the government's housing policy on the immigrants' choice of residence and their initial occupational integration.

A model is constructed that combines the job search decision with the choice of place of residence and employment. The model implies that relatively cheap housing in a given area may compensate the immigrant for poor job prospects there. The results indicate that an immigrant attributes greater weight to housing costs and labor market characteristics in each area than to nonmonetary characteristics.

Similar to the findings in the other chapters, we find that immigrants in scientific and academic occupations have difficulty finding appropriate jobs due to the small number of relevant job offers. This scarcity of job offers for these occupations is particularly noticeable in the Periphery relative to the Center. Moreover a difference of approximately 15 percent was found between wages offered in the Center and those offered for similar jobs in the Periphery. As a result the estimated model predicts that on the one hand, immigrants with an academic or technical education will tend to live in the Center and search for their first job in low-skilled occupations. On the other hand, immigrants who do not have an academic or technical education will have a greater tendency to locate in the Periphery, where they will enjoy lower housing costs and a supply of suitable jobs at least as large as that in the Center. Furthermore we find that given the housing costs and labor market conditions that existed in the early 1990s, the immigrants could expect an average wage loss of 12.3 percent relative to their potential wage. However, the simulation of an immigrant's expected wage loss given the housing costs as of 1995 indicated that the expected loss had risen to 20.5 percent.

The increased attractiveness of locating in the Periphery can be explained by, among other things, the government's policy of subsidizing housing costs in these areas, which was adopted as the wave of immigration began. According to the simulation, an alternative policy of fully subsidizing housing costs in the Periphery would had led to an increase of up to 30.2 percent in the mean expected wage loss. The simulations lead to the conclusion that although the policy of reducing housing costs in the Periphery did indeed induce immigrants to locate (and find employment) there, it had an adverse effect on their ability to fully utilize their human capital.

Chapter 7, which concludes the book, provides a descriptive summary of the integration process of the immigrants who arrived in Israel during the period 1989 to 1991, which we track for almost two decades, until 2009. It is shown that most of the wage dynamics and occupational mobility took place in the early years. In the longer run, immigrants had higher participation rates and lower unemployment than comparable native Israelis. However, their wages did not converge to those of comparable native Israelis. This is explained by the facts that immigrants earned less than natives in the same type of job and that some highly educated immigrants failed to find a white-collar job suited to their level of education. For instance, male immigrants who arrived from the FSU in 1990–91 aged 25 to 40 with a college degree who worked in a white-collar job in 2008 earned about 29 percent less than comparable native Israelis. Furthermore only 56 percent of these immigrants had a white-collar job in 2008, as compared to 74 percent of native Israelis with the same age and education profile. Consequently, on average, college-educated immigrants who arrived in 1990–91 aged 25 to 40 earned 42 percent less than comparable natives in 2008. Immigrants who arrived at an older age display a slower rate of occupational upgrading. Thus among immigrants who arrived between the age of 41 and 55 with a college degree, only 41 percent worked in a white-collar occupation after 19 years in Israel.

The total growth rates in wages of men over the period 1992 to 2008 were 67 percent for immigrants with a college degree (as compared to 41 percent for comparable natives) and 42 percent for immigrants without a college degree (as compared to 21 percent for comparable natives). There were also important changes in the wage distribution of immigrants over time due to occupational upgrading, which raised both the average wage and its variance among the immigrants. The explanation for these two related outcomes lies in the fact that immigrants were sorted out over time and eventually matched with jobs that better suited their local skills.

The rates of unemployment among immigrants declined continuously over time. For example, by 2009, rates of unemployment among immigrants who were aged 25 to 40 on arrival converged to between 2 and 6 percent depending on gender and education. These rates are equal to or less than those of comparable natives. In contrast to the convergence between immigrants and natives in employment, convergence is not achieved in occupation, conditioned on schooling and age. In addition immigrants who arrived at an older age display a slower rate of occupational upgrading.

Besides economic indicators, the chapter also presents broader social indicators of long-term integration, including place of residence (especially enclaves), home ownership, marriage patterns for those who married in Israel and finally the rate of out-migration. These indicators suggest that the large scale of this wave of immigration helped create a relatively supportive environment for FSU immigrants in Israel, which enabled them to continue using the Russian language and to maintain cultural traditions. Many of them arrived married while those who married in Israel tended to marry other immigrants from the FSU. This made it possible for them to avoid complete assimilation and a loss of identity. According to social surveys, immigrants from the FSU are generally satisfied with their jobs and dwellings and are characterized by about the same level of social interaction as native Israelis. In some respects they have adapted quickly to Israeli attitudes and norms. For instance, 89.5 percent of them believe that "personal contacts" are crucial in achieving economic and social success, which is also a typical belief among natives. However, even after 20 years, many of them are not fluent in Hebrew.

Finally, immigrants leaving the FSU in 1990 to 1992 had limited options in choosing a destination. Only Israel accepted FSU immigrants immediately, and in large numbers, and did not impose visa restrictions or eligibility criteria for welfare benefits. It is therefore of interest to determine whether Israel was a temporary or permanent destination for them. We show that survival rates, namely the proportion of immigrants remaining in Israel, as of 2004 for immigrants who arrived during 1990–91, conditional on them still being in Israel in 1995, are quite high. They range from 88 to 98 percent depending on age on arrival and schooling, and are very similar for men and women. The data suggests that younger immigrants are more likely to leave the country and that within the 16 to 25 and 26 to 35 age groups better-educated immigrants have a higher propensity to out-migrate.

1.4 Lessons

The main lesson to be learned from the large and unexpected wave of high-skilled immigrants from the FSU, as well as from earlier waves of immigration to Israel, is that even a very large and unanticipated wave of immigration can be integrated within the local labor market without any significant long-term adverse economic impact on natives. This was primarily achieved through an increase in the capital stock that was financed by direct foreign investment and a certain amount of government borrowing abroad. In addition the gradual matching of immigrants with high-skilled jobs mitigated the impact on wages and unemployment among natives. This gradual occupational upgrading was facilitated by the government assistance in learning the local language, vocational training in high-skilled occupations and housing subsides, with the choice of occupation and location left to the immigrant.

The mismatch between immigrants' skills and the local demand for labor is associated with frictions and search costs. The skills that the immigrants brought with them were not immediately put to their best use. We estimate that about 14 percent of the potential lifetime earnings of immigrants in Israel were lost due to nonemployment and the job distribution mismatch resulting from search frictions and other costs of adjustment.

The government assistance programs included family allowances, language courses, and vocational training, which alongside the free choice allowed to them in choice of occupation and residence, enabled immigrants to eventually upgrade to better jobs. In other words, immigrants could invest in local human capital and improve their match in the local labor market. While immigrants receive almost no return on imported human capital, the investment in local human capital enables them to adjust their imported skills to the host country's labor market. This dynamic process took about five years on average and provided an especially high rate of return for both the immigrants and the host country.

The main policy implication of the analysis is the importance of providing government assistance in the acquisition of local human capital, especially through the subsidization of vocational training. This assistance compensates for the inability of immigrants to borrow against future income without collateral. Facilitating investment in vocational training and skill conversion among high-skilled immigrants produces a high return both to the immigrants and to the host country and is an effective policy tool for integrating immigrants within the labor market.

The combination of learning by employers, the accumulation of local human capital and job search by immigrants leads to a highly nonlinear assimilation process, with upward job mobility in the early years followed by slower progress later on. It is important to note that this nonlinear process strongly depends on the immigrant's level of imported human capital. The dynamic stochastic structural models with explicit inclusion of search frictions, employer learning, and human capital provide insight into the potential gains and losses of alternative policies.

The research also provides some methodological innovations in the use of different data sources to examine the same economic phenomena. Thus use was made of aggregate data combined with dynamic macroeconomic models, as well as repeated cross-sectional data combined with dynamic simple models, in order to analyze the wage and occupational dynamics of natives and immigrants. Panel data was additionally used in dynamic stochastic models in order to analyze the complex quarter-by-quarter transition of immigrants in the labor market five to ten years after arrival. We show that a dynamic search framework combined with investment in human capital is the appropriate approach to the analysis of immigrant behavior in the labor market. Search and sorting are evidenced by several important features of the data, such as the decrease in wage variation among educated immigrants and their initially higher rate of unemployment relative to less-educated immigrants. Human capital acquisition can be seen in the positive interaction between formal training and language acquisition. Combining elements of search and human capital accumulation enables us to perform a dynamic cost–benefit analysis of policies from the perspectives of both the individual immigrant and society. This integrated approach should be useful to other researchers who wish to analyze the labor market implications of immigration.

2 The Aggregate Macroeconomic Impact of a Large Inflow of Immigrants

2.1 Introduction

Between October 1989 and the end of 2001, more than 900,000 immigrants arrived in Israel from the FSU (see table 2.1). For purposes of comparison, Israel's population at the end of 1989 was only 4.56 million. From 1989 to 1993 the population grew at an annual rate of 3.8 percent, which is almost three times the average rate (1.4 percent) of the 1980s (see table 2.2). The growth in the labor force from 1990 to 1992 was even larger and represents the most dramatic change in the Israeli economy since the 1960s.

In this chapter we summarize the aggregate time series evidence for the link between immigration, economic growth, employment, and wages. Holding other inputs constant, an increase in labor supply leads to a decline in the marginal productivity of labor and per capita GDP. Furthermore the decline in per capita GDP is even more pronounced if immigrants initially do not work or are less productive than natives. However, firms can be expected to increase their utilization of capital and their investment in response to the increase in labor supply (due to immigration). This response may offset the negative impact of immigration on per capita GDP, as well as its effect on the marginal productivity of labor.

Israel provides an interesting case study for exploring the correlation between population growth and economic growth since the latter has been based on successive waves of immigration. Table 2.2 and figure 2.1 provide a summary of the economy's main aggregate indicators since 1922.[1] The most striking insight provided by the data is that every period of population growth was characterized by growth in per capita GNP, regardless of how rapidly the population grew. Ben-Porath (1986) documented the positive correlation between immigration and per capita

Table 2.1
Immigrants from FSU by year of immigration and occupation in the FSU

		1990		1991		1992		1993		1994		1995	
		Number	Percent	Number	Percent	Number	Percent	Number	Percent	Number	Percent	Number	Percent
Total		185,227		147,839		65,093		66,145		68,079		64,847	
Aged 15+		142,944		117,395		52,037		52,569		54,706		52,382	
Worked in the FSU		a		79,743		33,696		33,141		35,145		36,338	
Occupation in the FSU[b]	1	a		31,693	39.7	12,242	36.3	10,214	30.8	11,563	32.9	11,089	30.5
	2	a		26,021	32.6	10,872	32.3	10,736	32.4	11,748	33.4	11,272	31.0
	3	a		22,029	27.6	10,582	31.4	12,191	36.8	11,834	33.7	13,977	38.5

		1996		1997		1998		1999		2000		2001		Total	
		Number	Percent	Number	Percent	Number	Percent	Number	Percent	Number	Percent	Number	Percent	Number	Percent
Total		56,049		54,591		46,033		66,848		50,817		33,600		905,168	
Aged 15+		47,960		44,536		37,220		53,747		41,394		27,550		724,440	
Worked in the FSU		32,009		31,026		26,243		44,173		35,798		23,534		410,846	
Occupation in the FSU[b]	1	10,771	33.6	9.926	32.0	8,284	31.6	14,815	33.5	12,159	34.0	7,641	32.5	140,397	34.2
	2	10,220	31.9	9,856	31.8	8,378	31.9	13,943	31.6	10,959	30.6	7,462	31.7	131,467	32.0
	3	11,018	34.4	11,244	36.2	9,581	36.5	15,415	34.9	12,680	35.4	8,431	35.8	138,982	33.8

Source: CBS Statistical Abstract 1990–2002.
a. Not available.
b. For details on occupational classification, see section 2.1 in the text.

Table 2.2
Annual growth rates of population, production, and capital, 1922 to 2001

	Population	GNP	Per capita GNP	Capital stock	Per capita consumption	Immigration (proportion of population)
1922–1932	8.0%	17.6%	7.8%	13.7%		8.2%
1932–1947	8.4%	11.2%	3.0%	9.8%		6.4%
1947–1950	21.9%					19.8%
1950–1951	20.0%	29.7%	10.0%			13.2%
1951–1964	4.0%	9.1%	4.9%	12.3%	5.1%	2.2%
1964–1972	3.0%	8.9%	5.5%	8.4%	3.6%	1.3%
1972–1982	2.1%	3.2%	0.8%	6.7%	3.2%	0.9%
1982–1986	1.4%	3.3%	1.7%	3.4%	2.4%	0.5%
1986–1989	1.4%	4.0%	2.3%	2.9%	2.7%	0.6%
1989–1993	3.8%	5.7%	1.9%	3.6%	2.7%	3.6%
1993–1997	2.1%	5.0%	2.4%	7.4%	3.8%	2.1%
1997–2001[a]	1.7%	2.7%	0.3%	6.5%	0.9%	1.6%

Sources: Ben-Porath (1986), CBS Statistical Abstract 2003 and ISDC Economic Time Series.
a. GNP and per capita GNP growth rates are for 1997 to 1999.

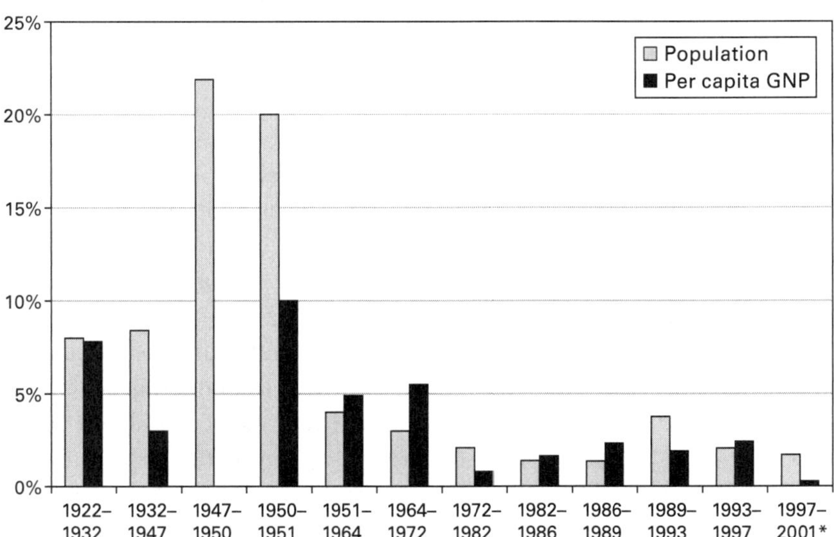

Figure 2.1
Growth rates of population and per capita GNP. *Per capita GNP growth rate is for 1997 to 1999. Sources: Ben-Porath (1986), CBS Statistical Abstract 2003 and ISDC Economic Time Series.

GNP, per capita consumption and the increase in the capital stock for earlier waves of immigration to Israel. For example, following the establishment of the State in 1948, the annual rate of population growth reached 20 percent over a period of two years (1950–51) and per capita GNP grew at about 10 percent annually. Surprisingly, table 2.2 and figure 2.1 show that the positive correlation between population growth and per capita GNP was maintained during the wave of immigration in the 1990s. During the early years of this wave (i.e., 1989–93), the population grew by 3.8 percent annually while the annual growth rate in per capita GNP was 1.9 percent. In addition table 2.2 shows that the growth in the capital stock kept pace with the increase in population, though with a lag.[2]

In contrast to the immigrants who arrived during the 1950s and 1960s, the most notable characteristic of the immigrants who began arriving in late 1989 was the high level of education they brought with them.[3] About 60 percent of the working-age immigrants were college educated, as compared to only 30 to 40 percent of native Jewish Israelis in 1989. This is reflected in the high proportion that were employed in occupations 1 and 2 in the FSU (table 2.1).[4] In contrast, 68 percent of native Israelis worked in occupation 3 in 1991. Notably, in certain high-skilled occupations, the stock of labor doubled within a short period.

The mismatch between the immigrants' occupational distribution and the local labor market distribution of jobs created an interesting dilemma for both the immigrants and policy makers. Overall, there was minimal intervention by the government in the occupational choice of the immigrants in the labor market. Residential location, participation in a Hebrew language course (Ulpan) and participation in government-provided vocational training courses were left to the discretion of the immigrant. In general, immigrants experienced occupational downgrading upon arrival and correspondingly their wages were lower than those of comparable natives.[5] This situation changed over time as immigrants eventually found better matches for their imported skills and accumulated local skills that were better-suited to the Israeli economy. In addition their productivity increased the longer they worked in Israel, and they became more similar to native Israelis with comparable schooling and work experience. The fact that this was a gradual process played a major role in mitigating the adverse effect of the immigration on native Israelis.

In order to explain the aggregate employment and wage trends in Israel following the wave of immigration, we follow the literature on economic growth (Solow 1956; Helpman 2004) by assuming a constant returns to scale production function. We then consider two different approaches to interpreting the data. The first is based on the observation that immigrant workers do not earn as much as native workers and thus may not be as productive as them on arrival. However, immigrants do eventually adapt to the Israeli labor market, although this is a gradual process due to search frictions. Consequently the large initial inflow of immigrants led to only a very gradual change in employment. The second approach is based on the assumption that an immigrant supplies the same number of labor efficiency units as a native worker but that there are costs for adjusting labor and capital that lead to a gradual adjustment in aggregate employment and the capital stock. These two approaches complement each other in explaining the observed patterns of real wages, the return on capital, investment and the inflow of capital.

In the first section of this chapter we present data on the main aggregate features of the Israeli labor market, namely participation, unemployment, and wages, while distinguishing between native Israelis and immigrants. We show that immigrants found employment relatively quickly and experienced high rates of wage growth, even while native employment remained almost constant. At the same time the wages of native workers declined at the peak of the immigration from the FSU, though they rebounded in later years. The following two sections present two complementary analytic approaches that are able to explain the data.

2.2   Natives and Immigrants in the Labor Market

This section describes the Israeli labor market before and after the major influx of FSU immigrants which began in 1989. In particular, we present indicators of the labor market outcome for native workers during the 1980s and for natives and immigrants during the period 1990 to 2000.

During the 1980s the participation rate of native Jewish males in Israel remained steady at 62 to 63 percent, while the participation of Jewish women increased from 39 to 47 percent.[6] There is some indication that during the large initial influx of FSU immigrants in 1990 and 1991 (see table 2.3) there was a small reduction in the participation rate of native Jewish men (to 61 percent in 1992), while the participation rate of Jewish women slightly increased from 1989 to 1992. Later in the 1990s, the participation of women further increased to 51 percent.

There are widely different trends in participation rates for native Jews according to schooling. Thus there was a sharp decline in the participation rate among native men with less than eight years of schooling in the 1980s, which continued into the 1990s. The participation rate for native

Table 2.3
Labor force participation rates among native Israelis and immigrants, 1990 to 2000

	1990	1991	1992	1993	1994	1995	1996	1997	1998	1999	2000
Men											
Native Israelis (Jews)[a]	61.86	61.52	60.84	61.73	61.88	62.16	61.39	60.53	60.23	60.28	60.66
By years of schooling											
0–8	53.69	53.13	50.42	48.70	48.25	44.64	40.78	39.19	38.93	39.29	39.50
9–12	60.22	59.70	59.05	60.51	59.92	60.11	59.49	58.35	57.40	57.57	58.51
13–15	70.21	69.06	69.22	71.36	71.18	70.86	70.04	68.22	68.43	67.61	68.36
16+	73.87	74.13	73.72	72.85	74.17	74.99	74.28	74.59	76.78	77.42	77.64
FSU immigrants[b]	29.98	56.89	64.42	66.15	66.11	63.58	62.78	62.61	61.05	61.81	62.46
Women											
Native Israelis (Jews)[a]	47.08	47.41	47.87	48.70	50.23	51.31	51.34	51.22	51.35	51.27	49.28
By years of schooling											
0–8	24.60	22.63	22.75	22.50	22.16	19.17	17.57	16.88	16.04	14.09	12.86
9–12	45.87	46.12	46.69	47.47	48.50	48.17	47.70	47.95	47.69	47.50	45.29
13–15	66.34	67.15	67.13	67.73	68.19	69.32	68.57	65.60	66.60	67.01	67.72
16+	80.03	80.69	79.81	78.99	80.80	80.98	82.50	81.96	81.59	81.71	82.05
FSU immigrants[b]	18.08	37.47	46.15	47.75	49.26	47.32	47.16	48.32	50.04	50.99	53.32

Source: CBS Labor Force Survey 1990–2000.
a. Born in Israel or immigrated prior to 1989, aged 15+.
b. Immigrated during 1989 to 2000, aged 15+.

Jewish women with less than eight years of schooling was constant during the 1980s but declined in the 1990s, from 25 percent in 1990 to about 13 percent in 2000 (see table 2.3). Although immigrants are characterized by a high level of education, most of the change in the labor supply of natives occurred among low-skilled Israelis.

Upon arrival in 1990, only 30 percent of the male immigrants from the FSU and 18 percent of the females participated in the labor market (see table 2.3). It is striking how quickly the FSU immigrants were absorbed into the Israeli labor market during the subsequent two years. By 1992, their participation rate was virtually identical (among women) or even higher (among men) than that of native Israelis. Contrary to some expectations, immigrants from the FSU were willing to accept any job. Thus they first entered low-skilled jobs and gradually climbed the occupational ladder.

The unemployment rate among Israeli men and women was relatively high in 1989, prior to the major influx of immigration.[7] Surprisingly, table 2.4 shows that the unemployment rate among native Jews declined during the first half of the 1990s while it increased during the second half. In contrast to the participation rate, there are only small differences in unemployment trends among native Jews according to schooling.

In 1990, 43 percent of the male immigrants and 53 percent of the female immigrants were unemployed (see table 2.4). The main reason for this is that most immigrants study Hebrew in Ulpan for an average period of six months soon after arrival. The unemployment rate among the immigrants dropped substantially after 1990, albeit at a slower rate than the rate of increase in the participation rate. The unemployment rate among male FSU immigrants fell from 43 percent in 1990 to 7 percent in 1995 and that of females fell from 53 to 12 percent during the same period.

The figures above provide little evidence that immigrants had an adverse effect on the participation and unemployment rates among native Jews. However, there is some evidence that during the influx of FSU immigrants there was a reduction in wages of native Israelis (table 2.5). Real hourly wages of natives, both men and women, grew by about 8 percent annually during the period 1980 to 1988. Subsequently, during the peak of the immigration inflow from 1990 to 1991, there was a small decline in wages of 1.8 percent for women and 2.7 percent for men. A more pronounced decline was observed for Israeli men with 9 to 12 years of schooling whose hourly wages declined by 4.3 percent (per year) during 1990–91 and for Israeli women with 16+ years of schooling whose

Table 2.4
Unemployment rates among native Israelis and immigrants, 1990 to 2000

	1990	1991	1992	1993	1994	1995	1996	1997	1998	1999	2000
Men											
Native Israelis (Jews) [a]	7.38	6.85	7.54	6.79	5.22	4.59	4.97	5.75	7.18	7.57	7.76
By years of schooling											
0–8	9.87	9.00	10.36	10.87	7.89	5.78	6.41	8.03	11.47	12.32	12.11
9–12	9.13	8.20	9.20	8.52	6.42	6.01	6.20	7.18	9.36	9.27	9.88
13–15	5.08	4.89	5.55	3.87	3.47	2.91	3.78	4.53	5.28	6.19	4.97
16+	2.22	2.89	2.58	2.03	2.14	1.99	2.50	2.71	2.41	3.27	3.71
FSU immigrants[b]	43.13	27.66	20.31	15.05	8.75	7.18	6.95	7.21	10.57	10.61	9.61
Women											
Native Israelis (Jews)[a]	11.09	11.11	11.45	10.40	8.90	7.28	6.62	7.14	8.25	8.79	8.66
By years of schooling											
0–8	11.82	12.67	12.88	11.92	10.84	6.57	5.64	8.10	10.17	8.91	11.02
9–12	15.39	16.17	16.51	15.08	13.14	10.75	9.78	10.36	11.41	12.85	13.08
13–15	7.23	6.35	6.70	6.07	4.89	5.12	4.65	5.06	6.88	7.30	6.38
16+	3.62	2.94	3.36	2.77	2.52	2.21	2.68	2.81	3.31	3.08	2.94
FSU immigrants[b]	53.36	50.71	38.32	23.49	17.53	11.72	9.71	10.69	12.67	12.45	11.27

Source: CBS Labor Force Survey 1990–2000.
a. Born in Israel or immigrated prior to 1989, aged 15+.
b. Immigrated during 1989 to 2000, aged 15+.

Table 2.5
Average growth rate of the real wage for natives and immigrants

	1980–1988		1989–1991		1992–1997		1997–2000	
	All sectors	Private sector[a]	All sectors	Private sector[a]	All sectors	Private sector[a]	All sectors	Private sector[a]
Men								
Native Israelis (Jews)[b]	7.98		−2.73		2.49		3.28	
FSU immigrants[c]					4.45		3.55	
Natives by years of schooling								
0–8	7.63	7.60	−2.65	−3.44	1.49	1.41	2.29	2.94
9–12	7.10	7.06	−4.34	−4.82	1.22	1.23	1.63	1.41
13–15	7.64	7.43	−0.54	−0.27	1.42	1.19	2.56	2.71
16+	8.11	7.47	−2.52	−4.13	2.31	1.02	2.99	3.11
Immigrants by years of schooling								
0–8					1.03	0.43	−2.01	−2.78
9–12					1.95	1.78	3.88	4.09
13–15					5.76	6.45	2.49	2.16
16+					5.65	6.74	5.55	5.91

Table 2.5
(Continued)

	1980–1988		1989–1991		1992–1997		1997–2000	
	All sectors	Private sector[a]	All sectors	Private sector[a]	All sectors	Private sector[a]	All sectors	Private sector[a]
Women								
Native Israelis (Jews)[b]	8.04		−1.82		3.11		3.28	
FSU immigrants[c]					4.93		4.35	
Natives by years of schooling								
0–8	9.27	9.91	−3.64	−5.32	1.90	2.65	5.78	5.95
9–12	7.32	7.66	−1.21	−1.69	1.89	1.82	2.58	2.57
13–15	7.45	8.88	−1.12	−1.14	0.90	2.70	3.41	3.26
16+	7.71	7.59	−5.93	−3.98	4.71	5.04	1.00	1.11
Immigrants by years of schooling								
0–8					2.77	2.59	3.58	3.49
9–12					4.53	4.75	4.41	4.00
13–15					4.05	5.27	3.59	3.75
16+					5.11	7.01	6.26	5.89

Source: CBS Income Survey 1980–2000.
Note: The sample includes men aged 18–65 and women aged 18–60. We exclude individuals whose last school is a yeshiva and individuals with more than 30 years of schooling or with no schooling indicated. We also exclude men with less than 25 weekly work hours and women with less than 20 weekly work hours. In 1980, we also exclude individuals who worked less than one month during the previous year. The growth rates represent the change in average log hourly wages.
a. Until 1994, excludes "public and community services"; from 1995, excludes "public administration" and "community, social, personal and other services."
b. Born in Israel or immigrated prior to 1990.
c. Immigrated during 1990 to 2000.

wages declined by 5.9 percent during the same period. However, these negative effects were transitory and the trend in wages resumed in 1992 and continued until the end of the decade (at a rate of 2.5 percent for men and 3.1 percent for women). During that period the wages of immigrants grew at a substantially faster rate (4.5 percent for men and 4.9 percent for women) and the wages of better-educated immigrants increased even more rapidly (at a rate of 5.6 percent for men and 5.1 percent for women).

The trends in participation, unemployment, and wage growth are evidence of the flexibility of the labor market, which contrasts with the market rigidities that many observers had claimed to exist in Israel. In addition it should be noted that the proportion of workers covered by collective wage agreements fell from 70 percent of employees in Israel during the period 1985 to 1989 to only 30 percent in 1997.[8] Overall, the evidence indicates that FSU immigrants had only a moderate and transitory adverse effect on the real hourly wages of native Israelis.

Several papers have analyzed the effect of the wave of immigration from the FSU on the Israeli economy, in general, and on labor market outcomes of natives, in particular, using various econometric techniques and data sets. All concluded that despite the extraordinary number of immigrants and their high level of skills, the effect on native workers was either transitory or of a small magnitude. For example, Friedberg (2001) found that the relative growth rate in wages of native Israelis in occupations that absorbed large numbers of FSU immigrants fell from 1989 to 1994. Since the occupational choice of the immigrants in Israel is endogenous, she uses the occupational distribution of FSU Jews prior to immigration as an instrumental variable for their current occupational choice in Israel and finds little evidence of occupational wage pressures on native Israelis. Cohen Goldner and Paserman (2011) used repeated cross-sectional data to estimate the impact of FSU immigrants on natives' employment and wages in a segmented labor market, in which segments are defined by various combinations of occupation and skills. Controlling for the distribution of immigrants among the various labor market segments, they found that immigration had a short-run adverse impact on the wages of natives, both men and women, with the effect dying out after 5 to 7 years. Gandal, Hanson, and Slaughter (2004) examined two possible open-economy mechanisms through which the increase in labor supply due to the arrival of FSU immigrants was absorbed: the adoption of global skilled-biased technological change and changes in the mix of traded goods produced in Israel. They argue that an increase in the rate of skill-biased technological change swamped any negative effect the FSU immigrants may have had on the skill premium in Israel. Overall, the above-mentioned papers found that the adverse effect of FSU immigrants on the labor market outcomes of natives was relatively small and transitory while the immigrants experienced positive wage growth during that period.

2.3 The Capital–Labor Ratio—Trends and Adjustment[9]

We begin the analysis by examining the macro implications of the gradual occupational upgrading of immigrants and the associated increase in immigrants' wages. In particular, we examine the implications for the aggregate capital–labor ratio.

The data shows that the capital–labor ratio in Israel declined during 1990–94 (see figure 2.2), which seems to contradict the CRS hypothesis. However, the capital–labor ratio as it is usually measured may have been underestimated during the early stages of the wave of immigration. In this section, we argue that the supply of labor from immigrants should be measured in terms of efficiency units, rather than number of individuals. Immigrants are not as productive as natives upon arrival and cannot replace natives in the production function on a one-to-one basis. Specifically, we assume that at each point in time, the iso-quants are linear but that the slope varies with time and approaches –1 as immigrants become increasingly similar to natives. Given the assumed linearity, the wage

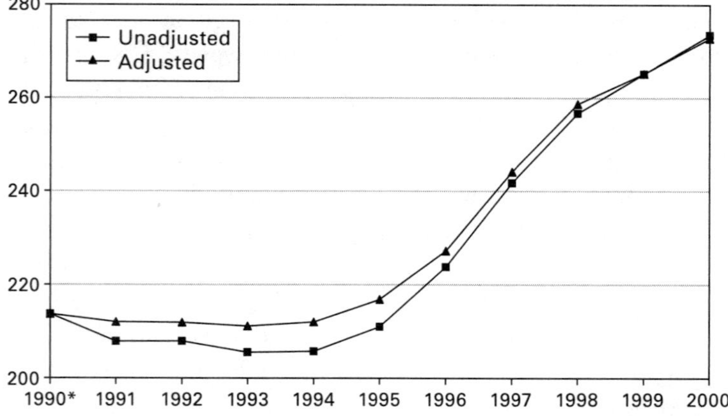

Figure 2.2
Adjusted and unadjusted capital–labor ratios. Gross capital stock in new Israeli shekels (NIS) millions (1995 prices); labor in thousands of workers. *We assume that there were no immigrants in 1990. Sources: CBS Statistical Abstract and Bank of Israel Annual Report.

ratio of natives to immigrants in each period must equal the slope of the iso-quant. Hence, the observed wage ratios reflect the relative productivities of native Israelis and immigrants in each year.

In order to account for the difference in productivity between immigrants and natives and to construct a quality-adjusted labor aggregate, we follow Jorgenson and Griliches (1967) who adopt a simple method of adjustment for the quality of employed immigrants. This procedure assumes that at each level of schooling, the difference in productivity between immigrants and natives is reflected in their wage differences. Therefore we first estimate a wage regression for immigrants in order to capture their wage growth over time in Israel according to their level of skills and then use the estimated wage profiles to create an adjusted measure of labor input (aggregated over levels of skill).[10] Appendix 2.1 presents the exact method and the data used to implement the quality-adjusted measurement of labor input for the Israeli economy during the period 1990 to 2000.

Figure 2.2 presents the actual and adjusted capital–labor ratios. As one would expect, during the initial influx of immigrants (from 1990 until 1994) the unadjusted capital–labor ratio in Israel declined. However, the adjusted capital–labor ratio is almost flat from 1990 to 1994. Under constant returns to scale technology and competitive conditions, a stable adjusted capital–labor ratio implies that the growth in inputs has no effect on wages. The only sources for growth in average wages are changes in quality, which reflect shifts in the composition of the labor force toward more productive workers, and growth in total factor productivity. Among immigrants, we find that there was a 20 percent increase in quality during the period 1990 to 1995, compared with only 2 percent among native Israelis. In this respect the aggregate data, when properly interpreted, are consistent with a stable average wage for native workers and a rising average wage for immigrants. Figure 2.2 reveals that within six years the adjusted and unadjusted capital–labor ratios are almost identical. This convergence reflects the higher quality of immigrants who came to Israel in the early 1990s and the declining number of new immigrants.

2.4   An Open-Economy Equilibrium Model with Adjustment Costs[11]

In this section we take a different approach to explaining the gradual adjustment of immigrants in the labor market. We now assume that natives and immigrants are perfect substitutes on a one-to-one basis, but that the capital stock and employment are only gradually adjusted due to the costs involved. We then examine whether the adjustment of the Israeli economy to the large influx of immigrants fits the predictions of an open-economy neoclassical model with a CRS production function. To answer this question, we use Israeli data to quantitatively calibrate a "back-of-the-envelope" growth model with capital and labor adjustment costs. We demonstrate that the model predicts the main patterns in the macro indicators of the Israeli economy. The main insight of the analysis indicates that the endogenous response of capital accumulation to an exogenous labor supply shock (the arrival of immigrants) can offset a significant part of the initial adverse effect of immigration on natives' wages. The short-run effect of an exogenous increase in a country's labor endowment is an immediate reduction in the capital–labor ratio, and consequently in real wages, and an increase in the return on capital. The increase in the return on capital does not trigger an infinite rate of investment due to the existence of adjustment costs. As a result the rate of investment increases and the capital–labor ratio gradually recovers, while the supply of labor from each worker and aggregate employment both rise.[12] For a small open economy that faces a constant and exogenous real interest rate, this induced capital accumulation continues until the return on capital and real wages return to their original levels. In addition, if households in this small open economy have standard preferences over their lifetime consumption, then capital accumulation should be financed through external borrowing rather than by an increase in domestic savings.

The patterns in Israel's main macroeconomic variables are in fact remarkably consistent with the neoclassical model of induced capital accumulation with adjustment costs. Figure 2.3 shows that the return on capital increased sharply from 1989 to 1992 and slowly returned to its 1988 level of 5 percent by 2001. The rate of investment in machinery and equipment (as a fraction of the stock of machinery and equipment) increased from 11 percent in 1989 to 21 percent in 1993 and slowly fell to roughly 15 percent in 1998 (see figure 2.4). As widely noted in Israel, the arrival of the FSU immigrants initiated a temporary housing boom in 1991 and 1992, with a return to normal levels by the late 1990s (figure 2.4). With a fixed international interest rate and an increase in the return on capital, direct foreign investment in Israel also increased in the early 1990s from $160 million in 1989 to $605 million in 1993 (figure 2.5). Finally, the current account deficit as a fraction of GDP increased by 8 percentage points from 1989 to 1996 before starting to decline (figure 2.6), which is in line with the predictions of the consumption-smoothing model. In the model specified below, we attempt to fit the data to these observed patterns.

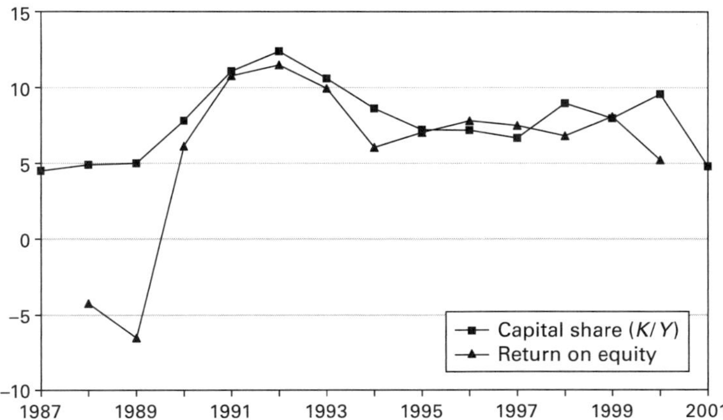

Figure 2.3
Return on capital (percent). Sources: CBS Statistical Abstract and Bank of Israel Annual Report.

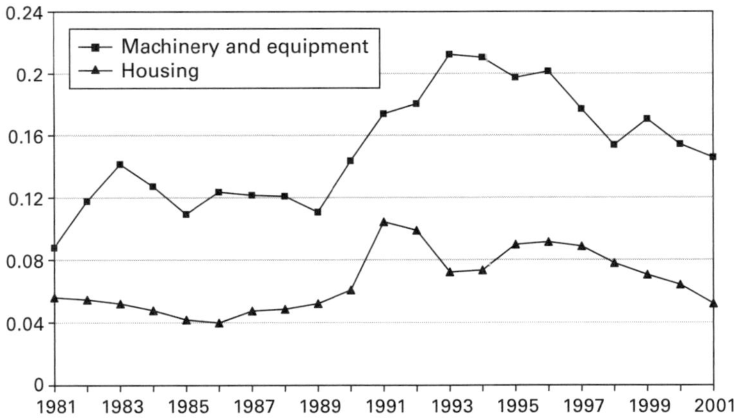

Figure 2.4
Ratio of gross investment to capital stock. Source: CBS Statistical Abstract.

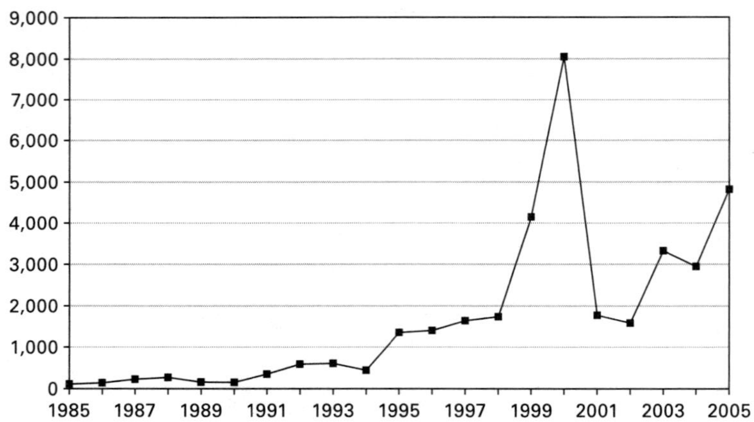

Figure 2.5
Total direct foreign investment in Israel ($millions in current prices). Source: CBS Time Series–DataBank.

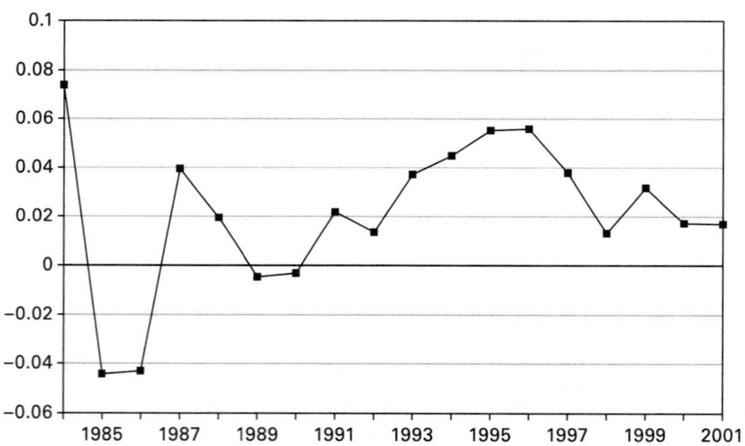

Figure 2.6
Ratio of current account deficit to GDP. Source: CBS Statistical Abstract.

2.4.1   Model Specification

The calibration uses a standard neoclassical model with a constant returns to scale aggregate Cobb–Douglas production function:

$$Y_t = BK_t^{\alpha} A_t L_t^{1-\alpha},\tag{2.1}$$

where Y_t is output in period t, K_t is the capital stock in period t, L_t is the aggregate amount of labor supplied by the N_t workers in period t (normalized to 1 before migration took place), A_t is the index of exogenous labor-augmenting technology in period t and B and α are positive parameters $(0 < \alpha < 1)$.

We will assume that it is costly for firms to adjust the amount of labor they use and that the adjustment costs are given by $(\tau/2)(dL_t^2/L_t)$, where τ is an exogenous positive parameter and dL_t is the change in the number of workers in period t. Similarly we will assume that the adjustment cost of capital is given by a standard convex function $(\chi/2)(I_t^2/K_t)$, where χ is an exogenous positive parameter and I_t is the quantity of gross investment in period t. In addition we assume that each firm faces a real interest rate r^* and real wage w_t, which are taken as given by the firm. Under these assumptions the value of the representative firm is given by the present discounted value of its profits:

$$V_o = \sum_{t=0}^{\infty} \frac{1}{(1+r)^t} \cdot \left[Y_t - w_t L_t - \frac{\tau}{2} \frac{dL_t^2}{L_t} - \frac{\chi}{2} \frac{I_t^2}{K_t} - I_t \right].\tag{2.2}$$

Finally, the capital stock depreciates at a constant rate δ, which implies that the evolution of the capital stock is given by

$$K_t = (1-\delta)K_{t-1} + I_{t-1}.\tag{2.3}$$

The aggregate supply of labor and aggregate consumption (and by extension, the current account) are determined by the preferences of the representative household, which are given by

$$U_o = \sum_{t=0}^{\infty} \frac{1}{(1+\rho)^t} \cdot [\log(C_t) + \phi \log(T - l_t)]dt,\tag{2.4}$$

where C_t is consumption in period t, T is the total labor (or leisure) endowment per household, l_t is the labor supply of a representative household in period t and ρ and ϕ are positive parameters $(0 < \rho < 1)$.

The budget constraint for the representative household in every time period t is given by

$$C_t + I_t + S_t^f = w_t l_t + r_t K_t,\tag{2.5}$$

where S_t^f is the net increase in foreign assets (or equivalently, the current account deficit). To capture the response of the current account to FSU immigration, we assume that households are able to borrow and save in international capital markets at a fixed interest rate r^*. We also assume that FSU immigrants do not own any capital or foreign assets when they immigrate to Israel but otherwise have the same preferences and labor endowment as native Israelis.

The competitive equilibrium in this economy is given by the sequence of $\{C_t, L_t, I_t, K_t, S_t^f\}$ such that (1) firms maximize the present discounted value of their profits (equation (2.2)) subject to the capital accumulation constraint (2.3), (2) households maximize the present discounted value of their lifetime utility (2.4) subject to their budget constraint (2.5), and (3) the following two equations of market-clearing conditions hold:

$$N_t l_t = L_t, \tag{2.6}$$

$$Y_t = C_t + I_t + S_t^f - \frac{\tau}{2} \frac{dL_t^2}{L_t} - \frac{\chi}{2} \frac{I_t^2}{K_t}, \tag{2.7}$$

where N_t is the number of households in the economy. N_t is the key exogenous variable in this analysis since we assume that immigrants and natives are perfect substitutes and hence we model the influx of FSU immigrants as an increase in N_t.

The existence of adjustment costs implies that the initial effect of an increase in the labor supply due to immigration is a decline in the amount of work l and in the wage w while aggregate employment given by L rises and the capital–labor ratio declines, since K is initially fixed. Hence, the return on capital rises, as does the long-run level of capital desired by firms. Consequently capital accumulation is associated with an increase in demand for labor and rising wages.

2.4.2 Calibration

In order to calibrate the model, we chose parameter values that capture key aspects of the Israeli economy prior to the wave of immigration. The weight on the log of leisure ϕ is set to 2, which implies that the labor supply is roughly one-third of a representative household's total labor endowment in the steady state. We set both the annual discount rate (ρ) and the interest rate (r) to 0.05 so that the optimal consumption path is constant over time. The annual rate of depreciation of physical capital δ is set to 0.10. For the Cobb–Douglas production function, we set $\alpha = 0.3$, $B = 0.5$, and $A_t = 1$ for all t in our baseline simulation. We assume that the initial number of households is 1 and increase N_t from 1990 to 1997 by the actual increase of the labor force in Israel as a result of the immigration from the FSU.[13]

Turning to the adjustment cost parameters, we set the adjustment cost parameter of labor, τ, equal to 4 which implies that firms close roughly 17 percent of the gap between desired and actual employment each year, which roughly translates into a mean adjustment lag of 4.8 years following a shock. This is approximately the amount of time it took for participation and unemployment rates among FSU immigrants to converge to that of native Israelis. The adjustment cost parameter for capital (χ) is assumed to be 5. Along with the other parameters of this model, this implies a steady state shadow price of capital (widely known in the literature as Tobin's Q) of 1.5, which is consistent with the estimates reported by Blanchard, Rhee, and Summers (1993).

2.4.3 Simulations

Our baseline simulation of the response of the Israeli economy to immigration from the FSU is shown in figure 2.7.[14] Note the deviation of logged wages, the profit rate, investment/capital stock and current account

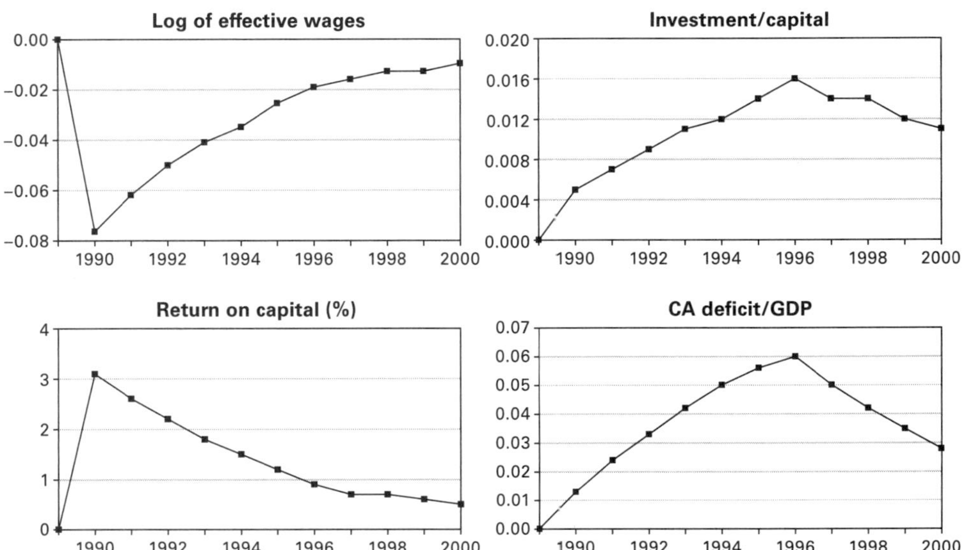

Figure 2.7
Simulated response to labor endowment shock (deviation from steady state). Source: Authors' calculations (for details, see section 2.4 in the text).

deficit/GDP from a steady state baseline in which the number of households is held constant. According to the simulation, wages initially fall by almost 8 percent and the profit rate increases by 3 percentage points in the first year of the immigration. In turn this stimulates a cumulative increase of 1.6 percent in the rate of investment (relative to the capital stock) up until 1996, followed by a gradual return to the steady state level. The investment boom almost doubled the capital stock, and thus by 1998 real wages were only 1 percent lower than pre-immigration levels. These results closely resemble the time pattern in the response of wages, the profit rate and the rate of investment in Israel after 1989. The actual increase in the profit rate is larger (though more gradual) than in the simulated results, as is the case for the rate of investment. Finally, the simulated current account deficit as a fraction of GDP increases by 6 percentage points from 1989 to 1996 and gradually declines subsequently, which is broadly consistent with the actual data.

Figure 2.8 presents simulations to assess the sensitivity of these calibrations to various assumptions about the capital adjustment cost parameter. As one would expect, a smaller capital adjustment cost results in a larger investment boom and a faster convergence to the steady state.

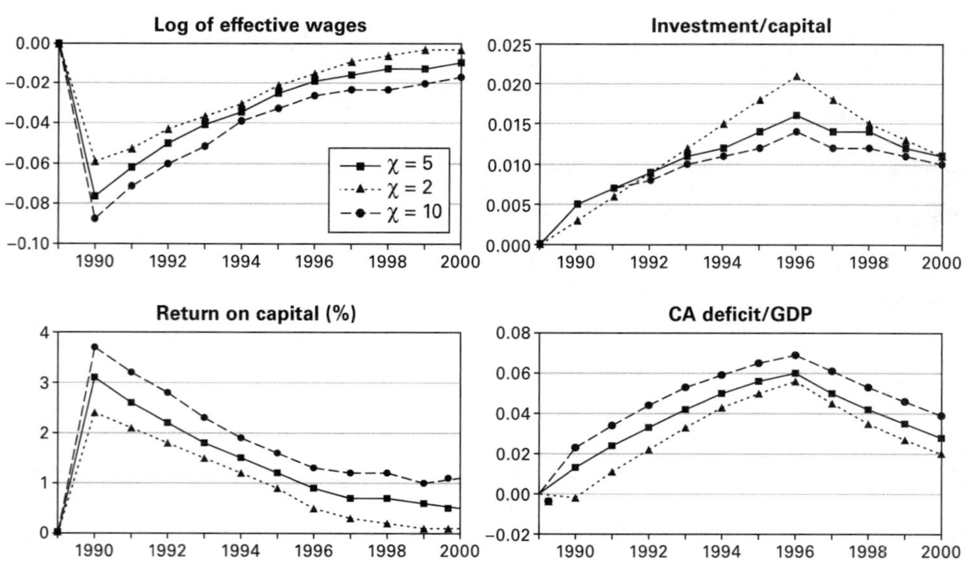

Figure 2.8
Simulated response to labor endowment shock under various assumptions for capital adjustment costs (deviation from steady state). Source: Authors' calculations (for details, see section 2.4 in the text).

2.4.4   Related Literature

The results obtained in this section, which support the CRS hypothesis, are consistent with the results reported in related papers. Razin and Sadka (1993) and Sussman (1998) use a simple aggregate model with a Cobb–Douglas production function to describe the co-movements of population, GDP, employment, wages, and the capital stock. Since the implication of this technology, under competitive conditions, is that the wage rate is proportional to output per worker, they view the continued rise in per capita GNP as an indication that the mass influx of immigrants was accompanied by a corresponding increase in other inputs and in productivity, without a substantial negative impact on the wages and employment opportunities of native Israelis.

Hercowitz and Yashiv (2002) studied the effect of FSU immigrants on the employment of native Israelis using the reduced form of a macro-economic model that assumes an open economy and perfect capital mobility. In this setting immigration does not affect the employment of natives and their relative wages since capital mobility eliminates the substitution between native and immigrant workers. However, in addition to the direct effect of immigration on labor supply, in the short run the gradual entrance of immigrants into the labor market leads to a change in the relative price of domestic goods, which in turn affects the demand for labor and as a result employment. The main finding is the negative effect of immigration on native employment a year after arrival. The delay is attributed to the positive impact of immigration on the excess demand for goods and thus on the demand for labor earlier on. Further evidence and an explanation for the gradual entry of immigrants into the labor market are provided in chapter 5.

2.5   Immigration and GNP Growth: A Puzzle?

This chapter has provided evidence on the unexpected positive link between immigration, growth in per capita income and consumption. Standard applications of modern growth theory (Solow 1956; Helpman 2004) emphasize technological progress and the accumulation of physical and human capital as sources of sustained growth. Moreover constant returns to scale in capital and effective labor are a required condition for growth theory. Using macroeconomic data for Israel, we have provided evidence supporting the CRS technology.

To explain the links between immigration and sustained growth is beyond the scope of this book. However, in this chapter we have obtained some insight into the relation between immigration and short-term growth. Immigrants from the FSU were on average more educated than native residents, but this extra human capital was not put to use immediately. The participation rate among immigrants increased rapidly and overtook that of native Israeli men by the year 1992 and that of women by 2000 (see table 2.3). In addition immigrants joining the labor force had fewer children than natives, thus raising the ratio of labor force to population. In fact a gradual adjustment process took place in which immigrants accumulated local human capital and gradually raised their productivity through better matching with local employers. This is reflected in the increased mean and variance of the immigrant wage distribution. In this book we emphasize the role of human capital investment as the main source of wage growth for immigrants (see chapters 3, 4, and 5). Finally, immigrants from the FSU entered high growth sectors, particularly hi-tech industries (Cohen Goldner 2006). Together, these factors can explain the positive correlation between immigration and growth in per capita income during the period 1989 to 2001. In contrast, this observed positive correlation between immigration flow and per capita GNP has not been fully explained in the existing macroeconomic literature.

2.6 Summary

In this chapter we have presented two methods for testing the hypothesis that the Israeli economy can be well approximated by a CRS production function with frictions. The first is based on the assumption that immigrants are not as productive as native Israelis upon arrival and therefore the labor input of immigrants should be quality-adjusted when calculating the aggregate labor supply. It was shown that the adjusted capital–labor ratio remained almost constant during the influx of FSU immigrants during the early 1990s, which under the CRS hypothesis is consistent with the fact that the wages of native workers declined for only a short period and that per capita income did not decline at all. In the second method we assumed that immigrants are as productive as natives and calibrated a neoclassical growth model with a CRS production function and adjustment costs for capital and labor. The calibration showed that the predictions provide a good fit for the observed changes in Israel's macroeconomic variables. The two approaches complement each other and yield similar results, with the main differences between them being the endogeneity of the response of capital and the fact that changes in capital and labor are jointly determined in the second method.[15]

We therefore conclude that the Israeli economy can be approximated by a competitive economy with a CRS production function. In this framework, the wage is proportional to the marginal productivity of labor in the long run, a result that underlies the analysis in the following chapters. The main focus of these chapters will be on a *micro* analysis of the wage and employment dynamics among immigrants, which are associated with their investment in local human capital in the form of training, language acquisition, work experience, and search strategy.

Appendix: Quality-Adjusted Labor

This appendix describes a simple procedure that can be used to adjust for the quality of employed natives and immigrants, based on the wage regressions reported in Eckstein and Weiss (2002).

Consider a constant returns to scale (CRS) production function $Y_t = A_t F(K_t, L_t^*)$, where Y_t is GNP, K_t is aggregate capital, L_t^* is the aggregate *quality-adjusted* supply of labor, and A_t is an index of total factor productivity. Let there be J types of labor where L_{jt} is the quantity of each type and w_{jt} is the wage of each type in year t. Then $L_t = \sum L_{jt}$ is the unadjusted aggregate and $w_t = \sum w_{jt} L_{jt} / L_t$ is the average wage in year t. We define the quality-adjusted index as $L_t^* = \sum_{j=1}^{J} \gamma_j L_{jt}$, where γ_j is a *fixed* positive weight of labor of type j. These weights are defined as the wage of labor type j relative to the average wage in some base year $t = 0$, that is, $\gamma_j = w_{j0}/w_0$. By construction, therefore, the unadjusted and adjusted indexes coincide in the base year, that is, $L_0^* = L_0$. Recall that under constant returns to scale, the marginal product of labor $A_t F_L(K_t, L_t^*)$ depends only on the adjusted capital–labor ratio K_t / L_t^*. Under competitive conditions, the linear aggregation rule implies that $w_{jt} = \gamma_j A_t F_L(K_t, L_t^*)$ and $w_t = A_t F_L(K_t, L_t^*)(L_t^*/L_t)$. Setting $A_0 = 1$, we see that the average wage equals the marginal product of labor in year 0. Notice that if labor quality rises due to a shift toward more productive workers, then the average wage may grow even if the adjusted capital–labor ratio is constant and no technical change occurs.

We now introduce immigrants into this simple framework. The population is divided between immigrants and natives and each of the two groups is cross-classified by four levels of schooling (0–8, 9–12, 13–15, and 16+ years), three occupational groups (as defined in section 2.1), and six levels of experience (0–4, 5–10, 11–20, 21–30, 31–40, and 40+ years) for a total of 72 cells. Within each cell, immigrants are further classified by years in Israel (between 1 and 6) and by cohort (1990–91 or 1992 to 1995).

We assume that immigrants that arrived before 1990 can be treated as Israelis. Immigrants in each occupation (j) are distinguished by their cohort (c) and time in Israel (τ). For $t = 1990, 1991, \ldots, 1995$, let $N_{jt}^0(\tau, c)$ be the number of working immigrants with τ years in Israel in cohort c in year t and let $w_{jt}^0(\tau, c)$ be their wage. We transform immigrants into equivalent Israelis in the cell by using *relative wages* as weights. Thus the adjusted number of working immigrants in each year, N_{jt}^*, is

$$N_{jt}^* = \frac{\sum_{c=0}^{2} \sum_{\tau=0}^{5} w_{jt}^0(\tau, c) N_{jt}^0(\tau, c)}{w_{jt}^n},$$

where w_{jt}^n is the wage of native Israelis in cell j in year t. The total number of "Israeli-equivalent" workers in each cell is $L_{jt} = N_{jt}^n + N_{jt}^{0*}$, where N_{jt}^n is the number of Israelis working as type j in year t. We define the weights for each type of labor j based on the relative wages of *Israelis* in 1991, that is, $\gamma_j = w_{j0}^n / w_0^n$, where w_{j0}^n and w_0^n are the wage of natives of type j and the average wage of natives in 1991, respectively.

A restrictive assumption implicit in this procedure is that the *relative* wages of Israeli workers of different types do not change over the period of the analysis. However, we do allow the weights for immigrants relative to Israelis to change over time since immigrants with different skill levels may adapt at different rates. An alternative log-linear specification $L_t^* = \exp\left(\sum_{j=1}^{J} \gamma_j \ln(L_{jt})\right)$, where γ_j are labor shares in the base year, can be used to allow for changes in relative wages (Young 1995).

The wages w_j^n and $w_{jt}^0(\tau, c)$ are calculated using the predicted wages from the regressions reported in the text of Eckstein and Weiss (2002), based on the Income Survey for 1991 to 1995. We use the midpoint in the cell for the conditioning variables. For example, for the years of schooling cell 13–15 we used 14 years. The average wages $w_{average}^n$ and $w_{t,average}^n$ are the average predicted wages of native Israelis using the regression reported in table 11.4 of Eckstein and Weiss (2002). The number of workers for each cell of natives and immigrants is taken from the Labor Force Survey for the years 1990 to 1995.

We assume that the Labor Force Survey is a representative sample of all cells in the population. Within each survey, we estimate the ratio L_t^* / L_t separately for immigrants and natives for the years 1990 to 1995. We then take aggregate data on employed immigrants and natives, as reported in the CBS Annual Report, multiply them by the corresponding adjustment factors and sum over the natives and immigrants to obtain the total adjusted labor force. The results are presented in table 3 of Eckstein and Weiss (1999).

Since we have estimated regressions only for male workers, *relative* wage differentials between male natives and male immigrants were imputed to females and within-group gender differences in wages were ignored. Based on cross-sectional data from the 1995 census, female workers earn about 20 percent less than males, adjusting for observed characteristics, and among immigrants this difference increases to almost 40 percent. Since the proportion of employed females is larger among immigrants, the required quality adjustment is underestimated. The procedure can be extended to include further adjustment for the difference between male and female workers, but this would require more resources than were available for this study.

3 On the Wage Growth of Immigrants[1]

3.1 Introduction

The macroeconomic analysis in chapter 2 concludes with the claim that wages of natives and immigrants in Israel during the early 1990s were proportional to the marginal productivity of labor. This conclusion has also been the underlying assumption in almost all the literature on the wage growth of immigrants and was the basis for the estimation of a Mincerian wage equation for immigrants.[2]

In the international literature on immigration, the typical pattern of immigrants' integration in a new labor market is characterized by initially low and relatively uniform wages followed by relatively rapid earnings growth. Over time, immigrants invest in local human capital and search for better matches with local employers while employers become less uncertain of the immigrant's potential quality. These processes combine to provide immigrants with increasing returns on their imported skills.

This chapter extends the classic human capital model (Becker 1975; Mincer 1974; Ben-Porath 1967) by including expected changes in the wages of immigrants that result from improved sorting and learning by employers. These expectations affect investment by immigrants in local human capital, and consequently we estimate a log wage equation that includes interactions between experience acquired in Israel and an immigrant's occupation in Israel, as well as imported schooling and experience. This specification extends the standard Mincerian log wage equation that is used for native Israelis, who are less affected by sorting and employer learning. Our estimation strategy yields a more flexible framework for the analysis of the convergence of immigrants' wages to those of natives than that to be found in most other studies, since we do not impose the same wage structure on both immigrants and natives. In this chapter, we will discuss only male immigrants for whom there is more complete wage data. Nonetheless, the employment and wages of female immigrants are discussed in chapter 4.

The labor market integration pattern for FSU immigrants in Israel is quite similar to that described above. However, in the Israeli case, the earnings growth of FSU immigrants is more pronounced due to their high levels of education and prior experience in high-skilled jobs (see table 3.1). Specifically, on arrival in Israel, immigrants start in low-skilled occupations and receive low wages that do not vary with years of

Table 3.1
Occupation, schooling, and experience of male native Israelis and immigrants who arrived in 1990–91

	Occupation[a]		
	Occupation 1 (%)	Occupation 2 (%)	Occupation 3 (%)
Israelis, 1991[b]	18.5	12.9	68.6
Immigrants in the FSU[c]	58.6	12.2	29.2
Immigrants in Israel, 1991–95[b]	14.6	9.3	76.1
Immigrants in Israel, 1996–2000[b]	19.1	10.0	70.9

	Schooling			
	0–12 (%)	13–15 (%)	16+ (%)	Mean
Israelis, 1991[b]	65.6	17.2	17.1	12.3
Immigrants on arrival[b]	32.0	37.5	30.5	14.1

	Experience[d]				
	0–5 (%)	6–15 (%)	16–24 (%)	25+ (%)	Mean
Israelis, 1991[b]	9.8	38.7	29.7	21.8	17.0
Immigrants on arrival[b]	11.8	34.3	31.8	22.1	17.1

Sources: CBS Income Survey and Brookdale Survey.
a. For details on occupational classification, see section 3.4 in the text.
b. Based on the CBS Income Survey. The sample includes males aged 25–65. For details on additional sample restrictions, see section 3.4 in the text.
c. Based on the Brookdale Survey. The sample includes 389 male immigrants who arrived during 1989–91, whose age on arrival was 25+ and whose age at the time of the interview was 65 or less. We exclude immigrants who did not work in the FSU and did not search for a job in Israel since arrival. Occupation in the FSU is based on the last job the immigrant held there.
d. Experience is calculated as age – years of schooling – years of army service – age at the start of school. Ages at the start of school are 6 and 7 for Israelis and immigrants, respectively. Years of army service are 3 for Israelis, 2 for immigrants with 11 years of schooling or less, and 0 for other immigrants.

Table 3.2
Monthly wages of male immigrants by schooling and years since arrival in Israel, 1991 to 2000

Year	Schooling ≤ 12		Schooling = 13–15		Schooling ≥ 16	
	Wage	Standard deviation	Wage	Standard deviation	Wage	Standard deviation
1	1,688	681	1,717	551	1,875	1,016
2	1,922	612	2,070	919	2,249	1,061
3	1,994	795	2,188	716	2,376	1,377
4	2,014	715	2,385	1,244	3,142	1,764
5	2,233	762	2,503	1,018	3,495	2,071
6	2,299	821	2,686	1,340	3,548	2,132
7	2,449	884	2,905	1,222	4,232	2,575
8	2,380	693	3,078	1,501	3,812	1,948
9	2,448	843	3,161	1,575	3,531	2,095
10	2,925	1,034	3,647	2,289	4,516	2,034
Annual growth rate	6.50%		8.86%		11.16%	

Source: CBS Income Survey.
Note: Wages are expressed in 1991 prices (NIS). The sample includes immigrants aged 25–65 who were aged 25+ on arrival. For details on additional sample restrictions, see section 3.4 in the text.

imported schooling. As time passes, they move into high-skilled occupations and as a consequence achieve higher wages. At the same time, wage disparity appears according to years of imported schooling (see tables 3.2 and 3.3). In each occupation immigrants initially receive wages that are below those of natives with the gap closing over time (see table 3.4). The wage growth we observe is closely linked to changes in occupation. The occupational distribution of first jobs held by immigrants is similar to the overall distribution of jobs in the Israeli economy, implying a substantial occupational downgrading. In the second phase, the more educated immigrants climb up the occupational ladder, thus obtaining better jobs and higher wages in each job. Thus the basic picture presented in the raw data is of substantial wage growth across occupations, though within occupations this is only seen in high-skilled occupations; there is almost no wage growth in low-skilled occupations.

An important goal of this chapter is to assess the importance of these two channels of wage growth. In particular, we distinguish between three sources of wage growth among immigrants and estimate their relative importance: (1) the increase in the return on imported human capital, (2) the impact of accumulated experience in the host country, and (3) the mobility up the occupational ladder in the host country.

Table 3.3
Occupational distribution of male immigrants, 1991 to 2000

Years in Israel		Age on arrival 25–40					Age on arrival 41–55				
		Occupation 1 (%)	Occupation 2 (%)	Occupation 3 (%)	Unemployed (%)	Observations	Occupation 1 (%)	Occupation 2 (%)	Occupation 3 (%)	Unemployed (%)	Observations
1	All	6.5	5.6	69.2	18.7	1,226	5.7	2.9	67.9	23.5	936
	Schooling 16+	21.5	8.8	48.3	21.5	228	16.0	3.0	49.3	31.7	268
2	All	10.1	7.8	71.1	11.1	1,290	8.3	5.2	69.9	16.6	872
	Schooling 16+	22.8	9.7	54.1	13.5	290	17.1	5.6	56.7	20.6	321
3	All	13.5	8.4	69.3	8.8	1,200	9.7	6.6	72.5	11.2	859
	Schooling 16+	32.3	10.1	47.5	10.1	297	20.8	8.4	58.1	12.8	298
4	All	15.2	10.2	68.0	6.6	1,078	11.2	8.1	71.5	9.3	807
	Schooling 16+	33.6	12.9	48.3	5.2	286	23.9	10.8	53.5	11.8	297
5–10	All	20.1	11.3	63.0	5.5	4,433	15.5	8.6	68.4	7.5	3,120
	Schooling 16+	43.6	14.1	38.4	3.9	1,299	29.7	11.9	51.6	6.8	1,282
11–15	All	19.8	10.3	65.7	4.2	359	27.3	11.2	55.9	5.6	143
	Schooling 16+	58.3	3.9	33.9	3.9	103	48.2	10.7	33.9	7.1	56

Source: CBS Labor Force Survey.
Note: Proportions of labor force participants. The sample includes immigrants aged 25–65. For details on additional sample restrictions, see section 3.4 in the text.

Table 3.4
Monthly wages of male immigrants and natives by work experience in Israel, 1991 to 2000

Years of schooling	All workers		Work experience ≤5		Work experience >5	
	Israelis	Immigrants	Israelis	Immigrants	Israelis	Immigrants
0–12	3,334	2,290	2,252	1,947	3,387	2,785
13–15	4,711	2,717	2,752	2,201	5,046	3,541
16+	6,377	3,727	4,026	2,726	6,926	5,006
Occupation in Israel						
Occupation 1	6,512	4,717	4,181	3,489	6,834	5,795
Occupation 2	4,555	3,574	3,185	2,857	4,791	4,303
Occupation 3	3,398	2,290	2,545	1,959	3,471	2,862

Source: CBS Income Survey.
Note: Wages are expressed in 1991 prices (NIS). The sample includes males aged 25–55, with no restriction on age on arrival. For details on additional sample restrictions, see section 3.4 in the text.

The theoretical model presented here contributes to the literature on the investment in human capital, as developed by Becker (1975) and Mincer (1974), through the introduction of explicit time trends that reflect the rising market returns on imported schooling and accumulated experience in the host country. Although the rising prices of skills and occupational transitions are given exogenously in our model, the investment in local skills is endogenous. We use the theoretical model to specify the wage equations for natives and immigrants, which are jointly estimated using the restrictions implied by the theoretical analysis. Using the estimated wage functions, we analyze the sources of wage growth and the assimilation of immigrants from the FSU.

The estimated earnings function confirms that upon arrival immigrants do not receive a return on imported human capital, defined in terms of schooling and experience. The prices of these skills rise with time in Israel, but a large gap remains between the prices obtained by immigrants and natives in the Israeli labor market. This is mainly reflected in a low return on schooling acquired abroad for immigrants, which we estimate to be 0.027 in the long run, substantially lower than the return of 0.069 on schooling for natives (Friedberg 2000 reports a similar finding). We are unable to reject the hypothesis that immigrants eventually obtain the same return on experience as natives and conclude that the importance of the unobserved part of earnings declines sharply with time spent in Israel. During the initial ten years following arrival, wages of immigrants who arrived in 1990 grew at a rapid rate of 6.6 percent annually (8.0 percent for immigrants with more than 16 years of schooling). Using the estimated wage equations, we find that *half* of this growth can be ascribed to a rising return on imported skills. Occupational transitions account for annual growth of 1.1 percent among immigrants with 16+ years of schooling and accumulated experience in Israel and the economywide rise in wages each account for about 1.5 percent annually. During that same period, the proportion of skilled immigrants (16+ years of schooling) working in occupation 1 in Israel rose from 21 to 44 percent.

We find evidence for reduced quality among more recent cohorts of immigrants from the FSU. This trend exists for both observable skills, such as schooling and occupation, and unobservable aspects of the wage. Accounting for this effect, we find that conditional on occupation, there is no long-run convergence of immigrants' wages to those of natives. In high-skilled occupations the final gap is small, but immigrants who remain in low-skilled jobs receive lower wages than comparable Israelis even after a long stay in Israel.

Most existing studies of immigrants in the United States focus on the rapid convergence of their wages to those of comparable natives of the same ethnicity. For instance, LaLonde and Topel (1991) report rates of convergence to the wages of comparable workers that range from 8 percent among Europeans to 24 percent among Asians (Borjas 1985 reports similar results).[3] We find that the wages of immigrants from the FSU converge at a rate of about 28 percent during the first ten years in Israel, which is similar to that of Asian immigrants in the United States during the 1970s, who also had a high level of schooling.[4]

The rest of the chapter is organized as follows: In the next section, we analyze a human capital model that justifies the wage equations derived in section 3.3. In section 3.4, we describe the data, and in section 3.5, we present the estimation results. Section 3.6 describes the decomposition of wage growth. Section 3.7 describes the occupational dynamics of immigrants and natives. Section 3.8 describes the convergence of wages, and section 3.9 concludes.

3.2   A Model for Immigrant Earning Equations

We now present a simple human capital model that allows us to compare patterns of earnings between immigrants and natives. The model describes the investment decisions of immigrants and natives and derives their implications for wage growth. The innovative feature of this analysis is the explicit introduction of time-since-arrival effects on prices of skills that influence immigrants' investment decisions. In the model the acquisition of new skills requires some sacrifice of current earnings. Investment decisions interact with changes in the market value of the immigrant's skills, and together they determine his growth in earnings. In particular, rising prices for imported skills provide an added incentive for investment since the sacrifice of current earnings is small relative to the growth in future earning capacity. A native faces a similar investment problem except that he does not possess skills acquired abroad that must be adapted to the host country's labor market.

To formalize the process, let x_s be the quantity of skill $s, s = 1, 2, \ldots,$ S, possessed by an individual. Human capital K is an aggregate that summarizes individual skills in terms of productive capacity. Skills are rewarded differentially in the various occupations, and we assume that this aggregate can be represented as

$$K_j = \exp(\sum \theta_{sj} x_s), \tag{3.1}$$

where θ_{sj} are nonnegative parameters that represent the contribution of skill s in occupation j (Welch 1969). Firms reward individual skills indirectly by renting human capital at the market-determined rental rate, R. Thus the parameter θ_{sj} is the proportional increase in earning capacity associated with a unit increase in skill x_s if the individual works in occupation j. Since θ_{sj} is independent of skill acquisition, each individual can view it as the implicit "price" (or "rate of return") of skill s.[5] In a frictionless economy each worker will apply his human capital to the occupation in which his bundle of skills yields the highest reward. However, we allow here for the possibility that occupational assignments are an outcome of a two-sided search process, whereby individuals may not end up in their most preferred occupation. Earning capacity is then

$$Y = RK, \tag{3.2}$$

where K is the worker's human capital in the chosen or assigned occupation. To simplify the analysis, we assume that moves up the occupational scale occur exogenously and are fully anticipated.[6]

In order to analyze immigrants' earnings, it is important to partition skills into two groups: locally acquired skills and imported skills. While imported skills are fixed in quantity, an immigrant can acquire additional local skills. A basic feature of the model is that the prices of imported skills rise with time spent in the host country relative to the prices of locally acquired skills.

We denote the subsets of skills acquired abroad and in Israel by S_0 and S_1, respectively, and assume that for all $s \in S_0$, the quantities x_s are fixed at $x_s(0)$ but that prices are allowed to vary with time in Israel, while for all $s \in S_1$, prices are fixed but quantities can vary. Accordingly we define $K_{0j}(t) = \exp\left[\sum_{s \in S_0} \theta_{sj}(t)x_s\right]$ and $K_{1j}(t) = \exp\left[\sum_{s \in S_1} \theta_{sj}x_s(t)\right]$. An immigrant can augment his local skills by training in school or on the job in the new country. We will focus here on investments while on the job. Assuming that the investments in any particular skill requires the same sacrifice of earnings and since prices of local skills are fixed, each immigrant will choose to invest only in that skill which maximizes his lifetime earnings. We denote the resulting value of local human capital by $K_1(t)$. In short, the immigrant's earning capacity is given by

$$Y = RK_1(t)K_0(t), \tag{3.3}$$

where $K_0(t)$ reflects the process of adaptation of a worker's imported skills through changing prices and occupational transitions and $K_1(t)$ reflects the process of investment in local skills. Note that the two types of human capital are *complementary* in their influence on the immigrant's earning capacity in the host country.

A specification suggested by Ben-Porath (1967) is used to characterize investment policy. The immigrant's local current earnings are defined as

$$y(t) = Y(t)(1 - x(t)) = Y(t) - I(t), \tag{3.4}$$

where $x(t)$ is the proportion of earnings forgone as a result of on-the-job investment and $I(t)$ is the quantity of sacrificed earnings. The accumulation of local human capital is given by

$$\dot{K}_1(t) = f(I(t)) - \delta K_1(t). \tag{3.5}$$

The function $f(I_t)$ is assumed to increase in I_t and is strictly concave, with $f(0) = 0$, and δ is the rate of depreciation of local human capital. The immigrant maximizes his lifetime earnings and the optimal investment policy is characterized by

$$\frac{RK_0(t)}{f'(I(t))} = R\int_0^{T-t} e^{-(r+\delta)\tau} K_0(t+\tau)d\tau, \tag{3.6}$$

where T is the end of the immigrant's working life, assuming an interior solution for the rate of investment. Condition (3.6) equates the marginal cost of an additional unit of K_1 at time t to the expected additional earnings that this unit will provide until the immigrant's retirement.

The current value of imported human capital $K_0(t)$ influences the marginal cost of investment, while the future value of imported capital $K_0(t + \tau)$ influences future benefits. Assuming that the local value of imported skills rises over time, that is, $K_0(t + \tau) > K_0(t)$, provides immigrants with an additional incentive for investment. To ensure that investment declines with experience, we will assume that the growth rate of imported human capital $\dot{K}_0/K_0$ declines with time spent in the new country.

Although the implications of changing prices for unobserved investment are clear, it is less obvious what their implications are for observed earnings. For the purposes of estimation, we will therefore use a different specification for the production function, as suggested by Blinder and Weiss (1976):

$$\frac{\dot{K}_1(t)}{K_1(t)} = g(x(t)) - \delta, \tag{3.5'}$$

where $g(x(t))$ is increasing and concave, with $g(0) = 0.$[7] If we parameterize this function as

$$g(x(t)) = \gamma - \gamma(1 - x)^{1/\alpha}, \tag{3.7}$$

with $0 < \alpha < 1$ and $\gamma > r + \delta$, then the optimal earning path satisfies

$$\frac{\dot{y}}{y} = \begin{cases} \dfrac{\left(\dot{K}_0/K_0\right) + \gamma - r\alpha - \delta}{1 - \alpha} & \text{if } t \leq t_1, \\[3mm] \dfrac{\dot{K}_0}{K_0} - \delta & \text{if } t > t_1. \end{cases} \tag{3.8}$$

Thus the growth rate of earnings is a simple piecewise *linear* function of the growth rate in the value of imported skills. During a period in which the worker does not invest in local skills, the change in prices translates into a change in earnings on a one-to-one basis. However, during a period in which the worker also acquires local skills, there is a "multiplier effect," given by $1/(1-\alpha)$, reflecting the impact of increasing prices of imported skills on the investment in local skills.[8]

We can now compare the earning paths of immigrants and natives. The basic difference between natives and immigrants is that the former bring with them skills that are not immediately applicable in the local market. Consider a native and an immigrant with identical skills. Assuming no occupational switches, their earnings during the investment period are given by

$$\ln y_m(t) = \ln K_0(0) + \ln(1 - x_m(0)) + \frac{1}{1-\alpha}(\ln K_0(t) - \ln K_0(0)) + \frac{\gamma - r\alpha - \delta}{1-\alpha} t$$

$$(3.9)$$

and

$$\ln y_n(t) = \ln K_1(0) + \ln(1 - x_n(0)) + \frac{\gamma - r\alpha - \delta}{1-\alpha} t, \qquad (3.9')$$

where m indicates an immigrant, n indicates a native, $K_0(0)$ is the initial local value of the immigrant's imported skills and $K_1(0)$ is the initial human capital of the native. During their early years in Israel, immigrants are paid lower prices for their skills and therefore $K_0(0) < K_1(0)$. In addition, because the immigrant expects a rise in these prices, he makes additional investments in local human capital and therefore $x_m(0) > x_n(0)$. Taken together, these facts imply that the immigrant's initial observed earnings, $y(0) = K(0)(1 - x(0))$, are lower than the native's. However, because of the rise in the prices of imported skills and a higher level of investment, the immigrant's earnings grow faster than the native's. After sufficient time in the host country, the prices of imported skills may converge to the prices obtained by the native so that $K_0(t)$ converges to $K_1(0)$. If this occurs, $y_m(t)$ can exceed $y_n(t)$ since

$$\ln K_0(0) + \frac{1}{1-\alpha}(\ln K_1(0) - \ln K_0(0)) > \ln K_1(0).$$

Thus an immigrant's earnings can *overtake* those of a comparable native if the price of imported skills converges to the *same* price obtained by natives for locally produced skills, since the increase in prices of imported human capital imply higher levels of investment by immigrants. However, if imported skills are of lower quality and their long-run price falls short of the value of locally acquired skills, then an immigrant's earnings may never catch up with those of natives. This is likely to occur when immigrants arrive from a less-advanced country as is the case of immigrants from the FSU in Israel. However, this is an empirical issue and will be investigated below.[9]

3.3   The Empirical Earning Function

The empirical earning function suggested by Mincer (1974) assumes static conditions and that investment declines linearly with remaining working life. According to the model in this chapter, investment is carried out under time-variant conditions and the investment rule is influenced not only by remaining working life but also by changes in the local value of imported skills.

We make the following functional form assumptions. Let $t - t_0$ be time since arrival. Then

$$\theta_{sj}(t - t_0) = e^{-\lambda(t-t_0)}\theta_{sj}(t_0) + (1 - e^{-\lambda(t-t_0)})\tilde{\theta}_s. \tag{3.10}$$

Thus the current price of imported skills $\theta_{sj}(t - t_0)$ is a weighted average of the initial price $\theta_{sj}(t_0)$ and the long-run price $\tilde{\theta}_s$. As the immigrant spends more time in the host country, the price of each imported skill approaches $\tilde{\theta}_s$. The specification imposed in (3.10) has the convenient property that the price of skill s in occupation j can be written as

$$\theta_{sj}(t - t_0) = d_{sj}e^{-\lambda(t-t_0)} + e^{-\lambda(t-t_0)}\theta_s(t_0) + (1 - e^{-\lambda(t-t_0)})\tilde{\theta}_s, \tag{3.10$'$}$$

where θ_s and $\tilde{\theta}_s$ can be interpreted as the prices that the immigrant receives when he reaches his "final" occupation, in which his skills are well matched with those required and d_{sj} is a constant that represents the initial difference between the prices of skill s in the first and final occupations. The parameter $\lambda > 0$ controls the speed of adjustment, which is given by

$$\dot{\theta}_{sj} = \lambda(\tilde{\theta}_s - \theta_{sj}(t - t_0)). \tag{3.11}$$

An important result of these assumptions is that the value of an immigrant's imported capital $K_0(t - t_0)$ can follow a different time path in the new country, depending on the *composition* of skills he brings with him and his success in climbing up the occupational ladder. Although we assume a common rate of adjustment among immigrants, the rate of change in the price of each skill may differ, depending on the distance between the current price and the long-term price. The value of the immigrant's imported skills rises continuously within each occupation and may jump discretely when he switches occupations. By construction, the rate of increase in the price of each skill declines as the price rises, implying that $\dot{K}_0/K_0$ declines with time spent in the new country.

It remains to specify the impact of the immigrant's age or remaining working life on his earnings. Equation (3.8) implies that if prices are fixed, logged earnings rise at a fixed rate until they reach a peak and then, when investment stops, decline at a fixed rate. Because workers switch jobs and reach their earnings peak at different ages, we will assume, as an approximation, that earnings grow according to

$$\frac{\dot{y}}{y} = a\frac{\dot{K}_0}{K_0} + b - ct, \tag{3.8'}$$

where the price and age effects are additive and the age effect declines linearly. We can now pool the two equations for immigrants and natives and jointly estimate the following earning function:

$$\ln y = b + \sum b_t\, year_t + b_{occ1}OCC1 + b_{occ2}OCC2 + \left(b - \frac{c}{2}exp_1\right)exp_1$$

$$+ b_s(s_1 + s_0) + D(IM)\Big\{[b' + de^{-\lambda exp_1}] + [b_{<90}C_{<90} + b_{92-2000}C_{92-2000}]$$

$$+ [(b'_{occ1} + d_{occ1}e^{-\lambda exp_1}]OCC1 + [b'_{occ2} + d_{occ2}e^{-\lambda exp_1}]OCC2$$

$$+ [b'_{exp} + d_{exp}e^{-\lambda exp_1)}]\left[\left(b - \frac{c}{2}exp_0\right)exp_0\right] + [(b'_s + d_s e^{-\lambda exp_1}]s_0\Big\} + \varepsilon,$$

$$\tag{3.12}$$

where $D(IM)$ is equal to one if the observation is of an immigrant and zero otherwise. Potential experience in Israel is denoted by exp_1 and potential experience in the FSU by exp_0. The number of years of schooling in the FSU is denoted by s_0, and in Israel by s_1. The occupational dummies $OCC1$ and $OCC2$ indicate whether the individual works in occupation 1 or 2 in Israel, respectively (occupation 3 is the reference group).[10] The year dummies indicate the year of observation, which ranges from 1991 to 2000. The cohort dummies $C_{<90}$ and $C_{92-2000}$ indicate whether the immigrant entered Israel before 1990 or between 1992 and 2000, respectively.[11]

The observed imported skills in equation (3.12) are schooling and experience acquired abroad. Schooling is measured simply by years spent in school. However, experience is not simply potential or actual work experience; rather, it is the amount of human capital or skills accumulated while employed. We measure this quantity by the expression $[bexp - (c\, exp^2/2)]$, where exp denotes experience, which is defined in the usual way (age minus years of schooling minus age of entry into school minus years of military service). We normalize by setting the price (in terms of logged earnings) paid to Israelis for their "true" experience to unity. We will *define* the "true" work experience immigrants bring with them as $[bexp_0 - (c\, exp_0^2/2)]$, using the *same* values for b and c as for Israelis. We then estimate the time pattern of the price that immigrants receive for this experience. Since we have no access to data on wages in the FSU, it is not possible to estimate these parameters directly. If both the parameters b and c differ between Israelis and immigrants, one cannot separate "quantity" from "price." Our specification implies that the restriction on "true" work experience is not binding and that the parameters b'_{exp} and d_{exp} measure the initial difference between the experience accumulated in Israel by natives and the experience accumulated by immigrants from the FSU, respectively. It is possible, however, for one parameter to differ across these groups, and we have allowed for this in the estimation. This coefficient c was found to be -0.00061 for immigrants and -0.00066 for Israelis. The difference between the two is statistically insignificant.

It should be emphasized that we do not restrict the returns on immigrants' imported schooling and experience to be equal to those of Israelis. We estimate all the human capital parameters in the immigrants' earning equations as deviations from the corresponding returns for Israelis. Specifically, the sum of the coefficients $b'_s + d_s$ measures the initial difference (at the time of arrival) between the rate of return (price) that immigrants obtain on their imported schooling and the rate of return that Israelis (and immigrants) receive on locally acquired schooling, b_s. The coefficient b'_s is the long-run difference in the rates of return. Similarly the sum $b'_{exp} + d_{exp}$ measures the initial difference between the rate of return (price) that immigrants obtain on their imported experience and the rate of return that Israelis (and immigrants) receive on locally acquired experience. The parameter λ describes the speed of adjustment between the short-term and long-term effects. The coefficients b' and d, which are associated with the immigrant's occupation in Israel, capture the variation in the evaluation of the immigrant's skills across occupations, which may also vary with time since arrival. Finally, the coefficients b' and d, which are associated with the immigrant dummy itself, capture the effect of an immigrant's unmeasured skills on the adjustment process.

Equation (3.12) allows us to describe and compare the parameters governing the dynamics and convergence properties of the earnings of immigrants and natives. Thus, if the parameter b'_k, corresponding to skill k, is not significantly different from zero, then the price of this skill converges to that of locally acquired skills. However, if this coefficient is negative, then there is no convergence. In addition, if the speed of adjustment, represented by λ, is too slow, then immigrants who entered the workforce at a late age will never catch up with similar Israelis within their working lifetime. We thus obtain a flexible specification that *allows* for convergence but does not impose it.

Equation (3.12) is nonlinear in its parameters and there are cross-equation restrictions implied by the human capital model of section 3.2

on the earning functions of immigrants and Israelis. Therefore we estimate it jointly using nonlinear least squares. In a previous draft we imposed the restrictions by using a two-step procedure, which yielded very similar results.[12]

3.4   Data

Although specification (3.12) is quite general, we will discuss here only male immigrants. The interrupted careers of women imply a more complex process of on-the-job investment and require an explicit analysis of labor supply.[13] For similar reasons we will not discuss young immigrants who may acquire schooling in Israel. We thus focus on the interactions between imported skills and on-the-job investment by immigrants in Israel.

The main sources of data for this chapter are the Central Bureau of Statistics (CBS) Income Survey and Labor Force Survey for the years 1991 to 2000. These surveys are annual random samples of the whole population.[14] The descriptive statistics are presented in table 3.5.[15] On average, immigrants are 3 years older than native workers, have one additional year of schooling (13.8 years for immigrants vs. 12.9 for natives) and earn about 65 percent of the monthly wage of native Israelis (and 67 percent of their hourly wage).[16]

For the analysis of wage assimilation, we further restrict the sample of male immigrants to those who were older than 25 upon arrival.[17] This is done to ensure that their schooling was acquired abroad.[18] As a result the rates of return on locally acquired schooling will be estimated primarily using data on Israelis. Our data source for the occupational transitions of immigrants is the CBS Labor Force Survey, from which the Income Survey is drawn. (Both surveys report occupation, but only the Income Survey contains wage data.) This is a relatively large sample with almost 15,000 observations (see table 3.5). We also use retrospective data contained in the Brookdale Engineers' Survey, which reports detailed work histories for 714 male engineers from the FSU who entered Israel in the most recent wave of immigration (1989 to 1992) and were surveyed in 1995.[19]

In order to analyze occupational transitions in Israel, we define three broad occupational categories: occupation 1 which includes engineers, physicians, professors, other professions requiring an academic degree, and managers; occupation 2 which includes teachers, technicians, nurses, artists, and other professionals; and occupation 3 which includes

Table 3.5
Summary statistics from the Income Survey and Labor Force Survey, 1991 to 2000

		Male natives		Male immigrants		Male immigrants aged 25+ on arrival	
		Income Survey	Labor Force Survey	Income Survey	Labor Force Survey	Income Survey	Labor Force Survey
Wage[a]	Monthly	4309.1		2815.3		2663.2	
		(3012.4)		(1856.9)		(1701.6)	
	Hourly	20.7		13.8		13.0	
Experience	Total	18.6	16.5	22.2	21.9	23.8	23.8
	Abroad			15.1	14.1	17.8	17.4
	In Israel	18.6	16.5	7.1	7.8	6.0	6.4
Age	Total	40.5	38.8	43.6	43.3	45.2	45.2
	On arrival			36.1	35.0	39.2	38.9
Schooling	Total	12.9	13.3	13.8	13.7	13.9	13.9
	On arrival			13.5	13.4	13.9	13.9
Occupation[b] (%)	Occupation 1	23.14	23.74	17.25	16.4	17.08	16.61
	Occupation 2	11.90	13.21	9.66	10.8	8.68	9.40
	Occupation 3	64.96	63.05	73.09	72.9	74.23	73.99
Cohort (%)	Before 1960			0.58	1.49	0.03	0.02
	1960–69			1.06	1.34	0.22	0.32
	1970–79			16.55	15.72	10.96	10.17
	1980–88			2.45	2.47	2.28	2.32
	1989–91			56.10	53.61	61.73	59.85
	1992–95			18.99	20.62	20.16	21.90
	1996–2000			4.26	4.75	4.62	5.42
Size of survey sample	1991	1,704	7,073	276	1319	212	1031
	1992	1,606	6,742	386	1,686	324	1,421
	1993	1,432	6,584	402	1,793	345	1,513
	1994	1,608	7,347	459	2,148	385	1,765
	1995	1,709	7,680	513	2,453	417	1,942
	1996	1,311	7,848	434	2,485	372	1,990
	1997	847	7,710	333	2,482	270	1,915
	1998	897	7,867	335	2,518	294	1,941
	1999	900	7,748	336	2,549	268	1,926
	2000	911	7,887	282	2,526	233	1,901
	Total	12,925	74,486	3,756	21,959	3,120	17,345

Sources: CBS Income Survey and CBS Labor Force Survey.
Note: The sample includes Jewish men aged 25–65. For details on additional sample restrictions, see section 3.4 in the text.
a. Wages are expressed in 1991 prices (NIS).
b. For details on occupational classification, see section 3.4 in the text.

blue-collar and unskilled workers. The occupational distribution of working immigrants is quite similar to that of working Israelis.

The immigration flows from the FSU were concentrated in three time periods: about 16 percent of the immigrants observed in 1991 to 2000 arrived in the early wave of 1970 to 1979, about 19 percent arrived in 1992 to 1995, and 56 percent arrived in the more recent wave of 1989 to 1991. Seventy-nine percent of the immigrants in the sample had been in Israel for less than ten years.

3.5   Estimation Results

In this section we report the estimation results for equation (3.12) using the data on natives and immigrants from 1991 to 2000.[20]

3.5.1   Results for Natives

The estimates of the model for native Israelis (presented in table 3.6) are similar to those obtained in other applications of Mincer's wage

Table 3.6
Nonlinear least squares estimation of the wage equation for male natives, 1991 to 2000

	With occupation dummies		Without occupation dummies	
	Coefficient	Standard error	Coefficient	Standard error
Constant	1.4431	0.0284	1.1707	0.0267
1991	−0.1455	0.0156	−0.1365	0.016
1992	−0.0856	0.0158	−0.0764	0.0162
1993	−0.1243	0.0163	−0.1187	0.0167
1994	−0.0931	0.0158	−0.0906	0.0162
1996	−0.0473	0.0167	−0.0468	0.0172
1997	−0.0395	0.0192	−0.0382	0.0197
1998	−0.0171	0.0188	−0.0156	0.0193
1999	−0.0782	0.0188	−0.0751	0.0193
2000	0.0041	0.0188	0.0042	0.0193
Occupation 1	0.2923	0.0122	—	—
Occupation 2	0.2056	0.0134	—	—
Experience	0.0418	0.0014	0.0433	0.0015
Experience^2	−0.0006	0.00003	−0.0006	0.00003
Schooling	0.0694	0.0017	0.0952	0.0014

Source: CBS Income Survey.
Note: The dependent variable is the log hourly wage in 1991 prices (NIS). The sample includes males aged 25–65. For details on additional sample restrictions, see section 3.4 in the text. The yearly dummies represent the real wage difference relative to 1995.

function. The only nonstandard feature is that we allow occupation to have a separate effect on wages, beyond that of schooling. This is mainly done to allow comparability with immigrants, for whom occupational transitions play an important role. The introduction of occupational dummies has little impact on the estimated coefficients, except for the schooling coefficient, which rises from 0.0694 to 0.0952 when occupation is omitted. The wages in occupations 1 and 2 are, respectively, about 29 and 21 percent higher than in occupation 3. There is a 4.2 percent increase of the hourly wage on the attainment of the first year of experience and about a 6.9 percent increase on the attainment of a year of education. The yearly dummies represent the difference with the wage in 1995. The estimated yearly dummies show that despite the mass immigration, the wage per hour for Israelis is *increasing* during this period. Controlling for schooling, occupation, and experience, the hourly wage in 1991 is about 15 percent lower than in 1995 and in all other years (except for 2000) the real hourly wages of natives were lower than in 1995. We interpret the yearly dummies as representing macroeconomic effects that to some extent may be related to the aggregate number of immigrants.

3.5.2 Results for Immigrants

As explained above, the wage equation for immigrants is estimated jointly with that of Israelis (results are shown in table 3.7). In this case the addition of occupational dummies influences all the coefficients, and we will therefore discuss the specification in which these variables are included.

The estimated speed of adjustment λ is 0.0995 per year, implying that within a period of ten years the price of each skill adjusts by 63 percent of the initial distance from its long-run value. However, convergence in prices also depends on the initial and long-term differences between the prices obtained by Israelis and immigrants for their skills.[21] We will separately discuss the prices for schooling, experience and unobserved skills.[22]

The initial difference upon arrival in the price (rate of return) of schooling between immigrants and Israelis is $b'_s + d_s = -0.0429 - 0.0288 = -0.0717$. Given the estimated rate of return of 0.0694 for native Israelis, the initial reward for schooling is slightly negative (but not significantly different from zero) for an average immigrant. The long-run difference in the rate of return on schooling is $b'_s = -0.0429$ and the rate of return that immigrants can expect in the long run is only $0.0694 - 0.0429 = 0.0265$. This substantial gap between natives and immigrants suggests that schooling acquired in the FSU is not fully transferable to

Table 3.7
Nonlinear least squares estimation of the wage equation for male immigrants, 1991 to 2000

	With occupation dummies		Without occupation dummies	
	Coefficient	Standard error	Coefficient	Standard error
b' – long-run difference in the rate of return on unmeasured skills	0.4191	0.0143	0.3270	0.0091
d	0.5136	0.0177	0.8834	0.0232
λ – speed of adjustment	0.0995	0.0031	0.1389	0.0033
$b_{<90}$ –immigrated prior to 1990	0.0498	0.0052	0.1418	0.0103
$b_{92-2000}$ –immigrated between 1992 and 2000	−0.0468	0.0042	−0.0608	0.0045
b'_{occ1} – long-run difference in the premium for occupation 1	0.3463	0.0318	—	—
d_{acc1}	−0.2530	0.0381	—	—
b'_{occ2} – long-run difference in the premium for occupation 2	0.1682	0.0288	—	—
d_{occ2}	−0.1425	0.0351	—	—
b'_{exp} – long-run difference in the rate of return on experience	−0.3630	0.0258	−0.6391	0.0370
d_{exp}	−1.0104	0.0528	−0.8435	0.0558
b'_{s} – long-run difference in the rate of return on schooling	−0.0429	0.0016	−0.0275	0.0014
d_s	−0.0288	0.0020	−0.0633	0.0028
Sum of squares residuals	3,062.606		3,276.919	
Number of observations	16,045		16,045	

Source: CBS Income Survey.
Note: The dependent variable is the log hourly wage in 1991 prices (NIS). The sample includes immigrants aged 25–65 who were aged 25+ on arrival. For details on additional sample restrictions, see section 3.4 in the text. $b'_k + d_k$ is the initial difference upon arrival between immigrants and Israelis in the rate of return (premium) on skill k.

Israel. After ten years, the rate of return reaches 0.0158 which is about 60 percent of its long-run value.

The initial difference upon arrival in the value of experience acquired abroad is $b'_{exp} + d_{exp} = -0.363 - 1.01 = -1.373$. Since the price of accumulated experience for Israelis is normalized to one, this means that the initial return on accumulated experience is $1 - 1.373 = -0.373$. Thus experience accumulated in the FSU has negative value in the Israeli labor market, at least initially. Over time, however, the price rises to $1 + b'_{exp} = 1 - 0.363 = 0.637$, which, given the high standard error of b'_{exp}, is not significantly different from one. Thus we cannot reject the hypothesis that in the long run immigrants obtain the same rate of return on experience as native Israelis.

The occupational dummies show that immigrants in occupations 1 and 2 obtain a higher premium (relative to occupation 3) than comparable Israeli workers. In the short run, the premium for occupation 1 is $[0.292 + (0.346 - 0.253)] = 0.385$ and for occupation 2 is $[0.206 + (0.168 - 0.142)] = 0.232$. In the long run, these increase to $0.292 + 0.346 = 0.638$ and $0.206 + 0.168 = 0.374$, respectively. However, a large part of these occupational effects is a consequence of the lower rate of return on schooling in occupation 3.

As seen in table 3.7, the coefficients b' and d are positive and large for both specifications, indicating that in the short run there is little difference between immigrants with different human capital indicators. However, over time the constant term declines and more weight is shifted to observable characteristics as their prices rise. Note that the cohort dummies indicate a reduction in the unobserved quality of immigrants. If observed characteristics are held constant, immigrants who arrived before 1990 earn 4.98 percent more than those who arrived in 1990–91 (the omitted group) who in turn earn 4.68 percent more than immigrants who arrived after 1992. This pattern is consistent with the observed deterioration in terms of schooling among later cohorts of immigrants, as noted by Borjas (1985) for the United States.

3.6 Decomposition of Wage Growth

The purpose of this section is to use the estimated earning equation in order to decompose the wage assimilation process according to the four sources of immigrants' earning growth after ten years in Israel. In particular, we assess the relative importance of the change in price of imported skills, local experience, occupational transition and the time effect on the wage growth of the first large cohort of immigrants. Table 3.8 provides a partition of the wage growth for immigrants in a synthetic cohort into four components: time, experience, price effects and occupational transition. Specifically, we select the cohort from the 1991 and 2000 cross sections of immigrants who arrived in 1990. Averaging logged wages for each cross section and taking the difference (divided by 10) yields the "average annual growth rate" for the 1990 synthetic cohort during the period 1991 to 2000. For each person in these two cross sections, we can generate the "average predicted growth rate" based on his *specific* characteristics and occupation. We then partition this prediction using the estimated coefficients in tables 3.6 and 3.7. This is done for the whole sample of immigrants who arrived in 1990 and for subsamples classified by schooling and age on arrival. We also repeat the calculations for the period 1991 to 1995.

The time effects are derived directly from the year dummies in table 3.6. The experience effect is the average "true" experience accumulated in Israel between 1991 and 2000 (1995) by members of the 1991 cross section. The price effect is defined as the average change in predicted wages, net of the year and experience effects, *holding occupation constant* from 1991 onward. In order to evaluate the occupation effect, we predict each immigrant's wages in 1991 and 2000 (1995) based on his occupation in those years and then divide the difference between the average predictions by 10(5). Since time in Israel is held constant in this comparison, the experience and price effects are accounted for and the only remaining factor is the difference in occupational choices.[23]

The results in table 3.8 show that the increase in skill prices is the most important factor in explaining wage growth during the initial five years following immigration. Forty percent of the average annual wage growth of 6.6 percent from 1991 to 2000 was due to the increase in prices of imported skills. Of course, the importance of this factor increases with schooling and experience. Changing occupation contributes 1.1 percent to wage growth; general growth contributes 1.5 percent; and the accumulation of experience contributes 1.4 percent. As expected, occupational transition is more important for immigrants with a higher level of imported schooling while experience effects are more important for younger immigrants. It is interesting that these features are not affected much by macro effects, as captured by the year dummies. Thus, although exogenous wage growth was primarily concentrated in the period 1991 to 1995 and was practically nil during 1996 to 2000, the effects of price, experience and occupation remained quite stable.

Table 3.8
Components of annual wage growth rates during 1991 to 2000 and 1991 to 1995 (percent)

	All immigrants		Schooling 13–15		Schooling 16+		Age on arrival 25–40		Age on arrival 41–55	
	91–2000	91–95	91–2000	91–95	91–2000	91–95	91–2000	91–95	91–2000	91–95
Actual	6.62	7.99	4.82	7.02	8.03	10.96	7.18	9.62	5.96	6.79
Predicted	6.48	8.07	5.38	7.70	7.48	9.56	6.60	7.89	6.17	8.20
Time[a]	1.46	2.91	1.46	2.91	1.46	2.91	1.46	2.91	1.46	2.91
Experience[b]	1.37	1.36	1.20	1.23	1.53	1.60	2.01	1.91	0.51	0.75
Prices[c]	2.52	2.84	2.51	2.83	3.42	3.84	1.88	2.10	3.18	3.51
Occupation[d]	1.13	0.96	0.21	0.73	1.07	1.21	1.25	0.98	1.02	1.03
Number of observations										
1991	119		50		29		60		59	
1995	135		51		46		76		51	
2000	64		19		30		36		28	

Source: Authors' calculation based on coefficients from tables 3.6 and 3.7.
Note: The sample includes male immigrants who arrived in 1990 and were aged 25+ on arrival. For details on additional sample restrictions, see section 3.4 in the text.
a. The time effect is the difference between the 2000 (1995) year dummy and the 1991 year dummy in table 3.6 divided by 10 (5).
b. The experience effect is the difference in average accumulated experience in Israel between 1991 and 2000 (1995) (averaged over members of the 1991 cross section and divided by 10(5)). The accumulated experience is defined as $[b(exp_0 + t - t_0) - (c/2)(exp_0 + t - t_0)^2]$, where $t - t_0$ equals 10 in 2000 (5 in 1995) and 1 in 1991. The coefficients b and c are taken from the wage equation for Israelis in table 3.6 (i.e., $b = 0.0418$ and $c/2 = 0.0006$ and exp_0 is the experience accumulated abroad by the immigrant).
c. For each immigrant in the 1991 cross section, we calculate predicted wages for 1991 and 2000 (1995), *holding occupation constant* at the 1991 level. We then average these two predictions (i.e., for 2000 (1995) and 1991) over all observations in the 1991 cross section, divide by 10(5) and deduct the time and experience effects.
d. For each immigrant in the 2000 (1995) cross section, we predict his wage based on his observed occupation. For each immigrant in the 1991 cross section, we calculate a predicted wage for 2000 (1995) based on his 1991 occupation. We then take the difference between the averages of these two predictions and divide by 10(5).

We can thus conclude that during the first ten years in Israel, rising skill prices were the main factor in the growth of immigrant wages and that acquired skills and occupational transitions were of secondary importance. However, the specification of the wage dynamics implies that the rate of increase in skill prices declines with time in Israel. Meanwhile the wage increase associated with occupational transition becomes increasingly important, as can be seen from a comparison of the 1991 to 1995 and 1991 to 2000 periods in table 3.8.

3.7 Occupational Transitions

In this section we focus on the occupational transitions of high-skilled immigrants in comparison to natives when schooling is set equal to 16– years. This is done in order to better understand the effect of occupational transition on the wage growth of immigrants and the potential convergence of their wages to those of Israelis. In interpreting the data, we assume that the occupation in which we observe an immigrant or a native is an exogenous draw from a given probability distribution, as explained in section 3.2.[24]

In figure 3.1 we present the predicted results from a simple logit regression of the estimated probability of being employed in occupation 1 conditional on age for an immigrant who arrived at age 30 with 16+ years of schooling.[25] As can be seen, the proportion of Israeli workers with

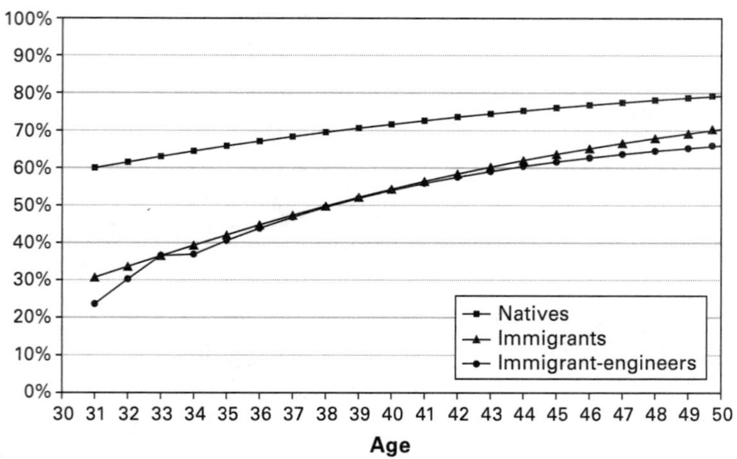

Figure 3.1
Predicted proportion of male workers with 16+ years of schooling employed in occupation 1. Source: Authors' calculations (for details, see section 3.7 in the text).

16+ years of schooling who actually worked in occupation 1, rises from about 60 percent at age 30 to about 80 percent at age 50. It can be predicted that over the same age (time) interval the proportion of immigrants who arrived in Israel with the most recent wave at age 30 with 16+ years of schooling and who work in occupation 1 will rise from about 30 percent to about 70 percent. In other words, based on the available information, it is expected that the occupational gap between recent immigrants and comparable Israelis will narrow substantially, though not completely, with time in Israel.

A similar pattern involving a rapid rise in the proportion of immigrants employed in occupation 1 is observed in the Brookdale Engineers' Survey data (see figure 3.1). This retrospective data allows us to calculate annual transition matrices for immigrants during their initial years in Israel.[26] Using monthly data, we calculate the annual transition rate (12 months ahead) for each month and then take the monthly average for immigrant engineers who had been in Israel for between 30 and 42 months. We use the estimated transition matrix to forecast the future occupational distribution of the immigrant engineers, as shown in figure 3.1.[27]

The various sources of wage growth tell the same story: initially only about 20 percent of the qualified immigrants found a job in occupation 1, while after 4 or 5 years this proportion rises to about 40 percent. The agreement between the predictions from the logit regressions based on the repeated cross-sectional data, the retrospective Engineers' Survey and the observed proportions in the pooled cross sections, suggests that all of them can be used, with some confidence, to calculate the occupational probabilities in order to generate expected wage profiles that are not conditioned on occupation.

3.8 Convergence of Wages

In order to evaluate the assimilation rate of immigrants' in the host country, it is common to ask whether immigrants' wages converge, overtake, or fall short of those of comparable natives. To answer this question, we now turn to the long-run behavior of immigrants' wages. We first look at convergence within occupation and wage residual dynamics and then examine the convergence of wages averaged across occupations.

As noted above, time in Israel has a different impact on observed skills than on unobserved components of the wage (unobserved skills and other sources). The average impact of the unobserved components declines with time in Israel while the average impact of observed skills increases, reflecting the rise in the price of these skills. We now consider the combined impact of these factors and ask whether or not the average wage of immigrants converges to the average wage of comparable natives in the same occupation. Figure 3.2, a to c, shows the predicted wage-age profiles for an immigrant with 16 years of schooling who arrived in Israel at the age of 30 and for an equivalent native. We consider three such comparisons—one for each occupational category—using the estimated parameters reported in tables 3.6 and 3.7.

As can be seen from the results, immigrants' wage-age profiles are generally below those of natives. In occupation 1, convergence is faster for members of the 1990–91 cohort than for later cohorts. In occupations 2 and 3, the wages of immigrants with 16 years of schooling do not converge to those of comparable natives, but rather to those of natives with the average level of schooling in those occupations (i.e., 14 and 12 years of schooling, respectively).[28] The predicted wage gaps between immigrants and natives with 16 years of schooling at age 55 are 5, 24, and 45 percent in occupations 1, 2, and 3, respectively, for the 1990–91 cohort.

3.8.1 Convergence of Residual Distributions

The increasing price of measured characteristics implies that, with the passage of time, immigrants become more distinct, based on their imported skills and, consequently, wage inequality rises. An interesting question is whether the same patterns apply to unobserved skills and other wage components. We have seen that the *average* impact of the unobserved components declines with time in Israel. We will now show that the *variability* of unmeasured characteristics of immigrants' earnings rises with time in Israel since the distribution of their residuals converges to that of natives.

The residuals for natives and immigrants are based on the regression coefficients in tables 3.6 and 3.7, respectively. To examine the effect of time in Israel for immigrants, we divide the sample into two subsamples based on experience in the Israeli labor market: those with less than five years and those with more. Figures 3.3 and 3.4 show the residual distributions for immigrants and natives in the two experience groups. It can be seen that among the less experienced, the residual distribution of immigrants is steeper, suggesting a lower variance while among those with more than five years of experience, the residual distributions of immigrants and natives are very similar.[29]

The declining mean and rising variability in immigrants' residuals over time reflects the presence of two types of learning with respect to immigrant skills. First, as employers learn about the measured characteristics of immigrants, the *average* role of unmeasured attributes is reduced. Second, as more is learned about each individual immigrant, immigrants are sorted out and variability rises (Farber and Gibbons 1996).

3.8.2　Convergence of Average Wages

We now bring together the results on wage dynamics and the dynamics of occupational transitions among immigrants in order to examine the convergence of the average wage, unconditioned on occupation. Figure 3.5 presents wage-age profiles, averaged over occupations, for an immigrant with 16 years of schooling who arrived in Israel at age 30, and for a comparable native. For immigrants, we combine the dynamic effects from the estimated wage equations reported in tables 3.6 and 3.7 with the occupational distribution predicted by the logit regressions (Eckstein and Weiss 2003).[30] Figure 3.5 shows that the wage differential between immigrants and comparable natives narrows substantially with time in Israel. An immigrant who arrived at age 30 with 16 years of schooling earns, on average, only 53 percent (58 percent for the 1990–91 cohort) of the wage of a comparable Israeli. After five years in Israel, the same immigrant earns 61 percent (68 percent for the 1990–91 cohort) of the wage of a comparable native and after 20 years 81 percent (90 percent for the 1990–91 cohort). As explained above, the growth in earlier years is primarily due to the increase in the returns on imported skills. Growth in later years is primarily due to occupational transitions, as reflected in the narrowing of occupational differences between immigrants and native Israelis. However, convergence is not attained due to incomplete convergence in the occupational structure and the lack of convergence within occupations.

Comparison to Findings for the United States
Studies of immigrants in the United States during the 1970s showed rapid rates of assimilation relative to natives of the same ethnicity (e.g., Chiswick 1978; Borjas 1985; LaLonde and Topel 1991). These studies defined the assimilation rate of immigrants during their first decade in the United States as the reduction in the difference between the log

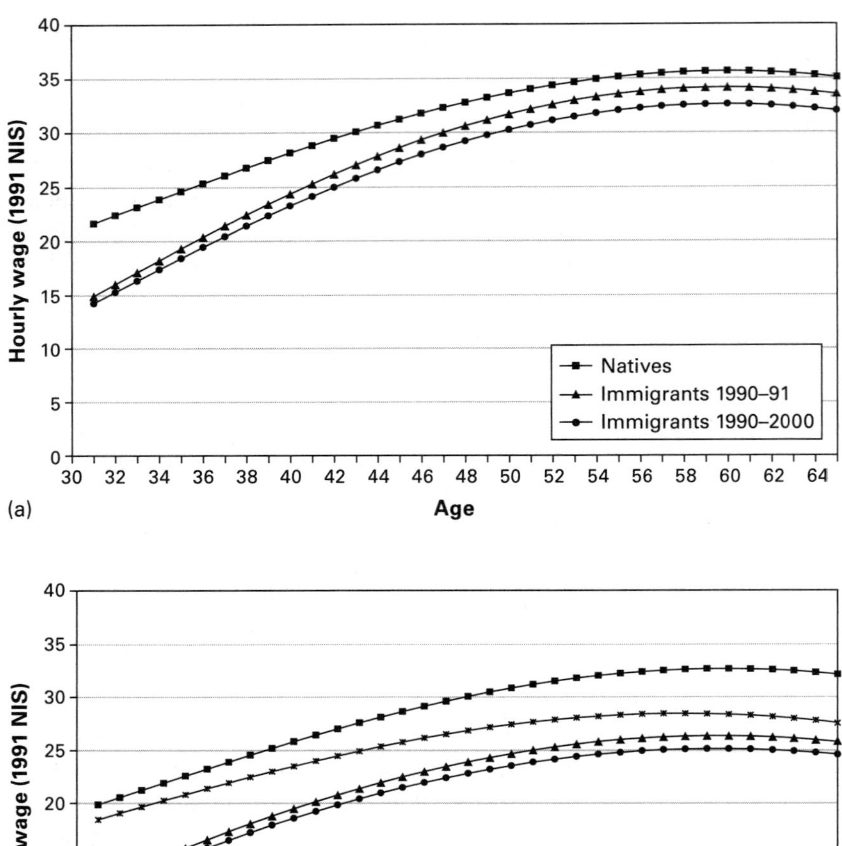

(a)

(b)

Figure 3.2
Simulated wage-age profiles for native and immigrant males: (a) In occupation 1; (b) in occupation 2; (c) in occupation 3. Predictions apply to males with 16 years of schooling who were aged 30 on arrival. Source: Authors' calculations based on coefficients from tables 3.6 and 3.7.

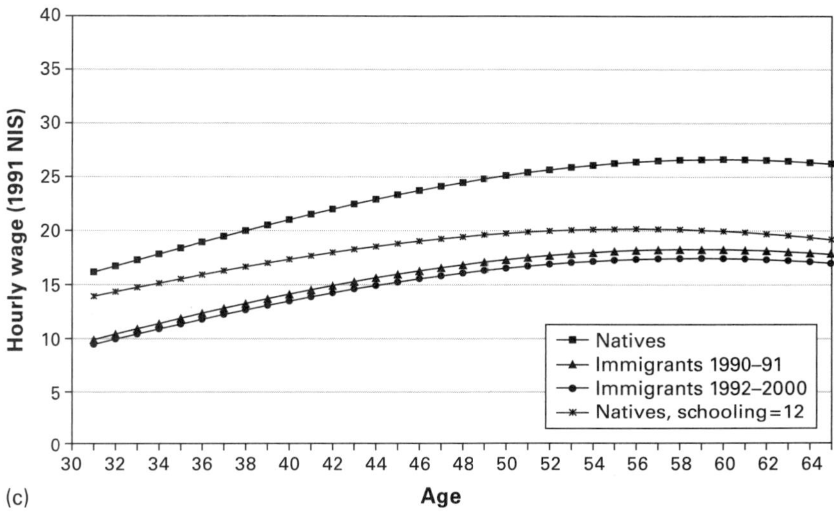

Figure 3.2
(continued)

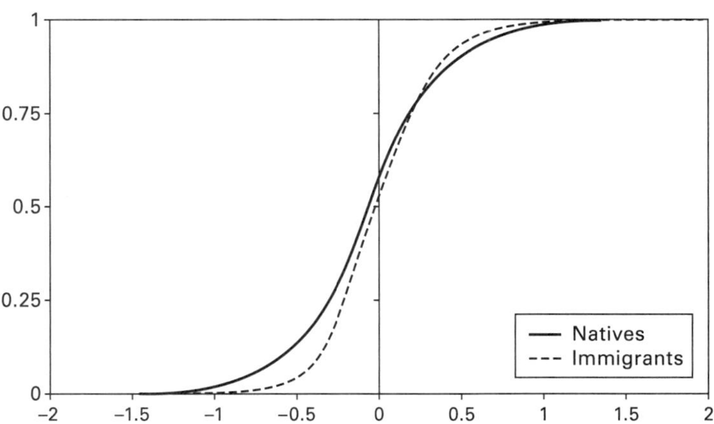

Figure 3.3
Residual distributions for natives and immigrants with five or fewer years of experience.
Source: Authors' calculations based on coefficients from tables 3.6 and 3.7.

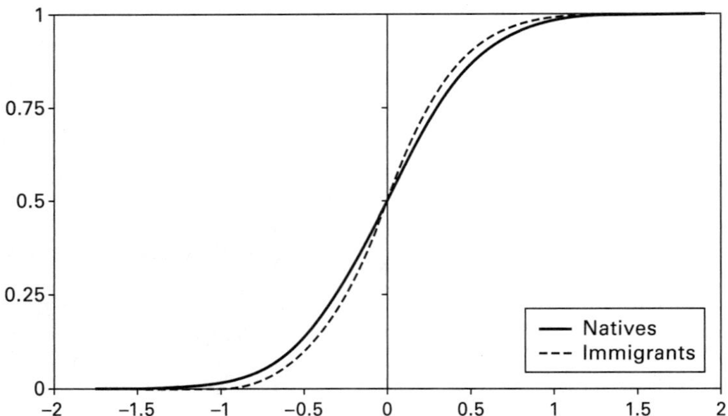

Figure 3.4
Residual distributions for natives and immigrants with six or more years of experience.
Source: Authors' calculations based on coefficients from tables 3.6 and 3.7.

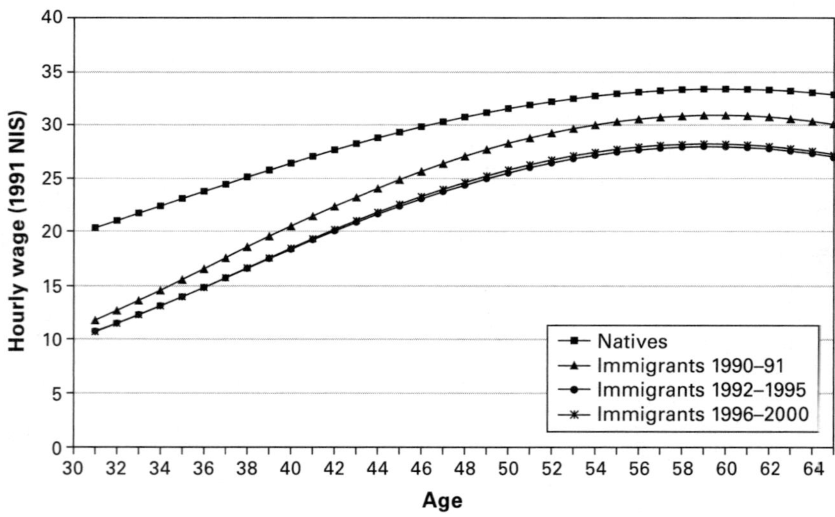

Figure 3.5
Simulated wage-age profiles averaged over occupations for native and immigrant males.
Predictions apply to males with 16 years of schooling who were aged 30 on arrival. Source:
Authors' calculations (see section 3.8.2 in the text).

wages of immigrants and those of equivalent natives of the same ethnicity. LaLonde and Topel (1991) find that the initial gaps between newly arrived immigrants and natives of the same ethnicity ranged from −0.05 for Europeans to −0.33 for Asians, while the ten-year assimilation rates ranged from 0.08 for Europeans to 0.24 for Asians during the decade 1970 to 1980. These studies use census data to estimate separate regressions for immigrants and natives, without the use of occupational dummies.

Measuring the difference in log wages, as in Lalonde and Topel (1991), we obtain an initial gap of −0.65 (−0.56 for the 1990–91 cohort) between immigrants on arrival and natives, which is substantially higher than that observed in the United States.[31] After ten years the difference has declined to −0.37 (−0.25 for the 1990–91 cohort). Thus, if we measure assimilation by the narrowing of the wage gap, then an immigrant from the FSU assimilates in Israel at a rate of 28 percent (30 percent for the 1990–91 cohort) during his first ten years in the country. This is similar to what has been observed among Asian immigrants in the United States during the 1970s, who also had a high level of schooling (about 14 years on average).

To further facilitate a comparison with these studies, we use simple descriptive regressions for immigrants and natives without occupational dummies and without imposing any restrictions of equal coefficients between the two equations.[32] However, we do allow for "years since migration" (ysm) to have a different slope after five years in the host country and to interact with schooling, as our theory suggests it does. According to these regressions, the initial gap between immigrants and natives with comparable schooling and work experience (16 and 6 years, respectively) is −47 percent. The annual growth rate for immigrants, evaluated at 16 years of schooling, is 0.093 per year during the first five years following migration. In later years it declines to 0.025, thus yielding a wage increase of 77 percent during the first ten years in Israel. The comparable growth rate for native Israelis is 37 percent, so that the gap is reduced to 19 percent after ten years and the assimilation rate since arrival is 28 percent. These results are similar to those obtained from the model estimated in this chapter and described above.

3.9 Summary

It is well known that immigrants enjoy high wage growth during the initial phase after arrival. The novel aspect of the model presented here is the attempt to identify the sources of this wage growth. We distinguish between three sources of wage growth for immigrants: (1) the increase in the return on imported human capital, (2) the impact of accumulated experience in the host country, and (3) the mobility up the occupational ladder in the host country. We find that the increase in the price of imported skills accounts for about half of the unconditional 6.6 percent annual growth in wages during the first ten years in the country. Occupational transitions are important mainly for high-skilled immigrants who arrived with academic degrees (accounting for 1.1 percent of the 7.5 percent annual growth rate) and for immigrants who arrived at a young age (accounting for 1.3 percent of the 6.6 percent annual growth rate). For high-skilled immigrants, experience in the host country accounts for 1.5 percent of the annual growth rate and aggregate wage growth accounts for another 1.5 percent.

The prices that immigrants receive for their imported schooling and experience are initially zero or negative. These rise with time in the host country but never reach the prices obtained by natives. The market "penalty" on observed imported skills is partially compensated for by a premium on the unobserved characteristics of these immigrants.

The increase in skill prices slows with time spent in the host country and occupational transitions become more important. Initially there is a substantial occupational downgrading and about half of the male immigrants with more than 16 years of schooling work in occupation 3 during the first three years in Israel. However, immigrants who arrived at a relatively young age, that is, 25–40, move up the occupational ladder and about 60 percent of them are working in occupation 1 after 11 to 15 years in the country. By way of comparison, the percentage of natives with 16+ years of schooling who work in occupation 1 is 62 percent (Eckstein and Weiss 2003, app. tab. A3). We can thus conclude that the occupational opportunities for immigrants who arrived at a young age with a high level of schooling almost converge to those of comparable natives. However, their wages are not expected to converge, primarily because the long-run return that immigrants obtain on their imported schooling (2.7 percent) is substantially lower than that obtained by natives for their locally acquired schooling (6.9 percent). This substantial gap in the returns on schooling, which was also documented by Friedberg (2000), may reflect either an inherent difference in quality of schooling or frictions in the labor market that lead qualified immigrants to "give up" in their search for suitable jobs.

The large windfall of human capital that Israel received is somewhat of a rare occurrence, yet it is relevant for policy makers in developed countries who wish to attract large inflows of skilled workers from less developed countries. In the European context, this can be achieved by either extending the borders of the European Union or through the introduction of new immigration policies that put greater emphasis on skill levels (Fertig and Schmidt 2002). According to the two main conclusions reached in this chapter, the absorption of high-skilled immigrants takes time and may involve a substantial waste of skills during the gradual process of matching between imported skills and local job opportunities. However, natives do not appear to suffer any loss even when immigration is on a large scale.[33] Although one should be cautious about drawing general conclusions, the Israeli experience is suggestive of the substantial opportunities associated with more open immigration policies.

4 Immigrants' Choice of Employment, Occupation, and Human Capital: Dynamic Stochastic Empirical Models[1]

4.1 Introduction

In chapter 3 we showed that wage growth in the early years following arrival is primarily due to the increase in returns on imported skills (schooling and work experience) while the growth in later years is primarily due to occupational transition. In addition, as the value of their imported skills rises, immigrants become increasingly differentiated and their wage distribution becomes less uniform. Furthermore, while the wages of low-skilled immigrants remain almost the same as during the first year following arrival, those of higher skilled immigrants increase significantly. This suggests that occupational mobility and the value of skills are important determinants of wage growth, a hypothesis that will be investigated in this chapter. More specifically, we examine the following questions: Which factors explain the transition from blue-collar (BC) jobs to white-collar (WC) jobs?[1] How valuable are imported schooling and pre-migration occupational skills and experience? Which is the more dominant factor: investment in local skills and the adaptation of imported skills to the local labor market or the availability of jobs in WC occupations? And finally, what is the net gain from migration?

The analysis in chapter 3 could not provide a clear answer to these questions since it is based on cross-sectional data, which is less detailed than the panel data to be used in this chapter.[2] For example, the cross-sectional data does not include information on immigrants' language

This chapter is based on Cohen Goldner and Eckstein (2008), Labor mobility of immigrants: Training, experience, language, and opportunities, *International Economic Review* 49 (3): 837–72, doi: 10.1111/j.1468-2354.2008.00499.x, © 2008 by the Economics Department of the University of Pennsylvania and the Osaka University Institute of Social and Economic Research Association, and on Cohen Goldner and Eckstein (2010), Estimating the return to training and occupational experience: The case of female immigrants, *Journal of Econometrics* 156 (1): 86–105, © 2009 by Elsevier B.V. All rights reserved.

skills, participation in vocational training programs and actual work experience in the host country and therefore does not facilitate an analysis of the investment by immigrants in local human capital, nor does it differentiate between the impact of accumulated local human capital and that of imported human capital. Panel data makes it possible to design a dynamic model of wage growth and occupational mobility that can separately identify the role of imported human capital and that of local human capital in determining labor mobility and earnings.

In this chapter we formulate two dynamic discrete choice models of labor supply and training, one for male immigrants and the other for female immigrants, and estimate them using a unique panel. The dynamic models are based on Ben-Porath's classic model of investment in human capital and follow the specifications of Keane and Wolpin (1997) and Eckstein and Wolpin (1999). The models incorporate two main determinants of occupational transition: (1) investment in local human capital in the form of experience, training, and language skills; and (2) employment opportunities in two broadly defined occupational categories, that is, WC and BC.

The models begin from the immigrants' arrival and track their labor market decisions. Each immigrant is nonemployed on arrival and either attends classes to learn the local language (i.e., Hebrew) for one or two quarters or searches for a BC job. From the third quarter onward, immigrants sequentially choose whether to work (in either a BC or WC occupation) or to attend government-provided training, where the availability of each option is subject to uncertainty. The availability of work and training depends on an immigrant's labor market history and it is assumed that choices are made optimally in order to maximize expected discounted utility. Immigrants who have learned Hebrew are eligible for one government-provided training program, and conditional on having participated in a training course, the immigrant decides whether to accept a WC or BC job, if one or both are offered. The job-offer rate and the associated wage depend on occupation, participation in a training course, actual experience and imported schooling.

Within this framework we measure the individual and social benefits from government-sponsored vocational training programs. Finally, the models incorporate initial observed heterogeneity at the time of arrival, which is reflected in marital status, number of children, years of schooling, age on arrival, and occupation in the FSU, as well as unobserved heterogeneity. The unique panel used to estimate the models includes relevant data that were not available to other studies of immigrants' labor market integration. Specifically, starting from time of arrival, the panel includes quarterly data on the participation of immigrants in government-provided vocational training programs and on actual work experience in various occupations. In addition it includes indicators of fluency in the local language and imported human capital, such as schooling and occupation prior to immigration. The main patterns of employment by occupation, nonemployment and training participation are similar for both males and females, although females have lower mobility.

We find that both the qualitative and quantitative results are similar for male and female immigrants. The main result is that WC job offers have relatively low availability and that participation in a training course significantly improves an immigrant's prospects. Hence the impact of training on job-search friction is an important channel through which human capital affects labor mobility. In addition we find that while training has no impact on wages in BC jobs, it has a large effect on wages in WC jobs. Finally, it is found that for both males and females the wage return on immigrants' imported skills is close to zero conditional on investment in local skills.

In order to measure the importance of training, we analyze several policy alternatives to the provision of training programs. We measure the individual benefit from the policy by the change in an immigrant's expected present value of utility and the resulting social benefit using a simple social cost–benefit calculation. We find that increasing the availability of training for female immigrants is beneficial both for the immigrant and for society, while for males the same policy produces no additional social benefit. This finding is primarily due to differences in the opportunity cost of training between males and females. For females, training is a substitute for nonemployment; that is, if a female immigrant does not participate in a training program, she is less likely to be employed. For males, training is a substitute for work; that is, if a male immigrant does not participate in a training program, he is more likely to be employed. Thus, if we simulate a counterfactual policy of no training, we obtain the following results: (1) higher budgetary costs in the case of females due to increased government expenditure for unemployment benefits since nonemployment increases; and (2) lower government expenditure in the case of males since nonemployment (including training) decreases, such that the net impact is slightly negative.

The dynamic programming model with endogenous choice of training and employment implies that the social and individual benefits of training cannot be measured *solely* by the coefficient of training in the wage function since both the costs and gains from training are affected by the immigrant's choices and labor market dynamics, as well as by the costs of the programs and the individual optional value. The finding that vocational training programs benefit females but not males is consistent with findings in the existing literature (Heckman, LaLonde, and Smith 1999).

We find that for females the distinction between WC and BC work experience plays a major role in explaining wage growth. On the one hand, the accumulation of BC work experience does not contribute to wage growth in either type of occupation and does not affect the probability of receiving BC job offers. On the other hand, an additional quarter of WC experience increases the probability of receiving a WC job offer by 9 to 20 percent and increases the wage in WC jobs by 4 percent.

In addition to the policy analysis, we use additional data not included in the estimation in order to verify the model's predictions for a ten-year period. The analysis shows that the model's predictions of labor market employment and training patterns are consistent with the out-of-sample data and provides strong support for the interpretation of the data provided by the model.

In section 4.8 we compare the present value of earnings in the FSU to the present value of earnings or utility under various scenarios of integration in Israel. The results show large economic gains for FSU immigrants (both males and females) who arrived in Israel during the period 1989 to 1992. This is due to the fact that the expected present value of earnings in Israel is 1.5 to 2 times higher than in the FSU. Nonetheless, we find that immigrants who are permanently nonemployed in Israel have negative utility, implying that immigrants dislike nonemployment.

The chapter is organized as follows: In the next section, we describe the data and present the main trends that the models are meant to fit. In the third section we formulate the model for females (4.3.1) and males (4.3.2), and in section 4.4 we present the solution and the estimation method. Section 4.5 summarizes the results for females and males, and in section 4.6 we conduct a counterfactual analysis of active labor market policies for females (4.6.1) and males (4.6.2). Section 4.7 provides a verification analysis of the female model using out-of-sample data, and in section 4.8 we discuss the gain from immigrating to Israel from the FSU in the early 1990s.

4.2 The Data

The data are based on a panel from two retrospective surveys of the same sample carried out by the Brookdale Institute.[3] The first survey was conducted during the summer of 1992 on a random sample of 1200 male and female immigrants from the FSU who arrived in Israel between October 1989 and January 1992. The second survey was done in 1995 and re-sampled 901 of the immigrants. The original sample consists of immigrants of working age (25–65) residing in 31 different locations in Israel at the time of the first survey. Both surveys contain a monthly history of employment and wages for each immigrant from date of arrival in Israel until the interview. The surveys also provide detailed information on participation in government-sponsored training programs, participation in Hebrew classes (called "Ulpan" in Hebrew) and Hebrew fluency at the time of the surveys. The immigrants also provided background information such as occupation in the FSU, years of schooling, knowledge of Hebrew before migration and place of residence in the FSU. For our purposes, we converted the monthly labor market data into a quarterly data set.

We use the two surveys to construct a panel of 502 female immigrants who were aged 25 to 55 on arrival and a panel of 419 male immigrants who were aged 23 to 58 on arrival.[4] The data tracks these immigrants for their first 20 quarters (at most) in Israel and enables us to construct their job profiles from arrival until the last interview. The data set contains information on the dates of employment, occupation, weekly work hours and wage for each job. In total, there are 7,205 (5,778) observations of labor market states and 649 (574) wage observations for females (males).[5] An important feature of our data set is the information on *actual* work experience accumulated in Israel in various occupations, which is essential in the study of life-cycle labor supply. We define two broad occupational categories: (1) WC jobs that include scientific and academic occupations, managers, technical workers, and other professional occupations,[6] and (2) BC jobs that include all other occupations.[7]

The surveys also gathered detailed information on participation in government-sponsored vocational training and in Ulpan. The training programs are offered by the Ministry of Labor and the Ministry of Absorption as part of the "absorption package" every immigrant is entitled to upon arrival in Israel. Government training programs in Israel take the form of classroom vocational training and are relatively intensive in comparison to similar programs in Western countries. They have an average duration of six months (as compared to three months in the United Kingdom and the United States) and involve 26 hours of study per week. Participants are not permitted to work while attending the program. During the program the participants study both the theoretical and practical aspects of the profession and at some point during the program visit potential places of employment or alternatively visit training centers to learn about skill requirements and job conditions. Thus participants are also exposed to potential work opportunities in the field they are studying. The training programs include courses such as sales, cosmetics, diamond cutting, and computers. Despite the long duration of the Israeli training programs, less than 5 percent of the participants dropped out,[8] which may be due to the importance attributed to training by the immigrants or perhaps their lack of alternatives.

4.2.1   (A) Females

Table 4.1A presents the averages of the key variables both for the full sample and according to whether the immigrant participated in a training

Table 4.1A
Summary statistics—Females

Variable	Full sample	Untrained	Trained[a]
Number of observations	502	284	218
Age on arrival	37.2 (8.5)	38.9 (8.9)	35 (7.4)
Years of schooling	14.5 (2.4)	13.9 (2.5)	15.2 (2)
Number of children	1.05 (0.8)	1.01 (0.9)	1.1 (0.8)
Number of jobs since arrival	1.9 (1)	1.6 (0.9)	2.1 (1)
Months in Israel	43.2 (14.1)	40.5 (15.6)	46.7 (10.9)
Nonemployed[b] (%)	15.1	21.1	7.3
White-collar[c] in the FSU (%)	75.7	69.4	83.9
Married (%)	76.5	77.1	75.7
Had knowledge of Hebrew prior to immigrating (%)	15.7	12.0	20.6
Hebrew fluency index—first survey[d]	2.99 (0.78)	2.71 (0.77)	3.36 (0.62)
Hebrew fluency index—second survey	3.3 (0.75)	3 (0.83)	3.62 (0.48)

Source: Brookdale Survey.
Note: Standard deviations appear in parentheses.
a. Participated in a training program since arrival.
b. Percentage of immigrants who never worked since their arrival.
c. For details on occupational classification, see section 4.2 in the text.
d. 1 = lowest; 4 = highest.

course. Around 43 percent (218) of the women in the sample participated in a training program since their arrival. The trainees are younger on arrival and have more years of schooling than the immigrants who do not train. About 97 percent of the women had worked in the FSU; 76 percent had worked in WC occupations while only 21 percent had worked in BC occupations. Of those who worked in WC occupations in the FSU, almost half attended a training program as compared to 24 percent of those who had worked in BC occupations.

The Hebrew fluency index variable is based on four questions that were asked in both surveys. The index ranges from one (no knowledge) to four (fluent in Hebrew). Knowledge of Hebrew is a prerequisite for participation in training courses, which are taught only in Hebrew. The share of female immigrants who possessed some Hebrew skills before migration is higher among participants than among nonparticipants (20.6 vs. 12 percent).

Labor Market States

Figure 4.1a presents the breakdown over time of female immigrants between four labor market states: WC employment, BC employment, nonemployment and participation in a training course.[9] The proportion of employed females increased sharply during the first two years in Israel and continued to increase subsequently at a moderate rate. A year after migration, 37 percent (= 0.069 + 0.299) of the women were employed, 46 percent were nonemployed and 17 percent were attending training courses. After four years in Israel, 82 percent of the immigrants were employed while 16 percent were nonemployed and only 2 percent were attending training courses. Training attendance increases following arrival, peaks after one year of residency in Israel and slowly declines in later periods. A substantial proportion (56 percent) of immigrants worked in BC jobs after four years in Israel. The substantial occupational downgrading during the first four years in the new country is subsequently reversed. Thus, during the fifth year in Israel, the share of female immigrants who work in BC jobs declines to 16 percent and the share of those employed in WC jobs increases by almost the same amount. Hence mobility across occupations is a prolonged dynamic process.

Transitions

Table 4.2A presents the total number and proportion of quarter-to-quarter transitions for female immigrants between the four labor market states. There is a high level of state dependence in occupation-specific employment, such that about 96 (93) percent of the immigrants who

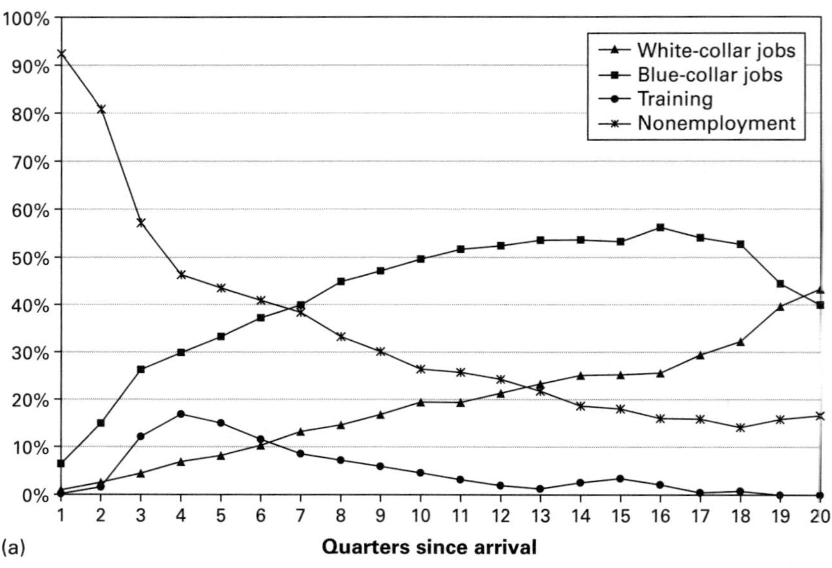

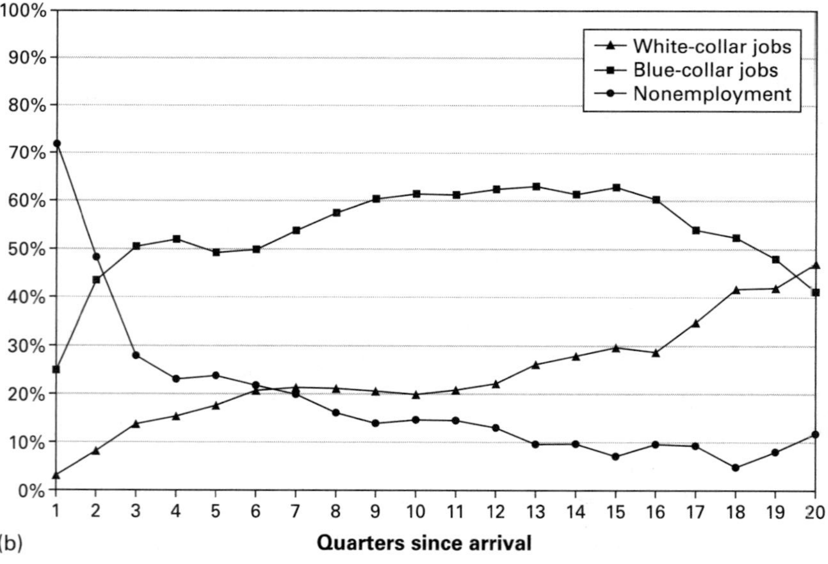

Figure 4.1
Actual choice distributions: (a) Females. (b) Employed and nonemployed males. (c) Males undergoing training. Source: Brookdale Survey.

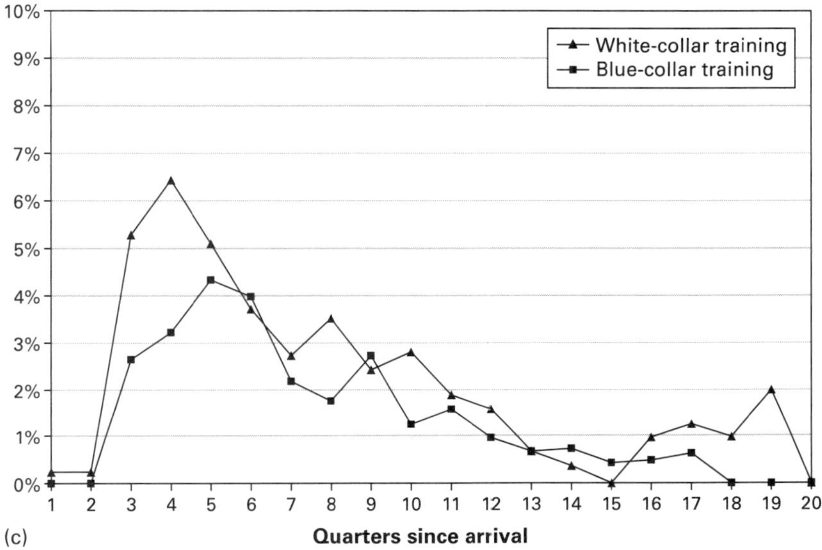

Figure 4.1
(continued)

worked in a WC (BC) occupation continue to do so in the subsequent quarter.[10] Transitions from one type of occupation to the other are rare. However, some transitions may occur indirectly through training and nonemployment. Direct transitions from training to WC and BC employment are considerably more common than transitions from nonemployment to either of the two employment states, which is an indication of the potential employment gain from training.

Wages

In the 1992 survey, the immigrant was asked about the last salary she had received. In the 1995 survey, she was asked about the salary she had received in each of the jobs she reported in that survey. Thus there are a total of 649 wage observations for females. The average wage in WC (BC) occupations is 12.5 (11.6) NIS per hour during the first year in Israel, which increases to 22.1 (10.8) NIS per hour by the fifth year.[11] Thus the average wage in WC jobs increases over time, whereas in BC jobs it remains roughly constant. Furthermore wages in WC jobs are more volatile than those in BC jobs.

The results of a standard OLS estimation of log hourly wage equations (with robust standard errors) are presented in table 4.3A.[12] Training enters as a dummy only for wages reported after the completion of the training program. The results indicate that imported human capital in the

Table 4.2A
Actual quarterly transitions—Females

From / To	White-collar		Blue-collar		Training		Nonemployment		Total
White-collar	918	95.6%	7	0.7%	12	1.3%	23	2.4%	960
Blue-collar	14	0.5%	2,414	92.9%	51	2.0%	120	4.6%	2,599
Training	33	7.7%	71	16.5%	222	51.5%	105	24.4%	431
Nonemployment	101	3.7%	330	12.2%	154	5.7%	2,128	78.4%	2,713
Total	1,066		2,822		439		2,376		6,703

Source: Brookdale Survey.
Note: Each row sums to 100%.

form of schooling and experience (age on arrival) imported from the FSU has no impact on the immigrant's wage in Israel.

Local occupational WC experience has a large effect on wages in WC occupations, while BC experience has a zero return in both occupations. The estimated impact of Hebrew fluency on wages is large and significant only in BC jobs. The data from the two surveys was used to measure each immigrant's knowledge of Hebrew (see table 4.1A) in order to construct a female immigrant's specific predicted Hebrew fluency in each quarter following arrival in Israel. Specifically, we use the following estimated pooled regression:

$$Heb_{it} = 1.906 + 0.5357 * Heb\_FSU_i + 0.459 * studied\_Ulpan_i$$

$$+ 0.1802 * finished\_Ulpan_i + 0.07924 * t - 0.0021 * t^2 + fe_i$$

where Heb_{it} is the level of Hebrew fluency of individual i in quarter t following arrival, Heb_FSU_i is a dummy for knowledge of Hebrew prior to migration (table 4.1A), $studied\_Ulpan_i$ is a dummy for studying in Ulpan, $finished\_Ulpan_i$ is a dummy for graduating the Ulpan and fe_i is the individual fixed effect.

The most important result of the wage regression for females (table 4.3A) is that the return on training in a WC occupation is very large (16

Table 4.3A
OLS estimation of wage equation—Females

Variable	White-collar wage	Blue-collar wage
Constant	1.7615*	1.8351*
	(0.7249)	(0.1376)
Schooling	0.0219	−0.0004
	(0.0208)	(0.0089)
Age on arrival	0.0057	0.0024
	(0.0066)	(0.0024)
WC experience (quarters)	0.0372*	0.0269
	(0.0115)	(0.0237)
BC experience (quarters)	0.0006	0.0045
	(0.0162)	(0.0046)
Hebrew[a]	0.0621	0.0943*
	(0.1443)	(0.0371)
Training	0.1605**	−0.0149
	(0.0897)	(0.0438)
Number of observations	168	481
R^2	0.09	0.02

Source: Brookdale Survey.
Note: The dependant variable is log hourly wage. Robust standard errors appear in parentheses. *Significant at 5% level; **significant at 10% level.
a. Predicted Hebrew fluency index, for details see section 4.2.1 in the text.

percent) and significant at the 10 percent level, while it is zero in BC jobs. Since the regressors are endogenous these estimates are biased and the correction for this potential bias is an important task of the structural estimation presented below.

4.2.2   (B) Males

As table 4.1B indicates, 30 percent (124) of the men in the sample participated in a training program since their arrival. As with females, we find that male trainees are younger on arrival and have more years of schooling. About 98 percent of the men in our sample worked in the FSU, of whom 68 percent worked in WC occupations while 30 percent worked in BC occupations. Knowledge of Hebrew was measured in both interviews: 12 percent of the immigrants were able to hold a simple conversation in Hebrew prior to arrival, 92 percent of the immigrants attended Ulpan and 79 percent completed it. Knowledge of Hebrew increased by

Table 4.1B
Summary statistics—Males

Variable	Full sample	Untrained	Trained[a]
Number of observations	419	295	124
Age on arrival	38.1	38.8	36.2
	(9.2)	(9.5)	(7.9)
Years of schooling	14.6	14.2	15.4
	(2.7)	(2.9)	(2.1)
Number of children	1.09	1.07	1.15
	(0.9)	(0.9)	(0.8)
Number of jobs since arrival	2.2	2.1	2.6
	(1.3)	(1.3)	(1.2)
Months in Israel	41.4	39.9	45.2
	(14.7)	(15.2)	(12.7)
Nonemployed[b] (%)	4.8	4.7	4.8
White-collar[c] in the FSU (%)	67.8	60.7	84.7
Married (%)	86.6	87.1	85.5
Had knowledge of Hebrew prior to immigrating (%)	11.9	9.8	16.9
Hebrew fluency index—first survey[d]	2.71	2.56	3.07
	(0.82)	(0.8)	(0.76)
Hebrew fluency index—second survey	2.98	2.86	3.24
	(0.83)	(0.87)	(0.69)

Source: Brookdale Survey.
Note: Standard deviations appear in parentheses.
a. Participated in a training program since arrival.
b. Percentage of immigrants who never worked since their arrival.
c. For details on occupational classification, see section 4.2 in the text.
d. 1 = lowest; 4 = highest.

an average of 10 percent between the two surveys. Note that the proportion of male immigrants who were nonemployed throughout the sample period (4.8 percent) is significantly lower than the proportion of female immigrants.

Labor Market States

In the case of males we classified an individual's labor market status according to the classification used in our model. In each quarter the immigrant can be in one of five labor market states: nonemployed, employed in a WC job, employed in a BC job, attending a training course in a WC occupation (WC training), or attending a training course in a BC occupation (BC training). Figure 4.1b and c presents the actual proportions of males in each state for the first 20 quarters since arrival in Israel. Immigrants who attend Ulpan during the first two quarters are considered to be nonemployed. The nonemployment rate reaches 23 percent after a year in Israel and stabilizes at about 10 percent after 13 quarters. A substantial number of immigrants work in BC jobs during their first two years in Israel. This proportion increases to more than 60 percent after two and a half years in Israel and remains at this level for almost two additional years (see figure 4.1b). These patterns of slow dynamic transition for males and females are similar to what is believed to be typical immigrant behavior (Chiswick 1992; Eckstein and Weiss 2004).[13] During the fifth year in Israel, the share of male immigrants who work in BC jobs declines by almost 20 percent and the share of those employed in WC jobs increases by almost the same magnitude (see figure 4.1b), which is similar to the trend for females. Does this change in trend for male and female immigrants reflect occupational upgrading during the fifth year following migration, or is it a result of the characteristics of the 1989–90 cohort of immigrants relative to those of the 1991–92 cohort? To answer this question requires a structural model that can distinguish between the two hypotheses.

Transitions

Table 4.2B presents the total number and proportion of quarter-to-quarter transitions by male immigrants between the model's five labor market states. As with females, males have a high level of state dependence in occupation-specific employment, such that almost all the immigrants who worked in a WC or BC occupation continue to do so in the subsequent quarter. Transitions from one type of occupation to the other are rare. However, some transitions may occur indirectly through training

Table 4.2B
Actual quarterly transitions—Males

From / To	White-collar		Blue-collar		WC training		BC training		Nonemployment		Total
White-collar	999	95.5%	15	1.4%	12	1.1%	4	0.4%	16	1.5%	1,046
Blue-collar	18	0.6%	2,646	93.6%	26	0.9%	28	1.0%	110	3.9%	2,828
WC training	24	17.6%	17	12.5%	70	51.5%	0	0.0%	25	18.4%	136
BC training	4	4.4%	19	20.9%	0	0.0%	47	51.6%	21	23.1%	91
Nonemployment	89	7.1%	275	21.9%	34	2.7%	19	1.5%	841	66.9%	1,258
Total	1,134		2,972		142		98		1,013		5,359

Source: Brookdale Survey.
Note: Each row sums to 100%.

and nonemployment. Direct transitions from training to WC and BC jobs are considerably more common than transitions from nonemployment to either of the two employment states, which is an indication of the potential employment gain from training.

Wages

There are a total of 574 wage observations for male immigrants. The results of a standard OLS estimation of log hourly wage equations are presented in table 4.3B. Training enters as a dummy only for wages reported after the completion of the training program. The results indicate that for both male and female immigrants human capital in the form of imported schooling has no impact on the immigrant's wage in Israel. However, experience (age on arrival) has a positive and significant impact on wages in WC jobs for male immigrants, while its effect on wages in BC jobs is negative and significant at the 10 percent level. The estimated coefficients of training have large standard errors indicating a small sample with high variance. However, the values of the coefficients indicate that the classification of training and jobs according

Table 4.3B
OLS estimation of wage equation—Males

Variable	White-collar wage	Blue-collar wage
Constant	1.1133*	2.1244*
	(0.3498)	(0.1212)
Schooling	0.0212	0.0084
	(0.0212)	(0.0059)
Age on arrival	0.0131*	−0.0031**
	(0.0045)	(0.0018)
Total experience (quarters)	0.0172*	0.0243*
	(0.0083)	(0.0033)
Hebrew[a]	0.1228*	0.0495**
	(0.0567)	(0.0258)
English	0.1318*	−0.0112
	(0.0359)	(0.0219)
WC training	0.1146	−0.0098
	(0.0837)	(0.0633)
BC training	−0.0445	0.0561
	(0.1133)	(0.0474)
Number of observations	132	442
R^2	0.23	0.15

Source: Brookdale Survey.
Note: The dependant variable is log hourly wage. Robust standard errors appear in parentheses. *Significant at 5% level; **significant at 10% level.
a. Predicted Hebrew fluency index, for details see section 4.2.1 in the text.

to two occupational categories is justified. Furthermore these results are similar to those obtained in many other studies that have attempted to assess the impact of training on wages (Heckman, LaLonde, and Smith 1999).

The level of Hebrew fluency in each quarter is the predicted index from the regression of the index of Hebrew fluency at the time of the first and second surveys on time since arrival, time since arrival squared, the duration of the Ulpan and the indicator for knowledge of Hebrew prior to migration:

$$\widehat{Heb}_{it} = \underset{(0.169)}{1.695} + \underset{(0.015)}{0.092} * Ulpan\_length_i + \underset{(0.089)}{0.657} * Heb\_FSU_i$$
$$+ \underset{(0.031)}{0.071} * t_i - \underset{(0.0013)}{0.0014} * t_i^2 .$$

Given this format, one can interpret the Hebrew index *Heb* as a given process of accumulation of local language and social norms. The estimated coefficients for knowledge of Hebrew and English are higher in WC jobs than in BC jobs and are significant in WC jobs, while in BC jobs only Hebrew is significant at the 10 percent level.[14] In addition accumulated general experience in Israel has a positive effect on wages in both occupations.[15]

Discussion

The data reveals both similarities and differences in the labor market integration of female and male immigrants. The similarities are reflected primarily in the rapid decline in nonemployment and the massive entry into BC jobs subsequent to arrival, followed by a gradual transition to WC jobs. The participation in training peaks during the first year in Israel for both males and females and subsequently declines. The transitions between labor market states are also similar for male and female immigrants, and we observe a high level of persistence in the two employment states for both genders. Moreover the implications of the wage regressions are similar for both males and females, such that the return on imported education is almost zero and local training and experience have high returns (particularly in WC occupations), though the standard errors are also high. Nevertheless, despite the similarities in *trends,* we find that the *level* of nonemployment among female immigrants is substantially higher than among males, and consequently the level of employment in BC and WC occupations is somewhat lower for females. Overall, the data suggest that we can use similar models for males and females and that household characteristics do not play a major role in the integration of female immigrants.

4.3 Model Specifications

In this section we formulate finite-horizon dynamic discrete choice models for the integrated labor supply and human capital investment decisions of female and male immigrants. As already mentioned, the labor market integration of female immigrants is quite similar to that of male immigrants, which suggests that the model for females should be similar to that of males. Nevertheless, we chose different specifications for males and females and used them as a tool to test the robustness of the results to different specifications of the structural models. The models resemble the dynamic programming models of labor supply and schooling (Keane and Wolpin 1997; Eckstein and Wolpin 1999) in which individuals sequentially choose among a finite set of mutually exclusive alternatives over a finite horizon in order to maximize discounted expected utility. The models incorporate initial observed heterogeneity at the time of arrival, such as marital status, number of children, years of schooling, age on arrival and occupation in the FSU. Since the models are estimated using immigrants who came to Israel in the initial wave of 1989 to 1992 and who had not previously expected to migrate, the standard initial condition problem is not a concern here. Hence we can treat the imported endowment of human capital (schooling and occupation prior to migration) and age on arrival as exogenous.

4.3.1 (A) Females

Each female immigrant in each period t, starting on arrival in Israel ($t = 1$) and ending at retirement ($t = T$), chooses an element a from the four alternatives in her choice set A: employment in a WC occupation ($a = 1$), employment in a BC occupation ($a = 2$), participation in a training course ($a = 3$) and nonemployment ($a = 4$).[16] The choice variable d_{at} equals one if the a element was chosen in period t and zero otherwise.[17] The four alternatives are mutually exclusive, implying that $\sum_{a=1}^{4} d_{at} = 1$ for every t. The periodic utility of a female immigrant, U_t, is assumed to be linear and additive in consumption and labor market state, such that

$$U_t = (\gamma_{1m}M_t + \gamma_{1c}N_t)(d_{1t} + d_{2t})$$
$$+(\gamma_{2m}M_t + \gamma_{2c}N_t + \gamma_{3l} + \varepsilon_{3t})d_{3t}$$
$$+(\gamma_{3m}M_t + \gamma_{3c}N_t + \gamma_{4l} + \varepsilon_{4t})d_{4t} \tag{4.1}$$
$$+C_t,$$

where M is an indicator equal to one if the immigrant is married and N is the number of children (both of which are assumed to be exogenous and constant) and C_t is the consumption of a composite good in period t.[18] The utility from children, marriage and leisure depends on the labor market state, that is, employment, participation in a training course, or nonemployment.

The female budget constraint in each period $t, t = 1, \ldots, T$, is given by

$$d_{1t}w_{1t} + d_{2t}w_{2t} + d_{3t}TW + d_{4t}UB + AI_t$$
$$= C_t + g_1N_t \cdot (d_{1t} + d_{2t}) + g_2N_t \cdot d_{3t} + g_3N_t \cdot d_{4t}, \tag{4.2}$$

where w_{at} is the immigrant's wage in a WC occupation ($a = 1$) or in a BC occupation ($a = 2$), TW is the subsidy received by the immigrant while attending training ($a = 3$), UB is the unemployment benefit, AI_t represents additional sources of income that do not depend on the immigrant's choice such as the husband's earnings, and g_aN_t denotes the cost of children, which takes on different values according to whether the immigrant works ($a = 1, 2$), participates in a training course ($a = 3$) or is nonemployed ($a = 4$). Given the linearity of preferences, we can write the periodic utility U_t as

$$U_t = \sum_{a=1}^{4} U_{at}d_{at}, \tag{4.3}$$

where U_{at} is the periodic utility associated with choosing alternative a at time t. Substituting C_t (obtained from equation 4.2) into (4.1), the alternative state-specific utilities at time t are

$$U_{1t} = w_{1t} - g_1N_t + \gamma_{1m}M_t + \gamma_{1c}N_t,$$

$$U_{2t} = w_{2t} - g_1N_t + \gamma_{1m}M_t + \gamma_{1c}N_t,$$

$$U_{3t} = TW - g_2N_t + \gamma_{2m}M_t + \gamma_{2c}N_t + \gamma_{3l} + \varepsilon_{3t}, \tag{4.4}$$

$$U_{4t} = UB - g_3N_t + \gamma_{3m}M_t + \gamma_{3c}N_t + \gamma_{4l} + \varepsilon_{4t},$$

where ε_{3t} and ε_{4t} are the time-varying utility shocks, which are assumed to be serially uncorrelated. Note that under the assumption that utility is additive and separable in consumption, the additional sources of income in (4.2), namely AI_t, are neutral across the four alternatives and do not affect immigrants' choices.[19]

The stochastic offered wage, w_{jt}, in occupation $j, j = 1, 2$ follows a standard Mincerian wage function with cross-experience terms

$$w_{jt} = \exp(\alpha_{0j} + \alpha_{1j}SC + \alpha_{2j}EX_{1t-1} + \alpha_{3j}EX_{2t-1} + \alpha_{4j}DT_t$$
$$+\alpha_{5j}AGE + \alpha_{6j}Heb_t + \varepsilon_{jt}), \tag{4.5}$$

where SC denotes the immigrant's imported years of schooling, EX_{jt-1} is the *actual* work experience the immigrant has accumulated in occupation j from the time of her arrival until period t, DT_t is an indicator that equals one if the immigrant has completed a training program prior to period t, AGE represents the immigrant's age on arrival, and Heb_t is the immigrant's knowledge of Hebrew at time t. The training evaluation literature has focused on the parameter α_{4j}, which is known as the mean return on training.[20]

The parameter α_{0j} measures the wage and the constant individual utility premium for occupation j (see equation 4.4). The parameters α_{2j}, α_{3j}, α_{4j}, and α_{6j} measure the contributions of various forms of human capital, which the immigrant has accumulated in Israel, to her potential earnings. The parameters α_{1j} and α_{5j} measure the contribution of imported schooling and experience (age on arrival) to potential earnings. ε_{jt} is a time-varying occupation-specific shock, which is assumed to be serially uncorrelated. Under this last assumption, time-dependence in wages is not random but rather is related to the immigrant's decisions via work experience and participation in a training course. The random elements $\varepsilon_t = [\varepsilon_{1t}, \varepsilon_{2t}, \varepsilon_{3t}, \varepsilon_{4t}]$ are assumed to have a joint normal distribution and to be serially independent, such that $\varepsilon_t \sim iidN(0, \Omega)$, where Ω is not restricted and allows for within-period correlations between the four choices.

The stocks of occupation-specific work experience evolve according to

$$EX_{1t} = EX_{1t-1} + d_{1t},$$
$$EX_{2t} = EX_{2t-1} + d_{2t}, \tag{4.6}$$

where the initial values of the endogenous human capital variables are given by the level of these variables on arrival in Israel, implying that $EX_{1,0} = EX_{2,0} = DT_0 = 0$. The immigrant's choices take into account that future job opportunities and wage offers depend on endogenously accumulated occupation-specific work experience and training status.

The objective of the immigrant is therefore to maximize

$$E\left[\sum_{t=1}^{T}\beta^t\sum_{a=1}^{4}U_{at}d_{at}I_{at}\mid S(0)\right] \tag{4.7}$$

by choosing a sequence of the control variables d_{at} for all $t = 1, \ldots, T$, where β is the discount factor. I_{at} is an indicator function that is equal to one if alternative a is available at time t.[21] The expectation operator $E[\bullet|S(0)]$ is defined over the distribution of ε_t and the probability of availability of labor market states as defined below. Finally, $S(0)$ is the individual's state space on arrival ($t = 0$), which contains all the variables that are known to the immigrant in this period and affect either her current or future utility.

The availability of labor states in each period t in the optimization of (4.7) is determined as follows. The immigrant can always choose to be nonemployed, such that $I_{4t} = 1$ for all t. In each period the immigrant can receive independent job offers in WC and BC occupations. Furthermore in each period t there is an exogenous probability, $1 - s_j$, that the worker remains in the same occupation, such that s_j is the exogenous probability that an employed immigrant is fired or quits her job in occupation $j, j = 1, 2$.

The probability of receiving a job offer in occupation $j, j = 1, 2$ at time t depends on the labor market activity that the immigrant engaged in during the previous period ($d_{a\,t-1}$), as well as the immigrant's years of schooling, age on arrival, participation in training, occupation in the FSU (denoted by UOC) and accumulated work experience in occupation j. We adopt the following logistic form for job-offer probability:

$$\lambda_{jt} = \frac{\exp(Q_{jt})}{1+\exp(Q_{jt})}, \qquad \text{where } j = 1, 2, \tag{4.8}$$

$$Q_{jt} = b_{10j}d_{3t-1} + b_{11j}d_{4t-1} + b_{12j}d_{-jt-1} + b_{2j}SC + b_{3j}AGE + b_{4j}DT_t$$
$$+ b_{5j}UOC + b_{6j}EX_{jt-1} + b_{7j}Heb_t,$$

where $d_{-j\,t-1} = 1$ if the immigrant was employed in an occupation other than j at $t - 1$.

The institutional design of training programs imposes restrictions on participation in training that are included in the model. Each immigrant is eligible to participate in only one government-sponsored training program during her first five years in Israel. In addition the individual is eligible to participate in training only after completing a Hebrew course or passing a Hebrew test. We impose these restrictions on the model directly using indicator functions that receive the value of zero or one conditional on the relevant state.

While there is in general no uncertainty regarding the availability of training programs, uncertainty does exist in each period since there is a significant amount of bureaucracy involved in the supply of programs and a particular program may not be offered in a specific period even if demand for it exists. Also the training programs are not always available in every location. This was particularly true in 1991 to 2000 when the immigrants arrived in Israel continuously while the training programs had a predetermined schedule. There were also institutional restrictions on immigrants' participation in training if they were older than forty. We model this process as a periodic probability of receiving an offer to participate in training that depends on the immigrant's age on arrival:

$$pt_1 = \frac{\exp(p_1)}{1 + \exp(p_1)} \quad \text{if} \quad AGE < 40,$$

$$pt_2 = \frac{\exp(p_2)}{1 + \exp(p_2)} \quad \text{if} \quad AGE \geq 40,$$

(4.9)

where p_1 and p_2 are parameters.[22]

Finally, in this setting, the state space in period t, which includes all the variables that are known up to time t and are relevant for the immigrant's future decisions, can be written as

$$S(t) = \{d_{1t-1}, d_{2t-1}, d_{3t-1}, d_{4t-1}, EX_{1t-1}, EX_{2t-1} \, DT_t,$$
$$SC, AGE, N, M, UOC, Heb_t, Heb\_FSU, \varepsilon_t\}.$$

(4.10)

4.3.2   (B) Males

We assume that a male immigrant who arrives in Israel at age AGE and is expected to live L periods faces a finite-horizon planning period of duration $T = L - AGE$ quarters. In each period since arrival $t, t = 1, 2, \ldots T$, he can choose one of five labor market alternatives $a = 0, 1, 2, \ldots, A, A = 4$. Let d_{at} equal one if alternative j is chosen at time t and zero otherwise.[23] The index $a = 1$ corresponds to working in a WC occupation and $a = 2$ corresponds to working in a BC occupation. When $d_{at} = 1$ and $a = 3, 4$, the individual acquires training relevant to occupation $a - 2$.

When $d_{0t} = 1$, the immigrant searches for work while nonemployed. We denote by d_t the row vector $\{d_t, a = 0, \ldots, A\}$.

The current utility from labor market state a at time t in Israel is denoted by U_{at} and is given by

$$U_{0t} = ne + \varepsilon_{0t},$$

$$U_{jt} = w_{jt} \quad \text{for} \quad j = 1, 2,$$

$$U_{jt} = tr_j + \varepsilon_{jt} \quad \text{for} \quad j = 3, 4. \qquad (4.11)$$

The immigrant's utility in (4.11) is measured in monetary terms due to the linearity of utility in wages in the two employment states ($a = 1$, 2). The monetary value of the utility associated with a training program is denoted by $tr_j, j = 3, 4$, and that associated with nonemployment ($j = 0$) by ne. The monetary units are determined by the wage definition which is the hourly wage rate in NIS.[24]

The offered wage in occupation $j, j = 1, 2$ in period t is a standard log linear function of the immigrant's occupation-specific human capital, K_{jt}, and a random $i.i.d$ shock, z_{jt}. That is,

$$\ln w_{jt} = K_{jt} + z_{jt}. \qquad (4.12)$$

The accumulation of human capital for each $j, j = 1, 2$, is determined by the following equation:

$$K_{jt} = \alpha_{0j} + \alpha_{ej}EX_t + \alpha_{cj}DT_{jt} + \alpha_{Hj}Heb_t + \alpha_{Fj}ENG + \alpha_{Aj}AGE + \alpha_{Sj}SC, \qquad (4.13)$$

where EX_t is general accumulated experience in the Israeli labor market and DT_{jt} is an indicator that equals one if the worker has completed a training course in occupation $j, j = 1, 2$, prior to period t.[25] Heb_t indicates the level of Hebrew at time t in Israel, which we assume to be exogenous. Imported human capital is represented by the immigrant's education level (SC), age on arrival (AGE) and knowledge of English on arrival (ENG). The random vector $\varepsilon_{it} = [\varepsilon_{0t}, z_{1t}, z_{2t}, \varepsilon_{3t}, \varepsilon_{4t}]$ is normally distributed as $N(0, \Omega)$ and Ω is not restricted, such that we allow for correlation in the errors of different labor market states within each period.

Each immigrant is assumed to maximize the expected present value of his lifetime utility,

$$E\left[\sum_{t=1}^{T} \beta^{t-1} \sum_{a \in A} U_{at} d_{at} \mid S(0) \right], \qquad (4.14)$$

by choosing d_{at} for all $t = 1, \ldots, T$, where S_1 is the vector of all the relevant state variables on arrival. E denotes the expectation taken over the joint distribution of ε_t and the transition probabilities P_{rat} as specified below, and β is the discount factor, $0 < \beta < 1$.[26]

We assume that for alternative a, $a = 1, 2, 3$, the immigrant either has or does not have the option of choosing this alternative, while nonemployment ($a = 0$) and training in a BC occupation ($a = 4$) are always available. However, we impose the institutional rules that both training programs are available only from the third quarter of residency in Israel for those immigrants who had no prior knowledge of Hebrew.[27] The immigrant is allowed to participate in only one training program during his lifetime. Formally, given that an immigrant chose alternative r in period $t - 1$, the conditional probability that he has the option of choosing alternative j, $j = 1, 2, 3$, is given by

$$P_{rjt} = P_{rj}(x_t, d_{t-1}, t),\tag{4.15}$$

where the matrix $\{P_{rjt} : r = 0, 1, 2, \ldots, 4; j = 1, 2, 3\}$ is the periodic conditional offer probability matrix.[28] The vector x_t represents individual characteristics. Specifically, the probabilities of receiving WC and BC job offers have the following logistic form:

$$P_{rjt} = \frac{\exp\{Q_{jt}\}}{1 + \exp\{Q_{jt}\}}, \qquad j = 1, 2,\tag{4.16}$$

where the specification of Q_{jt} depends on j. During the first two quarters in Israel, immigrants who have no knowledge of Hebrew on arrival do not receive a job offer in a WC occupation ($j = 1$). From the third quarter onward ($t \geq 3$), P_{r1t} is given by (4.16), such that

$$Q_{1t} = b_{011}d_{1,t-1} + b_{021}d_{2,t-1} + b_{031}(d_{0,t-1} + d_{3,t-1} + d_{4,t-1})$$

$$+ b_{111}I(1 \leq EX_t \leq 4) + b_{121}I(EX_t > 4) + b_{21}DT_{1t}\tag{4.17}$$

$$+ b_{31}AGE + b_{41}Heb_t + b_5ENG + +b_6UOC,$$

where $I(1 \leq EX_t \leq 4)$ is an indicator that equals one if the individual has accumulated between one and four quarters of work experience in Israel by time t, and $I(EX_t > 4)$ is an indicator that equals one if the individual has accumulated more than four quarters of work experience in Israel by time t. The law of motion for general accumulated experience in the Israeli labor market (EX_t) is given by $EX_t = EX_{t-1} + d_{j,t-1}$, $j = 1, 2$, and upon arrival $EX_1 = 0$. The indicator DT_{1t} is equal to one if the worker has completed a training course in a WC occupation prior to period t. As such, the probability of receiving a job offer in a WC occupation ($j = 1$) depends on the individual's labor market state in the previous period (r), accumulated experience in Israel, participation in a WC training course, age on arrival, knowledge of Hebrew, knowledge of English and an indicator for employment in a WC job in the FSU.

The probability of receiving a job offer in a BC occupation ($j = 2$), P_{r2t} is given by (4.16), such that Q_{2t} depends on which activity the individual engaged in during the previous period (r), accumulated experience in Israel, participation in a BC training course, age on arrival and knowledge of Hebrew. Specifically,

$$Q_{2t} = b_{012}d_{1,t-1} + b_{022}d_{2,t-1} + b_{032}(d_{0,t-1} + d_{3,t-1} + d_{4,t-1})$$

$$+ b_{112}I(1 \leq EX_t \leq 4) + b_{042}(d_{0,t-1} + d_{3,t-1} + d_{4,t-1})I(t < 2) \qquad (4.18)$$

$$+ b_{122}I(EX_t > 4) + b_{22}DT_{2t} + b_{32}AGE + b_{42}Heb_t + b_7 d_{2,t-1}I(t < 6),$$

where $I(t < 2)$ is an indicator that equals one during the first quarter in Israel. The parameter b_7 is meant to capture the possibility that the persistence in BC jobs during the first 18 months, when immigrants change jobs more frequently, may differ from that in later periods, which are characterized by greater stability.

The probabilities of receiving an offer to participate in a training program in a WC or BC occupation are zero during the first two quarters, unless the immigrant had prior knowledge of Hebrew. For $t > 2$, the probability of receiving a BC training offer is one and the probability of receiving a WC training offer is constant over time (and less than 1), though we allow it to depend on schooling. Specifically, the probability of a WC training offer takes the form

$$P_{r3t} = \frac{\exp\{\gamma_0 + \gamma_1 SC\}}{1 + \exp\{\gamma_0 + \gamma_1 SC\}}, \qquad j = 3. \qquad (4.19)$$

Both training-offer probabilities are independent of job offers. An immigrant who has already participated in a WC or BC training program since his arrival does not receive another training offer. Once the training program is available, the immigrant is randomly assigned to a one-, two- or three-quarter training program. The allocation is determined by a random draw from a simple three-point discrete probability distribution where the proportions are set to be equal to the actual observed proportion in each program. That is, 33 percent are allocated to a one-quarter training program, 42 percent to a two-quarter program and 25 percent to a three-quarter training program. The decision to participate in a training course (either WC or BC training) is based on the expected present value of this choice conditional on the three alternative durations of training, assuming the actual probabilities.[29]

The state vector at time t in Israel is given by

$$S(t) = [EX_t, DT_{jt}, Heb_t, ENG, AGE, SC,$$
$$UOC, d_{j,t-1}, \varepsilon_t, \text{ for } j = 0, 1, 2, 3, 4], \tag{4.20}$$

where UOC is an indicator for employment in a WC job prior to migration and ε_t is the realized value of the vector of shocks.

4.4   Solution and Estimation Methods

The optimization problem for females (4.7) and males (4.14) can be represented by a set of alternative-specific value functions, each obeying the Bellman (1957) equation:

$$V_a(S(t), t) = U_{at} + \beta E\{\max_{x \in A}(V_x(S(t+1), t+1)) \mid S(t), d_{at} = 1\}, \qquad a \in A,$$

$$\tag{4.21}$$

where $V_a(S(t), t)$ is the maximum expected present value of utility if alternative a is chosen at time t for a given element of the state space $S(t)$. As can be seen from (4.21), future decisions are assumed to be made optimally for any current choice $a, a \in A$.

At this stage it is important to outline the elements of the model that explain the observed dynamics in figure 4.1a for females and figure 4.1b and c for males and the patterns of wage growth, respectively. The immigrant starts with some given initial characteristics but with no job. The random arrival of job offers, training programs and the immediate and expected return that determine choices jointly impose the particular transition between states. Standard human capital theory emphasizes the impact of human capital (schooling) on earnings (Ben-Porath 1967). Both the wage return and the job-offer reward on investment in training are enjoyed for the duration of the immigrant's working life and therefore the model implies that training is most worthwhile soon after arrival in Israel. In our model, however, training can also be viewed as an alternative to nonemployment, and hence participation in a training course can also be expected in later periods. Moreover the availability of training is random, and therefore it is possible to observe participation in a training course in later periods as well. In addition the gain from local experience creates a high opportunity cost for working immigrants to attend training programs. These results imply that we can expect early training attendance among the nonemployed and transitions to jobs that are more frequently offered. Since individuals choose optimally between potential current and future states, the model predicts that over time the number of transitions will diminish and greater stability can be expected.

The accumulation of work experience and participation in a training program affects future wages faced by the individual as well as work possibilities, which in turn affect future participation and wages in the labor market. Assuming that the availability of BC jobs is higher than that of WC jobs (as is the case in the Israeli market), the model predicts that initially workers who arrive with high potential human capital (schooling) will initially invest by working in BC jobs and attending a training course and later will find a job in a WC occupation. These predicted patterns of participation in training courses and occupational choice were obtained from simulations of the model and are consistent with the observed data (see figure 4.1a–c).

4.4.1   Solution

In each period the immigrant chooses one element from within his/her choice set A for which the value function in (4.21) is maximized. The decision rules in a finite-horizon model are not stationary and depend on, among other things, the number of periods until retirement. The model is solved recursively from the last period back to the first.

To demonstrate the solution method, consider, for example, the state space of females described by (4.10). Now denote by $\bar{S}(t)$ its predetermined values that can be taken to be deterministic elements at t. Assuming that the immigrant enters the last decision period T with $\bar{S}(T)$, the value functions at T are known up to a random draw from the multivariate normal distribution of the alternative-specific shocks ε_T. Given a draw from this distribution, all the terminal value functions given by (4.21) can be calculated and the immigrant chooses the alternative a that achieves the highest realized value $V_a(S(T), T)$.

However, in order to calculate the value functions at $T-1$ given $\bar{S}(T-1)$, conditional on the availability of job offers and a training offer, the immigrant has to first calculate

$$E \max\{V_1(S(T),T), V_2(S(T),T), V_3(S(T),T), V_4(S(T),T) \mid S(T-1), d_{aT-1}\}$$

$$= \int\limits_{\varepsilon_{1T}} \int\limits_{\varepsilon_{2T}} \int\limits_{\varepsilon_{3T}} \int\limits_{\varepsilon_{4T}} \max\{V_1(S(T),T), V_2(S(T),T),$$

$$V_3(S(T),T), V_4(S(T),T) \mid S(T-1), d_{aT-1}\} \tag{4.22}$$

$$\times f(\varepsilon_{1T}, \varepsilon_{2T}, \varepsilon_{3T}, \varepsilon_{4T}) d\varepsilon_{1T} d\varepsilon_{2T} d\varepsilon_{3T} d\varepsilon_{4T}.$$

This calculation must be done for every possible a since each choice a in $T-1$ leads to a different point in the state space in T. Thus the E max in (4.22) should be calculated at each of the four attainable state space points in T, given $\overline{S}(T-1)$. After calculating the E max *for* each possible choice at $T-1$, the immigrant knows the value functions at $T-1$ up to a random draw from the multivariate normal distribution of ε_{T-1}. Given a draw from ε_{T-1}, the immigrant chooses the alternative a for which $V_a(S(T-1), T-1)$ is maximized. The same calculation is done as we move backward. The value functions in period t need to be computed for every possible point $\overline{S}(t+1)$ in the state space that can arise, given $\overline{S}(t)$ and the actual choice d_{at}.

Under the assumption that the alternative-specific shocks have a multivariate normal distribution, (4.22) does not have a closed-form expression. Full numerical computation of (4.22) requires high-dimensional integrations. Following Keane and Wolpin (1994), we use Monte Carlo integration to numerically approximate (4.22). In other words, we take D draws from the multivariate normal distribution of ε_T and calculate the maximum of the value functions for each. The maximum values are then averaged, implying that:

$$E \max\{V_1(S(T),T), V_2(S(T),T), V_3(S(T),T), V_4(S(T),T) \mid S(T-1), d_{aT-1}\}$$

$$= \frac{1}{D} \sum_{d=1}^{D} \max\{V_1(S(T),T), V_2(S(T),T), V_3(S(T),T),$$

$$V_4(S(T),T) \mid S(T-1), d_{aT-1}\}. \tag{4.23}$$

Full solution of the dynamic programming problem, from the immigrant's arrival until retirement, for all potential points in the state space that may arise involves an enormous computational burden, especially since we use quarterly rather than annual data. To reduce this burden, we split the horizon into two subperiods. During the first 20 quarters, the model is solved explicitly, as described above. The value functions in the 21st quarter, $V_a(S(21), 21)$, are assumed to be a parameterized function of $S(20)$, the state space in the 20th quarter.

In particular, for females we assume the terminal value function[30]

$$V_a(S(21), 21) = \delta_1 EX_{1,20} + \delta_2 EX_{2,20} + \delta_{3m}(60 - AGE) + \delta_4 DT_{20} + \delta_5$$

$$+ \delta_6 d_{1,20} + \delta_7 d_{2,20} + \delta_8 SC + \delta_9 N + \delta_{10} M + \delta_{11} UOC + \delta_{12} Heb_{20}, \tag{4.24}$$

and for males we assume

$$V_a(S(21), 21) = \delta_1 + \delta_2 EX_{21} + \delta_3 DT_{1,21} + \delta_4 SC + \delta_5 AGE \tag{4.25}$$

$$+ \delta_6 Heb_{21} + \delta_7 ENG + \delta_8 d_{1,20} + \delta_9 d_{0,20} + \delta_{10} DT_{2,21}.$$

4.4.2   Estimation Method

The models are estimated using smooth maximum likelihood (SML) following McFadden (1989) and Keane and Wolpin (1997). Let t_i be the length of time we observe immigrant i. Given data on the choices of individual i (d_{at}^i; t = 1, . . . , t_i; a = 1, . . . , 4 for females and a = 0, . . . , 4 for males) and the wage, w_{jt}^{io}, in occupation j ($t = 1, . . . , t_i$, j = 1, 2) if chosen, the solution of the dynamic programming problem serves as input in the estimation procedure. As such, all the parameters of the model enter into the likelihood function through their effect on choice probabilities and wages. Given the observed variance in wages, we allow for a multiplicative measurement error in observed wages (Keane and Wolpin 1997), such that ln w_{jt}^{io}, the log of the observed wage of individual i at time t in occupation j, is of the form: ln $w_{jt}^{io} = $ ln $w_{jt}^{i} + \eta_{jt}^{i}$, where $\eta_{jt}^i \sim N(0, \sigma_\eta^2)$ is the measurement error.

The likelihood for a sample of I individuals is given by

$$L(v) = \prod_{i=1}^{I} \Pr\left(d_{a1}^i, w_{j1}^{io}, d_{a2}^i, w_{j2}^{io}, \ldots, d_{at_i}^i, w_{jt}^{io} \middle| S^i(0)\right), \tag{4.26}$$

where v is the vector of parameters to be estimated. Given the assumption of joint serial independence of the vector of errors, the likelihood function (4.26) can be written as a product of within-period conditional joint probabilities of the immigrant's choices and observed wage. These probabilities are computed from the solution of the dynamic programming problem as explained above. To achieve asymptotically efficient estimators using the simulated probabilities, we smooth the conditional probabilities.[31]

We can incorporate unobserved heterogeneity into the models for both males and females as in Heckman and Singer (1984). As a starting point, we estimated the two models with two unobserved types. However, for females, we found that the proportion of one of the types is not statistically different from zero, and thus in the following sections we report the results obtained from the model for females with no unobserved heterogeneity. For males, the fit of the model with two unobserved types was not satisfying and therefore the results for males in the following section are based on the estimation of the model with four unobserved types. As a result of having introduced unobserved heterogeneity into the model for males, we solved the model for each type independently and the likelihood function is a weighted average of the likelihood of each type. Assuming that there are M unobserved types of individuals ($m = 1, \ldots, M$) and that the type probabilities depend on the individual's initial conditions and therefore vary across individuals, the likelihood function can be written as

$$L(v) = \prod_{i=1}^{I} \sum_{m=1}^{M} \Pr\left(d_{a1m}^{i}, w_{j1m}^{io}, d_{a2m}^{i}, w_{j2m}^{io}, \ldots, d_{at_im}^{i}, w_{jt_im}^{io} \big| S_m^i(0), type = m\right)$$
$$\times \pi_{im}\left(S_m^i(0)\right),$$

$$(4.27)$$

where $\pi_{im}\left(S_m^i(0)\right)$ is the probability of individual i being of type m, which depends only on education and age on arrival and is given by

$$\pi_{im} = \frac{\exp\{\pi_{0m} + \pi_{1m}SC_i + \pi_{2m}AGE_i\}}{\sum_{m=1}^{M} \exp\{\pi_{0m} + \pi_{1m}SC_i + \pi_{2m}AGE_i\}}. \qquad (4.28)$$

We allow the unobserved heterogeneity for males to affect the following parameters: the current utilities from nonemployment (ne) and training (tr_j) in equation (4.11); the constant term (α_{0j}) and return on training (α_{cj}) in the occupation-specific human capital function (equation 4.13); the constant terms for WC employment (b_{01j}), BC employment (b_{02j}) and nonemployment or training (b_{03j}) in the WC and BC job-offer probability functions (4.17) and (4.18); the constant term (γ_0) in the WC training-offer probability function (4.19); and the constant term (δ_1) and return on training (δ_3, δ_{10}) in the terminal value function (4.25).

4.4.3   Identification

Given the data on the immigrant's wages in WC or BC occupations during the period since arrival, all the wage parameters in (4.5) and (4.12) can be identified using the conditional mean moments of wages (OLS regression moments; see table 4.3A and B). These moments can potentially identify the return on occupational experience and training, as well as individual wage-fixed effects. The fact that we have (relatively) few wage observations limits the precision (i.e., results in large standard errors) of the estimated parameters of the earnings function and the possibility of estimating interaction terms between imported human capital (age on arrival and schooling) and local accumulated human capital indicators.

Given the wage parameters, the cross-sectional choices between the four states for females and five states for males in each period identify the utility parameters. This follows directly from a standard Heckman selection model.[32] The parameters of the job- and training-offer rates (equations 4.8 and 4.9 for females and equations 4.17, 4.18, and 4.19 for males) are identified from the transition rates (see table 4.2A and B). The terminal value parameters are identified by their joint restrictions on the transitions between states over time and the cross-sectional choice.

There is no need for additional instruments in order to identify the causal effect of training on wages. If the dynamic programming model's implicit selection equation for the choice of training is correct, then we can consistently estimate the probability of participation in a training course for each individual using the predicted training choice probability as an "instrument" in the wage equation for training status. The likelihood functions (4.26) and (4.27) use these moments and restrictions jointly in order to estimate the parameters of the model.

The rich transition moments are the main source for the identification of the job- and training-offer probabilities, as well as the utility parameters of training and nonemployment outcomes. It was also advantageous that the data includes a large number of observations on the transitions between the four labor choices for females and the five labor choices for males, conditional on individual state variables. The likelihood function is built on the products of these conditional probabilities for each individual. The match of the simulated conditional probabilities, which are generated by the offer rates above and the choices, with the actual observed transitions jointly identifies the impact of the state variables on these offer rates and the utility parameters, given the parameters of the earnings functions.[33]

4.5 Results

This section presents the SML estimates of the models' structural parameters. The solution of the dynamic programming problem serves as an input in the estimation procedure, as explained above. Hence, all the parameters of the model enter the likelihood function through their effect on the joint choice and wage probabilities. The programs were written in FORTRAN90 code, and they iterate between the solution of the dynamic programming (DP) problem and the calculation of the likelihood function. For example, for each of the 502 female immigrants in our sample, we calculate the E max at each point in the state space that may arise during the 20-period planning horizon. At each of these points, we use 150 simulated draws of the vector ε to calculate the E max.[34] In this section we first discuss the fit of the estimated models to the actual aggregate labor states, the transitions between these states, and wages. We then review the estimated parameters and their interpretation. The policy implications are discussed in the next section.

4.5.1   The Model's Fit

(A)   Females

Given the estimated parameters of the model (to be discussed below) and the assumed random errors, we simulated the one-quarter-ahead predicted proportion of the initial 502 women in our sample for each of the four labor market states and for each observation in the data.[35] The predicted proportions of female immigrants in each of the four labor market states are presented in figure 4.2a. The estimated model fits the aggregate proportions extremely well and succeeds in replicating the qualitative and quantitative patterns in the data. The simple χ^2 test of the fit for each quarter and for each choice for all periods confirms that the predicted and observed choices are statistically different only in the first and third quarters. No significant differences are found in a simple χ^2 goodness-of-fit test between actual and predicted choices for each alternative, both separately and for the model as a whole.

The predicted pattern of participation in a training course is consistent with the data. The model predicts the peak in training attendance during the fourth quarter although the predicted proportion is only 14.2 percent as compared to the observed rate of 16.9 percent. Furthermore the estimated model predicts that 200 immigrants would choose to attend training during the sample period as compared to the 218 immigrants who actually did.

It should be noted that a good fit of the estimated model to the *aggregated* choices does not necessarily ensure that the model can accurately explain each individual's choices. The model in fact correctly predicts 5,461 of the 7,205 observed choices, which implies that the estimated

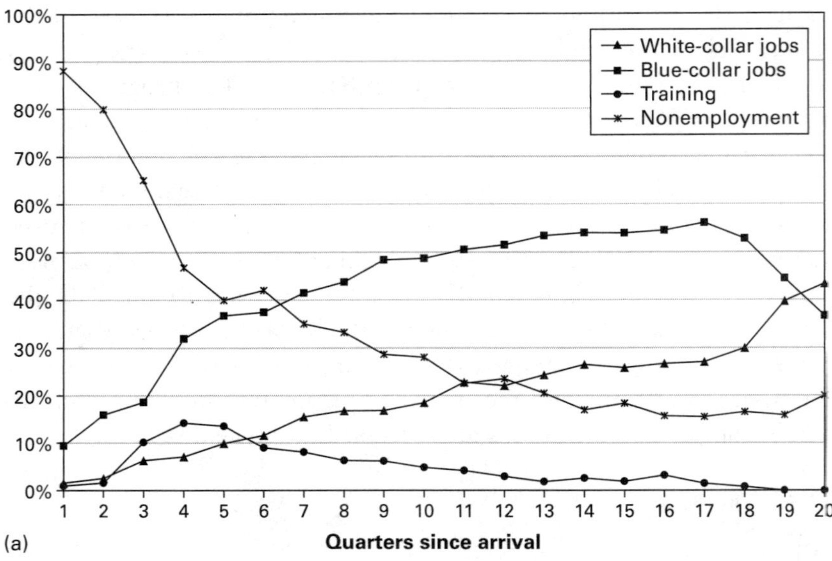

(a) **Quarters since arrival**

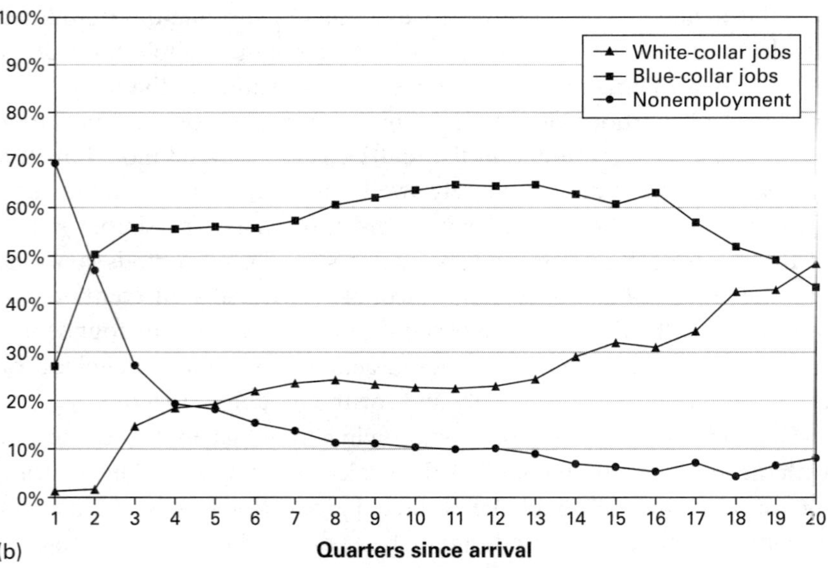

(b) **Quarters since arrival**

Figure 4.2
Predicted choice distributions: (a) Females. (b) Employed and nonemployed males. (c) Males undergoing training. Source: Authors' calculations based on the model's estimation and simulation.

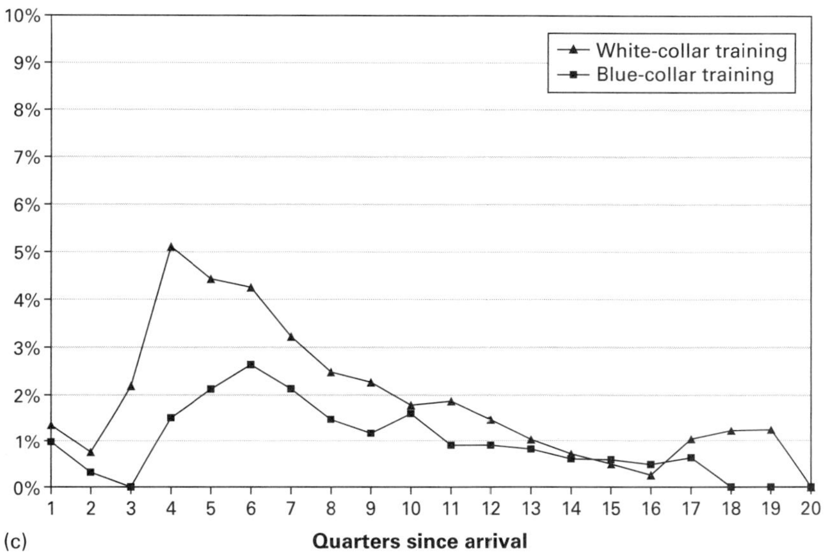

Figure 4.2
(Continued)

model "explains" 76 percent (pseudo-R^2) of the immigrants' choices within the sample period.

Transitions

Table 4.4A presents the predicted quarter-to-quarter transitions between the four states of the model based on the same simulations as above.[36] The estimated model captures the dominance of the elements on the diagonal remarkably well. However, it produces too few transitions from the two employment states to training and too many transitions from nonemployment to WC jobs.

Accepted Wages

The fit of the model to the average wage over time, occupation-specific experience and training is presented in table 4.5A. The estimated model accurately predicts the dynamic pattern and the level of wages by occupation. The substantial growth in wages with time since arrival in WC occupations is somewhat underpredicted by the model while the flat pattern of wages in BC occupations is captured accurately by the model, as is the same pattern by occupation-specific experience. The observed average wage growth of 27 (8) percent due to WC (BC) training is quite accurately predicted by the model, which predicts 14.7 (10) percent wage growth.[37]

Table 4.4A
Predicted transitions—Females

From To	White-collar		Blue-collar		Training		Nonemployment		Total
White-collar	929	96.8%	0	0.0%	3	0.3%	28	2.9%	960
Blue-collar	13	0.5%	2,434	93.7%	31	1.2%	121	4.7%	2,599
Training	44	10.2%	66	15.3%	208	48.3%	113	26.2%	431
Nonemployment	142	5.2%	310	11.4%	161	5.9%	2,100	77.4%	2,713
Total	1,128		2,810		403		2,362		6,703

Source: Authors' calculations based on the model's estimation and simulation (for details, see section 4.5.1 in the text).
Note: Each row sums to 100%.

Table 4.5A
Actual and predicted accepted wages by quarters since arrival, experience, and participation in a training course—Females

	White-collar		Blue-collar	
	Actual	Predicted	Actual	Predicted
Quarters since arrival				
1–4	12.52	13.38	10.22	8.01
5–8	17.26	17.29	10.36	8.47
9–12	17.92	18.69	9.73	8.99
13–16	26.17	19.94	10.56	9.37
Experience (relevant occupation, quarters)				
0–4	19.88	16.63	10.63	8.38
5–8	18.70	18.85	9.81	9.09
9–12	25.85	23.33	10.21	9.42
13–16	25.13	24.59	11.54	9.77
Participation in a training course				
Before training	18.10	17.49	10.07	8.60
After training	22.97	20.06	10.82	9.55

Sources: Brookdale Survey and authors' calculations based on the model's estimation and simulation (for details, see section 4.5.1 in the text).
Note: Hourly wage expressed in July 1995 prices (NIS).

Finally, in addition to the one-step-ahead predictions, in which the state space is updated according to the actual choice of the immigrant in each period, figure 4.3 presents the "unconditional" fit of the estimated model. This is based on simulations of the estimated model, assuming that all immigrants have zero experience in BC and WC jobs upon arrival in Israel and have not yet participated in a training course. Given these initial conditions and the exogenous values of the variables that make up the immigrant's state space (schooling, age on arrival, etc.), the immigrant chooses the alternative that gives her the highest value function during the first period in Israel and the state space is updated according to her simulated choices in each period. As the figure shows, the unconditional simulation also provides an excellent fit to the observed patterns, with the exception of the last two periods in which it fails to capture the change in trend in the proportions of immigrants working in WC and BC jobs.[38]

(B) Males

Given the estimated parameters of the model, we calculate the predicted proportion of immigrants in each of the five labor market states (see figure 4.2b and c).[39] The predicted proportions of immigrants provide a

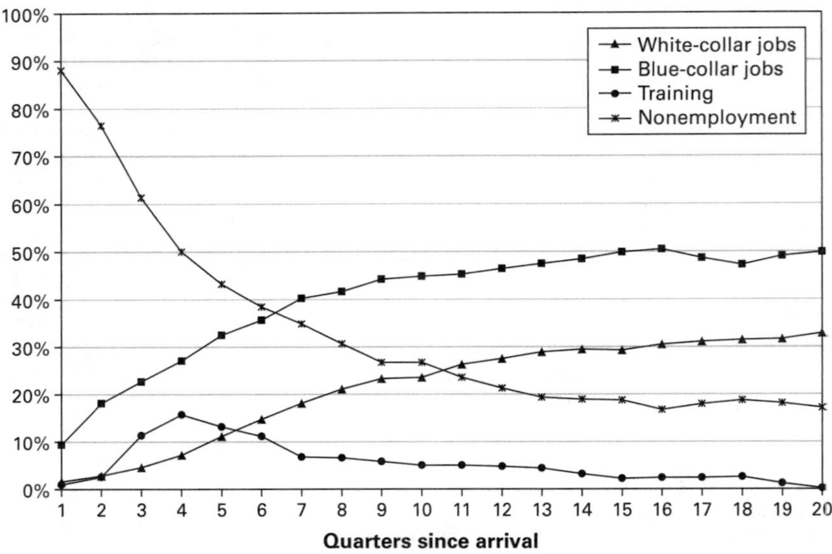

Figure 4.3
Predicted unconditional choice distributions: Females. Source: Authors' calculations based on the model's estimation and simulation.

good fit to the main dynamic patterns of aggregate nonemployment, employment, and training. Specifically, the model accurately predicts the rapid decrease in nonemployment during the first year in Israel and the level of nonemployment during the last two years of the sample. However, it underpredicts nonemployment during the second and third years, which largely corresponds to the overprediction of employment in BC jobs.

The predicted rise in the proportion of immigrants employed in WC jobs provides a good fit to the observed patterns and the predicted pattern of participation in a training course is roughly consistent with the data. The estimated model predicts a peak in participation in a WC (BC) training course of 5 (2.6) percent in the fourth (sixth) quarter, whereas the actual peak in WC training (6.4 percent) occurs in the fourth quarter and the actual peak in BC training (4.3 percent) occurs in the fifth quarter.

Based on a simple χ^2 Newman–Pearson test of fit for the first 20 quarters and the 5 labor market states, the hypothesis that there is no difference between the actual and predicted proportions in nonemployment, WC employment, WC training, and BC training is rejected when tested separately. This hypothesis is not rejected with respect to BC employment. The goodness-of-fit test for the model as a whole rejects the hypothesis at the one percent level. In addition we find a significant difference between the predicted and actual choice distributions for all the choices during the first 11 quarters and during the 16th quarter.[40]

The model accurately tracks the observed 20 percent decline in the proportion of immigrants employed in BC jobs and the increase in the proportion employed in WC jobs during the fifth year in Israel (see figure 4.1b).[41] This is a surprising and important result, and there are potentially three sources for this change in occupational choice: (1) endogenous accumulated human capital in the form of experience, training, and knowledge of Hebrew, which affect job-offer probabilities and wages; (2) the actual dynamic change in the stocks (proportions) of immigrants in each labor market state;[42] and (3) the differences between the exogenous characteristics of the 1989–90 and 1991–92 cohorts ("cohort effects").

Using unconditional predictions for the entire twenty quarters in Israel, the model predicts a higher proportion of immigrants in BC jobs and substantially fewer immigrants in training in comparison to the data and the one-step-ahead (conditional) predictions. In this case the reduction in the proportion of immigrants in BC jobs begins as nonemployment reaches a minimum toward the end of the third year in Israel and is predicted to decrease by 6 percent during the fourth and the fifth year. Simulations based on a sample of identical immigrants, with the same years of schooling and age on arrival as those of the 1989–90 cohort, also predict about a 6 percent reduction in the share of BC jobs during the fifth year in Israel. Hence we conclude that the cohort explanation (source 3 above) is not an important factor in explaining net transition into WC jobs during the fifth year in Israel. Therefore, of the 18 percent net increase in WC jobs, 6 percent is due to the first source mentioned above and the rest to the actual reduction in the stock of BC jobs, which caused a net move to WC jobs, both directly and through nonemployment (source 2 above).

The simulated average wages and reservation values always indicate a substantial gain from accepting a WC job offer. Hence the only reason for the low rate of increase in the proportion of immigrants working in WC jobs throughout the sample period is the relatively low WC job-offer rates conditional on not having worked previously in a WC job.

Transitions

Table 4.4B presents the predicted average transitions based on the same simulations and data presented in figure 4.2b and c. The model accurately

Table 4.4B
Predicted transitions—Males

From	To	White-collar		Blue-collar		WC training		BC training		Nonemployment		Total
White-collar		1,030	98.5%	1	0.1%	4	0.4%	1	0.1%	10	1.0%	1,046
Blue-collar		41	1.4%	2,713	95.9%	13	0.5%	4	0.1%	58	2.0%	2,828
WC training		13	9.9%	15	11.1%	77	56.8%	0	0.0%	30	22.2%	136
BC training		3	3.3%	12	12.8%	0	0.0%	52	57.5%	24	26.4%	91
Nonemployment		103	8.2%	417	33.1%	26	2.1%	3	0.3%	709	56.4%	1,258
Total		1,190		3,157		121		61		831		5,359

Source: Authors' calculations based on the model's estimation and simulation (for details, see section 4.5.1 in the text).
Note: Each row sums to 100%.

predicts the persistence in WC jobs, BC training and WC training. However, it underpredicts persistence in nonemployment and, accordingly, predicts too many transitions from nonemployment to BC jobs, as shown in figures 4.2b and c. The predicted transitions from training to the two employment states and to nonemployment match the observed transitions fairly well. The transitions to training occur primarily from nonemployment.

Accepted Wages

Table 4.5B shows that the predicted average annual compounded rates of wage growth (6 percent for BC jobs and 7 percent for WC jobs) during the first five years in Israel are consistent with observed wage growth.[43] This fact is also consistent with the average wage growth observed in cross-sectional data and the estimation results reported by Eckstein and Weiss (2004). The data show that wages are 11 percent higher for immigrants who participated in a WC training course and 6 percent higher for participants in a BC training course. The model, however, predicts that average accepted wages are 6.4 percent higher for those with WC training and 9.9 percent higher for those with BC training. Given the estimated wage parameters reported below, this result indicates that the model's selection process of individuals to employment by occupation dominates the estimated predicted return on training.

Table 4.5B
Actual and predicted accepted wages by quarters since arrival and participation in a training course — Males

	White-collar		Blue-collar	
	Actual	Predicted	Actual	Predicted
Quarters since arrival				
1–4	21.77	13.86	10.47	10.98
5–8	15.06	14.96	10.97	11.68
9–12	18.86	16.64	11.87	12.63
13–16	20.45	17.86	12.50	13.66
17–20	21.52	19.08	15.23	14.72
Participation in a training course (relevant occupation)				
Before training	17.93	16.14	11.99	12.18
After training	19.98	17.18	12.66	13.39

Sources: Brookdale Survey and authors' calculations based on the model's estimation and simulation (for details, see section 4.5.1 in the text).
Note: Hourly wage expressed in July 1995 prices (NIS).

4.5.2   Estimated Parameters

(A)   Females

Wage Parameters

The occupation-specific wage functions were estimated according to equation (4.12), and the resulting parameters (table 4.6A) are very close to the OLS parameters reported in table 4.3A. We find that immigrants from the FSU have (almost) zero return on their imported human capital in the form of schooling and experience when conditioned on investment in local accumulated human capital. The return on schooling is 2.3 (0.25) percent in WC (BC) occupations and is not significant at the 5 percent level and the impact of experience from the country of origin (using age on arrival as a proxy) is not significant for either type of occupation. The finding that female immigrants do not receive any return on the human capital they brought with them from the FSU is consistent with findings on male immigrants from the FSU (Cohen Goldner and Eckstein 2008; Eckstein and Weiss 2004).

The distinction between BC and WC occupation-specific experience is important in the analysis of the immigrants' wage growth. An addition of one quarter to WC experience significantly increases the WC wage (by 3.9 percent). WC work experience also has a large positive effect on the BC wage (2.7 percent), though this impact is statistically not significant. The return on BC experience in both BC and WC occupations is small and not significant. This last finding implies that the wage of immigrants who were absorbed into BC jobs is not expected to grow as the immigrants accumulate BC experience. However, the wage in WC jobs grows rapidly in the short run with the accumulation of WC work experience. Hence wage growth does not depend solely on previous employment, but also on occupation-specific experience. Studies that use age (or period of residence in the host country) as a proxy for experience are ignoring the possibility that occupation-specific experience may have a substantially different impact on wage growth.

Knowledge of Hebrew has a positive and significant return in both WC and BC occupations. The Hebrew fluency index ranges from 1 (no knowledge of Hebrew) to 4 (fluent in Hebrew), implying that the return on achieving fluency in Hebrew is 17 percent in WC jobs and 90 percent in BC jobs. The high return on Hebrew fluency in BC jobs may reflect the fact that the usage of Hebrew in BC jobs is more intensive than in WC jobs (gas station attendants, cashiers, salespersons, etc.).[44]

Table 4.6A
Estimated occupation-specific wage and job-offer probability parameters—Females

	White-collar, j = 1	Blue-collar, j = 2
Wage parameters		
α_{0j} – constant	1.7615	1.0696
	(0.007)	(0.1429)
α_{1j} – years of schooling	0.023	0.0025
	(0.0128)	(0.0071)
α_{2j} – WC experience	0.0388	0.0269
	(0.012)	(0.0236)
α_{3j} – BC experience	0.0006	0.0045
	(0.0234)	(0.0041)
α_{4j} – training	0.1951	−0.0149
	(0.0882)	(0.0334)
α_{5j} – age on arrival	0.0054	0.0024
	(0.0045)	(0.0022)
α_{6j} – Hebrew	0.0572	0.3033
	(0.0105)	(0.0423)
Job-offer probability parameters		
b_{10j} – attended training course in $t-1$	−5.856	−1.4962
	(0.2124)	(0.3808)
b_{11j} – nonemployed in $t-1$	−6.6306	−2.2585
	(0.1834)	(0.3369)
b_{121} – worked in blue-collar in $t-1$	−9.2383	
	(0.2916)	
b_{122} – worked in white-collar in $t-1$		−4.3348
		(0.5684)
b_{2j} – years of schooling	0.1551	0.0015
	(0.02)	(0.0201)
b_{3j} – age on arrival	0.0015	0.008
	(0.0079)	(0.0056)
b_{4j} – training	1.0797	0.7897
	(0.0048)	(0.1228)
b_{5j} – white-collar in the FSU	0.8719	−0.2684
	(0.1035)	(0.1198)
b_{6j} – experience in occupation j	0.1936	0.0434
	(0.0512)	(0.0229)
b_{7j} – Hebrew	0.0552	0
	(0.0177)	(0)
s_j – separation rate from occupation j	0.0336	0.0515
	(0.0068)	(0.0039)

Note: Standard errors appear in parentheses.

The return on training in terms of wage growth also depends on the immigrant's occupation. The wage-return on training in WC jobs (α_{41}) is 19.5 percent and is significantly different from zero at the 5 percent level. The OLS estimator in a similar specification is 16.1 percent and is not significant. Thus the OLS estimate is biased downward due to the selection to training and occupational choice. The wage-return on training in BC jobs (α_{42}) is not statistically different from zero.[45]

The finding that training has no impact on the wage in BC jobs is consistent with the prevalent finding in the United States that the return on government-sponsored training is close to zero. One of the main explanations given for this in the training literature is that government-sponsored training is usually targeted toward relatively unskilled and less-able individuals who work in low-skilled jobs and are poorly paid. As argued by Heckman, LaLonde, and Smith (1999), evidence on the complementarity between the return on training and skill (education) in the private sector suggests that the return on training in the public sector should be relatively small. Our findings suggest that only immigrants who have succeeded in climbing up the occupational ladder will obtain a high return on their investment in training. Thus our results on training for high-skilled workers provide a novel extension to the existing literature.

Job-Offer Parameters

The estimated parameters imply that job-offer probabilities by occupation are sensitive to the current labor market state and to human capital stocks (table 4.6A). The probability of job retention in the same occupation is close to one, though job-offer rates are much lower for both WC and BC occupations if the current state is different. Moreover the probability of a nonemployed immigrant receiving a job offer in either type of occupation is higher than from employment in the other occupation ($b_{12j} < b_{11j}$), $j = 1, 2$. These results are consistent with widely accepted assumptions concerning job-offer rates in models with on-the-job search.

Imported human capital, which had almost no effect on wages, turns out to have a significant and large impact on WC job opportunities. An additional year of schooling substantially increases the probability of receiving a WC job offer but has no effect on job-offer probabilities in BC occupations. For example, a nonemployed immigrant with 15 years of schooling faces a WC (BC) job-offer probability which is 16.1 (0.13) percent higher than that of a similar immigrant with 14 years of schooling. In contrast, age on arrival has zero impact on job-offer probabilities in both types of occupations. Furthermore an immigrant who worked in a WC job in the FSU receives a WC job offer with a probability that is 135 percent higher than that for an immigrant who held a BC job in the FSU. Similarly for an immigrant who worked in a BC job in the FSU the probability of receiving a BC job offer is 27 percent higher than that of an immigrant who worked in a WC job prior to immigrating.[46]

The impact of accumulated WC experience on WC job-offer probability is greater than that of BC experience on BC job-offer probability. Table 4.7A shows the impact of an immigrant's occupation-specific experience on the job-offer probabilities from different states with and

Table 4.7A
Estimated job-offer probabilities — Females

To		White-collar		Blue-collar	
From	Experience (quarters)	Untrained	Trained[a]	Untrained	Trained[a]
White-collar	0			0.014	0.030
	4			0.016	0.035
	8		0.966	0.019	0.042
	12			0.023	0.049
	16			0.027	0.058
	20			0.032	0.068
Blue-collar	0	0.003	0.007		
	4	0.005	0.016		
	8	0.012	0.034	0.948	
	12	0.025	0.071		
	16	0.053	0.142		
	20	0.109	0.264		
Training	0		0.181		0.343
	4		0.323		0.383
	8		0.509		0.425
	12		0.692		0.468
	16		0.830		0.512
	20		0.914		0.555
Nonemployment	0	0.033	0.092	0.100	0.196
	4	0.070	0.181	0.116	0.225
	8	0.140	0.323	0.136	0.257
	12	0.260	0.509	0.157	0.291
	16	0.433	0.692	0.182	0.328
	20	0.624	0.830	0.209	0.368

Source: Authors' calculations based on the model's estimation.
Note: Probabilities are for a female immigrant with 14 years of schooling, who worked in a WC job in the FSU, was 38 years old on arrival, and has a Hebrew fluency index of three.
a. Participated in a training program since arrival.

without training. We consider a female immigrant with 14 years of schooling, who was 38 years old on arrival, has a score of three in knowledge of Hebrew, and worked in a WC job prior to immigrating. As expected, the estimated model predicts a considerable difference between the availability of BC and WC job offers. On arrival, the immigrant described above receives a job offer in a WC (BC) occupation each quarter with a probability of 0.033 (0.1). This probability is not expected to change as long as the immigrant is nonemployed and has not accumulated local skills, such as work experience, training and knowledge of Hebrew. An additional quarter of WC experience increases the WC job-offer probability for a nonemployed immigrant by 8.0 to 20.5 percent, while an additional quarter of BC work experience increases the BC job-offer probability by only 3.5 to 4.0 percent.[47] The large impact of WC experience on WC job-offer probability leads to a situation in which the probability of a nonemployed immigrant who has accumulated 9 quarters of WC experience receiving a WC job offer is higher than that of an immigrant who has accumulated a similar amount of BC experience receiving a BC job offer (see table 4.7A, columns 1 and 3, bottom block).

The effect of training on job-offer probabilities can be broken down into a permanent effect, b_{4j}, $j = 1, 2$, and a transitory effect, b_{10j}, in the quarter following graduation from the training program. Both coefficients indicate that training has a significant and positive impact on job-offer probabilities in both types of occupation, though to a much larger degree for WC jobs. The permanent effect of training on WC job-offer probabilities ranges from 179 percent for a nonemployed immigrant without WC experience to 33 percent for an immigrant who has accumulated 20 quarters of WC experience. The permanent effect of training on BC job-offer probabilities is estimated at 76 to 96 percent. Since most of the female immigrants who participated in a training course had no prior experience of any kind in Israel, the permanent effect of training on their job-offer probabilities is enormous.

In addition training has a large and significant transitory impact on the probabilities in the quarter following graduation from the training program. The probability of a nonemployed immigrant with no work experience receiving a WC (BC) job offer in the quarter subsequent to training is 5.5 (3.4) times higher than that for an immigrant who has not attended training (table 4.7A). Given the negligible probability of receiving a WC job offer, participation in a training course appears to be an unavoidable step in the process of WC job search. Moreover, in the absence of WC experience, the effect of training on WC job-offer probability in the quarter following training is almost twice as large as the permanent effect.

What is the source of the immediate and transitory impact of training on job-offer probabilities? According to our data (taken from the Brookdale Surveys), about 46 percent of the participants visited factories or institutions related to their field of study during the training program. These included meetings with potential employers, which suggests that training provides an additional benefit beyond the occupational skills it provides. In addition about 55 percent of the trainees reported that the training program also provided information on the Israeli labor market and employment opportunities. Therefore it is possible that the effect of training on job-offer probabilities reflects the acquisition not only of vocational skills but also job-search skills. Although we are unable to distinguish between these two effects, the finding that training has a different impact on WC job-offer probability than on BC job-offer probability indicates that the immigrants indeed obtained job-search skills in addition to occupational skills.

The estimated quarterly separation rate (table 4.6A) from WC (BC) jobs is 3.36 (5.15) percent. These rates indicate a high rate of mobility in the new labor market, which is also characteristic of young workers.

Comment: The labor and immigration literature focuses on wage growth and the earnings-return on imported and locally accumulated human capital. The model presented here follows the dynamic labor supply literature (search and labor force participation models) with emphasis on job-offer probabilities as a source of friction in the labor market, which may depend on the characteristics of the individual's human capital. In this framework the wage data identifies earning growth conditional on the return on human capital, whether imported or locally accumulated. The labor market transitions to jobs and training identify the conditional impact of human capital on job-offer opportunities, which may end up to be of greater value to the individual than the potential return if the job is not accepted. It turns out that the increase in job-offer opportunities due to training is a more important benefit of human capital investment than the impact of training on potential wages since the earnings-return on training is realized only if the immigrant works in a WC job, which is a very low-probability event.

Furthermore it is interesting that nonemployment in this model can be either voluntary or involuntary. Simulations indicated that almost all nonemployment is a result of no offers of either jobs or training and therefore can be interpreted as involuntary.

Training-Offer Probability Parameters
The model predicts a substantial difference in training-offer probabilities according to the immigrant's age on arrival (table 4.8A). An immigrant who was 40 years old or younger on arrival receives an offer to participate in a training course each quarter with a probability of 0.136. In contrast, an immigrant who was over 40 years old on arrival receives such an offer with a probability of only 0.058. This difference reflects the selection made by the government training administrators in providing training programs and the self-selection by immigrants of different ages.

Terminal Value Parameters
The terminal value expresses the expected future value of the immigrant's utility after five years in Israel. We assume that this value depends on the state space in the 20th quarter, and specifically on the work experience accumulated by the immigrant in BC and WC jobs up to the 20th quarter, and participation in a training course. Every quarter of WC (BC) experience increases the terminal value by 633 (520) NIS (see table 4.8A). As expected, the terminal value decreases with age on arrival since the immigrant's labor period is shortened. Training increments the terminal value by 1,400 NIS. This means that the value of training in terms of terminal value is larger than that of two quarters of WC work experience and slightly smaller than that of three quarters of BC work experience. Every increment in Hebrew fluency (ranging from 1 to 4) contributes 35.98 NIS to the terminal value. WC employment during the 20th quarter increases the terminal value by 380 NIS. This premium for WC work experience reflects the fact that an immigrant in this type of occupation will remain there with a high probability and will benefit from a high wage.

Utility Parameters
The utility estimates (see table 4.8A) show that immigrants do not enjoy training or nonemployment. However, the disutility from attending training is much smaller than that from being nonemployed. This suggests that even if there is no gain associated with training, the immigrant will prefer it to being nonemployed. In addition we find a negative correlation between the preference shocks in nonemployment and those in training (see the Cholesky decomposition parameters in table 4.8A). This may make training more appealing while nonemployed.

Table 4.8A
Estimated parameters—Females

Training-offer probability parameters	
pt_1 (if age on arrival <40)	0.1361
	(0.0105)
pt_2 (if age on arrival ≥40)	0.0575
	(0.0072)
Terminal value parameters	
δ_1 – accumulated white-collar experience	633.3353
	(3.149)
δ_2 – accumulated blue-collar experience	520.4621
	(3.14)
δ_3 – age on arrival	−65.138
	(3.152)
δ_4 – training	1399.9682
	(3.162)
δ_5 – constant	1426.6797
	(3.162)
δ_6 – worked in white-collar during the previous period	379.1786
	(3.163)
δ_7 – worked in blue-collar during the previous period	−0.0934
	(3.154)
δ_8 – years of schooling	150
	(3.132)
δ_9 – number of children	100.0638
	(3.162)
δ_{10} – married	99.9792
	(3.162)
δ_{11} – white-collar in the FSU	99.3617
	(3.164)
δ_{12} – Hebrew	35.9821
	(3.1623)
Utility parameters	
Children – employment	−29.5124
	(0.0898)
Marriage – employment	124.9599
	(3.1551)
Constant – training	−15.9548
	(3.161)
Children – training	−2.7617
	(3.155)
Marriage – training	−12.6204
	(3.1591)
Constant – nonemployment	−591.6479
	(3.162)
Children – nonemployment	−1.3614
	(3.1594)
Marriage – nonemployment	40.4621
	(3.1613)
Cholesky decomposition parameters	
σ_{11}	0.286
σ_{22}	0.150
σ_{33}	0.051
σ_{44}	9.883
Cov_{34}	−0.476

Note: Standard errors appear in parentheses

(B) Males

Wage Parameters

The four types of immigrants face substantially different estimated rates of return on training in the two types of occupation (see table 4.6B).[48] The rate of return on WC training in WC jobs is 19 percent for a type-1 individual, 18 percent for a type-3 individual, and zero for types 2 and 4. The predicted weighted return across types for the average immigrant is 13.6 percent, which is higher than the OLS estimate of 11.6 percent.[49] Similarly the rate of return on BC training in BC jobs is 12.7 percent for type 1, 3.6 percent for type 3, and zero for types 2 and 4.[50] Hence most of the immigrants (types 1 and 3) gain substantially from any training program. The unobserved heterogeneity in the estimated return on training found here can explain the large variance in the estimated training coefficients to be found in the literature (Heckman, LaLonde, and Smith 1999). The dynamic programming model provides a complicated control for the selection of individuals to training and work by occupation and implies a higher estimate for the impact of training on wages than does the OLS regression. These estimated returns on training are large relative to the findings in the existing literature.[51]

Accumulated experience in Israel has a positive and significant impact on wages. An additional quarter of experience increases the wage in WC jobs by 2 percent and in BC jobs by 1.9 percent. These coefficients show that the actual experience effect is similar across occupations and is very close to the estimated coefficient from the OLS regressions. Knowledge of Hebrew has a significant and positive impact on wages in both occupations while knowledge of English has a positive effect on wages in WC jobs, but a negative effect on wages in BC jobs.[52] The Hebrew coefficient implies that the wage rate of return on average knowledge of Hebrew (compared to no knowledge of Hebrew) is between 15 and 19 percent, which is close to the OLS estimates.

The estimated parameters of the wage equation imply that the value of imported human capital in the form of schooling and experience abroad (age on arrival), conditional on local accumulated human capital, is zero. The only types of imported human capital that are highly rewarded in Israel are knowledge of English and knowledge of Hebrew. Our estimates suggest that the return on local Israeli human capital is a result of the accumulation of local experience, knowledge of the Hebrew language and training. The results with respect to imported human capital are roughly the same as the OLS estimates, but this might be due to the short period of time since arrival.

Table 4.6B
Estimated occupation-specific wage and job-offer probability parameters—Males

	White-collar, $j = 1$	Blue-collar, $j = 2$
Wage parameters		
α_{0j1} – type 1	1.6276 (0.2826)	1.8799 (0.077)
α_{0j2} – deviation of type 2 from type 1	−0.1804 (0.4733)	0.2316 (0.0845)
α_{03} – deviation of type 3 from type 1	0.0049 (0.2316)	0.0272 (0.1019)
α_{0j4} – deviation of type 4 from type 1	−0.3617 (4.2597)	0.1387 (0.0866)
α_{ej} – experience	0.0205 (0.0116)	0.0187 (0.0046)
α_{c11} – WC training, type 1	0.1908 (0.5505)	
α_{c12} – WC training, type 2	0.0004 (0.4247)	
α_{c13} – WC training, type 3	0.1792 (0.1309)	
α_{c14} – WC training, type 4	0.0042 (4.4721)	
α_{c21} – BC training, type 1		0.1275 (0.1842)
α_{c22} – BC training, type 2		0.0001 (4.2199)
α_{c23} – BC training, type 3		0.0364 (0.1243)
α_{c24} – BC training, type 4		0.0049 (0.2637)
α_{Hj} – Hebrew	0.0964 (0.0652)	0.11 (0.0296)
α_{Fj} – English	0.1386 (0.0436)	−0.0439 (0.0219)
α_{Aj} – age on arrival	0.005 (0.0059)	−0.0001 (0.0021)
α_{Sj} – years of schooling	0.0126 (0.0191)	0.009 (0.0071)
Job-offer probability parameters		
b_{01j1} – worked in white-collar at $t-1$, type 1	15.9959 (4.4721)	−2.1329 (0.4554)
b_{01j2} – worked in white-collar at $t-1$, deviation of type 2 from type 1	−0.0055 (4.4721)	0.7662 (1.0691)
b_{01j3} – worked in white-collar at $t-1$, deviation of type 3 from type 1	0.1002 (4.4721)	−6.9162 (4.472)
b_{01j4} – worked in white-collar at $t-1$, deviation of type 4 from type 1	0.1021 (4.4721)	−1.4027 (4.4708)
b_{02j1} – worked in blue-collar at $t-1$, type 1	−2.6507 (0.5027)	6.1483 (1.2434)

Table 4.6B
(Continued)

	White-collar, $j = 1$	Blue-collar, $j = 2$
b_{02j2} – worked in blue-collar at $t-1$, deviation of type 2 from type 1	−2.1937 (2.8183)	1.9236 (3.721)
b_{02j3} – worked in blue-collar at $t-1$, deviation of type 3 from type 1	−1.0537 (1.0295)	−1.5477 (1.3535)
b_{02j4} – worked in blue-collar at $t-1$, deviation of type 4 from type 1	−5.1863 (4.4543)	−0.2215 (1.3657)
b_{03j1} – nonemployed or attended training course at $t-1$, type 1	−1.749 (0.2142)	−0.4868 (0.1325)
b_{03j2} – nonemployed or attended training course at $t-1$, deviation of type 2 from type 1	0.5978 (0.6295)	1.0276 (0.3182)
b_{03j3} – nonemployed or attended training course at $t-1$, deviation of type 3 from type 1	−0.7524 (0.3376)	−0.9146 (0.2024)
b_{03j4} – nonemployed or attended training course at $t-1$, deviation of type 4 from type 1	−5.2264 (4.4693)	2.2431 (0.3663)
b_{11j} – work experience in Israel 1–4	−0.3489 (0.2215)	−0.144 (0.1085)
b_{12j} – work experience in Israel > 5	−1.0114 (0.2791)	−0.6512 (0.1755)
b_{2j} – training in occupation j	1.1161 (0.2377)	0.0193 (0.1165)
b_{3j} – age on arrival	−0.0259 (0.0071)	−0.0031 (0.0036)
b_{4j} – Hebrew	0 (0.0917)	0.0001 (0.058)
b_5 – English	0.2366 (0.0894)	
b_6 – white-collar in the FSU	0.6203 (0.2741)	
b_{042} – first period dummy from nonemployment or training		−0.6603 (0.1636)
b_7 – first 5 periods dummy from blue-collar		−2.273 (0.2717)

Note: Standard errors appear in parentheses.

Eckstein and Weiss (2004), who used cross-sectional data that included FSU immigrants from earlier waves, find that the return on imported human capital is zero on arrival but increases significantly with time in Israel. However, their cross-sectional data do not include actual experience, knowledge of Hebrew and English or training. In this chapter we use actual data on accumulated human capital in the host country and therefore are better able to measure the sources of wage growth.[53] In our specification locally accumulated human capital depends on imported skills through the effect of education and age on arrival on the type probabilities, which in turn affect the return on training and the availability of job offers and WC training offers.[54]

Job-Offer and WC Training-Offer Parameters

The estimated parameters of the logistic job-offer probabilities (equations 4.17 and 4.18) are presented in table 4.6B and the implied offer probabilities conditional on previous choice and weighted by type (for the average immigrant) are reported in table 4.7B. These probabilities are based on the average exogenous attributes in our sample and on the different levels of the endogenous human capital variables.[55] Due to institutional restrictions, we assume that WC job offers are not available

Table 4.7B
Estimated job- and training-offer probabilities—Males

To From	Experience (quarters)	White-collar		Blue-collar		WC training
		Untrained	Trained[a]	Untrained	Trained[a]	Untrained
White-collar	0	1.000	1.000	0.057	0.058	
	1–4	1.000	1.000	0.050	0.051	
	5+	1.000	1.000	0.032	0.032	
Blue-collar	0	0.034	0.094	0.994	0.994	
	1–4	0.024	0.069	0.993	0.993	0.039
	5+	0.013	0.037	0.989	0.989	
Nonemployment or training	0	0.114	0.264	0.381	0.384	
	1–4	0.084	0.208	0.355	0.358	
	5+	0.046	0.124	0.271	0.274	

Source: Authors' calculations based on the model's estimation.
Note: Probabilities are for a male immigrant with 14.6 years of schooling, who worked in a WC job in the FSU, was 38 years old on arrival, and has a Hebrew fluency index of 2.7 and an English fluency index of 1.76. Probabilities are weighted by type. The offer probability for BC training is assumed to be one if the state is "untrained."
a. Participated in a training program since arrival.

in the first quarter to immigrants who attend Ulpan and have no prior knowledge of Hebrew.

The large coefficients for remaining in the same occupation as in the previous period for all types and in both types of occupation imply that the individual almost always retains his job regardless of his other characteristics ($P^{11} = 1$ and $P^{22} > 0.98$). Immigrants who did not work in the previous quarter, either because they were nonemployed or in one of the training programs, are 3 to 6 times more likely to receive a job offer than immigrants who worked in the other occupation. For example, the offer rate from nonemployment or training with no experience to a WC job is between 11 and 26 percent per quarter (see table 4.7B) while from a BC job to a WC job it is between 3.4 and 9.4 percent. Hence job arrival rates from the other occupation are significantly lower for working individuals of all types.[56] We also find that the BC job-offer probability in the first quarter is significantly lower than in later periods (see b_{042} in table 4.6B).

General work experience accumulated in Israel has a negative effect on the probability of receiving WC and BC job offers. To understand this result, one needs to keep in mind that these marginal effects are conditional on the last period's state. Conditional on the fact that the immigrant is working, the estimated job-offer rate for the same occupation is one, independent of his level of experience (see table 4.7B). However, a nonemployed immigrant with some local experience has a lower job-offer rate. These results indicate that job-offer probabilities are sensitive to the individual's job-specific history, which is an intuitively appealing result.

Participation in a training course related to a particular occupation has a large positive effect on job offers in that occupation. Table 4.7B demonstrates that participation in a WC training course almost triples the WC job-offer probability from both the nonemployment (including training) and BC states. In particular, if the average immigrant has no experience in Israel, he will receive a WC job offer each quarter with probability 0.11; participation in a WC training course would increase this figure by 136 percent to 0.26. The same immigrant with no training but with five or more quarters of work experience in Israel will receive a WC job offer with a probability of 0.05; participation in a WC training course would increase this probability to 0.12, while participation in a BC training course increases the BC job-offer probability from nonemployment or training only slightly.

Knowledge of Hebrew does not affect WC and BC job-offer probabilities, though it affects wages in both occupations (see table 4.6B). This is a surprising result and may indicate that individuals who spend more time learning the new language put more effort into searching for a job; however, they are also more selective, such that these effects tend to offset each other.

We find that having worked in a WC job in the FSU and arriving with English skills (imported human capital) have a significant positive effect on the rate of WC job offers. However, the fact that the individual worked in a WC occupation in the FSU has much less impact on job-offer probabilities than training.

We assume that BC training is always available but find that the quarterly probability of receiving a WC training offer is negatively affected by schooling and differs according to the four types (see table 4.8B). For the average immigrant, the quarterly probability of receiving a WC training offer equals 0.027 if he is type 1, 0.084 if he is type 2, 0.049 if he is type 3, and almost zero if he is type 4. The weighted probability for all types is 0.039 (see table 4.7B). The fact that these rates are low is an outcome of the observed low rate of transition to WC training programs.

Net Utility from Nonemployment and Training
Utility while nonemployed or in training (whether BC or WC training) is negative (see table 4.8B) and varies significantly across types. This can be interpreted as being due to high search costs or other investment costs associated with the state of nonemployment or training. Type 1 prefers nonemployment to both WC and BC training, while type 2 prefers WC training to nonemployment and nonemployment to BC training. Since the utility of type 2, while attending WC training, is higher than the utility of being nonemployed, his participation in a WC training course might be motivated by the current gain in utility rather than by expected future returns.

The amount of government-provided income is the same for nonemployment and training. Hence the estimated lower value of utility in training indicates that there is additional disutility from training relative to nonemployment. The very low utility in both nonemployment and training may be due to the fact that immigrants have no access to credit, and therefore their consumption while not working is very low. Note that the disutility while training is an important reason for the observed low participation rates in training courses, and therefore the interpretation of the parameters has interesting policy implications.

Terminal Value
This is the most ad hoc part of the model. Nonetheless, table 4.8B shows that all the estimated parameters have the expected a priori

Table 4.8B
Estimated parameters — Males

WC training-offer probability parameters	
γ_{01} – type 1	−2.629
	(1.0421)
γ_{02} – type 2	−1.4268
	(1.0078)
γ_{03} – type 3	−2.0008
	(1.023)
γ_{04} – type 4	−6.7221
	(4.469)
γ_{1} – years of schooling	−0.0661
	(0.0625)
Terminal value parameters	
δ_{11} – type 1	1000.0271
	(4.4721)
δ_{12} – deviation of type 2 from type 1	−0.0001
	(4.4721)
δ_{13} – deviation of type 3 from type 1	0.1
	(4.4721)
δ_{14} – deviation of type 4 from type 1	−0.1
	(4.4721)
δ_{2} – experience	208.4056
	(4.3581)
δ_{31} – WC training, type 1	2156.473
	(4.47)
δ_{32} – WC training, deviation of type 2 from type 1	−758.8122
	(4.4716)
δ_{33} – WC training, deviation of type 3 from type 1	2.0396
	(4.4716)
δ_{34} – WC training, deviation of type 4 from type 1	−499.8875
	(4.4721)
δ_{4} – years of schooling	10.2756
	(4.4721)
δ_{5} – age on arrival	−8.7038
	(4.4721)
δ_{6} – Hebrew	60.0747
	(4.4721)
δ_{7} – English	60.0203
	(4.4721)
δ_{8} – worked in white-collar last period	116.0128
	(4.4703)
δ_{9} – nonemployed last period	−649.1533
	(4.4718)
δ_{101} – BC training, type 1	528.4895
	(4.4662)
δ_{102} – BC training, deviation of type 2 from type 1	−306.5896
	(4.4721)
δ_{103} – BC training, deviation of type 3 from type 1	−2.3251
	(4.4707)
δ_{104} – BC training, deviation of type 4 from type 1	−404.9197
	(4.4711)

Table 4.8B
(Continued)

Utility parameters	
ne_1 – nonemployment benefit, type 1	−252.913
	(4.3666)
ne_2 – nonemployment benefit, deviation of type 2 from type 1	−1249.2527
	(4.4719)
ne_3 – nonemployment benefit, deviation of type 3 from type 1	−14.6168
	(4.4521)
ne_4 – nonemployment benefit, deviation of type 4 from type 1	−1235.7882
	(4.4709)
tr_{31} – WC training benefit, type 1	−559.717
	(4.4612)
tr_{32} – WC training benefit, deviation of type 2 from type 1	218.4988
	(4.4696)
tr_{33} – WC training benefit, deviation of type 3 from type 1	17.8987
	(4.4697)
tr_{34} – WC training benefit, deviation of type 4 from type 1	−499.7519
	(4.4721)
tr_{41} – BC training benefit, type 1	−1116.4765
	(4.4436)
tr_{42} – BC training benefit, deviation of type 2 from type 1	−725.1144
	(4.4721)
tr_{43} – BC training benefit, deviation of type 3 from type 1	−22.4121
	(4.4651)
tr_{44} – BC training benefit, deviation of type 4 from type 1	97.7739
	(4.4674)
Type proportion parameters	
π_{01} – type 1	−0.2225
	(0.2383)
π_{02} – type 2	−0.9659
	(2.0798)
π_{03} – type 3	−1.7639
	(1.6554)
π_{04} – type 4	2.4068
	(1.5311)
π_{11} – years of schooling, type 1	−0.7068
	(0.1024)
π_{12} – years of schooling, type 2	−0.7533
	(0.141)
π_{13} – years of schooling, type 3	−0.5719
	(0.0898)
π_{14} – years of schooling, type 4	−0.8918
	(0.1264)
π_{21} – age on arrival, type 1	−0.0037
	(0.8754)
π_{22} – age on arrival, type 2	0.0078
	(0.8703)
π_{23} – age on arrival, type 3	−0.0087
	(0.8706)
π_{24} – age on arrival, type 4	−0.0238
	(0.8814)

Table 4.8B
(Continued)

Proportion of type 1	0.325
Proportion of type 2	0.121
Proportion of type 3	0.413
Proportion of type 4	0.141
Cholesky decomposition parameters	
ε_0 – variance of error nonemployment	11.434
z_1 – variance of error white-collar	0.163
Covariance (blue-collar, white-collar)	–0.057
z_2 – variance of error blue-collar	0.106
Covariance (WC training, nonemployment)	–0.781
ε_3 – variance of error WC training	1.727
Covariance (BC training, nonemployment)	–1.083
ε_4 – variance of error BC training	9.449

Note: Standard errors appear in parentheses. Type proportions are for the average male immigrant who has 14.6 years of schooling and was 38 years old on arrival.

sign and all the human capital variables have positive coefficients. Age and being nonemployed in the previous period reduce the terminal value of the immigrant's utility after 21 quarters in Israel. Since utility is measured in terms of hourly wage in NIS, the parameters can be interpreted accordingly. For example, WC training increments the terminal value by 2,156 NIS for types 1 and 3 and by 1,398 (1,650) NIS for type 2 (4), whereas training in BC increments the terminal value by around 528 NIS for types 1 and 3 and 222 (114) NIS for type 2 (4).[57]

The Interpretation of Types
The estimated distribution of types depends on the two main imported characteristics: age on arrival and education (table 4.8B). As noted, the estimated wage function (table 4.6B) indicates that types 1 and 3, who together constitute 73 percent of the sample, obtain a high wage-return on training in both occupations, while the wage-return on training is zero for types 2 and 4. From table 4.9 we see that the WC job-offer probability from nonemployment or training is highest for type 2 and almost zero for type 4. However, BC job-offer probability from nonemployment or training is highest for type 4 and lowest for type 3. Type 1's conditional probability of moving from a BC job to a WC job is significantly higher than for the other types while type 2's conditional probability of moving from a WC job to a BC job is significantly higher than for the other types.

Table 4.9
Estimated job-offer probabilities from nonemployment or training by type—Males

| Experience (quarters) | White-collar job-offer probability | | | | | | | |
| | Untrained | | | | Trained[a] | | | |
	Type 1	Type 2	Type 3	Type 4	Type 1	Type 2	Type 3	Type 4
0	0.155	0.250	0.079	0.001	0.359	0.504	0.209	0.003
1–4	0.114	0.190	0.057	0.001	0.283	0.418	0.157	0.002
5+	0.062	0.108	0.030	0.000	0.169	0.270	0.087	0.001

| Experience (quarters) | Blue-collar job-offer probability | | | | | | | |
| | Untrained | | | | Trained[a] | | | |
	Type 1	Type 2	Type 3	Type 4	Type 1	Type 2	Type 3	Type 4
0	0.354	0.605	0.180	0.838	0.358	0.609	0.183	0.840
1–4	0.322	0.570	0.160	0.817	0.326	0.575	0.162	0.820
5+	0.222	0.444	0.103	0.729	0.225	0.448	0.104	0.733

Source: Authors' calculations based on the model's estimation.
Note: Probabilities are for a male immigrant with 14.6 years of schooling, who worked in a WC job in the FSU, was 38 years old on arrival, and has a Hebrew fluency index of 2.7 and an English fluency index of 1.76.
a. Participated in a training program since arrival.

Table 4.10 presents the average predicted quarter-to-quarter transitions between the five alternative labor market states for all immigrants, conditional on the unobserved type.[58] The main result is that types 2 and 4 spend less time in nonemployment. While type 2 moves from nonemployment to both WC and BC jobs, type 4 moves only to BC jobs and has zero transitions to WC jobs. In addition type 4 has the highest frequency of direct movements from training (whether WC or BC training) to BC jobs while type 2 has the most frequent direct movements from training to WC jobs. It is interesting to note that the two types who remain the longest in nonemployment (types 1 and 3) also have the highest transitions from training to nonemployment.

These results indicate that only a small group of immigrants (made up of types 2 and 4) are well matched to market demand. Type-2 immigrants are better matched in both types of occupations while type 4 is well matched only to BC jobs; neither gains anything from vocational training programs. However, the largest share of the immigrants in the sample— type 3 (41 percent)—must make a major adjustment in order to meet the demands of the Israeli labor market. In other words, conditional on observed human capital, these immigrants face low job-offer rates;

Table 4.10
Predicted transitions by type (%)—Males

To	White-collar				Blue-collar				WC training			
From	Type 1	Type 2	Type 3	Type 4	Type 1	Type 2	Type 3	Type 4	Type 1	Type 2	Type 3	Type 4
White-collar	98.2	98.6	98.6	98.6	0.1	0.2	0.0	0.0	0.7	0.3	0.3	0.3
Blue-collar	3.0	0.4	1.1	0.0	95.2	99.3	94.3	98.6	0.8	0.1	0.5	0.1
WC training	13.8	19.2	7.8	0.3	9.0	12.8	5.6	34.6	56.8	56.8	56.8	56.8
BC training	4.7	7.5	2.3	0.0	11.7	18.7	6.3	33.5	0.0	0.0	0.0	0.0
Nonemployment	11.2	17.9	6.0	0.1	29.1	47.6	15.6	82.1	1.8	2.2	2.9	0.3
Total												

To	BC training				Nonemployment				
From	Type 1	Type 2	Type 3	Type 4	Type 1	Type 2	Type 3	Type 4	Total
White-collar	0.1	0.1	0.1	0.1	1.0	0.9	1.1	1.0	1,046
Blue-collar	0.1	0.1	0.1	0.1	0.9	0.1	4.0	1.2	2,828
WC training	0.0	0.0	0.0	0.0	20.4	11.2	29.8	8.4	136
BC training	57.5	57.5	57.5	57.5	26.1	16.3	33.9	8.9	91
Nonemployment	0.3	0.3	0.3	0.3	57.7	32.0	75.2	17.2	1,258
Total									5,359

Source: Authors' calculations based on the model's estimation and simulation (for details, see section 4.5.1 in the text).
Note: Each row sums to 100%.

however, they benefit substantially from investing in government-provided training programs. These training programs are costly in terms of time but provide significant wage compensation in later periods. Another large group of immigrants—type 1 (32 percent)—is similar to the type-3 group though they enjoy higher job-offer rates. They also must invest in training in order to improve their skills in WC jobs and thus obtain a higher wage.

4.6 Policy Analysis: Training

One of the primary motivations for estimating a structural model is to quantitatively evaluate the individual and social benefits of government policies that help immigrants integrate within the labor market. The best examples of such policies are language and training courses. In Israel all immigrants are eligible to attend Ulpan free of charge and almost all of them do so following arrival.

There are several reasons why human capital accumulated in the FSU is not fully transferable to the Israeli labor market. First, only a small proportion of immigrants know the local language on arrival. Second, immigrants in skilled occupations have to adapt to new methods and technologies while those in unskilled occupations face the same difficulties as any other displaced workers. In this chapter the acquisition of Hebrew is treated as an exogenous process that affects both wages and job-offer probabilities. The results show that the impact of language fluency is positive, significant and large for both wages and job offers. This is not a surprising result but nonetheless is important and can add to the existing knowledge on the gains from language acquisition by immigrants.

In this section we focus on the evaluation of occupation-related vocational training policy, which is conditional on language acquisition. Specifically, we consider policies that can potentially affect the supply side, such as an increase in the availability of training programs, and other popular intervention policies, such as wage subsidies that are intended to increase the demand for labor.

Policy makers view government-sponsored employment and training programs and other Active Labor Market Policies (ALMP) as tools for integrating the unemployed and economically disadvantaged into the workforce. Previous evaluations of such policies in OECD countries indicate that many programs have only a modest impact on participants' labor market prospects while others are totally ineffective. The main result is that there exists considerable heterogeneity in the impact of these programs. In a survey of the ALMP literature, Heckman, LaLonde, and Smith (1999) consider the question of whether government-provided training programs benefit the participants and society as a whole. Their answer is unambiguous: "As currently constituted, these programs are often ineffective on both counts." This claim, however, is based on vocational training programs that are primarily offered to low-skilled or displaced workers. Our data provides an opportunity to analyze the impact of vocational training programs on high-skilled workers. Furthermore, for immigrants who likely face binding liquidity constraints, subsidized training might be of greater benefit than for natives.

The link between training, work, and occupational choice embedded in our models enables us to estimate the impact of alternative government training policies on subsequent work and occupational choices. Thus an estimated structural model provides a setting in which to perform cost–benefit analysis of alternative training policies, as well as to evaluate the social and individual gains from training. The main contributions of our analysis in this section can be summarized as follows: First, training is analyzed for the first time in the framework of a structural model (Cohen Goldner and Eckstein 2008, 2010); second, the effect of ALMP on immigrants' *local* human capital accumulation is examined; and third, the individual and social gains from ALMP are measured in a life-cycle context.

The benefit from occupation-related training stems from its effect on future employment opportunities and wages. At the same time, the individual's preferences for training and the potential loss of earnings while attending the training course also affect her expected lifetime utility. Therefore the individual benefit from attending a training course is measured by the increase in expected lifetime utility from the existence of such training programs, which takes into account all these effects, including the optional value of the program being available even if the individual does not actually attend. The social return on training is measured by the expected increase in actual accepted wages less the cost of the program. The assumption adopted here is that the wage increase reflects the increase in output due to participation in a training course. The measure of the social gain used here differs slightly from the conventional one used in the literature, according to which the effect of training on potential wages is assumed to be fixed. That assumption is adopted here as well; however, in our analysis, the effect of training on actual wages changes over time since it depends on the sequential choices of the immigrants over the life cycle and on the job-offer rate, which is also a function of training.

The estimated individual and social benefits depend on both the estimated parameters of the models and on the predicted individual decisions conditional on these parameters. In estimating the effect of training on the average wage, the dynamic programming (DP) model provides conditional probabilities for both selection to the training program and the choice of jobs after training. In calculating the social benefit of a particular policy, we assume that active labor market policies aimed at immigrants do not reduce the employment of native Israelis. This assumption can be justified by results presented in the literature on recent immigration to Israel, which indicated that immigration from the FSU had no effect on the employment opportunities of native Israelis (e.g., Cohen Goldner and Paserman 2006, 2011).

Specifically, we use counterfactual simulations of the estimated models to quantitatively evaluate the effect of each alternative policy on the following outcomes: employment by occupation, nonemployment dynamics, participation in training programs, the expected present value of utility (individual benefit), and the expected present value of annual earnings over the first five years following arrival (gross social benefit). In addition we conduct a cost–benefit analysis of training-related policies using data on the costs of each policy. We use different policies for males and females in the analysis in order to demonstrate the potential uses for the estimated dynamic programming model.

4.6.1   (A) Females

In the case of females, we consider two training-related policies and two general labor market policies:

No training   In this scenario no training programs are offered to female immigrants. Although this is not the case in Israel, we believe that this is the standard case for host countries. This policy is simulated by setting the quarterly probability of receiving a training offer (equation 4.9) to zero, regardless of age. This probability is then compared to the estimated offer rates (in the "benchmark economy"), which are 0.136 for females younger than 40 on arrival and 0.056 for females older than 40 on arrival.

Always-available training   This case represents the other extreme, which assumes that training is always available to immigrants or, in other words, that the government offers a large variety of courses on an ongoing basis.

This policy is simulated by setting the quarterly probability of receiving a training offer (equation 4.9) to one, regardless of age.[59]

Doubling the WC job-offer probability   In this case we consider a policy that is not implemented directly, in which the government provides local employers with various incentives that result in the doubling of the WC job-offer probability (λ_{1t} in equation 4.8) for nonemployed immigrants who have no prior experience in WC jobs while leaving it unchanged for all other immigrants.[60] Essentially we assume that the government subsidizes WC job offers to these immigrants and that as a result employers increase their efforts to offer WC vacancies to immigrants without prior experience in WC occupations.

Wage subsidization   In this case we assume that the government subsidizes the wage offered to workers in WC jobs during their first two years in Israel. Specifically, we assume that offered wages (equation 4.5) are 6 NIS (in 1995 prices) higher than in the benchmark economy during the first year and 3 NIS higher during the second year.[61]

Each of these policies emphasizes a different channel through which the government can influence the employment outcomes and welfare of female immigrants. To evaluate the effect of each policy, we simulate each "economy" using the random sample of 502 female immigrants, assuming that they all remained in the sample for 20 continuous quarters.[62] The "benchmark economy" is based on the simulation using the estimated parameters of the model reported in the previous section. Table 4.11 reports the predicted policy effect on labor market outcomes, table 4.12 reports the predicted effects on average accepted wages and training, and table 4.13 presents the results of the cost–benefit analysis and the individual and social benefits of each policy.

Particular attention should be paid to the calculation of individual and social benefits for each case. Individual benefit is measured by the change in average expected present value of utility on arrival over the sample of 502 immigrants as a result of the policy and relative to the benchmark. Due to its linear form, utility is measured in NIS per hour expressed in 1995 prices. Social benefit measures the increase in output less the cost of the policy for the sample. We use the present value of earnings for each immigrant as the measure for output. The present value of earnings is presented in NIS in annual terms (in 1995 prices) per immigrant assuming that in each of the 20 quarters in Israel the immigrant works 500 hours.[63]

The cost of each policy is determined both directly and indirectly by a number of factors. First, each policy affects the number of nonemployed, and since nonemployed immigrants receive government benefits, government expenditure is directly affected.[64] Second, the cost of training consists of the direct cost of the program per participant, as well as the stipend the participant receives during the program. In calculating this cost, we assume that the quarterly training allowance is equal to the unemployment benefit, which is in fact the case for most immigrants. The cost of the two training policies, namely no training and always-available training, can therefore be calculated as the sum of the direct and indirect costs of training and the government expenditure on unemployment benefits.

As for the policy that involves doubling the WC job-offer probability, there is no direct method of calculating the cost of such a policy. The reason is that we do not model the offer rate as an endogenous determinant of the worker–firm matching function. Nonetheless, in order to evaluate this policy, we assume that employers would offer more WC jobs if they were offered an appropriate subsidy for each WC worker hired.[65] Specifically, we look for a "fixed-wage subsidy per hour" for all immigrants in WC jobs for five years that equates the present value of potential benefits due to doubling the WC job-offer rate to the present value of the costs (including the subsidy). The present value of the benefit is equal to the present value of the addition to wages relative to the benchmark. Since these benefits are uncertain, we discount the figures by a rate of 15 percent (annually) in order to capture the risk involved. The present value of the cost of this policy includes the change in training and nonemployment costs, as discussed above, as well as the present value of the cost of the subsidy calculated for a period of five years. The costs of the wage subsidy policy include the cost of training and unemployment benefits, plus the expenditure on the employee subsidy during the first two years.

Nonemployment and Wages
The impact of the no-training policy on nonemployment and employment in WC jobs among female immigrants after five years in Israel is substantial (table 4.11). The second policy, which makes training available with a probability of one, would increase participation in a training course by 60 percent (from 252 to 402 females), with most of the increase during the first year. Since training increases job-offer probabilities in both types of occupation, this policy has a positive effect on

Table 4.11
Effect of policy experiments on labor market outcomes—Females

	Benchmark[a]	Policy A No training	Policy B Always- available training	Policy C Doubled WC job-offer probability	Policy D Wage subsidy
In the 4th quarter					
WC employment (%)	7.2	7.4	9.0	14.7	7.2
BC employment (%)	27.1	29.5	28.1	24.5	27.1
Training (%)	15.7	0.0	36.9	15.5	15.7
Nonemployment (%)	50.0	63.2	26.1	45.2	50.0
In the 20th quarter					
WC employment (%)	32.9	21.7	38.3	50.0	32.9
BC employment (%)	49.8	51.0	47.0	36.7	49.8
Training (%)	0.2	0.0	2.0	0.0	0.2
Nonemployment (%)	17.1	27.3	12.8	13.4	17.1
Accumulated number of trained immigrants	252	0	402	268	252

Source: Authors' calculations based on the policy simulations (for details, see section 4.6.1 in the text).
a. The benchmark refers to the simulated choices of the 502 female immigrants over 20 quarters at the ML estimation point.

employment in general and on employment in WC jobs in particular. After five years in Israel, nonemployment would decline from 17.1 percent (in the benchmark economy) to 12.8 percent and the share of those employed in WC jobs would increase by 5.4 percent. Meanwhile the proportion of those employed in BC jobs would decrease by almost 3 percent.

The doubled WC job-offer probability policy would result in a substantial increase in WC employment and a decrease in nonemployment one year after its adoption. However, it also lowers BC employment (table 4.11). After a period of five years, the share of female immigrants employed in WC jobs would increase to 50 percent, while nonemployment would decline to 13.4 percent and employment in BC jobs to 36.7 percent. Participation in a training course increases only slightly (by less than 1 percent or 16 immigrants). Note that this policy has almost the same effect as the always-available training policy on nonemployment but has a much larger effect on the proportion of female immigrants working in WC jobs. The wage subsidy policy has no effect on the choice distribution of the immigrants and therefore has no effect on employment in WC jobs. The policy is ineffective in this regard since immigrants prefer WC jobs even in the absence of a wage subsidy and the main reason they are not employed in WC jobs is the low offer probability (i.e., low availability) of these jobs.

The no-training policy has a small negative effect on wages in WC jobs after 20 quarters, but has no effect on wages in BC jobs (table 4.12), while the always-available training policy has a large positive effect on accepted wages in WC jobs and almost no effect on accepted wages in BC jobs. There are two sources for the increase in WC wages. First, immigrants who participated in a training course and find a WC job earn more due to the high wage-return on training in WC jobs. Second, immigrants who work in WC jobs accumulate more WC experience and enjoy the high return on this specific type of experience. The wage increase is about 2.3 to 3.3 NIS, which represents an increase of 13.5 to 16.3 percent relative to the benchmark economy, depending on time since arrival. Since the return on training and BC experience in BC jobs is almost zero, this type of intervention has no significant effect on accepted wages in BC jobs.

Doubling WC job-offer probability has no effect on the average accepted wage in either BC or WC jobs. This policy accelerates the accumulation of WC experience, which has a positive effect on wages in WC jobs. However, more immigrants with less skills (i.e., education) will then be employed in WC jobs. This selection process implies a negative effect that offsets most of the positive effect of increased WC experience on wages in WC jobs. Finally, a wage subsidy has no effect on labor market outcomes or wages (tables 4.11 and 4.12). As such, this policy consists of a pure transfer of income to immigrants in WC jobs during their first two years in Israel, without having any real impact on the economy.

Cost–Benefit Analysis

The individual and social benefits of the various policies are reported in the lower part of table 4.13. The no-training policy is predicted to reduce annual output per immigrant by 19 percent due to the reduction in WC employment and the increase in nonemployment. Always-available training increases average annual earnings per immigrant by about 15 percent, which is about double the estimated return on a year of schooling for native Israelis (Eckstein and Weiss 2004). The average duration of training is about six months and its cost is lower than that of standard schooling. Hence it appears that the model predicts a very high social return on training programs, assuming that the increase in earnings reflects an increase in marginal product and therefore is proportional to the increase in output.[66] Overall, the gain from always-available training in comparison to no training implies annual earnings growth of 34 (= 15 + 19) percent.

Table 4.12
Effect of policy experiments on average accepted wages—Females

	Benchmark[a]		Policy A No training		Policy B Always-available training		Policy C Doubled WC job-offer probability		Policy D Wage subsidy	
	White-collar	Blue-collar	White-collar	Blue-collar	White-collar	Blue-collar	White-collar	Blue-collar	White-collar	Blue-collar
Time since arrival										
4th quarter	14.53	8.00	15.42	7.99	16.89	8.11	14.61	8.02	20.53	8.00
20th quarter	24.32	9.45	22.62	9.55	27.61	9.65	25.92	9.51	24.32	9.45
Before training	18.87	8.84	18.63	8.88	19.13	8.67	19.36	8.54	19.82	8.84
After training	22.45	8.80			22.70	9.00	22.10	8.99	22.82	8.80

Source: Authors' calculations based on the policy simulations (for details, see section 4.6.1 in the text).
Note: Hourly wages expressed in July 1995 prices (NIS).
a. The benchmark refers to the simulated choices of the 502 female immigrants over 20 quarters at the ML estimation point.

The large reduction (40 percent) in the welfare of female immigrants as a result of canceling training programs and the large increase (49 percent) in welfare as a result of always-available training demonstrate the substantial average gain from training (table 4.13). However, this gain varies widely within the sample. The largest gain is obtained for older and less-educated females who moved from nonemployment to employment due to their participation in a training course. The fact that the older females in the benchmark economy had a very low rate of training offers created the potential for a large gain as a result of training becoming available with a probability of one. This result suggests that interventionist policies have a larger impact on extensive margins (i.e., the move from nonemployment to employment) than on intensive margins (i.e., an increased rate of WC jobs).

Doubling the WC job-offer probability implies a predicted annual increase in earnings per female immigrant of about 21 percent, which constitutes a high social return, though it is lower than in the case of always-available training. The private gain from the doubled WC job-offer probability policy (24 percent) is also lower than that obtained in the always-available training case and is very close to the increase in earnings. The main advantage of always-available training, relative to the doubled WC job-offer probability policy, is that it directly affects both employment and wages (i.e., productivity). Doubling the WC job-offer probability affects only employment in WC jobs while its effect on wages is only secondary, through the accumulation of WC experience. The wage subsidy policy results in neither social nor private gain and even though money has been transferred, only a small fraction of the female immigrants are recipients.

Based on results in Eyal (2005), the per immigrant present value of the total annual cost of transfers to trainees, unemployment benefits and direct training is 6,436 NIS (in 1995 prices) in the benchmark economy. No training increases these costs by 10 percent; always-available training lowers them by 8 percent; and doubled WC job-offer probability lowers them by 9 percent. The subsidization of WC employees has no effect on participation in training courses and nonemployment and therefore does not affect their costs. As discussed above, the benefit from each policy is measured by the average increase in annual wages while the change in net benefit relative to the benchmark economy is equal to the change in benefit less the change in costs. The net benefit of the no-training policy is negative while the return on training provided in the benchmark economy is 43 percent under our assumptions. Always-available training

Table 4.13
Cost–benefit analysis of the policy experiments—Females

	Benchmark			Policy A No training	Policy B Always-available training	
	Transfer payments—trainees[a]	Transfer payments—non-employed[b]	Direct training cost[c]	Transfer payments—non-employed[b]	Transfer payments—trainees[a]	Transfer payments—non-employed[b]
Years since arrival[d]						
1	670	6,024	296	6,594	1,953	4,667
2	822	3,214	212	4,358	605	2,740
3	448	2,144	129	3,340	222	1,766
4	265	1,609	72	2,740	270	1,179
5	139	1,570	45	2,536	544	979
PV of costs for five-year period[d]						
	2,141	13,320	693	17,741	3,307	10,390
PV of annual costs per immigrant[e]						
	853	5,307	276	7,068 (33)	1,318 (55)	4,139 (−22)
PV of total annual costs per immigrant[f]						
		6,436		7,068 (10)		5,900 (−8)
PV of annual earnings per immigrant[g]						
		13,889		11,300 (−19)		15,923 (15)
Benefit net of cost[h]		7,453		4,232		10,023
Change in benefit net of cost[i]				−3,221 (−43)		2,570 (34)
Expected present value		5,121		3,047 (−40)		7,638 (49)

Source: Authors' calculations based on the policy simulations (for details, see section 4.6.1 in the text).
Note: The benchmark refers to the simulated choices of the 502 female immigrants over 20 quarters at the ML estimation point. Costs and wages are expressed in July 1995 prices (NIS). Percentage change relative to the benchmark appears in parentheses.
a. Number of trainees during four quarters × transfer payments per individual per quarter, zero for the no training policy.
b. Number of nonemployed during four quarters × transfer payments per individual per quarter.
c. Number of new trainees during four quarters × direct cost per trainee, zero for the no training policy. Transfer payment per individual is 1,450 NIS per month or 4,350 NIS per quarter, assuming that each trainee receives payment for 6 months. Direct training cost per trainee is 2,992 NIS for the entire training course. Costs are based on Eyal (2005, n.1).

| | Policy C | | | Policy D | | |
| Direct training cost[c] | Doubled WC job-offer probability | | Direct training cost[c] | Wage subsidy | | Direct training cost[c] |
	Transfer payments— trainees[a]	Transfer payments— non-employed[b]		Transfer payments— trainees[a]	Transfer payments— non-employed[b]	
778	687	5,759	296	670	6,024	296
81	852	2,718	233	822	3,214	212
78	553	1,692	150	448	2,144	129
84	265	1,331	75	265	1,609	72
183	135	1,274	48	139	1,570	45
1,112	2,275	11,726	736	2,141	13,320	693
443 (61)	906 (6)	4,672 (−12)	293 (6)	853 (0)	5,307 (0)	276 (0)
		5,871 (−9)			6,436 (0)	
		16,859 (21)			13,889(0)	
		10,988			7,453	
		3,535 (47)			0 (0)	
		6,340 (24)			5,124 (0)	

d. Thousands.

e. Cost for five years / number of immigrants (502) / number of years (five).

f. Transfer payments to trainees and nonemployed + direct training cost.

g. Present value over 20 quarters of (number of workers × hourly wage) / number of immigrants (502) / number of years (five) × number of hours per quarter (500). The hourly wage in the wage subsidy policy does not include the subsidy.

h. PV of annual earnings per immigrant — PV of total annual costs per immigrant — cost of subsidy (for the wage subsidy policy only).

i. Relative to the benchmark. In policy D, the cost is that of the subsidy.

is estimated to increase net benefit by 34 percent. The doubled WC job-offer probability increases the benefit by 47 percent if one ignores the subsidy that employers receive in order to offer more WC jobs. We calculate the upper bound of the subsidy by solving for the value that equates the additional benefit to the additional cost, including the subsidy. The result is a subsidy of 5.37 NIS per hour where the hourly wage (see table 4.12) in WC jobs starts at 15 NIS and increases to about 25 NIS after 20 quarters. Hence it appears that a subsidy of 5.37 NIS might substantially increase the potential number of job offers for immigrants and that this policy is potentially feasible with a positive social rate of return.

4.6.2   (B) Males

The estimated model for males distinguishes between WC and BC training. Therefore, the policy analysis will focus on policies that change the availability of each type of training program relative to the estimated existing policy. In addition the gain from training can be calculated for each of the two types of program in order to determine which is more efficient. To do this, we compare the outcomes of simulating the estimated model (i.e., the existing policy) to those of simulating the four alternative training policies. It should be noted that in the estimated model, which serves as our benchmark, the probability of receiving a BC training-offer is set to one, which implies that it is always available, while the estimated probability of receiving a WC training offer is constant over time (and less than 1) and depends on the immigrant's schooling and unobserved type according to equation (4.19).

The four policies to be considered are as follows:

No training   This policy is identical to the corresponding one for females and implies that neither WC nor BC training is available. This policy is considered in order to estimate the gain from the estimated benchmark model.

No WC training   This policy implies that WC training is not available and that BC training is available with a probability of 1, as in the benchmark economy. This case is intended to measure the gain from the estimated positive availability of WC training in the benchmark economy.

No BC training   The BC training probability, which was assumed to be one in the benchmark economy, is now set to zero while WC training is available with the same probability as in the benchmark economy. This case is intended to measure the gain from the continuous availability of BC training.

Doubled availability of WC training   In this case the offer probability of BC training is assumed to be one, as in the model while the WC training-offer probability, which depends on schooling and unobserved types, is doubled for each immigrant according to his WC training-offer probability in the benchmark economy.

First, we measure the effect of the policy experiments on wages and nonemployment for an average immigrant (table 4.14). Second, we measure the aggregate predicted wage growth due to the policy experiments (table 4.15). Finally, we measure the effect of the policies on the immigrant's welfare and perform a social cost–benefit analysis (table 4.16). The simulation outcomes are all conditional on each individual's state on arrival, but not on the actual subsequent outcomes.

Nonemployment and Wages
Table 4.14 reports the predicted differences in average accepted wages and the average nonemployment rate between the benchmark economy and the outcome of the simulated alternative policy during the fourth and fifth years in Israel. We find that the policy experiments have only a small impact on the predicted long-term nonemployment rate among immigrants. Thus the nonemployment rate after three years is predicted to be less than 4 percent and remains close to that level thereafter. Earnings are affected in the predicted direction, such that average earnings in WC jobs decrease due to the nonavailability of training programs and increase as the availability of WC training increases. Meanwhile the impact of the availability of WC training programs on BC wages is small. Finally, there is almost no difference in the effect of these policies on immigrants according to background (i.e., education and occupation in the FSU).

It is interesting that the availability of WC training has a large impact on accepted wages and affects the predicted average accepted wage in both WC and BC jobs to about the same extent. The increase in the average accepted BC wage is a result of the selection of different types of immigrants into WC training programs and subsequently into WC jobs.

The availability of BC training has zero impact on average accepted wages and nonemployment and therefore the no–BC-training policy is identical to the situation in the benchmark economy. This is derived from the estimation result that male immigrants unconditionally prefer to avoid BC training even though it is always available. The reason for this

Table 4.14
Effect of policy experiments on average accepted wages and nonemployment during the 4th and 5th years following arrival—Males

| | Case 1: No training | | | Case 4: Doubled WC training-offer probability | | |
| | Percent change | | Change | Percent change | | Change |
Immigrant	White-collar wage	Blue-collar wage	Nonemployment rate	White-collar wage	Blue-collar wage	Nonemployment rate
BC in the FSU, schooling = 12	−3.4	−0.4	0.4	1.6	0.4	−0.2
WC in the FSU, schooling = 15	−3.1	−0.3	0.4	1.7	0.2	−0.4

Source: Authors' calculations based on the policy simulations (for details, see section 4.6.2 in the text).
Note: Percentage change in wages and nonemployment rate relative to the benchmark. Results are for a male immigrant who was 30 years old on arrival, had no knowledge of Hebrew on arrival and has an English fluency index of 1.76.

Table 4.15
Annual effect of training availability on average accepted wages — Males

	Total	White-collar	Blue-collar
Year 1	0.09	0.18	0.06
Year 2	0.67	1.40	0.23
Year 3	1.12	2.12	0.23
Year 4	1.40	2.40	0.29
Year 5	1.61	2.46	0.43
All years	1.16	2.35	0.19

Source: Authors' calculations based on the policy simulations (for details, see section 4.6.2 in the text).
Note: Percentage change in the estimated model relative to the economy without training (case 1).

preference is that the potential gain from BC training is lower than the potential loss from not working, which is in agreement with the conclusion reached by Heckman, LaLonde and Smith (1999). As a consequence the effects of a no-training policy and a no–WC-training policy are identical, and therefore we do not report the results of the second and third policies separately. The main result is that only WC training programs produce benefit. The availability of these training programs has a very large impact on participation and predicted wage growth, though only a minor predicted impact on nonemployment. Finally, the endogeneity of all these outcomes is critical in generating the main result.

It is common to view the predicted aggregate increase in wages as the gross rate of return to the economy on the investment in training programs.[67] In table 4.15 we report the predicted annual effect of training availability on average accepted wages as a percentage change relative to an economy with no training (the first policy experiment listed above). We use the sample of 419 males in order to calculate the effect of such a policy. The calculation of the aggregate rate of wage growth due to training differs from the estimated coefficient of training in the wage equations since it includes the effect of dynamic choices made by the workers, in addition to the impact of training on wages and the random opportunities.

The predicted average aggregate wage growth due to training during the first five years following arrival is about 1.16 percent (table 4.15). The most important result of the analysis is that the total rate of return increases over time. In the first year the effect is almost zero since few immigrants are predicted to participate in a training course. Most training occurs between the end of the first year and the third year following arrival in Israel. Therefore it is not surprising to observe that the return on training increases during this period. The large increase in return during the fifth year is due to the large shift of workers from BC jobs to WC jobs, as discussed above. The main gain from training is enjoyed by type-1 immigrants who eventually find WC jobs. Finally, since the predicted wage growth of 1.12 to 1.61 percent occurs between the third and fifth years following arrival, it is safe to conclude that the increase in the present value of wages due to training is greater than one percent.

Cost–Benefit Analysis

The individual and social gains in each of the four experiments are measured for two representative immigrants who differ in their stock of imported human capital: age on arrival (30 and 45), years of schooling (12 and 15), and occupation in the FSU. Knowledge of Hebrew and English are set at the sample averages. The results are presented in table 4.16.

Recall that one of the main results of the unconditional predictions of the policies considered here is that no male immigrants will participate in a BC training course. Hence changing the availability of BC training produces no individual or social benefits. This result is consistent with the conclusion by Heckman, LaLonde, and Smith (1999) that BC training for low-skilled men has no social or individual benefits. Thus, we present the analysis only for the no-training and doubled WC training-offer probability policies.

If no training is available, then annual output is reduced by one percent due to the reduction in the present value of annual earnings per immigrant. The welfare of an immigrant who is 30 years old and has 12 years of schooling on arrival declines by 3 percent as a result of the no-training policy, while the welfare of an immigrant who is 45 years old and has 15 years of schooling on arrival declines by 4 percent. These figures imply that male immigrants gain little from the availability of training. Using the approximated costs of the government provision of training as we did for females, we obtain that a no-training policy reduces government costs by 5 percent for the first representative immigrant and by 4 percent for the second, relative to the benchmark. This is the opposite result to that obtained for females, according to which government expenditure was increased by the adoption of this policy. This is because males will accept whatever jobs are available if no training is offered due to their higher job-offer rates and therefore the government expenditure on unemployment benefits is reduced. In contrast, females have lower job-offer rates and are more likely to be nonemployed. Thus the individual and social benefits of WC training are zero or negative, despite the very high potential wage return on WC training in the estimated wage function.

Implementation of the doubled WC training-offer probability policy leads to a one-percent increase in annual output. The welfare of the 30-year-old immigrant with 12 years of schooling on arrival increases by 2 percent under this policy, while the welfare of the 45-year-old immigrant with 15 years of schooling on arrival increases by 3 percent. Thus the reason that male immigrants do not train is not the limited availability of courses, but rather the high opportunity costs, namely the loss of potential work experience while attending a training course. The doubled WC training-offer probability policy increases costs by 5 percent for the younger representative immigrant and by 3 percent for the older one and the policy's net benefit (see table 4.16) is zero for both. This implies that for males, unlike females, training programs in Israel provide no social benefits.

4.6.3   Summary

The policy analysis provides some insight into the potential individual and social gains from training programs. Despite the similar magnitudes of the estimated parameters for males and females, we find substantial differences between the genders. Specifically, always-available training for female immigrants is beneficial for both the immigrant and for society, whereas for males training programs provide no benefits. This is primarily due to differences in the opportunity costs of training between males and females. For females, training is a substitute for nonemployment; that is, if a female immigrant does not train, she is less likely to be employed. For males, training is a substitute for work; that is, if a male immigrant does not train, he is more likely be employed. Thus the no-training policy for females implies higher costs due to higher government expenditure on unemployment benefits. Yet the same policy for males results in lower government costs since nonemployment (including training) decreases, such that the net impact is slightly negative. The individual benefit of WC training for males is positive with a 3 or 4 percent increase in present value (table 4.16, last row).

The DP model with endogenous choice of training and employment implies that the social and individual benefits of training cannot be measured *only* by the coefficient of training in the wage function. Both the costs and the gains from training are affected by the immigrants'

Table 4.16
Cost–benefit analysis of the policy experiments—Males

	BC in the FSU, schooling = 12, age on arrival 30					
	Benchmark			Policy A No training	Policy D Doubled WC training-offer probability	
	Transfer payments—trainees[a]	Transfer payments—non-employed[b]	Direct training cost[c]	Transfer payments—non-employed[b]	Transfer payments—trainees[a]	Transfer payments—non-employed[b]
Years since arrival[d]						
1	117	2,753	54	2,827	243	2,680
2	145	802	39	831	222	800
3	45	359	14	395	51	349
4	12	246	6	285	33	223
5	27	262	7	288	44	251
PV of costs for five-year period[d]						
	319	4,129	112	4,313	548	4,020
PV of annual costs per immigrant[e]						
	152	1,971	53	2,059 (4)	262 (72)	1,919 (–3)
PV of total annual costs per immigrant[f]						
		2,176		2,059 (–5)		2,274 (5)
PV of annual earnings per immigrants[g]						
		20,727		20,572(–1)		20,832(1)
Benefit net of cost[h]		18,551		18,513		18,558
Change in benefit net of cost[i]				–38 (0)		7(0)
Expected present value		3,243		3,153 (–3)		3,310 (2)

Source: Authors' calculations based on the policy simulations (for details, see section 4.6.2 in the text).

Note: Costs and wages are expressed in June 1995 prices (NIS). Percentage change relative to the benchmark appears in parentheses. Results are for a male immigrant who had no knowledge of Hebrew on arrival and has an English fluency index of 1.76.

a. Number of trainees during four quarters × transfer payments per individual per quarter, zero for the no training policy.

b. Number of nonemployed during four quarters × transfer payments per individual per quarter.

c. Number of new trainees during four quarters × direct cost per trainee, zero for the no training policy. Transfer payment per individual is 1,446 NIS per month or 4,339 NIS per quarter, assuming that each trainee receives payment for 6 months. Direct training cost per trainee is 2,985 NIS for the entire training course. Costs are based on Eyal (2005; see n.1).

	WC in the FSU, schooling = 15, age on arrival 45						
	Benchmark			Policy A — No training		Policy D — Doubled WC training-offer probability		
Direct training cost[c]	Transfer payments—trainees[a]	Transfer payments—non-employed[b]	Direct training cost[c]	Transfer payments—non-employed[b]	Transfer payments—trainees[a]	Transfer payments—non-employed[b]	Direct training cost[c]
111	152	3,361	70	3,446	250	3,291	117
55	160	1,090	38	1,120	249	1,057	63
17	50	453	15	508	60	448	20
15	18	301	10	361	31	279	15
11	17	300	5	345	43	297	10
194	367	5,141	128	5,387	585	5,017	210
93 (75)	175	2,454	61	2,571 (5)	279 (59)	2,395 (−2)	100 (64)
		2,690		2,571 (−4)		2,774 (3)	
		21,368		21,068 (−1)		21,489(1)	
		18,678		18,497		18,715	
				−181 (−1)		37(0)	
		3,000		2,889 (−4)		3,086 (3)	

d. Thousands.
e. Cost for five years / number of immigrants (419) / number of years (five).
f. Transfer payments to trainees and nonemployed + direct training cost.
g. Present value over 20 quarters of (number of workers × hourly wage) / number of immigrants (419) / number of years (five) × number of hours per quarter (500).
h. PV of annual earnings per immigrant — PV of total annual costs per immigrant.
i. Relative to the benchmark.

choices and by the dynamics of the model, as well as by the costs of the programs and the individual optional value benefits. In conclusion, we find that vocational training programs benefit only females, which is largely consistent with the findings in the literature (Heckman, LaLonde, and Smith 1999).

4.7 Verification of the Model: Out-of-Sample Predictions[68]

Todd and Wolpin (2006) proposed the idea of model verification to evaluate social policies. They estimated their model for a control group and a treatment group but for the latter used only data for the period prior to treatment. They then verified the model by comparing the predictions of the estimated model for the treated group to the data for the period of treatment. Their method provides a direct way of evaluating interventionist policies.

In our case the model for females is verified using additional data not included in the estimation. Specifically, the model for females was originally estimated using the available data on immigrants' choices and wages during, at most, the first 20 quarters in Israel. Additional data for up to ten years (40 quarters) following arrival in Israel became available in 2001–2 when some of the immigrants were re-surveyed.

In this section we use the additional data to extend the model's solution to a period of ten years and then verify the model's out-of-sample predictions using actual data for the period between the 5th and 10th year of residence in Israel. In addition two other data sources are used to evaluate the predictions of the extended ten-year model.

Table 4.17 presents summary statistics for the four data sources: (1) the full Brookdale Employment Survey used for the estimation of the model (502 immigrants; summary statistics include additional data for these immigrants from the 2001–2 survey); (2) the partial Brookdale Employment Survey, which includes 235 females from the full Employment Survey for whom the sample period was extended to ten years based on a third interview (in 2001–2); (3) the Engineers' Survey, which includes 304 female immigrants from the FSU who arrived during the period 1989–94 and reported that they hold an engineering diploma from the FSU (for more details, see chapter 5; these immigrants were first interviewed in 1995 and then again in 2001–2, such that a retrospective ten-year panel was created); and (4) the Labor Force Survey (LFS), which contains annual cross-sectional data on female immigrants who arrived in Israel from the FSU during the period 1989 to 1992. The summary statistics in

Table 4.17
Summary statistics for the four samples—Females

Variables	Full Employment Survey[a]			Partial Employment Survey[b]			Engineers' Survey			LFS[c]
	All	Untrained	Trained[d]	All	Untrained	Trained[d]	All	Untrained	Trained[d]	All
Number of observations	502	239	263	235	94	141	304	188	116	15,379
Age on arrival	37.21	38.99	35.59	38.09	41.07	36.11	41.3	42.24	39.77	37.29
	(8.5)	(8.9)	(7.7)	(8.1)	(7.3)	(8)	(8.6)	(8.8)	(8)	(7.7)
Years of schooling	14.47	13.72	15.16	14.69	13.89	15.23	16.04	16.11	15.93	14.42
	(2.4)	(2.4)	(2.1)	(2.4)	(2.5)	(2.1)	(1.4)	(1.4)	(1.4)	(2.7)
Number of children	1.05	0.99	1.11	1.08	1.03	1.11				
	(0.8)	(0.9)	(0.8)	(0.8)	(0.9)	(0.8)				
Knew Hebrew prior to migration (%)	15.7	10.9	20.2	17.4	11.7	21.3				
White-collar in the FSU (%)	75.7	66.5	84.0	78.3	64.9	87.2	98.7	98.4	99.1	
Married (%)	76.5	76.2	76.8	79.6	80.9	78.7	75.7	74.5	77.6	77.4
Hebrew fluency index—first survey[e]	2.99	2.66	3.29	2.99	2.64	3.22				
	(0.8)	(0.8)	(0.6)	(0.7)	(0.7)	(0.7)				
Hebrew fluency index—second survey	3.3	2.95	3.56	3.25	2.88	3.5	3.24	3.12	3.44	
	(0.8)	(0.9)	(0.5)	(0.7)	(0.8)	(0.6)	(0.7)	(0.8)	(0.6)	

Sources: Brookdale Survey, Engineers' Survey, and CBS Labor Force Survey.
Note: Standard deviations appear in parentheses.
a. The sample used for estimation. Summary statistics include additional data from the 2001–2 survey.
b. Immigrants from the full Employment Survey who were re-sampled in 2001–2.
c. Annual cross-sectional data from the CBS Labor Force Survey during the period 1989 to 2002. The sample includes immigrants from the FSU who arrived in Israel during the period 1989 to 92, were aged 25 to 55 on arrival, participated in the labor force and resided in Israel for up to 11 years.
d. Participated in a training program since arrival.
e. 1 = lowest; 4 = highest.

table 4.17 show that the various samples share similar demographic characteristics (age on arrival, years in Israel, number of children, etc.) and stocks of human capital (schooling and knowledge of Hebrew). Immigrant engineers are the only exception due to the fact that they are older on arrival and have more years of schooling.

4.7.1 Out-of-Sample Predictions

The model was estimated using the sample of 502 immigrants who were tracked for up to five years (20 quarters) in Israel. The data in the partial Employment Survey of 2001–2 makes it possible to study the dynamics of immigrant assimilation and transition in the labor market over a period of ten years on a quarterly basis and to compare those patterns to the predictions of the estimated model.[69] In order to provide predictions of labor market states from the 6th to the 10th year following arrival, we first must solve the model for females for a period of ten years. This involves modifying the estimated terminal value for the 21st quarter in Israel (equation 4.24) in order to produce the desired terminal value for the 41st quarter. In other words, we seek an approximation for the terminal value after ten years in Israel that is consistent with the requirement that it declines to zero as the individual approaches retirement at age 65. Thus our approximation adjusts the estimated coefficients of the linearly estimated terminal value for the 21st quarter, such that each coefficient reaches a value of zero at the age of retirement.[70]

Figure 4.4 presents the actual and predicted labor market states for the ten-year period based on the partial employment sample of 235 immigrants. The predicted states are the result of a conditional one-step-ahead forecast based on the estimated parameters and the approximated terminal value for the 41st quarter. The model accurately reproduces both the trends and levels of actual employment by type of occupation, nonemployment, and training for the entire ten-year period. The fit for the first five years in Israel is as good as that of the estimated model within the sample period. The most striking result is that the out-of-sample predictions accurately recreate the dramatic stability in employment and nonemployment that characterizes the data starting from the 21st quarter in Israel.

The data show that the transition to a new labor market takes about five years of adjustment and that immigrants are characterized by a relatively stable distribution across labor market states following that period. These transitions are accurately predicted by our estimated dynamic

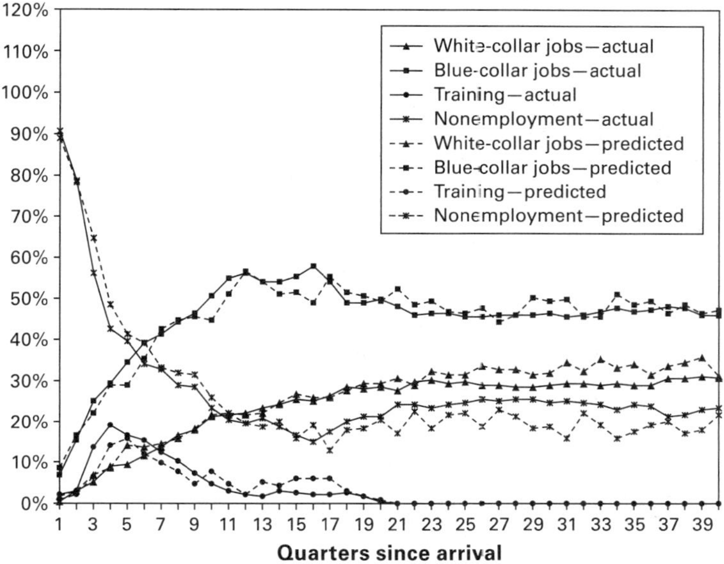

Figure 4.4
Actual and predicted choice distributions during the ten-year period following arrival:
Partial Employment Survey (235 observations). Sources: Brookdale Survey and authors'
calculations.

model based only on the first five years following arrival, thus providing
strong verification for our framework of analysis and for the estimated
parameters.

4.7.2   Aggregate Trends

Table 4.18 compares the annual aggregate data from the LFS with the
unconditional prediction of the estimated model for a ten-year period,
using all 502 observations in the employment sample.[71] The model accurately predicts both the level and trend of WC employment up to the 5th
year following arrival and the trend in nonemployment (including training) for the entire ten-year period. Furthermore the model predicts the
decrease in BC employment after seven years in Israel. However, there
are some significant deviations from the actual levels of WC and BC
employment during the second five-year period in Israel.

It should be noted that the model abstracts from aggregate macro
changes in the Israeli economy that affect individuals in the nationally
based LFS sample, such as the slowdown in the growth of the Israeli
labor market during the relevant period (1996 to 2000) relative to 1990

Table 4.18
Actual and predicted choice distribution during the ten-year period following arrival—comparison between the Labor Force Survey[a] and the unconditional prediction[b] of the model—Females

Years since arrival	Number of observations	White-collar LFS	White-collar predicted	Blue-collar LFS	Blue-collar predicted	Unemployment LFS	Nonemployment predicted[c]
1	268	0.0485	0.0438	0.3246	0.2082	0.6269	0.7480
2	1485	0.1044	0.1445	0.4444	0.3476	0.4498	0.5080
3	1571	0.1878	0.2206	0.5379	0.4358	0.2731	0.3437
4	1655	0.2495	0.2749	0.5813	0.4801	0.1674	0.2450
5	1600	0.2869	0.3292	0.5963	0.4711	0.1156	0.1997
6	1612	0.2636	0.3615	0.6576	0.4935	0.0775	0.1449
7	1587	0.2665	0.3860	0.6440	0.4995	0.0876	0.1146
8	1533	0.2942	0.4109	0.6308	0.4836	0.0724	0.1056
9	1387	0.3129	0.4427	0.6099	0.4438	0.0757	0.1136
10	1352	0.3336	0.4736	0.5836	0.4447	0.0791	0.0817

Sources: CBS Labor Force Survey and authors' calculations.
a. Annual cross-sectional data from the CBS Labor Force Survey during the period 1989 to 2001.The sample includes immigrants from the FSU who arrived in Israel during the period 1989 to 1992 and were aged 25 to 55 on arrival. Proportions of labor force participants.
b. Based on the initial conditions of the full Employment Survey (502 observations).
c. Includes training.

to 1995 and the aggregate increase in unemployment. However, the model does capture the trends due to the individual's transitions in the labor market as they are reflected in the aggregate data.[72] The model's good out-of-sample fit to the trends in the cross-sectional data provides additional verification of the empirical model as a good approximation of the immigrant's dynamic choice problem.

4.7.3   High-Skilled Immigrants

The availability of the Engineers' Survey creates an additional opportunity to verify the model's predictions by providing a ten-year quarterly panel of high-skilled immigrants. Engineers have an average of 16 years of schooling (and almost all have more than 14 years of schooling; see table 4.17). This survey, which includes 304 female immigrant engineers, was not used in the estimation and contains almost all the data (on a quarterly basis) required to produce unconditional predictions for each individual in the sample for a ten-year period.

Table 4.19 summarizes the data and the unconditional simulated prediction of the model for the sample on an annual basis (the annual figures are obtained by averaging over four quarters). The model predicts with relative accuracy the observed patterns of WC and BC employment, as well as nonemployment (including training). The fit for the first five years is superior to that for the second five years in terms of levels and trends. The model underpredicts nonemployment (including training) and BC employment and overpredicts WC employment from the 5th to the 10th year in Israel, though it accurately predicts the observed decrease in BC employment after the 5th year in Israel.

The model predicts that 171 female immigrant engineers will participate in a training course as compared to only 116 who actually did so.[73] Overall, the sample contains lower quality labor state outcomes than those predicted. One plausible explanation is that this particular sample represents a subsample with a high reservation wage for BC employment. The main observation that supports this claim is the very high rate of un(non)employment (more than 20 percent) from the 4th to the 10th year in Israel. In addition the actual number of trainees is lower than predicted and is also lower than that in the full employment sample.

4.7.4   Summary

This section shows that the model's predictions of labor market employment and training patterns are consistent with the out-of-sample data.

Table 4.19
Actual and predicted[a] choice distribution during the ten-year period following arrival—Engineers' Survey—Females

Years since arrival	Number of observations	White-collar data	White-collar predicted	Blue-collar data	Blue-collar predicted	Nonemployment data[b]	Nonemployment predicted[b]
1	304	0.0436	0.0650	0.2286	0.2122	0.7278	0.7229
2	304	0.1628	0.1941	0.4704	0.3701	0.3668	0.4359
3	304	0.2245	0.2887	0.5082	0.4310	0.2673	0.2804
4	304	0.2566	0.3470	0.5058	0.4112	0.2377	0.2418
5	304	0.2837	0.4219	0.5058	0.4013	0.2105	0.1768
6	304	0.3002	0.4770	0.4720	0.4054	0.2278	0.1176
7	304	0.3289	0.5008	0.4622	0.3627	0.2089	0.1365
8	286	0.3512	0.5444	0.4267	0.3545	0.2221	0.1012
9	248	0.3627	0.5880	0.4050	0.3281	0.2324	0.0839
10	209	0.3783	0.5864	0.4051	0.3100	0.2165	0.1036

Sources: Engineers' Survey and authors' calculations.
a. Unconditional prediction based on the initial conditions of the Engineers' Survey (304 observations).
b. Includes training.

This provides strong support for the interpretation of the data provided by the model and therefore for its policy conclusions as well. Based on this analysis, we can more confidently proceed in the next section to use the results in order to measure the value of immigrating from the FSU to Israel.

4.8   The Value of Immigrating to Israel

The possibility of migrating from the FSU to Israel appeared suddenly and unexpectedly in late 1989 and was exogenous to economic conditions in Israel and prior choices of the relevant Jewish population. This section attempts to make a simple comparison between the present value of earnings in the FSU and the present value of earnings or utility under several scenarios of integration in Israel. In order to calculate the value of staying in the FSU, we consider only the present value of earnings since we do not have a valuation of utility in the FSU. For the scenarios in Israel, the model allows us to distinguish between the valuation of utility and earnings.[74] Thus we are able to compare the present value of expected income in the FSU to that in Israel. Specifically, we assume that the immigrant did not know Hebrew before immigrating to Israel (which was true of about 88 percent of males and 85 percent of females) and consider two possible scenarios for integration in the Israeli labor market:

1. The immigrant actively searches for a job upon arrival in Israel and faces the estimated (benchmark) economic conditions. For this scenario we compute the expected present value of utility and of income.

2. The immigrant is nonemployed following arrival and does not accumulate any experience or participate in a training course. In this case we measure the present value of utility from living in Israel and the present value of unemployment benefits.

The results are presented in table 4.20 for males and females.

The present value of hourly earnings in the FSU for a 25(40)-year-old male is 956 (684) NIS.[75] For an average male immigrant who has actively searched for a job in Israel, is 25 years old on arrival and has 12 (15) years of schooling, the model predicts an expected present value of earnings of 1,534 (1,608) NIS, while the corresponding figure for a 40-year-old immigrant is 1,090 (1,149) NIS. For the same cases, the expected present values of *utility* are 3,322 (3,345) NIS and 3,086 (3,086) NIS. These results

Table 4.20A
Value of immigrating to Israel—Females

	BC in the FSU, schooling = 12		WC in the FSU, schooling = 15	
	Age on arrival 25	Age on arrival 40	Age on arrival 25	Age on arrival 40
Expected present value, simulated choices	5177.00	3820.42	6243.30	4678.51
Expected value of income, simulated choices[a]	1021.79	752.43	1422.81	994.37
Expected present value, nonemployed in all periods	−8495.11	−9294.26	−8045.78	−8844.94
Expected value of income, nonemployed in all periods[b]	688.73	545.98	688.73	545.98
Expected value of income, stayed in the FSU[c]	698.93	500.14	698.93	500.14

Source: Authors' calculations.
Note: Incomes and value of immigrating are hourly and expressed in July 1995 prices (NIS). Results are for a married female immigrant with one child who had no knowledge of Hebrew on arrival and finished Ulpan. The discount factor is 0.99 per quarter.
a. In periods 1–20, income is calculated as (proportion in WC × average wage in WC) + (proportion in BC × average wage in BC) + (proportion nonemployed or in training × transfer payments). From period 21 onward, income is equal to the average wage in period 20 plus quarterly wage growth of 0.5 percent, assuming the individual always works.
b. Transfer payments are 8.70 NIS per hour per quarter.
c. Income is equal to the average wage in 1989 (based on Katz 1997) plus quarterly wage growth of 0.5 percent, assuming that the individual always works.

suggest that a male immigrant who has actively searched for a job in Israel experiences a substantial gain in earnings by moving to Israel. The expected present value of earnings in Israel is about 1.6 to 1.7 times higher than that in the FSU. Furthermore the expected present value of utility in Israel is about twice the expected present value of earnings in Israel for the younger immigrant while it is almost threefold higher for the older one.

However, the expected present value of unemployment benefits for an immigrant who is permanently nonemployed in Israel is lower than the present value of earnings for a working individual in the FSU. The expected present value of income for a permanently nonemployed immigrant who is 25 (40) years old on arrival is 687 (545) NIS which is about 72 (80) percent of the expected present value of earnings in the FSU. Furthermore the expected utility of a permanently nonemployed male in Israel is negative and large (in absolute value). This disutility ranges between −9,937 to −13,149 NIS and tends to be lower for the younger and less-educated immigrant.

Table 4.20B
Value of immigrating to Israel—Males

	BC in the FSU, schooling = 12		WC in the FSU, schooling = 15	
	Age on arrival 25	Age on arrival 40	Age on arrival 25	Age on arrival 40
Expected present value, simulated choices	3322.15	3085.79	3345.14	3085.81
Expected value of income, simulated choices[a]	1533.77	1089.54	1607.56	1148.82
Expected present value, nonemployed in all periods	−13148.78	−12698.79	−10049.04	−9936.77
Expected value of income, nonemployed in all periods[b]	687.05	544.65	687.05	544.65
Expected value of income, stayed in the FSU[c]	955.96	684.07	955.96	684.07

Source: Authors' calculations.
Note: Incomes and value of immigrating are hourly and expressed in June 1995 (NIS) prices. Results are for a male immigrant who had no knowledge of Hebrew on arrival and has an English fluency index of 1.76. The discount factor is 0.99 per quarter.
a. In periods 1–20, income is calculated as (proportion in WC × average wage in WC) + (proportion in BC × average wage in BC) + (proportion nonemployed or in training × transfer payments). From period 21 onward, income is equal to the average wage in period 20 plus quarterly wage growth of 0.5 percent, assuming the individual always works.
b. Transfer payments are 8.68 NIS per hour per quarter.
c. Income is equal to the average wage in 1989 (based on Katz 1997) plus quarterly wage growth of 0.5 percent, assuming that the individual always works.

The present value of hourly earnings in the FSU for females is about 73 percent of that for males. Thus, the present value of hourly earnings in the FSU for a 25(40)-year-old female is 699 (500) NIS. However, according to the estimated models, female immigrants are expected to earn less than males in Israel as well. For a female immigrant who has actively searched for a job in Israel and is 25 years old on arrival, the model predicts an expected present value of earnings of 1,022 NIS if she has 12 years of schooling and 1,423 NIS if she has 15 years of schooling, while the corresponding figures for a 40-year-old immigrant are 752 and 994 NIS, respectively. Thus a female immigrant who actively searches for a job in Israel experiences a considerable gain from moving to Israel. Although female immigrants can expect lower earnings in comparison to similar male immigrants, their utility gain from moving to Israel is substantially higher. For the same cases as above, the expected present values of *utility* are 5,177 (6,243) NIS and 3,820 (4,679) NIS.

Another interesting result is that the present value of income for a female immigrant who is permanently nonemployed in Israel and whose only income is from unemployment benefits for all periods is almost identical to the expected present value of earnings for an employed female in the FSU. The expected present value of income for a permanently nonemployed immigrant who is 25 years old on arrival is 689 NIS as compared to 546 NIS for a female immigrant who is 40 years old on arrival. Does the immigrant prefer working in the FSU to being nonemployed in Israel? There is no way for us to know. However, the calculation of the present value of utility from being permanently nonemployed in Israel showed it to be negative and substantial (between −8,046 and −9,294 NIS), suggesting that female immigrants dislike permanent nonemployment.

Overall, the results clearly show the large economic gains in migrating from the FSU to Israel during the period 1989 to 1992. These calculations in fact underestimate the gain since they do not include the benefit from increased life expectancy as a result of improved medical care.

4.9 Concluding Remarks

The main results can be summarized as follows:

• The main transition process to the new labor market lasts about five years and is characterized by early investments in classroom skills (language and training) and later by the accumulation of local experience and transitions from nonemployment to employment and between occupations. The transition to WC jobs is the most important source of hourly wage growth, and it is a gradual and continuous process of more than five years' duration.

• One of the main effects of training is to significantly increase job-offer rates in both BC and WC occupations.

• While training has a major impact on WC wages, its impact on BC wages is almost zero.

• The cost–benefit policy analysis stresses the difference in the impact of training between males and females. For females, training benefits both the immigrant and society, while for males, it provides no benefits. According to our models, this result reflects the difference in the opportunity cost of training between males and females.

• Learning the local language results in a major benefit for both males and females. For males, English fluency is important as well (we didn't estimate the return on fluency in English for females).

• Conditional on their investment in local human capital, immigrants receive a very low return on imported skills. This may provide one explanation of the nonconvergence of immigrants' wages to those of comparable natives, which was discussed in chapter 3.

In the next chapter we use similar panel data to formulate and estimate a dynamic discrete choice model in order to perform a more in-depth analysis of the potential expected lifetime earnings loss for immigrants due to the only partial adjustment of their imported skills.

5 Job Search and Loss of Skills

5.1 Introduction

The two previous chapters described the difficulties faced by FSU immigrants in finding high-paying jobs in white-collar occupations. Given the large number of high-skilled migrants, it is not surprising that many of them were forced into low-skilled occupations. Among males who were 25 to 55 years on arrival, only 26 percent of those who had worked as scientists or engineers in the FSU found similar jobs within their first three years in Israel. The extent of occupational downgrading was even higher among females and older males.[1]

As in chapter 4, this chapter investigates the job transitions of immigrants in a search environment with frictions. The main focus is on calculating the immigrants' loss of human capital and its implications for both the immigrants themselves and the economy as a whole. To this end, a model of on-the-job search is constructed and estimated using panel data on the labor market experience of 1,086 male immigrants during the period 1990 to 1995. The model is designed to describe the process of matching between immigrants and jobs where workers differ in skills and jobs vary in skill requirements. The jobs in the economy are assumed to be arranged in a "job hierarchy"[2] and within each occupation can be ranked according to the *minimal* level of schooling required to perform the job. Finding a suitable job, which maximizes the immigrant's output (and wages) given his schooling endowment, requires job search. An immigrant is qualified for a job he has found only if his level of schooling exceeds its minimal requirement. A high-skilled immigrant may decide

This chapter is based on Weiss, Sauer, and Gotlibovski (2003), Immigration, search and loss of skill, *Journal of Labor Economics* 21 (3): 557–92 © 2003 by The University of Chicago.

to accept a job offer in a low-skilled occupation due to the scarcity of offers in high-skilled occupations and the fact that he can continue to search while employed. In general, workers will select occupations and job acceptance criteria that do not fully exploit their formal schooling. However, immigrants find better matches over time and their wages rise accordingly.

The panel data on recently arrived immigrants from the FSU are used to estimate the distribution of wage offers and job-offer arrival rates in various occupations in Israel, assuming that immigrants choose jobs according to the optimal solution of a dynamic programming problem under uncertainty. The results are used to compute the loss of human capital, which is defined as the difference between expected actual lifetime earnings and the expected potential lifetime earnings that the immigrant would have obtained had he been employed in the same jobs and earned the same wages as comparable Israelis. The expected discounted present value of the difference between actual earnings and potential earnings is US$253,200 on average, which constitutes 57 percent of the present value of potential earnings over the immigrant's remaining working life (25 years, on average). Nearly 75 percent of this estimated loss ($190,900) can be attributed to the fact that in each job immigrants initially earn wages that are about *two-thirds* less than those of comparable native Israelis. Immigrants' wages rise sharply with time in Israel but do not fully catch up to those of natives (after 30 years in Israel immigrants are predicted to earn only 15 percent less in the same jobs). The remaining 25 percent of the loss ($62,300) can be attributed to frictions associated with nonemployment and job distribution mismatch. The estimated loss is probably an upper bound of the social loss associated with the transfer of human capital since differences in the quality of schooling and macro effects can cause the potential earnings of immigrants to fall short of the earnings of comparable natives.[3]

While the analysis focuses on a particular episode—the recent wave of immigration to Israel—the methods developed can be applied to other situations that involve major occupational restructuring due to aggregate labor market shocks (e.g., technological innovations and changing trade patterns).[4] In the model, losses in human capital occur when workers with a predetermined level of schooling find themselves nonemployed and become willing to accept jobs with schooling requirements below their schooling endowment. Even in a smoothly operating economy, in which individuals can select their schooling and firms can choose their job offers, the model predicts some "natural" loss of skills, akin to the natural rate of unemployment.[5]

5.2 Data

The data are drawn from two surveys conducted by the Brookdale Institute. The first, conducted between April and August 1992, consists of a random sample of 1,118 immigrants who arrived from the FSU after 1989. Of this representative sample, 910 immigrants were surveyed again during 1994. The second survey, conducted between June and December 1995, consists of a random sample of 1,432 immigrants who arrived after 1989 and reported being engineers in the FSU. The two samples are pooled and the analysis is restricted to males between the ages of 25 and 55 at the time of arrival, yielding a sample of 1,086 immigrants. The respondents' length of stay in Israel ranges from 6 to 77 months. Each immigrant supplied information on his occupational and educational background in the FSU and a detailed history of his work experience in Israel. Average sample values for the variables used in the analysis are presented in appendix table 5.A1.

The possible occupations in Israel and the FSU are classified into three broad categories, based on schooling requirements: (1) scientific and academic occupations, including government officials; (2) other professional occupations, including technical workers, teachers, nurses, and artists; and (3) all other occupations. Tables 5.1 and 5.2 describe the distribution of immigrants in the sample by occupation in the FSU and in Israel. The tables show an initial occupational downgrading from occupations 1 and 2 in the FSU to occupation 3 in Israel, followed by a gradual recovery. About 89 percent of the immigrants in the combined sample worked in occupations 1 and 2 in the FSU (see table 5.2), but only 20 percent of them found their first job in these occupations in Israel. Most of the immigrants (75 percent) started their career in Israel as unskilled workers (see table 5.1). However, with the passage of time, the percentage of immigrants who work in occupation 1 rises sharply from 11.6 in month 12 to 36.7 percent in month 60. Nonemployment declines sharply from 26.2 percent in month 12 to 7.8 percent in month 60.

Within each broad occupational category, each job requires some minimal level of schooling. The minimum schooling requirement for a reported two-digit occupation is defined as the second decile of the native Israeli distribution of completed schooling levels in that occupation. Table 5.3 shows the schooling requirements of the jobs held by

Table 5.1
First occupation in Israel by occupation in the FSU

Occupation in the FSU[a]	First occupation in Israel[a]				
	Occupation 1 (%)	Occupation 2 (%)	Occupation 3 (%)	Nonemployment (%)	N
Representative sample					
Occupation 1	18.7	10.0	66.7	4.6	219
Occupation 2	4.0	20.0	74.0	2.0	50
Occupation 3	0.0	5.8	89.2	5.0	120
All occupations					
Representative sample	11.0	10.0	74.6	4.4	389
Engineers' sample	15.4	4.9	76.3	3.4	697
Combined sample	13.8	6.7	75.7	3.8	1,086

Sources: Brookdale Survey and Engineers' Survey.
Note: The sample includes males aged 25 to 55 on arrival.
a. For details on occupational classification, see section 5.2 in the text.

Table 5.2
Occupational distribution in Israel by year since arrival

Occupation in Israel	Occupation 1 (%)	Occupation 2 (%)	Occupation 3 (%)	Nonemployment (%)	N
Year 1	11.6	5.6	56.6	26.2	1,058
Year 2	17.4	6.9	57.7	17.9	929
Year 3	22.3	7.2	57.5	13.0	793
Year 4	27.6	7.5	52.7	12.2	583
Year 5	36.7	7.8	47.7	7.8	218
Occupation in the FSU:	84.3	4.6	11.0	0.0	1,086

Sources: Brookdale Survey and Engineers' Survey.
Note: The sample includes males aged 25 to 55 on arrival.

Table 5.3
Average minimal schooling requirements of jobs held by immigrants by year since arrival and schooling acquired in the FSU

	Schooling acquired in FSU				
	5–12	13–14	15	16	17–22
Immigrants					
Year 1	8.9	9.6	10.6	10.7	10.2
Year 2	9.0	9.8	11.3	11.5	10.7
Year 3	9.1	9.8	11.7	11.9	10.9
Year 4	9.2	10	12.1	12.5	11.4
Year 5	9.5	10.5	12.5	13.1	11.7
Year 6	[a]	11.3	12.3	13.7	12.8
Israelis	9.9	11.4	12.0	13.3	14.4

Sources: Brookdale Survey, Engineers' Survey, and CBS Income Survey.
Note: The sample includes males aged 25 to 55 on arrival. The distribution of completed schooling for native Israelis in each two-digit occupation is based on pooled cross-sectional data from the CBS Income Survey during the period 1991 to 1995.
a. There are no observations in this group.

immigrants in comparison to their imported schooling endowment and the schooling requirements of jobs held by Israelis with the same schooling. The figures indicate that immigrants upgrade their jobs steadily over time and after 6 years in Israel, the average schooling requirement of their jobs is similar to that of jobs held by comparable Israelis, except in the case of immigrants with 17 to 22 years of schooling who hold jobs that require less schooling than comparable Israelis.

Although immigrants change jobs quite frequently, most of the sample reported only one accepted wage offer in their employment history. Of the 697 immigrants in the engineers' sample, 571 reported their wage at the time of the survey. Of the 389 immigrants in the representative sample, 102 reported one accepted wage offer and 233 reported two or more, yielding another 646 wage observations. The total number of wage observations is thus 1,217. Approximately 45 percent of the reported wages are net of taxes.[6] Average wages, according to years in Israel, are displayed in table 5.4. The figures show that immigrants in occupations 1 and 2 obtain higher wages than those in occupation 3. There is a sharp increase in real wages within the sample period. Immigrants who reported wages during their sixth year in Israel have an average real wage which is 78 percent higher than the average wage reported during their first year. This growth reflects wage growth within jobs (58 percent in occupation 3) and the gradual shift to higher paying jobs and occupations.

Table 5.4
Average monthly reported wages of immigrants by occupation and years since arrival

| | Occupation in Israel | | | | | | | |
| | Occupation 1 | | Occupation 2 | | Occupation 3 | | All occupations | |
Year	N	Wage	N	Wage	N	Wage	N	Wage
1	6	3,856	1	2,764	71	2,322	78	2,445
2	26	3,422	32	2,764	189	2,416	247	2,567
3	38	3,623	11	3,288	155	2,732	204	2,911
4	41	4,562	14	3,337	163	2,861	218	3,211
5	92	5,047	29	3,575	202	3,413	323	3,893
6	57	5,340	10	4,263	83	3,688	150	4,354

Sources: Brookdale Survey and Engineers' Survey.
Note: NIS/$ = 0.33 in 1995. The sample includes males aged 25 to 55 on arrival.

Before specifying the model and estimation procedure, it is worth looking at some descriptive regressions that illustrate several important features of the data. First, imported skills, such as schooling and work experience, have virtually *no* effect on wage outcomes during the *early* years in Israel. Rather, the determining factors are the immigrant's job and occupation in Israel (see top panel of table 5.5). It is therefore important to explicitly model the process by which immigrants find jobs as well as the decision to accept job offers. Second, if one controls for the (endogenous) occupational variables, then knowledge of Hebrew[7] has a small and insignificant effect on wages.[8] Moreover knowledge of Hebrew is highly correlated with occupational history in Israel, suggesting that language acquisition might also be endogenous (see bottom panel of table 5.5). Thus, given the lack of sufficient information on *changes* in knowledge of Hebrew, it is not incorporated into the analysis.

5.3   The Model

In order to describe the process by which immigrants gradually find a job appropriate to their imported skills, a model of on-the-job search is developed. The search model is cast as a finite-horizon discrete choice dynamic programming problem under uncertainty and corresponds to the decision problem of a single individual. At the same time individuals can be heterogeneous in both observed and unobserved dimensions.

Suppose that immigrants vary in their skill endowments and local jobs vary in their *minimal* skill requirements. The output achieved by employ-

Table 5.5
Monthly wage OLS regression and knowledge of Hebrew logit regression

Variable name	Coefficient	t-Statistic	Coefficient	t-Statistic
Log wage regressions				
Constant	7.729	64.460	7.754	62.977
Months in Israel	0.0058	8.322	0.0056	7.897
Job requirement	0.0275	3.223	0.0258	2.996
Occupation 1	0.1836	3.025	0.1853	3.022
Occupation 2	0.0196	0.445	0.0155	0.338
Schooling_0[a]	−0.0071	−1.484	−0.0061	−1.227
Experience_0	0.0006	0.105	−0.0024	−0.044
Experience_0^2	−0.0002	−1.418	−0.0001	−0.964
Physician_0	−0.1586	−2.273	−0.1755	−2.480
Engineer_0	0.0129	0.034	0.0137	0.377
Representative sample	−0.0950	−2.547	−0.0970	−2.506
Representative sample × net[b]	−0.1307	−4.274	−0.1246	−4.016
Engineers' sample × net	−0.2084	−6.328	−0.2071	−6.307
Knowledge of Hebrew			0.0172	0.659
N	1,217		1,164	
Adjusted R^2	0.3548		0.3503	
Knowledge of Hebrew logit				
Constant	1.239	1.793		
Months in occupation 1	0.060	6.450		
Months in occupation 2	0.062	3.844		
Months in occupation 3	0.023	3.773		
Months nonemployed	0.025	2.937		
Schooling_0	−0.034	0.926		
Experience_0	−0.013	−6.180		
Hebrew course	1.1635	5.541		
N	990			
Pseudo R^2	0.2310			

Sources: Brookdale Survey and Engineers' Survey.
a. A subscript of 0 indicates value on arrival.
b. Net indicates that the reported wage is net of taxes.

ing a particular worker in a particular job depends on the match between the worker and the job. Specifically, a worker with less skill than the required minimum cannot perform the job. A worker with more than the required minimum can perform the job and receives a wage that depends both on the minimal requirement and the worker's skill level.

Workers meet employers randomly and receive job offers. The arrival rate of job offers and the distribution of jobs by skill requirements differ across occupations. Jobs within each occupation j are ranked according to the job's minimal skill requirement s where $s = 0, 1, \ldots, S$. Occupations are also ranked from 1 to J, based on the frequency distribution of jobs by skill requirements, where 1 is the occupation containing the highest frequency of jobs with the highest minimal skill requirements. J is the occupation with no skill requirements and a single wage, which is interpreted as the nonemployment state. Firms offer a different wage for a given s, depending on technology and demand conditions. A local employer with job s in occupation j who meets a worker with skill $s*$ extends a job offer if and only if $s* \geq s$. If the worker is acceptable to the firm, the worker then chooses whether or not to accept the offer.

Workers have a finite working life T and time is discrete, $t = 1, 2, \ldots,$ T. In any period, a worker can be in one of $J * S$ states. In any given state the worker receives a flow of wages and nonmonetary returns. He may also receive an alternative job offer and/or a notice of immediate job termination. It is assumed that, at most, one job offer arrives in each period. This offer may be from any one of the $J * S$ jobs. The probability of receiving a job offer in any period t is modeled as the product of three components: λ_{jkt}, $P_k(s)$, and $\Phi_k(s* \geq s)$. λ_{jkt} is the probability of meeting an employer in occupation k, given that the current state involves a job in occupation j. Specifying the probability of meeting an employer in occupation k as a function of the previous occupation j allows for state dependence and the choice of search intensity. When $j = k$, λ_{jkt} is the probability of meeting a different employer in the same occupation. An immigrant may be more likely to meet a new employer in the occupation in which he is currently working. There is also a positive probability, given by $1 - \sum_{j=1}^{J} \lambda_{jkt}$, that a person in occupation j receives no job offers in period t. Given that a worker has met an employer in occupation k, the probability that the minimal skill requirement for the job is s is denoted as $P_k(s)$.[9] The last component of the job-offer probability, $\Phi_k(s* \geq s)$, denotes the probability that the worker is acceptable to the firm, namely that $s* \geq s$. If a job offer arrives, which occurs with probability $\lambda_{jkt}P_k(s)\Phi_k(s* \geq s)$, the individual then decides whether or not to accept the offer by comparing its discounted present value to that of other feasible alternatives, which include nonemployment and the immigrant's current job, unless terminated. Termination of his current job is also stochastic and occupation specific. The job termination probability is denoted as δ_j.

The current period returns on each job are specified as the sum of a job-specific wage w_{sjt} and a job-specific monetary equivalent of nonmonetary returns n_{sjt}. While the distribution of possible realizations is known at time t, the value of future wages plus nonmonetary returns is not. The worker thus faces a problem of decision under uncertainty in several dimensions. It is assumed that in each period the worker seeks to maximize his remaining expected lifetime income, inclusive of the nonmonetary value of nonmonetary returns.

The remaining expected lifetime income of the individual in each state at time t can be calculated recursively using the following system of Bellman (1957) equations:

$$V_{sjt} = w_{sjt} + n_{sjt} + \Delta(1-\delta_j)$$

$$\left\{ \begin{aligned} \sum_{k=1}^{J-1} \lambda_{jk,t+1} \sum_{s'=0}^{S} P_k(s') \{ \Phi_k(s^* \geq s') E_t \max[V_{sj,t+1}, V_{s'k,t+1}, V_{J,t+1}] \\ + (1-\Phi_k(s^* \geq s')) E_t \max[V_{sj,t+1}, V_{J,t+1}] \} \\ + \left(1 - \sum_{k=1}^{J-1} \lambda_{jk,t+1}\right) E_t \max[V_{sj,t+1}, V_{J,t+1}] \end{aligned} \right\} \tag{5.1}$$

$$+ \Delta\delta_j \left\{ \begin{aligned} \sum_{k=1}^{J-1} \lambda_{jk,t+1} \sum_{s'=0}^{S} P_k(s') \{ \Phi_k(s^* \geq s') E_t \max[V_{s'k,t+1}, V_{J,t+1}] \\ + (1-\Phi_k(s^* \geq s')) E_t[V_{J,t+1}]\} + \left(1 - \sum_{k=1}^{J-1} \lambda_{jk,t+1}\right) E_t[V_{J,t+1}] \end{aligned} \right\}.$$

V_{sjt} denotes the discounted present value of remaining lifetime income in job s in occupation j in month t. $\Delta = 1/(1+r)$ is the discount factor, and r is the monthly interest rate. The first term in brackets is the value of expected future returns given that the current job has not been terminated, and the second term in brackets is the value of expected future returns given that the current job has been terminated.

The process of transition from the initial state of nonemployment to subsequent jobs implied by the dynamic optimization problem has several salient features. First, transition leads to an improvement in income (broadly defined to include both wages and nonmonetary returns) as long as the worker can maintain his current state. Second, it is possible for a worker to accept a job with a lower wage and/or nonmonetary returns if he is compensated in terms of expected future income. In choosing jobs, workers examine not only current income but also future income prospects that depend on wage growth and alternative job-offer and layoff probabilities. Finally, because of the frictions embedded in the model and the possibility of on-the-job search, a worker will usually not wait until he gets the best job for which he is qualified but rather will accept jobs for which he is overqualified. Thus the model naturally captures the phenomenon of occupational downgrading and loss of skill, while at the same time allowing for a gradual climb up the occupational ladder in a dynamic context.

It should be noted that the model is nonstationary since wages *rise* over time and there is a finite horizon.[10] These features are crucial for the understanding of the behavior of immigrants who arrive in Israel with different skills and at different stages of the life cycle. The rewards that immigrants obtain for their imported skills are initially very low but then rise as immigrants adapt to the new labor market.

5.4 Implementation of the Model

For purposes of empirical implementation, the length of each period t is assumed to be one month. This implies that job offers and job terminations occur at the beginning of each month and that wages adjust monthly. The length of the planning period is assumed to be the remainder of the immigrant's working life (65 minus age on arrival). However, the model is solved for each individual for only the first 72 months following his arrival in Israel. Terminal values at month 73 are specified to approximate the value of anticipated events in subsequent periods. Since it is difficult, in general, to find analytical solutions to dynamic programs of this type, the model is solved numerically by backward recursion, starting with the terminal value functions in month 73.

In each month the immigrant can hold a job in one of four broad occupational categories: scientific and academic occupations ($j = 1$), other professional occupations ($j = 2$), all other occupations ($j = 3$), and nonemployment ($j = 4$).[11] The first component of the job-offer probability λ_{jkt} is specified as

$$\lambda_{jkt} = \frac{\exp(a_{jk}x_{it})}{1 + \sum_{k=1}^{3} \exp(a_{jk}x_{it})} \tag{5.2}$$

for $j = 1, 2, 3, 4$, and $k = 1, 2, 3$, where x_{it} is a vector of individual characteristics and a_{jk} is a vector of parameters. The measured characteristics in x_{it} are occupation in the FSU, employment as an engineer in the FSU, employment as a physician in the FSU, age on arrival in Israel, and year of arrival in Israel (cohorts 1989 to 1990, 1991, and 1992 to 1995).[12]

Schooling is assumed to be the parameter relevant to employers in assessing the quality of the job–worker match. Each occupational category thus includes a hierarchy of jobs indexed by their minimal schooling requirement s, where s is assumed to range from 0 to 21. As noted earlier, the second decile of the native Israeli distribution of completed schooling levels within each two-digit occupation determines the minimum schooling requirement for that two-digit occupation.[13] The resulting empirical frequency of minimum schooling requirements, ranging from 0 to 21, varies widely across occupational categories. The second component of the job-offer probability $P_j(s)$ is derived from this empirical distribution. $P_j(s)$ is thus estimated outside the model.[14]

The third component of the job-offer probability $\Phi_j(s^* \geq s)$ is the probability that the immigrant's "true" schooling endowment s^* exceeds the local employer's required minimum s in occupation j. Each employer's assessment of the immigrant's "true" schooling level is idiosyncratic, time variant, and assumed to be a linear function of the immigrant's imported schooling s_0.[15] That is,

$$\Phi_j(s^* \geq s) = \Pr(\alpha + \beta_j s_0 + u \geq s) = \frac{\exp\left[(\beta_j s_0/v) - (s/v) + (\alpha/v)\right]}{1 + \exp\left[(\beta_j s_0/v) - (s/v) + (\alpha/v)\right]}, \tag{5.3}$$

where u is assumed to be logistically distributed with zero mean and variance $v^2\pi^2/3$. The parameters α and β_j provide a simple linear translation of schooling acquired abroad into equivalent local units. Thus the expected "true" schooling of an immigrant who acquired s_0 in the FSU and who meets an Israeli employer in occupation j is given by

$$s^* = \alpha + \beta_j s_0, \tag{5.4}$$

which is expressed in years. The translation parameters α and β_j are identified from the acceptance rates of immigrants with imported schooling level s_0 into jobs with minimal schooling requirement s.[16]

The wage offer in a job requiring a minimum of s years of schooling in occupation j at month t is given by

$$w_{sjt} = \exp(\gamma_{0j}s + \gamma_{1j}x_t), \tag{5.5}$$

where γ_{0j} is the impact of the minimal schooling requirement on output in occupation j, x_t is a vector of individual characteristics, and γ_{1j} is a vector of coefficients. The measured characteristics in the wage offer function are schooling and experience acquired in the FSU, occupational category in the FSU, employment as an engineer in the FSU, employment as a physician in the FSU, year of arrival in Israel (cohorts 1989 to 1990, 1991, and 1992 to 1995) and time (months) since arrival.

The wage offer functions are assumed to follow a deterministic path for a given job; nonetheless, the estimation procedure does incorporate measurement error in observed wages, which is assumed to be normally distributed with variance σ^2. The mean of the measurement error is specified as a linear function (with interactions) of the subsample from which the observation was taken (engineers or representative) and whether the reported wage is net of taxes.[17]

The model also incorporates unobserved heterogeneity among individuals. Each immigrant can be one of three discrete types where the distribution of types in the population can differ between the two subsamples (engineers and representative), thus allowing for heteroscedasticity in the distribution of unobserved heterogeneity. The conditional distributions of types, along with the impact of type on wages and arrival rate of job offers, are estimated jointly with the other parameters of the model. The use of three types is sufficient to distinguish between absolute and comparative advantages in the unobserved ability of immigrants in the various occupations.[18]

An additional source of uncertainty in the model arises from *iid* shocks to the nonmonetary returns in each job, as given by

$$n_{sjt} = b_{jt} + v\varepsilon_{sjt}, \tag{5.6}$$

where $b_{jt} = (e^{k_j} - 1)w_{sjt}$ in occupations 1, 2, and 3. b_{jt} is specified in this manner so that nonmonetary returns remain a fixed proportion of the wage in any period t. b_{4t} is assumed to be constant and normalized to 580 NIS per month for purposes of identification.[19] However, only low-skilled immigrants who worked in occupation 3 in the FSU receive this level of benefits when nonemployed. Immigrants with a higher level of skills may attribute a higher value to nonemployment, primarily because they can exploit the period of nonemployment for training. Nonemployment benefits are thus specified as $b_{4t} = 580e^{k_{41}occ_01+k_{42}occ_02}$, thus making it possible to estimate the implicit average value of training for immigrants who worked in occupations 1 and 2 in the FSU.[20]

The error term ε_{sjt} in (5.6), which takes a different value in each of the 19 ($J * S$) elements of the choice set in month t, enters linearly into the value functions and is assumed to follow the type-*I* extreme value distribution with zero mean and variance $\pi^2/6$. These assumptions enable the use of a closed-form expression for expected maximum future returns. In particular,

$$E_t \max\left[V_{sj,t+1}, \; V_{s'k,t+1}, \; V_{4,t+1}\right]$$

$$= v \ln\left\{\exp\left(\frac{\overline{V}_{sj,t+1}}{v}\right) + \exp\left(\frac{\overline{V}_{s'k,t+1}}{v}\right) + \exp\left(\frac{\overline{V}_{4,t+1}}{v}\right) \right\} \tag{5.7}$$

where $\overline{V}_{sjt}$ denotes the mean value of being in job s in occupation j in period t and v is a parameter that regulates the relative importance of nonmonetary returns or the variance of the shocks (Rust 1994).

For reasons of parsimony, the terminal value functions for each element in the choice set are assumed to be proportional to the current period returns in month 73, with a correction for finite life or retirement at age 65. Specifically,

$$V_{sj73} = \frac{1+q^T}{1-q}\left(w_{sj73} + n_{sj73}\right)\exp(\gamma_j) \qquad \text{for } j = 1, 2, 3, \tag{5.8}$$

where $q = 1/(1+r)$, $(1+q^T)/(1-q) = \sum_{t=1}^{T}(1+r)^{t-1}$, and $T = 65$ minus age on arrival. The monthly interest rate is fixed at 6 percent, which is relatively high and is chosen to reflect the fact that immigrants had almost no initial assets on arrival and face borrowing constraints.[21] The proportionality constants $\gamma_j, j = 1, 2, 3$ are estimated parameters and capture the implicit value of future events.

The model is estimated using full information maximum likelihood. For a given vector of trial parameters, the dynamic program is solved by backward recursion for each immigrant and for each unobserved type, starting with the terminal value functions in month 73. Given the type-specific expected value functions for each individual in every state in each month, the estimation problem is reduced to a static panel data multinomial logit with unobserved heterogeneity. That is, given the assumptions on the shock to nonmonetary returns, the choice probabilities can be calculated according to the following closed form:

$$\Pr\left(V_{s'kt} \geq V_{sjt}, V_{s'kt} \geq V_{4t}\right)$$
$$= \left\{\frac{\exp\left[(\overline{V}_{s'kt} - \overline{V}_{4t})/v\right]}{1 + \exp\left[(\overline{V}_{sjt} - \overline{V}_{4t})/v\right] + \exp\left[(\overline{V}_{s'kt} - \overline{V}_{4t})/v\right]}\right\}. \tag{5.9}$$

Observed wages are incorporated into the estimation by multiplying the choice probability in month t by the measurement error density in the reported wage. The choice probability is thus conditional on the true wage. If no wage is observed, only the choice probability enters the type-specific likelihood contribution.

The unconditional likelihood contribution for each individual is constructed by taking a weighted average over the three type-specific likelihood contributions (Heckman and Singer 1984). The weights are specified to be a (logistic) function of the subsample indicator. The parameters of the model are recovered by re-solving the dynamic program and re-constructing the likelihood contributions for each iteration of the optimization algorithm. The solution to the dynamic program, the incorporation of unobserved heterogeneity and the joint estimation of the wage functions and choice probabilities correct the wage function estimates for biases due to self-selection.[22]

5.5 Results

Since there are a total of 104 estimated parameters, this section only discusses specific parameter estimates of interest and highlights the main features of the model. The parameter estimates and their associated standard errors are presented in appendix table 5.A3.[23]

5.5.1 Wages

The estimated parameters of the wage offer functions show that the returns obtained by immigrants in Israel on work experience in the FSU are very low in occupations 1 and 3. In occupation 2, returns are higher but still relatively small in magnitude. In contrast, experience accumulated in Israel during the first 6 years, as proxied by time in Israel, has a substantial positive effect of 0.00665 per month, (8.0 percent annually) in occupations 1 and 2. In occupation 3, experience accumulated in Israel has a slightly smaller but still substantial positive effect of 0.00649 per month (7.8 percent annually). The impact of imported schooling on wages, in any given job for which schooling exceeds the minimal requirement, is negligible in occupation 3, slightly negative in occupation 1 and somewhat more negative in occupation 2. However, higher imported schooling levels are associated with a higher probability of obtaining a job with a higher minimal schooling requirement. Immigrants who find jobs with higher schooling requirements attain a rate of wage increase of 3.3 percent per year of required schooling in occupations 1 and 2 and 1.1 percent in occupation 3. The model thus captures the two main features of the wage data: increasing average wages over time and rising inequality. The latter is due to the gradual move of immigrants with higher schooling levels into jobs that have higher minimal schooling requirements.

Other imported characteristics do not generally have a statistically significant effect on wage offers. The exceptions are the significant positive effect of having worked as an engineer in occupation 2 and the significant negative effect of having worked as a physician in occupation 3. The results also indicate that unobserved types 1 and 2 attain substantially lower wages than unobserved type 0 in all occupations. Type 1 is penalized primarily in occupations 2 and 3 while type 2 is penalized primarily in occupation 1.

5.5.2 Nonmonetary Returns

The variance component v of nonmonetary returns is estimated to be 3,267 NIS. Thus a nonmonetary shock of one standard deviation, which under the extreme value distribution occurs with a probability of about 13 percent, has an effect that is approximately equal to the average wage in the sample, namely 3,304 NIS. This suggests that nonmonetary shocks can play an important role. One feature of the data that determines this result is the presence of transitions, mainly within occupation 3, into jobs with lower minimal schooling requirements and hence lower wages.

The estimates of the systematic components of nonmonetary returns $k_j, j = 1, 2, 3$, imply that average nonmonetary benefits are zero for jobs in occupation 1. In occupation 2, nonmonetary benefits increase current period returns by 16 percent of the wage and in occupation 3 by 18 percent. The estimates of average nonmonetary returns are not significantly different from zero.[24] The estimate of the nonemployment benefit shifter k_{41} implies that immigrants who worked in occupation 1 in the FSU value current nonemployment benefits by 45 percent more than unskilled immigrants who worked in occupation 3 in the FSU. The estimate of k_{42} implies that immigrants from occupation 2 value current nonemployment benefits by only 5.3 percent more than unskilled immigrants. The additional benefit among skilled immigrants may reflect the value of training programs in which many of them participate.[25]

5.5.3 Job-Offer and Job-Termination Probabilities

Table 5.6 presents the estimated values of λ_{jkt} for each of the three unobserved types of immigrants. There are large differences in these probabilities between the three unobserved types: type-0 immigrants meet substantially more employers in occupation 1, type-1 immigrants meet very few employers outside of occupation 3, and type-2 immigrants meet more employers in occupation 3 than either type-0 or type-1 immigrants.

The table also shows that λ_{jkt} is generally higher in nonemployment. For example, the probability of meeting an employer in occupation 1 is higher from nonemployment than from jobs in occupation 3 and occupation 2 for all types $\left(\hat{\lambda}_{41t} > \hat{\lambda}_{31t} > \hat{\lambda}_{21t}\right)$. However, being already employed

Table 5.6
Estimated monthly job-offer probabilities by current occupation and type

Current occupation	Offer in occupation 1 Type			Offer in occupation 2 Type			Offer in occupation 3 Type		
	0	1	2	0	1	2	0	1	2
Occupation 1	0.032	0.002	0.013	0.003	0.000	0.002	0.003	0.001	0.003
Occupation 2	0.016	0.001	0.005	0.023	0.003	0.019	0.014	0.003	0.018
Occupation 3	0.005	0.000	0.002	0.004	0.000	0.003	0.039	0.008	0.049
Nonemployment	0.032	0.002	0.011	0.013	0.002	0.011	0.125	0.029	0.158

Source: Authors' calculations based on the model's estimation.

in occupation 1 and being nonemployed yield similar estimated probabilities $\left(\hat{\lambda}_{41t} \cong \hat{\lambda}_{11t}\right)$. An exception to this pattern occurs in occupation 3 where the probability of meeting an employer in occupation 3 is higher from nonemployment.

The estimated values of λ_{41t} for types 0, 1, and 2 are 0.032, 0.002, and 0.011, respectively. The estimated values of λ_{43t} are much higher – 0.129, 0.029, and 0.165 for the three types, respectively. Thus, from nonemployment, a type-0 immigrant's expected waiting time to meet an employer in occupation 1 is 29 months, while in occupation 3 it is only 8 months. These estimates reflect the market conditions that immigrants face upon entry and the fact that it is much easier for them to find jobs as unskilled workers.

Based on the estimated parameters λ_{jkt}, it is further noted that older immigrants and those who arrived in Israel in later years have lower probabilities of meeting employers in occupations 1 and 2. This reflects possible changes in cohort quality and "congestion" effects in Israel. As expected, the occupational category in the FSU is an important signal for Israeli employers. Immigrants who worked in occupation 1 in the FSU meet substantially more employers in occupation 1 in Israel. In comparison, engineers meet fewer employers than the average in occupation 1 while physicians meet more.

The estimated coefficient for $\Phi_j(s^* \geq s)$, namely the probability of being accepted to a job after having met an employer, yields the following quality adjustment equations for imported schooling:

$$s_1^* = 10.072 + 0.456s_0,$$
$$s_2^* = 10.072 + 0.270s_0, \qquad\qquad (5.10)$$
$$s_3^* = 10.072 + 0.080s_0.$$

The *marginal* effect of imported schooling is thus 0.456 in occupation 1, 0.270 in occupation 2, and 0.080 in occupation 3. The corresponding "breakeven" levels are 19, 14, and 11 years of schooling in occupations 1, 2, and 3, respectively. For purposes of comparison with Israelis, imported schooling is adjusted downward (upward) if it is above (below) the breakeven level.

The acceptance probabilities, which depend also on the estimated variances, are displayed in figure 5.1a to c. In occupation 1, immigrants are accepted with a probability close to 1 to jobs that require less than their level of imported schooling s_0. They are also accepted with a positive probability into jobs requiring slightly more schooling than they possess. For example, an immigrant with 15 years of imported schooling is accepted with probabilities of 0.909, 0.451, and 0.063 to jobs requiring 16, 17, and 18 years of schooling, respectively.

These results reflect the fact that in the FSU one could become an engineer (physician) by going to elementary and high school for a total of 10 years, followed by 5 (6) years of university training. Immigrants who find jobs in occupation 1 as doctors or engineers are treated as if they have schooling comparable to Israelis, that is, 16 (18) years of schooling. In occupation 3, practically all immigrants are accepted to jobs requiring 10 years of schooling or less, though the best jobs in this occupation, which require 12 years of schooling, are generally not available to immigrants, even those with a high level of schooling. Similarly immigrants with a high level of schooling have only a small probability of being accepted to jobs requiring 16 years of schooling in occupation 2. Stated differently, immigrants have a lower probability than Israelis of receiving the top job offers in occupations 2 and 3.

The model also allows for involuntary separations due to job termination. The estimates of δ_j are 0.0035, 0.0081, and 0.0052 in occupations, 1, 2, and 3, respectively. The termination probability estimates are small but highly significant. The estimates imply that immigrants are able to hold on to their jobs for long periods of time (24, 10, and 16 years, respectively) unless they decide to quit.

5.5.4 Choice Probabilities and Types

Table 5.7 presents the predicted occupational choice distribution by unobserved type for selected months following arrival. The choice frequencies are calculated by drawing from the distributions of the model's random elements, simulating choice histories for each individual 10,000 times and finally averaging over all simulations and individuals.

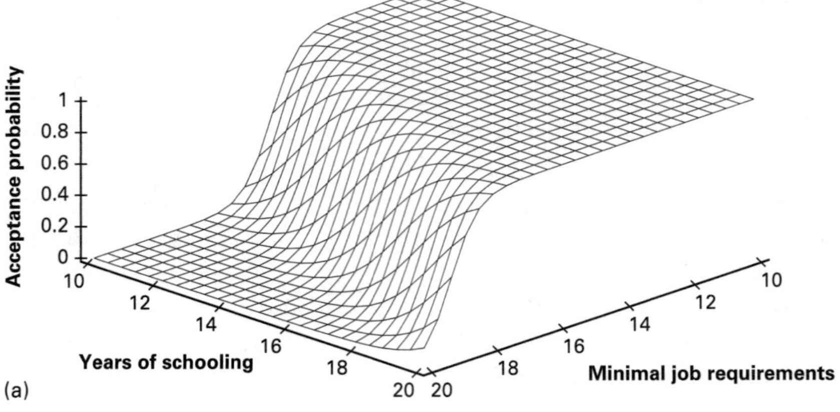

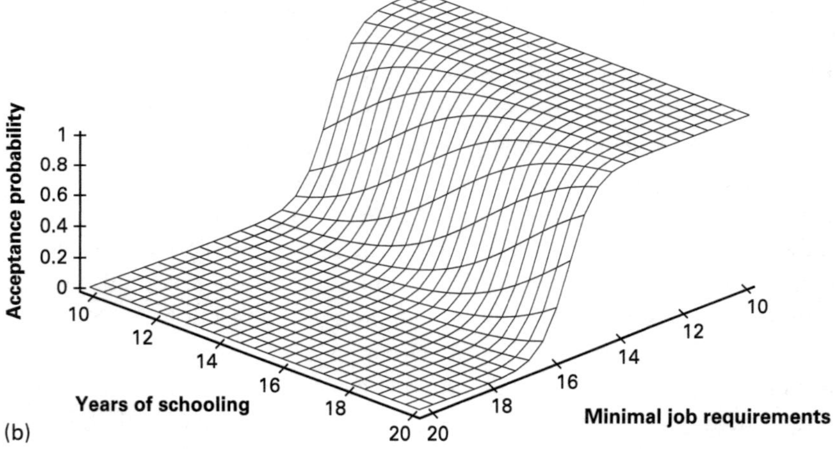

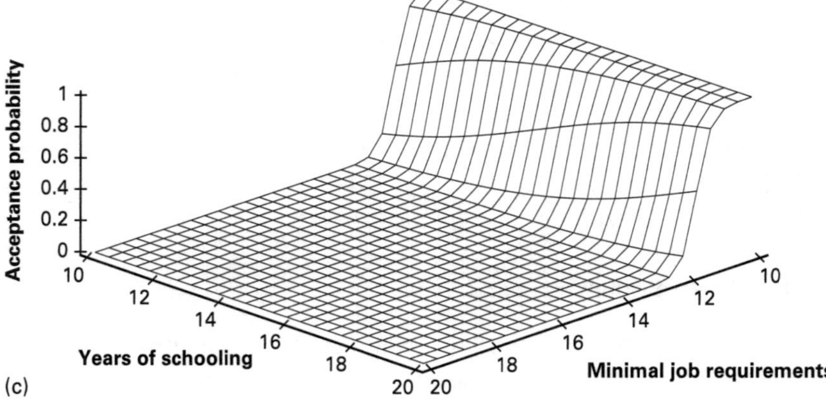

Figure 5.1
Acceptance probabilities by years of schooling and minimal job requirements. (a) Occupation 1; (b) occupation 2; (c) occupation 3. Source: Authors' calculations based on the model's estimation.

Table 5.7
Predicted occupational distribution by type (percent, selected months)

	Occupation 1			Occupation 2			Occupation 3			Nonemployment		
	Type			Type			Type			Type		
Month	0	1	2	0	1	2	0	1	2	0	1	2
12	16.4	1.7	4.8	5.5	1.5	6.0	56.4	16.8	58.3	21.6	80.0	30.9
24	22.9	3.4	6.6	6.0	2.7	9.2	62.7	24.5	64.3	8.5	69.4	20.0
36	27.8	5.0	8.0	5.8	3.8	11.5	61.0	29.8	65.4	5.4	61.5	15.1
48	33.3	6.7	9.9	5.6	4.9	14.7	56.9	32.1	64.5	4.2	56.3	10.9
60	38.6	8.3	10.9	5.6	5.9	17.5	52.0	30.1	63.4	3.7	55.7	8.1

Source: Authors' calculations based on the model's estimation and simulation.

The figures show that the proportion of each type of immigrant in occupation 1 grows over time but that there is a much higher proportion of type-0 immigrants in this occupation in all months. Moreover the proportion of type-0 immigrants in occupation 1 increases at a much faster rate. The proportion of each type of immigrant in occupation 2 is also nondecreasing. Type-2 immigrants form the highest proportion of occupation 2 and also have the fastest rate of increase. In occupation 3 the proportion of each type of immigrant rises to a peak and subsequently falls and the peak occurs earlier for type-0 and type-2 immigrants. In nonemployment, the proportion of type-1 immigrants is clearly the highest. In addition nonemployment falls sharply for types 0 and 2 and only gradually for type-1 immigrants.

The choice frequency patterns in table 5.7 can be explained by the fact that a nonemployed type-0 immigrant accepts almost any job offer in the early months following arrival. However, as his occupational status in Israel improves, he accepts fewer offers outside of occupation 1. A type-1 immigrant is reluctant to accept offers in occupation 3 in which his wage penalty is the highest. A type-1 immigrant waits for offers in occupation 1, although they arrive with a very low frequency. In contrast, a type-2 immigrant accepts offers mainly in occupation 2 in which his wage penalty is the lowest.

Based on the sign patterns of the estimated parameters in the wage offer functions and on the job-offer probabilities for each type, type 0 can be considered to have the highest ability, type 1 the lowest ability, and type 2 an intermediate level of ability. Type-0 immigrants obtain higher wages and receive more job offers in occupation 1. The penalties for a lower level of ability, in terms of lower wages and/or fewer job offers, are substantial. Despite an *absolute* disadvantage in occupation 1, type 1 has a *comparative* advantage in this occupation, while type 2 has a *comparative* advantage in occupation 2. The estimated probabilities of being type 0, 1, or 2 in the representative sample are 0.55, 0.04, and 0.41, respectively. The corresponding probabilities in the engineers' sample are 0.76, 0.07, and 0.17 for types 0, 1, and 2, respectively.

5.6   The Model's Fit

Figure 5.2a to d displays the actual and predicted choice frequencies in the four occupational alternatives over the first 60 months following arrival.[26] The model tracks the dynamics of occupational choice relatively well. Thus the sharp decline in nonemployment, the rise and subsequent fall in the proportion of workers in unskilled jobs and the gradual increase in the proportion of skilled workers are all captured by the model. In later months, for which there are fewer observations, there is a mild underprediction of the proportion of immigrants in occupation 1 and an overprediction in occupation 3. On the basis of a chi-square test, which compares the actual and predicted choice distributions in each month, the hypothesis that the actual and predicted choice distributions are identical is not rejected in 54 out of the 72 months.[27]

Table 5.8 presents the actual and predicted monthly transitions across occupations, averaged over the sample period. The fit is relatively good and on the basis of a chi-square test, the hypothesis that the actual and predicted transition matrices are identical is not rejected. The matrix shows that entry into occupation 1 occurs most often from nonemployment. Workers in occupations 2 and 3 enter occupation 1 indirectly, namely through nonemployment. Voluntary transitions into nonemployment occur when there are large random shocks to nonmonetary returns. However, these shocks primarily influence mismatches, namely type-2 immigrants working in occupation 1 and type-1 immigrants working in occupation 3. These movements also reflect, in part, participation in training programs.

The model is also able to capture the time patterns in transitions during the sample period. Figure 5.3a and b shows the actual and predicted transition rates between employment and nonemployment during the first 60 months following arrival. The model reproduces the decline in the exit rate from nonemployment and in the re-entry rate into nonemployment without reliance on time effects in the arrival rate of job offers. The decline in the re-entry rate into nonemployment is concurrent with a sharp rise in wages over time. Meanwhile, the opportunity cost of

Table 5.8
Actual and predicted monthly transitions, months 1 to 71

| | Month $t + 1$ | | | |
Month t	Occupation 1	Occupation 2	Occupation 3	Nonemployment
Occupation 1				
Actual	99.4%	0.0%	0.1%	0.5%
Predicted	99.2%	0.0%	0.1%	0.7%
Occupation 2				
Actual	0.6%	97.5%	0.3%	1.5%
Predicted	0.7%	97.3%	0.4%	1.7%
Occupation 3				
Actual	0.2%	0.1%	97.8%	1.9%
Predicted	0.2%	0.2%	97.9%	1.7%
Nonemployment				
Actual	1.8%	0.9%	9.3%	88.1%
Predicted	1.8%	0.9%	10.1%	87.2%

Sources: Brookdale Survey, Engineers' Survey, and authors' calculations based on the model's estimation and simulation.
Note: Each row sums to 100 percent.

voluntarily quitting and searching more efficiently in nonemployment rises, thus discouraging these types of transition. The decline in the exit rate from nonemployment is explained by the changing mix of unobserved types in the nonemployed population over time. Type-0 and type-2 immigrants constitute the majority of the nonemployed in the early months following arrival and these immigrants have relatively high exit rates. In later months the population of the nonemployed consists mainly of type-1 immigrants who have very poor employment prospects and thus low exit rates from nonemployment. On the basis of a chi-square test for each month, the hypothesis that actual and predicted exit rates from nonemployment are identical is not rejected in 66 out of 72 months. Similarly the hypothesis that actual and predicted entry rates into nonemployment are identical is not rejected in 68 out of 72 months.

Table 5.9 presents the actual and predicted average accepted wages in each occupation-job category for which there are wage observations. As shown in the table, predicted wages track observed wages relatively well for the cells in which there are a substantial number of wage observations. For all immigrants with wage observations, the simple correlation between actual and predicted logged wages is 0.602. Although the maximum likelihood estimation adjusts the coefficients of the wage functions to fit both wages and occupational choices, it yields a fit to wages

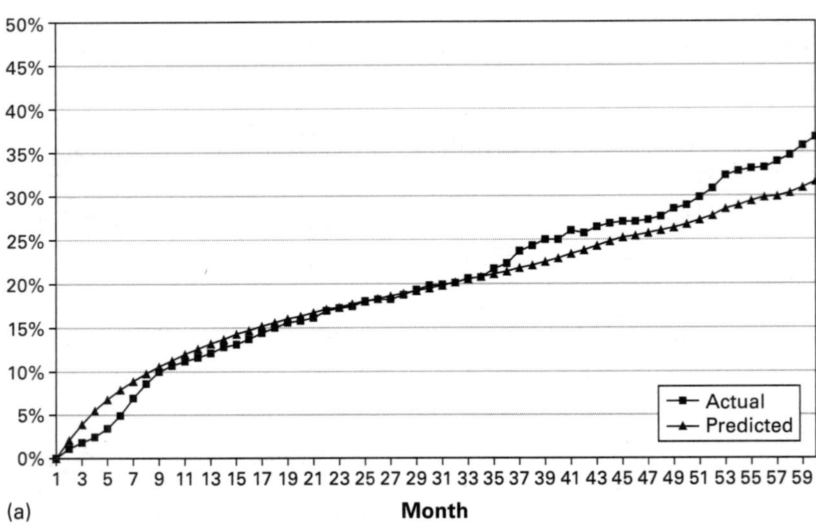

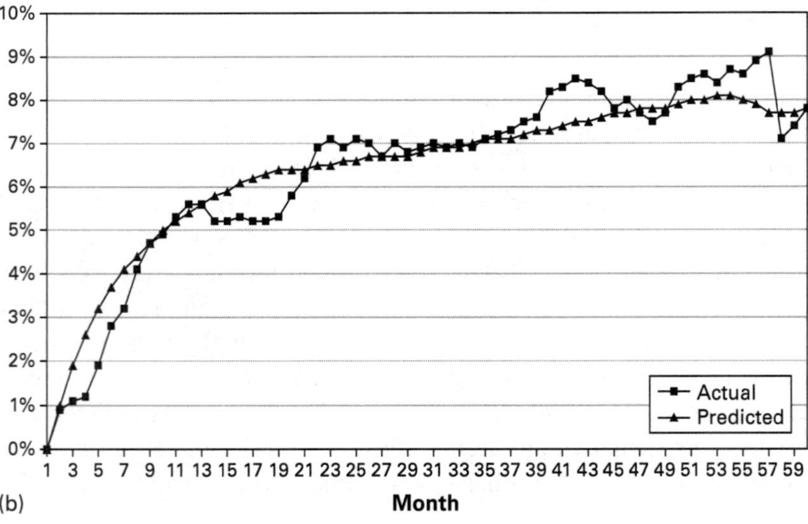

Figure 5.2
Actual and predicted proportion of immigrants. (a) Occupation 1: (b) occupation 2; (c) occupation 3; (d) nonemployed immigrants. Sources: Brookdale Survey, Engineers' Survey, and authors' calculations.

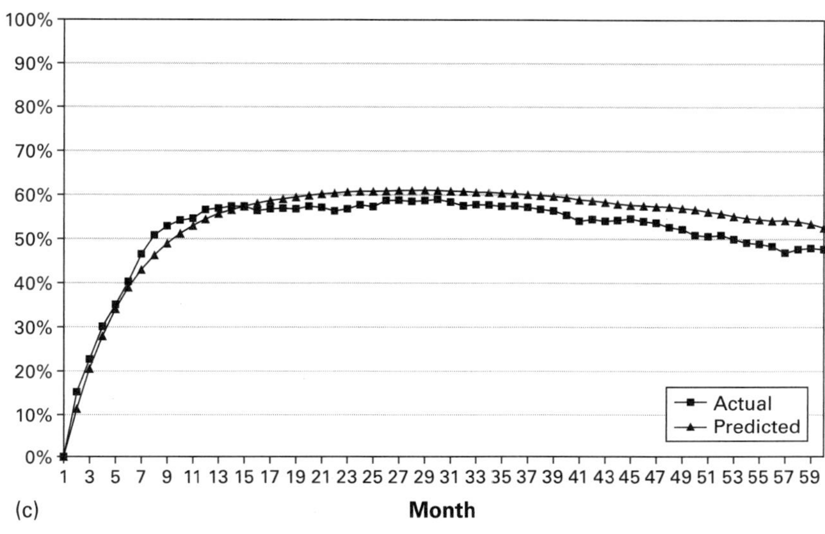

(c)

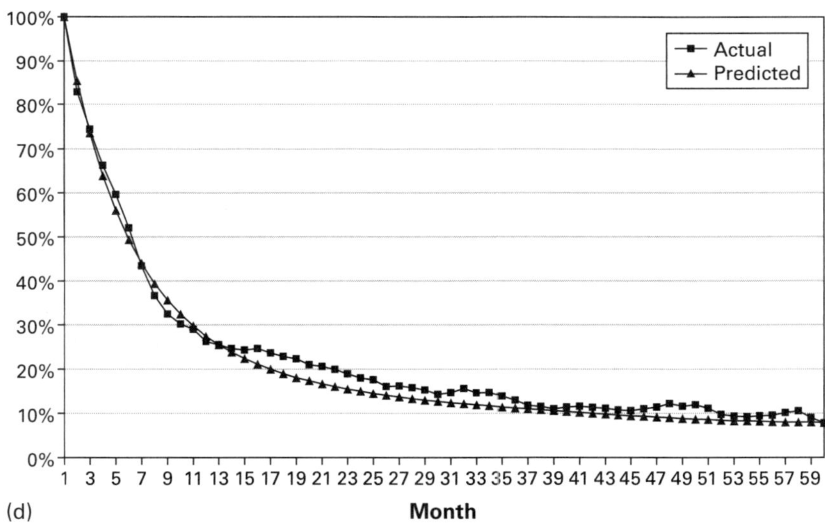

(d)

Figure 5.2
(Continued)

Table 5.9
Actual and predicted monthly wages by occupation, job, and type

Occupation and job	Number with wages > 0	Actual wages	Predicted wages				
			Type 0	Type 1	Type 2	All	OLS
3, 2	5	2,023	2,920	1,004	2,070	2,587	3,047
3, 6	3	2,983	3,093	1,058	2,193	2,734	2,538
3, 8	294	2,649	3,193	1,080	2,250	2,855	3,043
3, 9	126	3,184	3,252	1,092	2,287	2,928	3,353
3, 10	304	2,909	3,315	1,106	2,329	2,999	3,308
3, 11	116	3,178	3,377	1,118	2,374	3,073	3,472
3, 12	15	3,656	3,429	1,130	2,419	3,145	3,818
2, 12	82	3,290	3,521	1,726	2,996	3,267	3,517
2, 14	14	3,421	3,857	1,848	3,227	3,617	3,120
2, 16	1	2,742	3,983	1,913	3,323	3,761	2,871
1, 12	12	3,761	3,861	3,465	2,568	3,738	4,314
1, 15	11	3,878	4,355	3,823	2,957	4,210	4,125
1, 16	209	4,799	4,568	3,960	3,107	4,426	4,485
1, 17	6	4,908	4,752	4,089	3,216	4,618	3,606
1, 18	17	3,950	4,850	4,173	3,269	4,708	3,496

Sources: Brookdale Survey, Engineers' Survey, and authors' calculations based on the model's estimation and simulation.
Note: NIS/$ = 0.33 in 1995.

that exceeds that of a reduced form log-linear regression of wages on the same logged exogenous variables that appear in the structural model (0.519). For purposes of comparison, the predicted values from the second OLS regression specification in table 5.5, which includes the endogenous job choice variables, are also displayed.[28]

Table 5.9 also reveals large differences in predicted wages by type. Type-1 immigrant earns a very low wage in occupation 3, while in occupation 1 (in the rare case that he finds a job in occupation 1) his wage is substantially higher. A type-2 immigrant obtains the highest wage in occupation 2 while a type-0 immigrant obtains the highest wage in occupation 1.

Table 5.10 illustrates the impact of job transition on wage growth. In this framework, employed workers are classified into stayers and movers. The former do not change job from period t to period $t + 1$. The latter, who do change jobs from period t to period $t + 1$, are subdivided into movers within and across occupations. The table presents the actual and simulated proportions of such transitions and the associated predicted wage changes[29] averaged over individuals and sample months. The model mimics the sample proportions of movers and stayers relatively well. The predicted wage growth among stayers is a weighted average of the

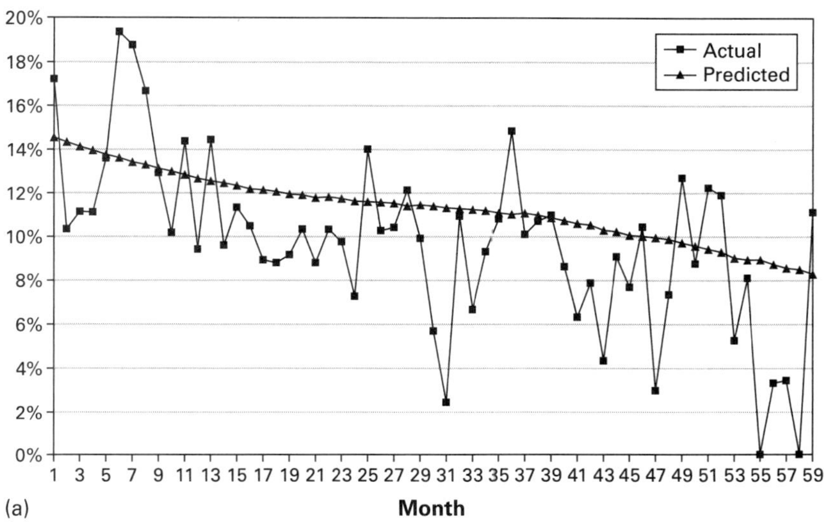

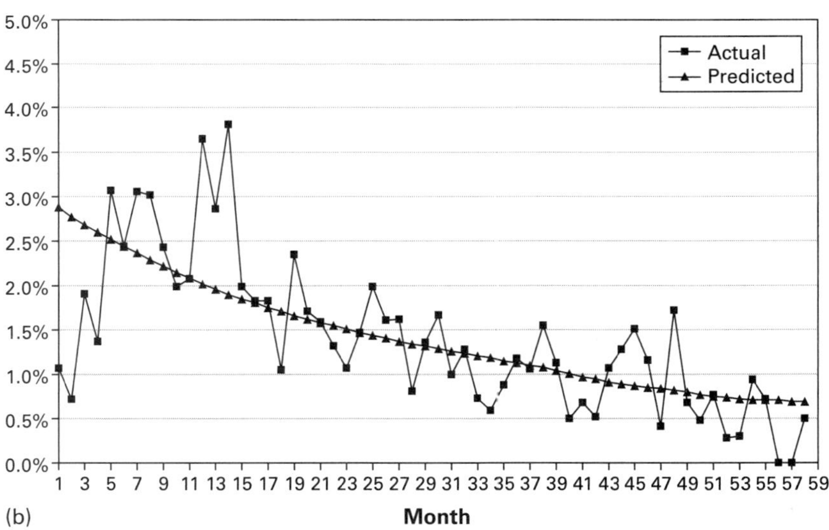

Figure 5.3
Actual and predicted monthly transition probabilities. (a) From nonemployment to employment; (b) from employment to nonemployment. Sources: Brookdale Survey, Engineers' Survey, and authors' calculations.

Table 5.10
Predicted wage growth of stayers and movers within and across occupations

| | Stayers | Movers | |
		Within occupations	Across occupations
Actual proportion	72.3%	0.4%	0.3%
Predicted proportion	73.3%	0.8%	0.3%
Predicted wage growth	0.7%	2.0%	18.3%

Source: Authors' calculations based on the model's estimation and simulation.

estimated monthly wage growth parameters in occupations 1, 2, and 3. Movers within an occupation have a predicted average monthly wage growth of 2 percent while movers across occupations have a substantial average wage growth of 18.3 percent. The predicted impact of job changes on wage growth is thus quite large. However, such transitions are rare and occur in only 1.1 percent of the time periods. The majority of transitions are to and from nonemployment. Ignoring the impact of these transitions on wages, which occur in 25.6 percent of the time periods, we have the average annual growth rate in wages for employed workers at 8.82 percent. Approximately 18 percent of the annual wage growth (1.32 percentage points) can be attributed to job transitions. These results are similar to the reduced form estimates presented in Eckstein and Weiss (1998), which are based on pooled cross-sectional data for the period 1991 to 1995. In that study, 17 percent (1.13 percentage points) of the predicted annual wage growth of 6.71 percent could be attributed to occupational transitions. Among immigrants with 16+ years of schooling, 17 percent (1.44 percentage points) of the predicted annual wage growth of 8.28 percent can be attributed to occupational transitions. The main methodological difference with the study presented here is that occupational transitions are *endogenously* determined.

5.7 Loss of Human Capital

Immigration entails the transfer of human capital from one labor market to another. Human capital is to some extent country specific. That is, skills acquired abroad are valued differently from those acquired locally, both because immigrants have limited information on local market conditions and the location of jobs and because employers are uncertain about the abilities of the newcomers. As a consequence immigrants do not immediately find the job for which they are most suitable, nor do they immediately receive the same wages as natives in the same job. Rather, there is a *gradual* process of adjustment in which immigrants start in low-paying jobs at the lower end of the occupational scale. This is followed by a sequence of job transitions that lead to rising wages over time. In addition the wage within each job rises over time. The speed of adjustment depends on market conditions, particularly the number of jobs in relation to the number of workers searching for them, which affects the speed at which immigrants meet local employers. It also depends on the *choices* made by immigrants, particularly with respect to which job offers to accept and how long to wait for a suitable job.

In order to assess the magnitude of the costs of immigration associated with frictions and the imperfect transferability of skills, the average simulated earnings (actual earnings) of each immigrant are compared to two hypothetical values in each period. The first (potential1 earnings) is the immigrant's mean potential earnings in each period over a counterfactual job distribution (i.e., the distribution of minimal schooling requirements among native Israeli workers with the same years of schooling as the "true" schooling endowment of the immigrant, s^*). The predicted wages for each job in the counterfactual job distribution are computed according to the estimated immigrant wage offer functions.[30] The second hypothetical value (potential2 earnings) is the immigrant's average potential earnings over the same counterfactual job distribution as for potential1 earnings, except that the predicted wages in each job are computed according to the parameters of a native Israeli wage regression.[31] The difference between potential1 earnings and actual earnings is a measure of earnings loss due to frictions (i.e., job distribution mismatch) while the difference between potential2 earnings and potential1 earnings is a measure of earnings loss due to a lower market valuation of imported skills.

In order to assess long-run outcomes, the actual and potential earnings are computed from the age on arrival until retirement at age 65 for each immigrant. In order to calculate actual and potential earnings past month 72 in Israel (the horizon of the model) in a computationally practical way, a period length of one year is assumed in the simulation of the model beyond that point. Furthermore, since it is not possible to identify quadratic effects on wage growth within the sample period and to thus reliably predict wage offers beyond month 72, the wage offer functions in the annual model are replaced by wage functions estimated separately using data on the annual earnings of previous waves of immigrants from the Soviet Union.[32] Nonetheless, the imported wage functions in the annual model do not contaminate the simulated job choices in terms of months. That is, the monthly model and the annual model are disconnected by separate backward recursions. The backward recursion and the subsequent simulation of the monthly model use the terminal value functions, as in the estimation.[33] The estimated monthly wage offer functions do, however, influence job choices in the annual model. The ratio of the wage offer according to the estimated monthly model to that according to the out-of-sample regression is used to adjust the annual wage offers for each job in month 73. We denote this ratio by $w_{sj73}^{m}/w_{sj73}^{y}$. The annual wage offers in each job are multiplied by $w_{sj73}^{m}/w_{sj73}^{y}$ for each year.[34]

Figure 5.4a displays the time paths of simulated actual and potential earnings averaged over immigrants who worked in occupation 1 in the FSU and were 40 years old or younger on arrival. Figure 5.4b displays the corresponding time paths for immigrants who were older than 40 on arrival. The simulated actual earnings of immigrants are always below their simulated potential earnings, though the gap closes as time in Israel increases. The change over time in potential2 earnings is driven by the increase in local work experience, where the impact of total experience (i.e., imported plus local) is evaluated using the native Israeli regression coefficients. The sharp rise in potential1 earnings reflects the *higher* return that immigrants obtain on local work experience. This is primarily due to the rising returns on imported skills and complementarity between local and imported human capital (Eckstein and Weiss 1998). The even sharper rise in simulated actual earnings occurs as immigrants move into higher paying jobs and occupations.

There are marked differences in the time paths of actual and potential earnings between the two age groups. Younger immigrants initially earn half of their potential wage but gradually close the gap, and after 25 years in Israel they earn 70 percent of what they would have earned as native Israelis. The gap in earnings in year 25 is evenly divided between job distribution mismatch and a lower market valuation of imported skills. Immigrants who arrive at an older age initially earn the same as younger immigrants; however, this represents only one-third of their potential, indicating negligible initial returns on imported work experience. As time in Israel increases, the rewards for imported skills rise for both younger and older immigrants, although the occupational status of older immigrants is substantially lower, and they remain locked in low-skilled occupations. After 10 years in Israel, older immigrants earn only half as much as comparable native Israelis. The rates of occupational upgrading by age on arrival are shown in table 5.11. Among immigrants who worked

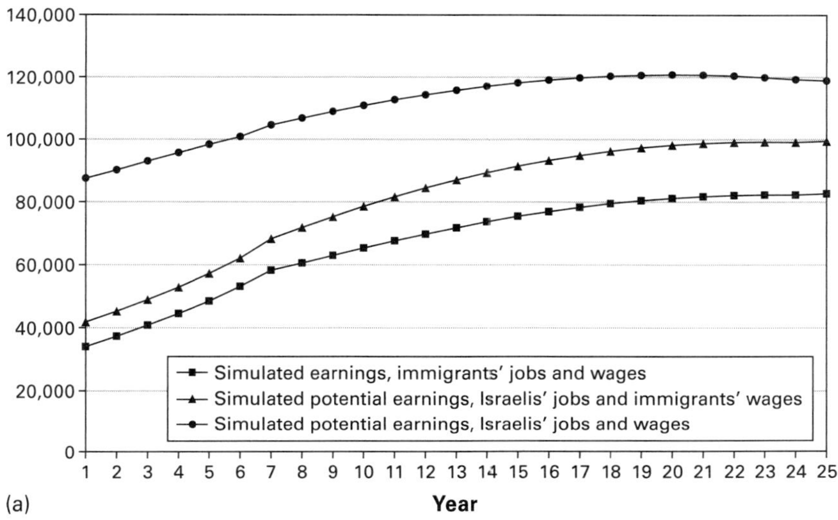

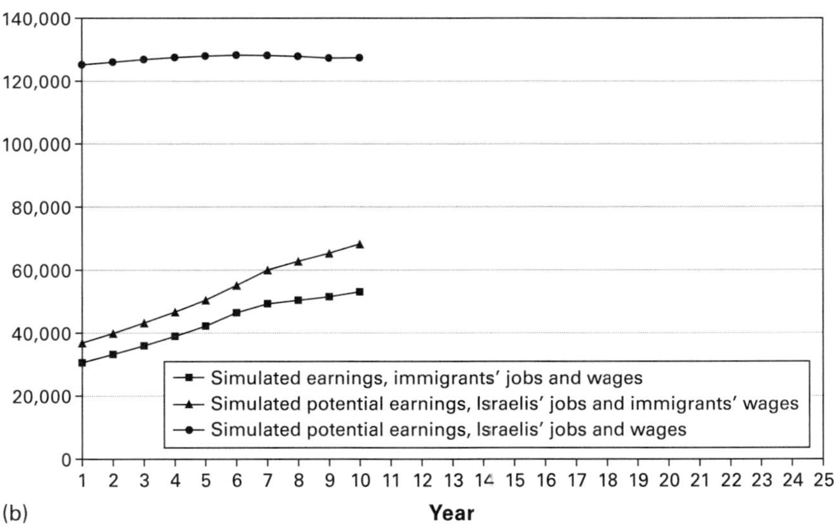

Figure 5.4
Simulated actual and potential annual earnings. (a) Immigrants younger than 40 on arrival; (b) immigrants older than 40 on arrival. NIS/$ = 0.33 in 1995. Source: Authors' calculations (for details, see section 5.7 in the text).

Table 5.11
Occupational choice distribution of immigrants who worked in occupation 1 in the FSU, by age on arrival

Year	Younger than 40 (%)				Older than 40 (%)			
	Occupation 1	Occupation 2	Occupation 3	Nonemployment	Occupation 1	Occupation 2	Occupation 3	Nonemployment
1	17.5	6.9	48.3	27.3	12.3	3.9	56.0	27.7
2	24.6	8.7	52.2	14.5	15.9	4.3	64.7	15.0
3	28.9	9.2	51.4	10.5	17.7	4.2	66.8	11.3
4	32.0	9.0	50.6	8.4	18.7	4.0	67.8	9.4
5	34.2	8.6	49.8	7.3	19.5	3.8	68.2	8.5
6	34.7	8.5	49.5	7.3	19.7	3.8	68.0	8.5
7	39.7	8.7	43.5	8.1	23.9	4.8	63.5	7.8
8	41.8	8.8	41.7	7.6	26.1	5.2	61.9	6.9
9	43.7	8.9	40.0	7.3	28.0	5.5	60.1	6.4
10	45.5	8.8	38.5	7.1	30.5	5.8	57.7	6.1
11	47.2	8.7	37.1	7.0				
12	48.7	8.6	35.9	6.8				
13	50.1	8.4	34.9	6.6				
14	51.4	8.2	33.9	6.4				
15	52.6	8.1	33.1	6.3				
16	53.6	7.9	32.4	6.1				
17	54.6	7.7	31.7	6.0				
18	55.4	7.6	31.1	5.8				
19	56.3	7.4	30.6	5.7				
20	57.0	7.3	30.2	5.6				
21	57.6	7.1	29.8	5.5				
22	58.2	7.0	29.5	5.3				
23	58.8	6.8	29.1	5.3				
24	59.3	6.7	28.9	5.2				
25	59.6	6.6	28.7	5.1				

Source: Authors' calculations based on the model's estimation and simulation.

in occupation 1 in the FSU and were 40 years old or less on arrival, 60 percent are predicted to be employed in occupation 1, 25 years after arrival. This is almost identical to the rate of 58 percent among similar immigrants from the FSU who arrived during the 1970s (Eckstein and Weiss 2002).

Due to the major changes in earnings over time in Israel and the endogeneity of wages and jobs, whereby currently low wages may be traded for higher wages in the future, the appropriate summary statistic of earnings loss is the difference in the expected discounted *present value* between actual and potential earnings over the immigrant's remaining working life. Table 5.12 describes the main findings for this statistic.[35] The

Table 5.12
Discounted present value of lifetime earnings loss

Sample attributes	Loss due to frictions		Loss due to prices		Total loss	
	Absolute	Relative	Absolute	Relative	Absolute	Relative
Years of schooling						
5–12	95,478	12.09	199,138	25.22	294,616	37.31
13–14	107,339	10.71	388,671	38.77	496,010	49.48
15	217,551	16.16	463,901	34.47	681,452	50.63
16	201,460	14.44	597,821	42.85	799,281	57.29
17–22	191,544	12.38	797,774	51.54	989,318	63.92
Occupation in the FSU						
1	211,498	14.63	619,855	42.88	831,353	57.51
2	112,560	10.12	531,082	47.77	643,642	57.89
3	46,930	5.91	282,630	35.58	329,560	41.49
Engineer	215,763	14.94	606,737	42.01	822,500	56.95
Physician	150,934	9.46	880,462	55.18	1,031,396	64.64
Age on arrival						
<=40	219,501	15.35	445,472	31.15	664,973	46.50
40+	160,201	12.40	702,088	54.36	862,289	66.76
Year of arrival						
1989–90	184,479	13.39	564,693	40.99	749,172	54.38
1991	171,185	13.23	557,145	43.06	728,330	56.29
1992–95	214,196	15.44	625,247	45.07	839,443	60.51
Type						
0	157,342	11.58	512,606	37.72	669,948	49.30
1	547,577	40.34	639,111	47.08	1,186,688	87.42
2	184,155	13.57	753,139	55.49	919,294	69.06
All						
$r = 0.06$	188,759	13.89	578,506	42.59	767,265	56.48
$r = 0.03$	262,438	14.37	722,253	39.55	984,691	53.92

Source: Authors' calculations (for details, see section 5.7 in the text).
Note: NIS/$ = 0.33 in 1995. The calculations apply to males aged 25 to 55 on arrival.

estimated lifetime earnings loss (potential2 minus actual) is US$253,200. This represents 57 percent of the lifetime earnings that these immigrants would have obtained had they been native Israelis with the same measured attributes. The estimated lifetime loss is thus quite substantial.

Most of the loss (US$190,900) can be attributed to the fact that immigrants are paid lower wages than Israelis in the same job, especially in the early years following arrival. This loss represents 43 percent of total potential lifetime earnings. The lifetime loss of earnings due to frictions in the labor market (nonemployment and job distribution mismatch) is US$62,300, which represents 14 percent of total potential lifetime earnings.

The estimated lifetime earnings loss varies substantially between immigrants. Immigrants with more schooling tend to experience higher total losses. Given the strong correlation between schooling levels and occupation, this is also true for immigrants who worked in occupations 1 and 2 in the FSU. The figures lead to the following conclusions: physicians experience higher losses than engineers, older immigrants experience higher losses than younger immigrants, losses increase with later arrival, and type-1 immigrants suffer exceedingly large losses.

In order to gauge the relative importance of job distribution mismatch and a lower market valuation of imported skills, the table decomposes the total loss into that due to frictions and that due to prices. The estimates indicate that the loss due to prices is, generally, far more significant. This is primarily due to the lower returns on imported schooling.[36] The difference between the loss due to frictions and that due to prices is greatest for physicians. Immigrants who worked as physicians in the FSU obtain jobs in the medical profession relatively quickly in Israel though they earn much lower wages than native physicians.[37] The smallest difference between the loss due to frictions and that due to prices is for engineers and type-1 immigrants. The large number of immigrants with engineering degrees nearly doubled the total stock of engineers in Israel. This group thus faces particular difficulty in finding a job in their field. Type-1 immigrants suffer a relatively large loss due to frictions since they constitute a high proportion of the permanently nonemployed. It should be noted that there is a discontinuity in the ranking of relative losses due to prices across schooling levels and occupations. Immigrants with 13 to 14 years of schooling suffer higher relative losses due to prices than immigrants with 15 years of schooling. Correspondingly, immigrants who worked in occupation 2 in the FSU suffer higher relative losses due to prices than immigrants who worked in occupation 1 in the FSU. This result is due to the relatively lower actual earnings of this group in occupation 3, in which many of these immigrants find employment.

The lifetime earnings loss calculations are meant to estimate the target country's social loss of output resulting from the movement of human capital across labor markets. For this reason they do not include the benefits that immigrants receive when nonemployed nor the monetary value of nonmonetary benefits when employed. In addition the wages of Israelis are used as a benchmark. Although the model contains an equivalence scale that translates the immigrants' schooling abroad into local schooling, there may still be unaccounted-for differences in quality between the two types of schooling. Moreover the counterfactual exercises do not account for possible macro effects on the Israeli labor market and wage structure. For these reasons the potential earnings of recent immigrants may be overstated when the current earnings of Israelis with the same *observable* characteristics are attributed to them. Therefore, the estimated losses of the various groups constitute an upper bound on actual losses. Biases in the separately estimated immigrant and Israeli wage functions due to sample selection and/or unmeasured characteristics also reduce the accuracy of the estimates. We thus have more confidence in the ranking of the losses across groups of immigrants with different attributes than in their actual magnitudes.

Recall that the model assumes a relatively high real annual discount rate of 6 percent in order to capture the borrowing constraint facing immigrants who arrive in Israel with no assets. This should not negate the use of an appropriate "social" discount rate in order to evaluate the social loss associated with immigration. As can be seen in the last two rows of table 5.12, the relative losses are affected only slightly by a reduction of the real annual discount rate to 3 percent. Clearly, if immigrants had better access to the capital market and had faced an interest rate of only 3 percent, there would have been a marked effect on their choices and the estimated parameters of the model.

5.8   Summary

This chapter examines the process of entry of high-skilled immigrants into the Israeli labor market using panel data on several cohorts of recent immigrants from the FSU. The main emphasis of the analysis is on the occupational *choices* of immigrants who arrive with various skill levels and at different points in their life cycle. The analysis does not investigate the factors that determine wage growth within occupations and jobs, but rather explicitly models how immigrants adjust their choices to the expected rise in their wages with the passage of time.

As demonstrated, a simple on-the-job search model cast as a finite-horizon discrete choice dynamic programming problem under uncertainty captures the observed dynamics of occupational choice during the first six years in Israel quite accurately. These dynamics are characterized by a rapid entry into the labor force and an initial phase of employment in a low-skilled occupation, followed by a gradual occupational upgrading. The model explains the changing proportions of immigrants in various occupations without relying on time effects in job-offer probabilities. The sharp increase in the proportion of immigrants with the equivalent of a high school education and previous work experience in high-skilled occupations in the FSU in low-skilled jobs is due to their willingness to work in such jobs in Israel. The subsequent decrease in this proportion is due to their gradual transition to jobs in high-skilled occupations. Permanent unobserved heterogeneity among immigrants is shown to be important in explaining the observed decline in exit rates from nonemployment. Immigrants with high exit rates from nonemployment constitute the majority of those without jobs in the early months following arrival. As these immigrants leave nonemployment, the population of the nonemployed is increasingly made up of immigrants with very poor employment prospects. The model is also capable of explaining the declining re-entry rates into nonemployment, which decline over time as wage growth on the job raises the opportunity cost of searching efficiently for better job opportunities from nonemployment.

The estimated parameters of the behavioral model, together with information on the wages of immigrants from earlier waves, are used to examine the speed of wage convergence between immigrants and natives. The simulation of an occupational path and associated wages for each immigrant upon arrival in the host country and until retirement suggests that the earnings of recently arrived immigrants will gradually approach those of comparable natives. However, the sharp growth in earnings, combined with the heterogeneity in age on entry into the labor market, suggest the use of discounted present value of lifetime earnings as a better summary measure of economic performance in the new country. The lifetime earnings predicted by the model are thus compared to the hypothetical lifetime earnings that immigrants would have obtained had their imported observable skills been valued, from the time of arrival, in the same way as comparable natives with the same labor market experience and schooling. The results indicate a large gap between actual and potential lifetime earnings. On average, immigrants from the FSU can expect lifetime earnings in Israel to fall short of the lifetime earnings of comparable natives by 57 percent. Of this figure, 14 percentage points reflect frictions associated with nonemployment and job distribution mismatch, and 43 percentage points reflect the gradual adaptation of schooling and experience imported from the FSU to the Israeli labor market.

According to our interpretation of these findings, the lack of information among employers regarding the quality of newly arrived immigrants and among immigrants regarding opportunities in the new labor market and the need for complementary local capital (e.g., language, social connections, and familiarity with local institutions) leads to a process of adjustment and adaptation that is necessarily *gradual*. The speed of adjustment depends on market conditions and the choices made by the immigrants, which interact in a complicated way. It is not clear whether, and to what extent, market failures affect this process and whether there is some policy that could reduce the social loss. It is possible that limited borrowing capacity prevents immigrants from making the required local investment in on-the-job training, which should be the main vehicle for the acquisition of local *general* human capital. There is, however, no way to ascertain the quantitative importance of this phenomenon.[38]

Appendix: Supplementary Tables

Table 5.A1
Sample means and standard deviations

Variable name	Representative sample		Engineers' sample		Combined sample	
	Mean	Standard deviation	Mean	Standard deviation	Mean	Standard deviation
Schooling_0[a]	14.6	2.7	16.4	1.6	15.8	2.2
Experience_0	16.6	8.3	18.6	8.4	17.8	8.4
Age_0	38.5	8.3	42.0	8.7	40.8	8.7
$\text{Age}_0 > 40$	40.1		58.4		51.8	
Occupation_0 1	56.3		100.0		84.3	
Occupation_0 2	12.9		0.0		4.6	
Occupation_0 3	30.8		0.0		11.1	
Engineer_0	25.7		100.0		73.4	
Physician_0	5.7		0.0		2.0	
Cohort 1989–90	59.4		41.5		47.9	
Cohort 1991	37.8		19.5		26.1	
Cohort 1992–95	2.8		19.0		26.0	
Knowledge of Hebrew	76.8		69.3		71.5	
Months in Israel	41.4	14.6	46.7	16.5	44.8	16.0
Months nonemployed	1 1.7	10.3	1 1.4	10.9	1 1.5	10.7
Months in occupation 1	5.1	12.4	9.3	18.1	7.8	16.4
Months in occupation 2	3.0	9.3	2.5	9.3	2.7	9.3
Months in occupation 3	21.6	18.0	23.5	19.3	22.8	18.8
Wage observations = 0	54		126		180	
Wage observations = 1	102		571		673	
Wage observations > 1	233		0		233	
Monthly wage	2,919	1,392	3,740	1,738	3,305	1,616
Wage observations	646		571		1217	
% Net wages	60.8		26.3		44.6	
Number of immigrants	389		697		1,086	

Sources: Brookdale Survey and Engineers' Survey.
a. A subscript of 0 indicates value on arrival.

Table 5.A2
Distribution of completed schooling and minimal schooling requirements, by occupation

s	% Workers with completed schooling s				% Jobs requiring completed schooling s $(P_j(s))$				Average minimal schooling requirements among workers with schooling s			
	Occupation				Occupation				Occupation			
	1	2	3	All	1	2	3	All	1	2	3	All
0–8	0.5	1.0	15.8	12.4	0.0	0.0	22.5	15.3	12.6	12.1	8.9	9.0
9	0.0	0.6	2.9	2.1	0.0	0.0	25.1	17.1	–	12.0	9.2	9.4
10	0.9	3.5	14.8	10.7	0.0	0.0	24.5	16.6	12.0	12.2	9.4	9.6
11	0.7	4.0	11.6	8.5	0.0	0.0	11.8	8.0	12.4	12.0	9.5	9.8
12	3.2	22.2	36.2	27.7	10.7	75.9	16.2	28.0	12.9	12.2	9.9	10.3
13	2.0	7.6	3.6	4.1	0.0	2.1	0.0	0.4	13.6	12.3	10.2	11.1
14	2.7	16.2	4.8	6.7	0.0	15.9	0.0	3.3	14.1	12.3	10.5	11.5
15	7.0	13.5	4.6	6.3	15.1	0.0	0.0	1.7	15.1	12.6	10.6	12.0
16	24.6	14.7	2.8	7.1	54.5	6.1	0.0	7.4	15.9	13.4	11.0	13.7
17	16.2	7.0	1.2	3.8	4.0	0.0	0.0	0.4	15.9	13.2	10.9	14.0
18	13.2	4.2	0.9	2.9	15.7	0.0	0.0	1.8	16.3	12.8	10.9	14.2
19	8.2	1.8	0.3	1.5	0.0	0.0	0.0	0.0	16.5	12.7	10.7	14.8
20	9.8	1.6	0.3	1.9	0.0	0.0	0.0	0.0	16.3	13.2	10.7	15.0
21+	11.5	2.1	0.2	4.3	0.0	0.0	0.0	0.0	16.6	12.8	10.8	14.9

Source: CBS Income Survey 1991–94.
Note: The sample includes male Israeli workers aged 25 to 55.

Table 5.A3
Maximum likelihood estimates and asymptotic t-values

	Occupation 1		Occupation 2		Occupation 3		Nonemployment	
	Coefficient	t-Value	Coefficient	t-Value	Coefficient	t-Value	Coefficient	t-Value
Wage-offer functions — $\ln w_{sjt}$								
Constant	7.64762	13.13	7.70313	40.23	7.79090	76.02		
Job (s)	0.03308	3.63	0.03308		0.01059	4.46		
Month (t)	0.00665	4.93	0.00665		0.00649	7.52		
Type 1	−0.15661	−0.42	−0.73910	−1.65	−1.12593	−11.41		
Type 2	−0.38857	−10.00	−0.16286	−2.02	−0.35763	−13.07		
Schooling$_0$ (s_0)[a]	−0.01363	−2.01	−0.02899	−2.58	−0.00540	−1.05		
Experience$_0$	0.00370	0.58	0.01354	1.82	0.00190	0.35		
Experience$_0^2$	−0.00037	−2.13	−0.00064	−2.83	−0.00023	−1.59		
Occupation$_0$ 1	0.19038	0.33	0.05910	0.90	0.06580	1.81		
Occupation$_0$ 2	0.03306	0.05	0.05190	0.64	−0.09450	−1.91		
Engineer$_0$	0.05546	1.29	0.23359	3.79	0.06949	1.83		
Physician$_0$	−0.21246	−1.94	0.02834	0.10	−0.24827	−2.42		
1991$_0$	0.00117	0.05	0.00117		−0.00116	−0.05		
>1991$_0$	0.00162	0.05	0.00162		0.01011	0.28		
Representative sample	0.08997	2.33	0.08997		0.08997			
Representative sample × net[b]	−0.13315	−3.86	−0.13315		−0.13315			
Engineers' sample × net	−0.20042	−5.80	−0.20042		−0.20042			
$\ln(\sigma)$	−1.08153	−21.53	−1.32353	−12.79	−1.27618	−46.52		
Nonmonetary returns — n_{sjt}								
k_j	0.00387	0.01	0.15442	0.36	0.16576	0.40		
k_{41}							0.36891	1.24
k_{42}							0.05173	0.12
v	3,267	2.03	3,267		3,267		3,267	

Table 5.A3
(Continued)

	Occupation 1		Occupation 2		Occupation 3		Nonemployment	
	Coefficient	t-Value	Coefficient	t-Value	Coefficient	t-Value	Coefficient	t-Value
	Terminal value functions — V_{sj73}							
γ_j	−1.49330	−6.38	−1.51262	−5.85	−1.40043	−6.39		
	Job-offer probabilities — λ_{jkt}							
Nonemployment	−5.19917	−5.61	−3.84230	−9.86	−1.69416	−19.57		
Occupation 1	−5.52473	−5.93	−5.51386	−8.88	−5.51386			
Occupation 2	−6.10825	−6.68	−3.55543	−7.79	−3.94459	−8.83		
Occupation 3	−7.19802	−7.66	−5.25765	−12.68	−3.01802	−33.34		
Type 1	−2.83216	−2.85	−2.05430	−2.56	−1.60270	−9.15		
Type 2	−1.02175	−3.05	−0.24861	−0.83	0.21600	2.62		
$Age_0 > 40$	−0.27582	−2.57	−0.36479	−1.98	−0.02991	−0.56		
$Occupation_0$ 1	2.48364	2.65	−0.01723	−0.03	−0.28822	−2.90		
$Occupation_0$ 2	0.62551	0.51	0.52499	1.20	−0.04304	−0.36		
$Engineer_0$	−0.27344	−1.40	0.00486	0.01	−0.15502	−1.83		
$Physician_0$	0.12819	0.35	−0.05532	−0.09	−1.21266	−3.87		
1991_0	0.00737	0.05	−0.40283	−1.86	0.33688	5.94		
$>1991_0$	−0.28445	−1.79	−0.34133	−1.21	0.47355	6.60		
	Job-offer probabilities — $\Phi_j(s^* \geq s)$							
α	10.07162	34.73	10.07162		10.07162			
β_j	0.45638	22.26	0.27028	9.96	0.08005	4.28		
sqrt(v)	0.40057	4.85	0.40057		0.20905	10.68		
	Job-termination probabilities — δ_j							
α_j	−5.62635	−24.63	−4.50681	−20.17	−5.14436	−22.72		

Table 5.A3
(Continued)

| | Type probabilities | | | |
| | Type 1 | | Type 2 | |
	Coefficient	t-Value	Coefficient	t-Value
Constant	−2.43253	−10.28	−1.51139	−5.36
Representative	−0.05924	−0.14	1.21765	3.77

Note: Representative sample, Engineers' sample, and net appear in the measurement error density but not in w_{sjt}.
$n_{sjt} = b_{jt} + v\varepsilon_{sjb}$ where $b_{jt} = (e^{k_j} - 1)w_{sjt}$, $j = 1, 2, 3$, and $b_{4t} = 580e^{k_{41occ_0}1 + k_{42occ_0}2}$.
$$V_{sj73} = \frac{1+q^T}{1-q}(w_{sj73} + n_{sj73})\exp(\gamma_j).$$
$$\lambda_{jkt} = \frac{\exp(a_{jk}x_{it})}{1 + \sum_{k=1}^{3}\exp(a_{jk}x_{it})}.$$
$$\Phi_j(s^* \geq s) = \frac{\exp[(\beta_j s_0/v) - (s/v) + (\alpha/v)]}{1 + \exp[(\beta_j s_0/v) - (s/v) + (\alpha/v)]},$$
$\delta_j = \exp(\alpha_j)/[1 + \exp(\alpha_j)]$.
The type probabilities are multinomial logit.
a. A subscript of 0 indicates value on arrival.
b. Net indicates that the reported wage is net of taxes.

Table 5.A4
Wage regressions for out-of-sample predictions

Variable name	Israelis		Immigrants	
	Coefficient	Standard deviation	Coefficient	Standard deviation
A_{cons}	6.3033	0.0441		
A_{year91}	−0.0061	0.0159		
A_{year92}	0.0477	0.0158		
A_{year93}	0.0117	0.0158		
A_{year94}	0.0363	0.0151		
A_{occ1}	0.2663	0.0204		
A_{ooc2}	0.1380	0.0196		
A_{exp}	0.0530	0.0019		
$A_{exp\ sq}$	−0.0009	0.0001		
$A_{years\ schooling}$	0.0670	0.0026		
$A_{min\ schooling\ requirement\ of\ job}$	0.02359	0.0036		
B_{dummy}			0.3720	0.2234
λ			−0.1193	0.0365
B_{occ1}			0.0930	0.0739
B_{occ2}			0.0962	0.0569
$B_{cohort<89}$			0.0220	0.0626
$B_{cohort92\text{-}95}$			−0.0131	0.0367
C_λ			0.6516	0.2743
B_{expFSU}			−0.1425	0.2320
C_{expFSU}			−1.0893	0.2714
$B_{years\ schooling}$			−0.0288	0.0118
$C_{years\ schooling}$			−0.0508	0.0140
$B_{s\ min}$			−0.0062	0.0095
Mean dependent variable	8.0666		7.6160	
R^2		0.3892		
Number of observations	8,184		1,818	

Source: CBS Income Survey 1991–94.
Note: The effect of variable j for immigrants is $A_j + B_j + (e^{-\lambda t} * C_j)$ and $expFSU = (A_{exp} - (A_{exp\ sq} * exp_0)) * (exp_0)$, where exp_0 is the number of years worked in the FSU.

6 The Joint Choice of Residential Location and Employment by Immigrants

6.1 Introduction

Upon arrival in the new country, immigrants make two main choices: their area of residence and their first job. Needless to say, the two decisions are interdependent. In the case of Israel, the government's immigration policy allowed each FSU immigrant to freely choose his area of residence. Also as part of this policy, the government provided immigrant households with a package of financial and nonfinancial benefits, including a rent subsidy during their initial period in the country. The analysis in this chapter focuses on the effect of the housing policy adopted by the Israeli government at the beginning of the wave of immigration on the immigrants' choice of residence, and as a consequence on the success of their initial occupational integration.

The early 1990s were characterized by massive government intervention in the housing market, which involved the construction of tens of thousands of housing units. Housing construction was concentrated mainly in the peripheral areas and in areas lacking employment infrastructure, due to the greater availability of land there. Furthermore housing in these areas was marketed to the immigrants at attractive prices. For example, between April 1990 and November 1991, the Ministry of Housing initiated the construction of 62,000 housing units, of which only 26.6 percent were located in the Center, where most of the places of employment are concentrated. Thus the mismatch between areas with a high concentration of employment opportunities and the areas of residence chosen by FSU immigrants upon arrival is another possible source for the initial occupational downgrading of FSU immigrants in Israel.

This chapter is based on Gotlibovski (1997), Absorption of 1990–92 immigrants in Israel: Interaction between housing and labor markets, PhD dissertation, Tel Aviv University.

The data shows that the residential choices of immigrants vary with year of arrival. Thus, according to the Central Bureau of Statistics, 26.4 percent of immigrants who arrived in 1990 chose to reside in the Tel-Aviv district upon arrival while only 10.9 percent chose the southern district. The proportion of those arriving in 2000 that chose Tel-Aviv as their first place of residence fell to 19 percent, while the proportion choosing the south rose to 21.7 percent. A similar shift to the south at the expense of Tel-Aviv is also apparent according to time in Israel: only 13 percent of the 1990 cohort were residing in the Tel-Aviv district in 2000 (as compared to 26.4 percent in 1990), whereas 22.9 percent resided in the southern district (as compared to 10.9 percent in 1990).

This transition away from the Center may partly be explained by the significant increase in housing costs in the early 1990s. Housing costs during this period increased by a cumulative real rate of approximately 30 percent, with a somewhat larger increase in the Center than in the Periphery. However, in light of the higher housing costs in the Center, a uniform rate of increase in all areas may still have led to a shift in the choice of residence from the Center to the Periphery.

The analysis in this chapter is based on an infinite-horizon dynamic structural model, in which each immigrant maximizes his expected utility from expected earned income while employed, net of housing costs. The model makes it possible to identify the characteristics of the labor market in different areas and to estimate the effect of housing market characteristics on the immigrants' choice of residence and consequently on their integration in the labor market and the utilization of their human capital.

The explicit formulation of the immigrant's decision problem with regard to location and employment also facilitates the simulation of alternative government housing policies on the immigrants' choice of residence and their success in the labor market. The model is not restricted to immigrant populations and can be expanded to describe the joint choice of residence and employment for any population that is moving from one area to another, whether willingly or otherwise.

The model is estimated using data from the 1992 Brookdale Survey of FSU immigrants who arrived between 1989 and 1992. According to the main result, it may be worthwhile for immigrants to compromise in their choice of residence and to reside in areas where the probability of utilizing their human capital is lower. The results further show that immigrants are sensitive to housing market conditions when choosing their first place of residence in Israel and that educated immigrants tend to choose metropolitan areas where their probability of finding a job compatible with their skills is higher, despite the higher housing costs in those areas.

The rest of the chapter is organized as follows: Section 6.2 presents the theoretical model. Section 6.3 presents the empirical specification of the model, and section 6.4 discusses the estimation strategy and identification. Section 6.5 describes the data and Section 6.6 summarizes the results. Section 6.7 provides a verification analysis using additional data sources, and section 6.8 concludes.

6.2 The Theoretical Model

We use an infinite-horizon search model in order to describe an immigrant's joint decision regarding residential location and occupation.[1] Each immigrant is assumed to maximize his expected utility by simultaneously choosing his area of residence, the occupation in which he will search for a job (if he has decided to do so) and the threshold rule for accepting job offers during each period, while taking into account the effect of his current choice on his future possibilities.[2] Using a search model to explain the immigrant's location and choice-of-occupation decisions would seem to be the correct method in view of the government's policy of leaving the choice of area of residence and of occupation to the immigrant.

The existence of a preferred choice for each immigrant can be the result of a lack of equilibrium between the labor market conditions and rent in the different regions and/or the existence of heterogeneity between individuals. The lack of equilibrium is a reasonable assumption for the Israeli market in the early 1990s in light of the scope of immigration during that period.

6.2.1 The Housing Market

We assume here that immigrants can change their place of residence at the beginning of each period. Immigrant families face the market price of housing (rent), R_d, which varies between regions and is assumed to be constant over time (in real terms).[3]

6.2.2 Production Technology

We assume that there are many types of jobs available in the economy that differ in their level of productivity. Productivity is defined as the minimal years of schooling (s) required by the job. The wage paid to an employee in a given job is derived from his level of productivity and his characteristics. However, a level of education beyond that required for the job (i.e., overqualification) does not increase productivity and therefore does not increase the employee's wage either. Jobs are distributed among the various regions of the country (d) and the production technology for a given product does not vary between regions.

Occupations are divided into three broad categories, $j = 1, 2, 3$, where $j = 1$ refers to scientific, academic, and managerial occupations; $j = 2$ refers to technical and licensed occupations; and $j = 3$ refers to all other occupations.[4] Within each category there are jobs that vary in their educational requirements. The difference between the occupations is reflected in the importance of education in the production process (and therefore in determining the return on education as well).

6.2.3 The Labor Market

The labor market in each period is characterized by a variety of vacated or newly created positions, dispersed throughout the various regions, which the firms wish to fill. Each vacant position offers a wage that may depend on the type of job (education required, type of occupation, and the area in which the job is located) and on the candidate's characteristics.

The distribution of firms across regions is assumed to be exogenous to the location of potential workers (whether immigrants or natives), at least in the short run.[5] Therefore the distribution of jobs across regions will be constant in the short run. The distribution of firms may be thought of as reflecting an equilibrium that existed prior to the wave of immigration from the FSU.

6.2.4 Wages

An immigrant's productivity, and thus his wage, is determined by his age on arrival in Israel, his fluency in Hebrew and English upon arrival, and his work experience in the Israeli labor market, which reflects his general human capital accumulation. In order to maintain a stationary framework, it is assumed that the increase in wage as a result of the accumulation of work experience is random and occurs with a constant probability each period and a constant magnitude according to a Poisson distribution (such that the probabilities of a jump in wage and its magnitude are uniform for all immigrants). The number of possibilities for promotion as a result of accumulating experience is finite.

Firms are indifferent between immigrants with different characteristics (as long as they have the minimal level of education required for the position) since the wage paid to an immigrant reflects his marginal productivity. The wage paid in each position may also be influenced by the firm's location. For example, if a remote area is characterized by high transportation costs, firms there may offer their employees a lower wage since the selling price of the product is identical for all firms in the industry.

6.2.5 Job-Offer Probabilities

An immigrant's probability of receiving a job offer in each region and in each occupation while nonemployed is assumed to be constant over time, but may vary between immigrants with different characteristics (e.g., between immigrants who worked in different occupations in the FSU). We assume that the distribution of job quality (as reflected in the minimal years of schooling required) by occupation is identical to the actual distribution in Israel (see appendix table 6.A3).

An employed immigrant who is searching for a new job receives job offers at a rate that is linearly related to the intensity of his search and depends on his current place of residence, since the distance to the area in which he is searching may reduce his access to job offers.

6.2.6 Job Search

We assume that due to search costs, an immigrant can search for a job in only one area and in only one occupation during each period. The immigrant can search for a job in an area different from his current area of employment (and residence). However, once he finds a job, it is worthwhile for him to move to the area in which he will be employed.[6] Any job search while employed involves costs, which are expressed in the loss of a certain percentage of his current wage according to the effort invested in the search. However, it is assumed that there exists a limit to the effort that can be invested in the search, beyond which the immigrant will be fired.

6.2.7 Utility

Upon arrival, each immigrant wishes to maximize the current expected value of his utility in Israel. He does this by consuming an aggregate product Y and housing services. We assume that an immigrant's utility from the aggregate product is linear, that the demand for housing (i.e., the desired size of his apartment) does not depend on income or housing costs and is identical in all areas and that both components of the utility function are identical for all immigrants. However, immigrants also have nonmonetary preferences regarding their first place of residence in Israel and the occupation in which they first search following arrival in Israel. These are assumed to be random and heterogeneous, and unknown to the researcher. The income of an employed immigrant is his wage net of search costs, while an immigrant who does not find a job, either because he does not receive an offer or rejects the offers he does receive, is entitled to receive unemployment benefits, which are determined exogenously by the government.

6.2.8 The Immigrant's Problem

Under the assumptions above, the immigrant's problem upon arrival in Israel can be represented as the maximization of the present value of his income net of housing costs, plus nonmonetary utility. The immigrant's behavior in each period is characterized by the following joint decision rules: his place of residence, the occupation in which he will search for a job during that period, the intensity of his job search, and the lowest level of job quality (i.e., years of schooling required) that he will accept. The variables that determine the decision rules in each period include: housing costs, the probability of receiving job offers, the wage levels in the different areas and occupations, the cost of search, the level of unemployment benefits, the interest rate, the immigrant's labor market state at the beginning of the period, and his beliefs regarding future developments in the exogenous variables. It should be mentioned that since the model is stationary, the immigrant's choice of behavior strategy does not change solely as a result of the passage of time.

6.2.9 The Model's Predictions

Analyzing the theoretical model makes it possible to characterize several patterns of immigrant behavior in the labor and housing markets:

1. The monetary value of searching while nonemployed increases with the immigrant's years of schooling. This result stems from the fact that an immigrant with more years of schooling can use any decision rule used by an immigrant with fewer years of schooling, but he has a higher probability of finding a job using any given decision rule (since he is also suited for positions that require more years of schooling).

2. A nonemployed immigrant will not necessarily accept a job offer even if the wage offered is higher than his unemployment benefits since accepting the job raises the cost of searching for other jobs. Therefore

nonemployment in this model has two sources: lack of job offers and rejection of job offers.

3. There exist two ways for an immigrant to increase his wage: switching to a higher paying job and accumulating general work experience in the labor market while employed. Therefore the immigrant's situation is expected to improve with the length of time he is in the country.

4. An immigrant with a higher level of education will not necessarily search for his first job in the higher quality occupations, in which there may be a lower probability of receiving a job offer.

5. Each employed immigrant invests maximal effort (i.e., the greatest effort that will not lead to him being fired from his present job) in on-the-job search or does not search at all while employed. This is a result of the assumption that the probability of receiving a job offer while being employed and the lost wages while searching are a linear function of the effort invested in the search.

6. An employed immigrant who is searching for a job may accept a lower paying job if it is located in an area with lower housing costs.

6.3 Model Specification

6.3.1 The Value Function

The monetary value attributed by the immigrant to employment in occupation j in area d in a position that requires s years of schooling after receiving e promotions as a result of accumulating work experience in the Israeli labor market, while searching for a job in occupation k in area m, is denoted by $N_{ijd}^{km}(s,e)$. This value is calculated by finding the threshold positions in the current period and assuming that from now on the immigrant will behave in an optimal manner:

$$
\begin{aligned}
(1+\rho)\,N_{ijd}^{km}(s,e) = &\max_{\tau=0,1,r\leq s_i,\,rr\leq s_i}\ (1+\rho)\big[(1-\tau Q)w_{ijd}(s,e)-R_d\big] \\
&+\tau\lambda_{ik}^{dm}\delta\left[\sum_{x=r}^{s_i}p_k(x)N_{ikm}(x,e+1)+\left(1-\sum_{x=r}^{s_i}p_k(x)\right)N_{ijd}(s,e+1)\right] \\
&+\tau\lambda_{ik}^{dm}(1-\delta)\left[\sum_{x=rr}^{s_i}p_k(x)N_{ikm}(x,e)+\left(1-\sum_{x=rr}^{s_i}p_k(x)\right)N_{ijd}(s,e)\right] \\
&+\delta(1-\tau\lambda_{ik}^{dm})N_{ijd}(s,e+1)+(1-\delta)(1-\tau\lambda_{ik}^{dm})N_{ijd}(s,e),
\end{aligned}
\tag{6.1}
$$

where ρ is the interest rate, $r \in (0, 1 \ldots, S_i)$ is the possible choice of the threshold rule in a situation where the immigrant simultaneously receives a promotion and a job offer in occupation k, $rr \in (0, 1 \ldots, S_i)$ is the possible choice of the threshold rule in a situation where the immigrant receives a job offer in occupation k but no promotion, $p_k(x)$, $x \in (0, 1 \ldots, S_i)$ is the distribution of job-offer quality in occupation k (see table 6.A3), which does not depend on the area of employment, and

$$N_{ikm}(x, e) = \max_{j,d} N_{ikm}^{jd}(x, e), \qquad k, j \in \{0, 1, \ldots, J\}, m, d \in \{0, 1, \ldots, D\},$$

$$e \in \{0, 1, \ldots, E\},$$

$$N_{ijd}(s, e) = \max_{k,m} N_{ijd}^{km}(s, e), \qquad j, k \in \{0, 1, \ldots, J\}, d, m \in \{0, 1, \ldots, D\},$$

$$e \in \{0, 1, \ldots, E\},$$

$$N_{ikm}(x, e+1) = \max_{j,d} N_{ikm}^{jd}(x, e+1), \quad k, j \in \{0, 1, \ldots, J\}, m, d \in \{0, 1, \ldots, D\},$$

$$e \in \{0, 1, \ldots, E\},$$

$$N_{ijd}(s, e+1) = \max_{k,m} N_{ijd}^{km}(s, e+1), \qquad j, k \in \{0, 1, \ldots, J\}, d, m \in \{0, 1, \ldots, D\},$$

$$e \in \{0, 1, \ldots, E\}.$$

The first row in equation (6.1) represents a situation of employment in occupation j in a position that requires s years of schooling in area d after receiving e promotions, while paying the market rate of rent in that area. The second row represents a situation where the immigrant simultaneously receives a promotion and a job offer in the occupation in which he is searching. In this case the immigrant must decide whether to accept the offer. The third row represents a situation where the immigrant receives a job offer but no promotion and must decide whether to accept the offer, while the fourth row represents a situation where he receives a promotion but no job offer and a situation where he receives neither a promotion nor a job offer. $N_{ijd}(s, e)$ is the value of the optimal action in any given situation.[7]

6.3.2 The Wage Function

Offered wages depend on the location of the job, the occupation involved, the level of education required and the immigrant's personal characteristics and experience in the labor market. Specifically,

$$w_{ijd}(s, e) = (1+\delta)^e w_{ijd} exp^{\alpha_{j}s} \quad \text{if } S_i \geq s,$$

$$w_{ijd}(s, e) = 0 \quad \text{if } S_i < s,$$

(6.2)

where e is the number of promotions the individual has received as a result of his experience in the labor market, Δ is the rate of wage growth for each promotion received by the individual since he began working, α_j is the occupation-specific return on each year of schooling required by the job, and S_i is the individual's education (measured by years of schooling).[8]

The initial wage is given by

$$\ln(w_{ijd}(0,0)) = a_{0dj} + a_1 immage_i - a_2 immage_i^2 + a_{3j} english_i, \tag{6.3}$$

where a_{0dj} is a constant that depends on the location of the job and on the occupation, $immage_i$ is the immigrant's age on arrival, and $english_i$ measures the immigrant's weighted fluency in English.[9] Fluency in English can affect the wage differently in the various occupations. Fluency in Hebrew at the time of arrival is not included in the final equation since in preliminary estimations it was not found to affect the wage (note that as a result of the model's stationary framework, fluency in Hebrew at the time of the survey cannot be included in the wage equation). The parameters a_{0dj}, a_1, a_{3j}, and α_j were estimated in the full model.[10]

In order to simplify the estimation problem, it is assumed that each immigrant receives a promotion only once during his working life. The timing of the promotion is assumed to be a random variable that reflects the immigrant's success in assimilating within the labor market. It is assumed that the probability of receiving a promotion during each period is derived from a Poisson distribution. Therefore immigrant i's expected wage after T periods of working in occupation j and in area d is given by

$$E_0(w_{ijd}^T) = w_{ijd0}(s)exp^{-\delta T} + w_{ijd1}(s)(1 - exp^{-\delta T}), \tag{6.4}$$

where w_{i0} represents the immigrant's wage at the time of arrival, which depends on his personal characteristics, while w_{i1} is the wage following his promotion, which is attained only after accumulating experience $((w_1/w_0) - 1 = \Delta)$.[11]

During the estimation of the structural model, the wage received by the immigrant in his first full-time job was compared to the wage predicted by the structural model for the immigrant's actual area of residence and the occupation of his first job.[12]

6.3.3　Areas of Residence, Occupations, and Job Search

The number of occupations and areas of residence (and employment) were minimized in order to simplify the estimation problem. The occupations in which immigrants can search for a job in Israel were divided into two broad categories: (1) scientific, academic, and managerial occupations, and (2) technicians, licensed and other occupations, while the division into three categories described in section 6.2.2 was preserved for occupation in the FSU.[13]

The areas of residence (and employment) were divided into two categories: Center and Periphery, where the Center consists of towns in a given close radius of the three major metropolitan centers in Israel and the Periphery includes the rest. In other words, the criterion for classifying the areas of residence was proximity to the main areas of employment. In most cases the areas of residence closest to the main areas of employment are characterized by higher housing costs. A list of the cities included in the two categories is presented in appendix table 6.A2.[14]

Furthermore an immigrant's search possibilities while employed were restricted, such that only immigrants employed in occupation 2 could search while employed. They could search in a different area or in a different occupation in either of the areas. It is also assumed that immigrants who were employed in occupation 3 in the FSU can only search for a job while employed in occupation 2 since they do not have a real chance of receiving a job offer in occupation 1.

6.3.4 Job-Offer Probabilities

As mentioned, each immigrant can search for a job according to four combinations of area and occupation. A nonemployed immigrant's probability of receiving a job offer in any given month, λ_{ij}^{d}, depends on the area and occupation in which he is searching, the occupation in which he was employed in the FSU[15] and his age and fluency in Hebrew and English at the time of his arrival in Israel. Specifically,

$$\lambda_{ij}^{d} = L\left(\beta_{j} AGE40_{i} + c_{j} Hebrew_{i} + \omega_{j} Denglish_{i} + \sum_{k} \psi_{jR_{k}}^{d} occ_{ik}^{R} \right) \tag{6.5}$$

$$j \in \{1, 2\}, d \in \{1, 2\}, k \in \{1, 2, 3\},$$

where $L(l)$ is the logistic function given by $L(l) = exp^{l}/(1 + exp^{l})$, $AGE40_{i}$ is a dummy variable that takes the value 1 if the immigrant arrived in Israel at age 40 or older and 0 otherwise, $Hebrew_{i}$ is a dummy variable that takes the value 1 if the immigrant knew Hebrew at the time of his arrival and 0 otherwise, $Denglish_{i}$ is a dummy variable that takes the value 1 if the variable $english_{i}$ (defined in section 6.3.2) is less than 7 and 0 otherwise (as mentioned, a lower value for $english_{i}$ indicates greater fluency in English), and occ_{ik}^R is a dummy variable that takes the value 1 if the immigrant was employed in occupation k in the FSU and 0 otherwise.

For the purposes of estimation, it is assumed that the cost of job search is identical whether the immigrant is employed or nonemployed and that the probabilities of receiving a job offer are as well.[16] However, the probability of receiving a job offer when employed may depend on the current area of residence. Specifically, it is assumed that the probability of receiving a job offer in a given occupation in the Center for an immigrant residing in the Periphery is lower than the probability for an immigrant residing in the Center. The monthly probability of receiving a job offer for immigrant i who is searching for a job in area m in occupation j while employed in area d is given by

$$\lambda_{ij}^{dm} = \Theta\lambda_{ij}^m, \Theta = \frac{\varphi}{1+\varphi} \quad \text{if} \quad d = \text{peripheral}, m = \text{central}, \Theta = 1 \text{ otherwise.} \tag{6.6}$$

The monthly probability of finding a job for a nonemployed immigrant who is searching for a job in occupation j in area d is the product of the probability of receiving a job offer and the probability of him accepting it:

$$\gamma_{ij}^d = \lambda_{ij}^d \sum_{s=r_{ij}^{*d}}^{s_i} p_j(s), \tag{6.7}$$

where r_{ij}^{*d} is the immigrant's optimal threshold rule.

The monthly probability of switching to a new job for an immigrant who is employed in occupation 2 in a job that requires s years of schooling in the Periphery (area d) and is searching for a job in occupation j in the Center (area m) is given by

$$\gamma_{ij}^{dm}(s) = \lambda_{ij}^{dm} \sum_{s=r_{ij}^{*dm}(s)}^{s_i} p_j(s). \tag{6.8}$$

The following parameters were estimated: β_j, c_j, ω_j, $\psi_{jR_k}^d$, and φ.

6.3.5 The Immigrant's Choice on Arrival in Israel

It is assumed that the immigrant did not search for a job in Israel before his arrival. Therefore, upon arrival, he must choose his first place of residence before finding a job and the first occupation in which he will search (if he indeed decides to search). This dual choice will hereafter be referred to as a "path." The immigrant will choose the path providing the highest expected utility, where utility is derived from the path's monetary and nonmonetary benefits. Immigrant i's expected utility from a path that begins in area of residence d and with job search in field j is given by

$$U_i^{jd} = V_i^{jd} \exp(\theta \varepsilon_{ijd}), \tag{6.9}$$

where V_i^{jd} is the monetary value of the path (described below) and ε_{ijd} represents the nonmonetary utility from any possible first choice.

The monetary value that immigrant i attributes to residence in area d and job search in occupation j in that same area is given by

$$V_i^{jd} = \max_{r \le s_i} \frac{(b - R_d)(1 + \rho) + \lambda_{ij}^d \sum_{s=r}^{s_i} p_j(s) N_{ijd}(s, 0)}{\rho + \lambda_{ij}^d \sum_{s=r}^{s_i} p_j(s)}, \tag{6.10}$$

where b represents unemployment benefits (or income support) per period, λ_{ij}^d is the probability of receiving a job offer in the area and in the occupation that the individual chose to search in, and $\sum_{s=r}^{s_i} p_j(s)$ is the probability that the job offer that the individual receives is compatible with his skills ($s \le S_i$) and that he will agree to work at the offered wage.[17]

The monetary value for immigrant i of residing in area d without searching for a job is given by

$$V_i^{0d} = \frac{b - R_d}{\rho}. \tag{6.11}$$

This result is derived from the stationarity of the model.

The nonmonetary utility (which is unobservable from the researcher's point of view) that the immigrant attributes to each possible first state, ε_{ijd}, is added to the monetary value of each first state. This utility is derived from the immigrant's preferences for first area of residence and first occupation in which he will search.[18] ε_{ijd} is assumed to be iid, with an expectation of 0, according to the extreme value distribution, and θ is a vector of parameters to be estimated which represent the relative importance attributed to nonmonetary utility by immigrants who were employed in the various occupations in the FSU ($\theta = \theta_1, \theta_2, \theta_3$).

An immigrant will choose his first place of residence and the first occupation in which he will job search according to the total utility he derives from each situation. Given the structure of the nonmonetary utilities, the probability that an immigrant who was employed in occupation k in the FSU will choose a path that begins with residence in area d and job search in occupation j is given by

$$g_{ijd} = \frac{\left(V_i^{jd}\right)^{1/\theta_k}}{\sum_{j=1}^{2}\sum_{d=1}^{2}\left(V_i^{jd}\right)^{1/\theta_k}}. \tag{6.12}$$

From this equation it can be seen that when the value of θ is large, the importance of the nonmonetary component in the immigrant's decision increases, though the path with the highest monetary value has the highest probability of being chosen. Furthermore the probability of choosing any given path does not depend on proportional changes in V_i^{jd}. Thus, for example, it does not depend on the units in which the search value is measured (shekels, dollars, etc.). In the event that the observed value of all paths is identical, the probability of choosing each path is identical (i.e., 0.25).

6.4 Estimation and Identification

The model was estimated structurally using the maximum likelihood method. Structural estimation makes it possible to identify parameters that reflect labor market conditions in the different areas, as well as the behavioral parameters that reflect the immigrants' preferences regarding area of residence and occupation. Note that structural estimation requires simultaneous fitting of the model's outcomes (i.e., duration of nonemployment, occupation, area of residence, and wage) to the data.

The probability that immigrant i will find employment in area d in occupation j after a period of nonemployment lasting t_i months is given by[19]

$$l_{ijd} = g_{ijd}\gamma_{ij}^{d}(1-\gamma_{ij}^{d})^{t_i}. \tag{6.13}$$

When information also exists on the wage he received in his first full-time job, w_i, the expression becomes

$$l_{ijd} = g_{ijd}\gamma_{ij}^{d}(1-\gamma_{ij}^{d})^{t_i}\frac{\sum_{r_{ij}^{*d}}^{S_i}p_j(s)\phi\{(\ln(w_i)-\ln[\hat{w}_{ijd}(s,0)])/\sigma_d\}}{\sigma_d\sum_{r_{ij}^{*d}}^{S_i}p_i(s)}, \tag{6.14}$$

where $\phi(.)$ represents the probability of each event according to a normal standard distribution, $\hat{w}_{ijd}(s,0)$ is the initial wage (at the time of accepting the job) as predicted by the model, and σ_d is the standard deviation of the wage's measurement error in area d.[20] Because the quality of the job that the immigrant found is unknown, the deviation of the predicted wage from the actual one should be weighted over all possible alternatives.

The probability that immigrant i, who lives in area d and has been searching for a job for T_i periods, does not find a (full-time) job during the sample period is given by

$$l_{id} = \sum_{j=1}^{2} g_{ijd} (1 - \gamma_{ij}^{d})^{T_i}. \tag{6.15}$$

The calculation is performed over j because if the immigrant did not find a job, then the occupation in which he was searching is unknown (though his area of residence is known).

Thus the likelihood function for immigrant i is given by

$$
\begin{aligned}
&L_i(a_{0dj}, a_1, a_{3j}, \alpha_j, \sigma_d, \beta_j, c_j, \omega_j, \psi_{jR_k}^{d}, \varphi, \theta) \\
&= \prod_{d=1}^{2} \prod_{j=1}^{2} [l_{ijd}]^{Z_{ijd}} \times \prod_{d=1}^{2} [l_{id}]^{DDD_{id} - \sum_{j=1}^{2} Z_{ijd}},
\end{aligned}
\tag{6.16}
$$

where DDD_{id} is a dummy variable equal to 1 if the immigrant's first area of residence in Israel was area d, and 0 otherwise, and Z_{ijd} is a dummy variable equal to 1 if the immigrant was employed in occupation j and in area d in his first job in Israel, and 0 otherwise.

In order to explain the sources of identification, it is useful to divide the estimated parameters into three groups: (1) wage function parameters, (2) job-offer parameters, and (3) parameters representing the relative weight of nonmonetary components.

The wage function parameters are identified through the use of the actual wage in the estimation and because the estimated wage affects the immigrant's choice between areas of residence and the various occupations. The actual wage also makes it possible to identify the variance of the measurement error in the reported wage.

Identification of the job-offer parameters in the various occupations and areas is accomplished simultaneously with the identification of the immigrant's threshold rules (in terms of years of schooling) for accepting job offers. This is made possible by the data on the period of time until the first job was found, the location of the first job and its occupational category, and the heterogeneity between the immigrants with respect to those characteristics included in the job-offer supply function. The immigrants' threshold rules are obtained by solving their utility maximization problem for given parameters.

The monetary/nonmonetary weight parameters can be identified under the assumption that the distribution of nonmonetary preferences follows an extreme value distribution and as a result of the fact that the data includes the immigrant's first choice of area of residence and occupation.

6.5   Data

The main source of data is the Brookdale Survey of 1992.[21] The immigrants in the first sample lived in about thirty different cities, which approximately coincide with the geographical distribution of these cohorts during the first sampling period. The data includes demographic characteristics, such as occupation in the FSU and fluency in Hebrew and English, and area of residence.

Employment history was obtained through retrospective questions on jobs held by the immigrant since his arrival in Israel. The wage reported in the 1992 survey is that of the last job held. All employment data were expressed in monthly terms for the estimation.

The research focuses on a subsample of 328 men under the age of 56, who worked in the FSU before immigrating and who were surveyed again in 1995.[22] Since the empirical model was formulated using only the data on the immigrants' first choice of occupation and area of residence (see section 6.3), only the data from the first survey was used for estimation, while the data from the second survey was used for testing the model's predictions.[23]

Tables 6.1 and 6.2 present the distribution of the immigrants by occupation in the FSU and first full-time job in Israel (at least 25 weekly hours) according to area of residence and the distribution of other selected characteristics.

The difference between the occupations can be expressed in the time it takes to receive a job offer, in the distribution of the positions according to minimal required quality (s) and in the returns on the immigrant's characteristics (e.g., the return on fluency in English is probably higher in occupation 1 than in occupation 2).[24]

The main conclusions from table 6.1 are as follows:

1. A high percentage (43 percent) of the immigrants in the sample were employed in occupation 1 in the FSU (142 out of 328).

2. Upon arriving in the country, 63.4 percent of the immigrants chose to reside in the Center. This tendency was highest among immigrants who were employed in occupation 1 in the FSU and lowest among those employed in occupation 3. This reflects the decisions of immigrants who worked in occupations 1 or 2 for whom residing in the Center may be worthwhile in terms of labor market outcome despite the higher cost of housing.

The nonemployment rate in the sample is 11.9 percent (39 out of 328).[25] This rate is higher among immigrants who worked in occupations 1 and

Table 6.1
Distribution of immigrants by occupation in the FSU and in Israel and by area of residence in Israel

Occupation in Israel[a]	Area of residence	Occupation in the FSU[a]							
		1		2		3		Total	
		Number	Percent	Number	Percent	Number	Percent	Number	Percent
1	Center	17	12.0	5	5.5	0	0.0	22	6.7
	Periphery	10	7.0	0	0.0	0	0.0	10	3.0
2 (2 + 3)	Center	70	49.3	47	51.6	50	52.6	167	50.9
	Periphery	27	19.0	25	27.5	38	40.0	90	27.4
Nonemployed	Center	11	7.7	5	5.5	3	3.2	19	5.8
	Periphery	7	4.9	9	9.9	4	4.2	20	6.1
All	Center	98	69.0	57	62.6	53	55.8	208	63.4
	Periphery	44	31.0	34	37.4	42	44.2	120	36.6
	Total	142	100.0	91	100.0	95	100.0	328	100.0

Source: Brookdale Survey 1992.
a. For details on occupational classification, see section 6.2.2 in the text. Occupations 2 and 3 in Israel were combined in order to simplify the estimation.

Table 6.2
Distribution of choices by area of residence in Israel

Area of residence	Months in Israel	Nonemployment rate by occupation in the FSU				Employment in Israel			
						Occupation 1		Occupation 2 (2 + 3)	
						Nonemployment duration	Mean wage	Nonemployment duration	Mean wage
		1	2	3	Total	(months)	(NIS)	(months)	(NIS)
Center	21.9	11.2	8.8	5.7	9.1	5.9	2,618	3.8	1,599
Periphery	21.7	15.9	26.5	9.5	16.7	6.9	2,315	3.2	1,491

Source: Brookdale Survey 1992.

2 in the FSU (12.6 and 15.4 percent, respectively) than among immigrants who worked in occupation 3 in the FSU (7.4 percent). The higher non-employment rate among immigrants who worked in occupation 1 may indicate an attempt to find work in their occupation in Israel, which sometimes involves a relatively long period of nonemployment or professional training. The difficulty of finding a job in occupation 1 in Israel is reflected by the fact that only 19.1 percent (27 out of 142) of the immigrants who worked in this occupation in the FSU were working in the same occupation in their first job in Israel.

Table 6.2 shows that the probability of being nonemployed in the Periphery is higher for all groups of immigrants and that the mean wage is higher in the Center than in the Periphery for all occupations. Furthermore the average time required for an immigrant to find his first job in occupation 1 (for those who found employment) is shorter in the Center than in the Periphery. The data indicate that the labor market for occupation 1 in the Center is superior in all parameters to that in the Periphery, whereas for occupation 2 there is no dominance of one area of residence over the other (since the time until finding employment is shorter in the Periphery, but wages are higher in the Center).[26]

In addition to the Brookdale Survey, other data series, which are published by the Central Bureau of Statistics, were also used for estimation. The first is the 1993 Income Survey, which was used to estimate a supplementary model for the probability of receiving a promotion and the rate of promotion as a function of experience in the Israeli labor market. The survey included immigrants who came to Israel from the FSU in earlier waves of immigration (prior to 1989), thus making it possible to examine the longer run effects of work experience. The survey included 501 immigrants from the FSU who had lived in Israel for an average of 8.2 years.

Data on housing costs faced by the immigrants upon arrival in Israel were obtained from the Survey of Homeowners. The calculation of monthly housing costs (rent) in each of the areas of residence was based on the assumption that the value of an apartment is equal to the present value of the total monthly rent payments (using a mortgage interest rate of 6 percent) over an infinite horizon and assuming that the immigrants' apartments have 2.5 to 3.0 rooms. Based on this calculation, the monthly cost of housing in 1991 was 950 NIS in the Center and 630 NIS in the Periphery. Unemployment benefits were set at 1,000 NIS per month for the estimation and the (real) annual interest rate faced by the immigrants was set at 6 percent (which was found to best explain their behavior).

6.6   Results

Many of the parameters estimated in the structural model do not have a direct economic interpretation due to the model's nonlinear structure. Discussion of the results will therefore focus on the economic interpretation of the parameters rather than the estimated values (which are presented in appendix table 6.A4 along with their t-values).

6.6.1   Wage Parameters

The estimation results indicate that the constants for both occupation 1 and occupation 2 are higher in the Center than in the Periphery.[27] The model therefore predicts that the wage in the Center will be higher for any given job in all the occupations and for all immigrants (since the other parameters in the wage equation do not depend on the area of employment).

The estimated parameters indicate that the immigrants receive a low return on the experience they acquired in the FSU, which is represented in the model by their age at the time of arrival. The initial return on each year of experience is approximately 2 percent, whereas the effect of age squared is –0.00039.[28] This result indicates that the Israeli labor market does not consider experience from the FSU as relevant in Israel. The effect of the work experience accumulated by immigrants in Israel is captured by the possibility of a one-time wage increase, which was estimated through a supplementary model. The estimation results of that model indicate that the annual probability of receiving a promotion is 0.20 (i.e., a monthly probability of approximately 1.5 percent), whereas the (real) rate of promotion is 67 percent (both parameters are significant at a 5 percent level; R-squared = 0.34).

The effect of education (utilized years of schooling) on the immigrant's wage differs significantly between the two occupations: each utilized year of schooling in occupation 1 adds approximately 5.6 percent to the immigrant's wage whereas in occupation 2 it adds only 0.71 percent (the coefficient is not significant at a 5 percent level of significance). If an immigrant's wage reflects his productivity, then the immigrants who are employed in occupation 2 are not utilizing their human capital.

Another individual characteristic included in the wage function is fluency in English at the time of the survey. The estimation results indicate that perfect fluency in English adds 38.4 percent to the wage of an immigrant in occupation 1 relative to a complete lack of fluency. In contrast, the effect of fluency in English in occupation 2 is negative and significant. Complete fluency in English reduces the wage in this occupation by 18.4 percent. Fluency in English is apparently also an indicator of the immigrant's general abilities, the quality of his education and the quality of the experience he accumulated in the FSU. However, this explanation does not shed any light on the reason for negative returns on fluency in English for those employed in occupation 2. Fluency in Hebrew at the time of immigration was found to have no effect on wages, possibly because the immigrants learned Hebrew after their arrival.

The immigrants' mean predicted wage in any potential first job in Israel and in their actual first job (in both cases, before receiving a promotion as a result of accumulated experience), as well as data on their actual wages (expressed in terms of a 45-hour work week), are presented in table 6.3. The average predicted wage in occupation 1 was found to be higher than in occupation 2 for all groups. Table 6.3 also shows that the average predicted wage for each immigrant group in any occupation is higher in the Center than in the Periphery. The average predicted wage in occupation 1 in the Center for immigrants who were employed in occupation 1 or 2 in the FSU is 14 percent higher than the average wage predicted for these same immigrants in occupation 1 in the Periphery. Immigrants who were employed in occupation 1 in the FSU have a predicted wage in occupation 2 that is approximately 23 percent higher in the Center than in the Periphery. The average predicted wage in occupation 2 for immigrants who were employed in occupation 2 or 3 in the FSU is approximately 13 percent higher in the Center than in the Periphery. The estimated standard deviation of the measurement error is 0.31 in the Center and 0.26 in the Periphery.

6.6.2 Job-Offer Probability Parameters

One of the main factors determining the success of an immigrant' integration in the Israeli labor market and his first choice in employment is the supply of jobs in the various occupations and areas. However, not every job offer that an immigrant "receives" is relevant to him due to the minimum requirements of the position. Nonetheless, it is not necessarily optimal for an immigrant to accept any job offer that comes along.

The monthly probability of receiving a job offer for a nonemployed immigrant is a function of the occupation in which he was employed in the FSU, the occupation and area in which he is searching, and his

Table 6.3
Predicted and actual wages

Occupation in Israel	Area of residence		Occupation in the FSU			
			1	2	3	All
1	Center	Predicted wage	2,340	2,049	1,728	
		Predicted wage in actual first job[a]	2,607	2,368		
		Actual wage	2,632	2,584		
	Periphery	Predicted wage	2,047	1,790	1,528	
		Predicted wage in actual first job[a]	2,208			
		Actual wage	2,315			
2 (2 + 3)	Center	Predicted wage	1,624	1,539	1,560	
		Predicted wage in actual first job[a]	1,649	1,544	1,543	
		Actual wage	1,608	1,731	1,460	
	Periphery	Predicted wage	1,318	1,361	1,383	
		Predicted wage in actual first job[a]	1,326	1,370	1,409	
		Actual wage	1,513	1,479	1,484	
All		Predicted wage	1,780	1,576	1,469	1,634
		Actual wage	1,818	1,740	1,470	1,689

Sources: Brookdale Survey 1992 and authors' calculations based on the model's estimation.
Note: Wages expressed in 1992 prices (NIS).
a. Predicted wage for immigrants whose first job in Israel was in occupation j in area d.

individual characteristics, which include age[29] and fluency in Hebrew and English at the time of arrival in Israel. If the immigrant is employed in the Periphery while searching for a job in the Center, his probability of receiving a job offer may also be affected.

The estimated probability of receiving a job offer while nonemployed and that of receiving an offer that is suited to the immigrant's education (defined as the "effective probability") are presented in table 6.4. The results show that the effective probability of receiving a job offer is much higher in the Center than in the Periphery in every occupation (except in occupation 2 for immigrants who were employed in occupation 3 in the FSU). The gap between the areas is especially large for occupation 1 and indicates the low probability of receiving a job offer in this occupation in the Periphery. Furthermore it appears that the effective probability of receiving a job offer in a given area for all groups of immigrants is much higher in occupation 2 than in occupation 1. This helps explain the fact that the first job in Israel for an immigrant who worked in occupation 1 in the FSU is often in occupation 2.[30]

Table 6.4
Estimated job-offer probabilities while nonemployed

| Area | Occupation in Israel | Occupation in the FSU | | | | | |
| | | 1 | | 2 | | 3 | |
		Probability	Effective probability	Probability	Effective probability	Probability	Effective probability
Center	1	0.220	0.107	0.091	0.027	0.004	0.000
	2(2 + 3)	0.212	0.200	0.289	0.254	0.235	0.169
Periphery	1	0.129	0.063	0.003	0.001	0.000	0.000
	2(2 + 3)	0.177	0.167	0.163	0.143	0.320	0.230

Source: Authors' calculations based on the model's estimation.

The estimation results also demonstrate that the probability of receiving a job offer in the Center in each occupation while employed in the Periphery is 60 percent less than when searching while nonemployed or while employed in the Center. Consequently immigrants who choose to reside in the Periphery will find it difficult at a later stage to obtain job offers in the Center, especially in occupation 1.

Surprisingly, the effect of age on the probability of receiving a job offer in the two occupations was found to be positive (though significant only for occupation 2).[31] The positive effect of age may stem from the fact that only immigrants up to the age of 55 are included in the sample and that the older age group (40–55) also includes relatively young immigrants (around age 40). The effect of fluency in English on the probability of receiving a job offer in occupation 1 was found to be positive and significant, while the effect of fluency in Hebrew at the time of arrival was found to have a positive but not significant effect on the probability of receiving a job offer in occupation 1 (at the 5 percent level of significance).

6.6.3   Weight of the Monetary Component in Immigrants' Choices

The model includes three parameters that represent the importance attributed by immigrants to the monetary component of utility according to their occupation in the FSU. It was found that the highest importance was attributed by the immigrants employed in occupation 1 for whom θ_1 = 0.0726 (a smaller value indicates greater importance) while the weights attributed by those employed in occupations 2 and 3 in the FSU were θ_2 = 0.1277 and θ_3 = 0.1185, respectively. However, this parameter was not significant at the 5 percent level, such that the null hypothesis that these immigrants relate only to the monetary component of utility cannot be rejected. The values obtained are evidence of the low weight attributed by the immigrants to nonmonetary components.

The estimated coefficients can also be interpreted in another way, according to which they represent the estimated variances of the immigrants' errors in their maximization calculations. According to this interpretation, the weight of the error in the maximization calculations of the three groups is relatively low since the choice of path is made primarily on the basis of monetary value.

6.6.4   The Probability of Search on Each Path

Table 6.5 presents the probabilities of choosing each path, which are derived from a combination of the path's expected monetary value and

Table 6.5
Probabilities of choosing areas of residence and type of employment

Area of residence	Occupation in Israel	Occupation in the FSU		
		1	2	3
Center	1	0.207	0.132	0.002
	2 (2 + 3)	0.466	0.524	0.476
Periphery	1	0.083	0.000	0.000
	2 (2 + 3)	0.244	0.344	0.522

Source: Authors' calculations based on the model's estimation.
Note: Each column sums to 1.

its expected nonmonetary utility. The results show that the highest probabilities are obtained for the choice of occupation 2 in the Center by immigrants who were employed in occupation 1 or 2 in the FSU. This finding reflects the high probability of finding employment in this occupation and the immigrants' hope of finding a better job in the future (i.e., in occupation 1). The probability of this group choosing occupation 2 in the Periphery is also relatively high due to the low housing costs in that region. However, as shown by the parameters of the job-offer function, choosing employment in occupation 2 in the Periphery may prevent immigrants from later switching to a job in occupation 1. With regard to first location in Israel, the probability of choosing the Periphery for immigrants who were employed in occupation 1 or 2 in the FSU is lower than that of choosing the Center since the probability of receiving a job offer and the expected wage in occupation 1 are lower there than in the Center. The lower housing costs in the Periphery apparently do not fully compensate for the weakness in the labor market. Taking into account the skills of immigrants who were employed in occupation 3 in the FSU, their relevant options are to job search in occupation 2 in either the Center or the Periphery. Of these two, there is a higher probability of them choosing the path that begins in the Periphery than the one that begins in the Center (52 percent versus 48 percent).

6.6.5　Nonemployment

The mean monthly probability of finding employment is the product of the monthly probability of finding employment in each of the occupations and the monthly probability of choosing to search in each occupation. Table 6.6 presents the monthly probabilities of finding employment in the various occupations, as well as the predicted probability of not finding a job after having been in Israel for 24 months.

Table 6.6
Monthly probability of finding employment by first occupation and area of residence in Israel

| Occupation in the FSU | Monthly probability of finding employment | | | | Waiting period until start of job search (months)[a] | Probability of remaining nonemployed after two years in Israel |
| | Center | | Periphery | | | |
	Occupation 1	Occupation 2 (2 + 3)	Occupation 1	Occupation 2 (2 + 3)		
1	0.057	0.200	0.044	0.167	3.24	0.110
2	0.020	0.252	0.001	0.141	2.59	0.096
3	0.000	0.169	0.000	0.208	1.85	0.040
All	0.031	0.205	0.019	0.172	2.71	0.086

Source: Authors' calculations based on the model's estimation.
a. According to the Brookdale Survey.

The data indicate that for nonemployed immigrants who were employed in occupation 1 or 2 in the FSU, the monthly probability of finding employment is highest in occupation 2 in the Center. This is due to the high probability of receiving a job offer in occupation 2 in the Center and the willingness of immigrants searching in this occupation to accept almost any offer they receive. For immigrants who were employed in occupation 1 in the FSU and are searching for their first job in Israel in, for example, occupation 2 in the Center, the monthly probability of finding employment is 0.2, which implies an average period of nonemployment lasting five months.

The lowest probability of finding employment is expected for immigrants who are searching for their first job in occupation 1 in the Periphery. The estimation results indicate that the probability of remaining nonemployed after being in Israel for two years is highest for those employed in occupation 1 in the FSU and lowest for occupation 3. These results are apparently due to the tendency of better-educated immigrants to search in occupation 1, which is characterized by a low rate of job offers. As indicated in table 6.6, the immigrants in the sample joined the labor force soon after arrival: the mean "waiting period" was only 2.71 months. The waiting period is highest for those employed in occupation 1 in the FSU and lowest for occupation 3, which may indicate that better-educated immigrants first invest in human capital upon arrival.

6.6.6 Distribution of Immigrants by Area of Residence and Occupation

Table 6.7 presents the model's predictions for the distribution of the immigrants according to first area of residence and first type of job and compares it to the actual data in order to evaluate the model's fit.[32] The results indicate that for each occupation in the FSU, the model's predicted distribution (across areas of residence and occupations) cannot be rejected (at a 5 percent level of significance). However, the model is rejected when the distribution of all immigrants is tested simultaneously.

6.6.7 The Probability of Moving between Areas of Residence and Occupations

The choice of whether to search in the Center or the Periphery for immigrants searching for their first job in occupation 2 is influenced by the possibility of later changing their area of residence and/or switching to occupation 1. Although the observations of immigrants who moved from

Table 6.7
Actual and predicted distribution of first area of residence and first type of employment in Israel (number of immigrants)

Occupation in Israel	Area of residence	Occupation in the FSU							
		1		2		3		Total	
		Actual	Predicted	Actual	Predicted	Actual	Predicted	Actual	Predicted
1	Center	17	18	5	5	0	0	22	23
	Periphery	10	6	0	0	0	0	10	6
2 (2 + 3)	Center	70	60	47	45	50	39	167	144
	Periphery	27	30	25	26	38	44	90	100
Nonemployed	Center	11	18	5	10	3	6	19	34
	Periphery	7	10	9	5	4	6	20	21
Q-statistic for χ^2-test		8.31		5.83		6.09		14.05	
All	Center	98	96	57	60	53	45	208	201
	Periphery	44	46	34	31	42	50	120	127
	All	142	142	91	91	95	95	328	328

Sources: Brookdale Survey 1992 and authors' calculations based on the model's estimation.

one region to another or between occupations were not used in the estimation, the direct estimation of the maximization problem makes it possible to calculate the probabilities from the viewpoint of the immigrant upon arrival in Israel.

The results indicate that the immigrants had high expectations of improving their occupational situation in Israel. For example, the model predicts that an immigrant who was employed in occupation 1 in the FSU and was employed in occupation 2 in his first job in Israel, expected a 3.6 percent monthly probability (before receiving a promotion) of switching to occupation 1 (and a 3.9 percent monthly probability after receiving a promotion).

However, data collected in later years on FSU immigrants indicate a more modest rate for switching occupations. In the follow-up survey conducted by the Brookdale Institute in 1995, it was found that only about 18 percent of the immigrants who worked in occupations 1 or 2 in the FSU and who were employed in occupation 2 in their first job in Israel[33] were employed in occupation 1 at the time of the follow-up survey (when 33.8 percent of those who worked in occupation 1 in the FSU were employed in occupation 1, as compared to 19.0 percent of those in their first full-time job). In the Engineers' Survey, which was conducted by the Brookdale Institute in 1995 among approximately 1,500 engineers who came from the FSU during 1989 to 1994, approximately 24 percent of the men who were ever employed in Israel in nonengineering occupations were employed as engineers by the time of the survey.[34] In contrast to the immigrants who worked in occupation 1 in the FSU, the model estimates that the expectations of immigrants who were employed in occupation 2 in the FSU of moving from occupation 2 to occupation 1 were less optimistic: less than 1.2 percent per month before receiving a promotion and 1.4 percent subsequently. However, the follow-up survey also indicates that these expectations were not fully realized. Only 13.8 percent of the immigrants who worked in occupation 2 in the FSU who were employed in occupation 2 in their first full-time job in Israel were employed in occupation 1 at the time of the follow-up survey.

In addition the data of the follow-up survey indicate that in several cases the path for changing area of residence differs from that predicted by the model. Table 6.8 presents the proportion of each group of immigrants who actually changed area of residence by the time of the follow-up survey (only the first move between areas of residence is taken into account).

Table 6.8
Proportion of immigrants who changed area of residence

Occupation in the FSU	Path			
	P2 → C[a]	P1 → C	C2 → P	C1 → P
1	11%	10%	28%	18%
2	16%	[b]	40%	40%
3	3%	[b]	34%	[c]
All	9%	10%	33%	23%

Source: Brookdale Survey 1995 (follow-up).
a. Immigrants whose first job was in occupation 2 (2 + 3) in the Periphery who later moved to the Center.
b. The sample does not include any immigrants who were employed in occupation 2 or 3 in the FSU and whose first (full-time) job was in occupation 1 in the Periphery.
c. The sample does not include any immigrants who were employed in occupation 3 in the FSU and whose first (full-time) job was in occupation 1 in the Center.

Only about 10 percent of the immigrants who were employed in occupation 1 in the FSU and who upon arrival in Israel lived in the Periphery had moved to the Center by the time of the follow-up survey (after approximately four years on average in Israel; see table 6.8). This is in contrast to the model's prediction, according to which the monthly probability of these immigrants moving from the Periphery to the Center (after finding a job)[35] is 1.9 percent before receiving a promotion and 2.0 percent subsequently. Similar deviations from the model's predictions were found for the other immigrant groups.

The deviation of the model's prediction for the probability of immigrants who worked in occupation 1 in the FSU moving between the different regions is consistent with its overestimation of the probability of these immigrants moving from occupation 2 to occupation 1. However, while the model predicts that this immigrant group is not expected to move from the Center to the Periphery, the results of the follow-up survey indicate that over 25 percent of the immigrants who lived in the Center upon arrival in Israel had in fact moved to the Periphery since then.[36]

The model's overestimation of the probability of moving to the Center and its underestimation of the probability of moving to the Periphery may be due to the significant real increase in housing costs that took place during the sample period. Housing costs in both the Center and the Periphery increased by a nominal rate of approximately 75 percent between the last quarter of 1991 and the second quarter of 1995. However, since housing costs are lower in the Periphery, the same rate of increase

Table 6.9
Simulated probabilities of choosing the various paths and changing area of residence and occupation, assuming 1995 housing costs

Probability of choosing a path

Occupation in the FSU	Occupation 1				Occupation 2 (2 + 3)			
	Center		Periphery		Center		Periphery	
	Before[a]	After[a]	Before[a]	After[a]	Before[a]	After[a]	Before[a]	After[a]
1	0.207	0.147	0.083	0.121	0.466	0.386	0.244	0.345
2	0.132	0.103	0.000	0.000	0.524	0.503	0.344	0.394
3	0.002	0.000	0.000	0.000	0.460	0.476	0.522	0.539
All	0.127	0.092	0.036	0.053	0.485	0.440	0.352	0.415

Monthly probability of changing area of residence and occupation after receiving a promotion

Occupation in the FSU	P2 → C1	P2 → P1	P2 → C2	C2 → C1	C2 → P1	C2 → P2
1	0.010	0.021	0.004	0.036	0.005	0.000
2	0.008	0.000	0.000	0.016	0.000	0.008
3[b]			0.000			0.072
All[c]	0.007	0.009	0.000	0.020	0.002	0.023

Sources: Authors' calculations.
a. Before and after the increase in housing costs.
b. The model does not allow for immigrants who were employed in occupation 3 in the FSU to search for a job when employed in occupation 1.
c. The mean is calculated for the entire immigrant population.

in both regions may increase the attractiveness of housing in the Periphery.

In order to estimate the effect of the change in housing costs between the last quarter of 1991 and the second quarter of 1995 on the immigrants' choices, a simulation was carried out using the model's parameters.[37] The simulation results (table 6.9) indicate that housing costs have a large effect on the immigrants' behavior and on their probability of moving between areas of residence. In general, the real increase in housing costs led to a higher probability among all immigrant groups of choosing to live in the Periphery upon arrival in Israel. This change is especially large for immigrants who were employed in occupations 1 or 2 in the FSU (the simulation was performed assuming the labor market conditions that existed between 1990 and 1992).

For example, the mean probability that an immigrant would choose to live in the Periphery upon arrival in Israel and to search for his first job in occupation 2 increased from 35.2 percent for 1991 housing costs to

41.5 percent for 1995 housing costs. Similarly the mean probability of an immigrant choosing to reside in the Periphery increased from 38.8 to 46.8 percent.

Similar changes occurred in the probability of moving between areas of residence (and employment). Thus there was an increased probability of moving from the Center to the Periphery and a decreased probability of moving in the other direction. For example, the mean monthly probability of an immigrant in the Periphery, who was employed in occupation 1 in the FSU and in occupation 2 following his arrival in Israel, later finding employment in the Center decreased from 2.8 to 1.4 percent (after receiving a wage promotion). Furthermore the mean monthly probability that an immigrant from this group would move from the Center to the Periphery, which was negligible under the old housing costs, increased to a monthly rate of approximately 0.5 percent.

For the sample as a whole, there is a mean probability of 53 percent that an immigrant will choose to reside in the Center upon arriving in Israel and a 47 percent probability that he will choose the Periphery. The mean monthly probability that an immigrant who lives in the Center will move to the Periphery is 2.5 percent, whereas the probability of moving in the opposite direction is 0.7 percent.

In order to determine the quality of the predictions, the results were compared to the actual geographical distribution of the immigrants at the time of the follow-up survey (although, as mentioned above, the simulation does not accurately reflect the situation of immigrants who arrived in the early 1990s). The survey data indicate that at the time of the survey 52 percent of the immigrants resided in the Periphery and 48 percent in the Center.

In light of these results it is clear that the main factor accounting for the deviation of the model's predictions is the real change in housing costs, which led to an increase in the tendency to live in the Periphery. This can also explain the difficulty encountered by immigrants who worked in occupations 1 or 2 in the FSU in finding employment in occupation 1 in Israel since the probability of receiving a job offer in this occupations is lower in the Periphery than in the Center.

6.6.8   Utilization of the Immigrants' Human Capital in Israel

Both the survey data and the model's results indicate that many of the immigrants who came to Israel didn't expect to receive "full compensation" for their human capital during an initial period following arrival, that is, the potential wage an immigrant would receive if he were to find a job in his occupation in the Center immediately upon arrival in Israel. Nonetheless, not every loss in wage is expressed in a loss of utility since in certain cases it can be compensated for by unemployment benefits or lower housing costs (if the immigrant chooses to live in the Periphery). Still the nonutilization of human capital may have a social cost if the immigrants' tendency to reside in the Periphery is a result not only of market forces but also government intervention in the housing market.

Given the model's wage estimations, the present value of each immigrant's potential wage at the time of arrival can be calculated. Since the present value of the immigrant's expected wage in Israel can be also calculated, it is possible to calculate each immigrant's expected wage loss, which is expressed as a percentage of his potential wage.

Table 6.10 shows that the mean expected wage loss is 12.3 percent.[38] It is highest for immigrants who were employed in occupation 3 in the FSU and lowest for immigrants who were employed in occupation 1 in the FSU. When the first occupation on the path is taken as given, the loss is higher for paths that begin in the Periphery than those that begin in the Center. The difference in the expected wage loss between job search in the Center and job search in the Periphery is particularly noticeable for those searching in occupation 1 as a result of the differences in wages and in the probabilities of receiving job offers between the regions.[39]

The wage losses were calculated based on the immigrant's expected behavior, given the housing costs that existed in 1991. However, as indicated above, housing costs increased by tens of percent during the first half of the 1990s. This increase may have affected their behavior and as

Table 6.10
Expected wage loss as a percentage of the potential wage in Israel for each path

| Occupation in the FSU | Initial situation | | | | |
	Center occupation 1	Center occupation 2 (2 + 3)	Periphery occupation 1	Periphery occupation 2 (2 + 3)	Mean[a]
1	13.1%	5.8%	27.8%	12.3%	9.8%
2	36.4%	9.7%	88.7%	17.5%	13.6%
3	93.1%	13.9%	99.4%	15.3%	14.7%
All	42.7%	9.2%	65.4%	14.7%	12.3%

Source: Authors' calculations.
a. The mean expected wage loss for each immigrant group is calculated by multiplying the expected loss for each immigrant included in the group for each of the paths by his probability of choosing each path and then averaging over all immigrants included in the group.

Table 6.11
Expected wage loss as a percentage of the potential wage in Israel for each path, assuming 1995 housing costs

Occupation in the FSU	Initial situation				
	Center occupation 1	Center occupation 2 (2 + 3)	Periphery occupation 1	Periphery occupation 2 (2 + 3)	Mean
1	13.1%	27.0%	27.8%	17.7%	20.5%
2	36.4%	10.5%	88.7%	18.3%	14.3%
3	93.1%	14.4%	99.4%	36.4%	26.3%
All	42.7%	18.8%	65.4%	23.3%	20.5%

Source: Authors' calculations.

a consequence the utilization of their human capital as well. Therefore table 6.11 presents the same calculation of expected wage loss as that in table 6.10, except that the housing costs used in the calculation are for 1995.[40]

According to table 6.11, the rise in housing costs increased the immigrants' expected wage loss. The expected loss given 1995 housing costs is 20.5 percent, as compared to 12.3 percent given 1991 housing costs. The difference is explained, as already mentioned, by the immigrants' tendency to choose to live in the Periphery.

The data presented in tables 6.10 and 6.11 indicate the existence of a negative correlation between residence in the Periphery and the extent to which the immigrants utilize their human capital in Israel. The increased attractiveness of residing in the Periphery since the early 1990s may be explained by, among other things, the subsidization of housing costs (through the subsidization of construction costs, mortgages, etc.), a policy that was introduced at the start of the wave of immigration.

Table 6.12 presents the immigrants' expected wage loss at different rates of subsidization (beyond the subsidization that actually existed) in order to obtain an estimate of the effect of housing cost subsidization on the immigrants' wage loss in the Periphery. The results indicate that a significant loss of human capital occurred as a result of encouraging residence in the Periphery (even though the immigrants' behavior was optimal given the conditions they faced). This may also have had a negative effect on economic welfare since as a result of the heavy subsidization of the housing market in the Periphery immigrants did not take into account the real cost of housing in that region and became "too" concentrated in the Periphery.

Table 6.12
Simulated effect of rent subsidization in the Periphery on wage loss

Rate of subsidization as a percentage of rent in the early 1990s	Wage loss
0	12.3%
20	22.2%
40	26.7%
60	28.7%
80	29.4%
100	30.2%

Source: Authors' calculations

6.7 Comparison of the Model's Prediction to Other Data Sources

In this section the model's predictions of area of residence are compared to data from sources other than the Brookdale sample. The first comparison utilizes data published by the Central Bureau of Statistics on first area of residence for immigrants who arrived in Israel from the FSU in 1990. Although this data does not make it possible to identify each immigrant's precise place of residence (which is possible in the Brookdale sample), a crude sorting of the data into Center/Periphery indicates that approximately 56 percent of these immigrants reported that their first area of residence in Israel was in the Center (the remaining 44 percent reported that it was in the Periphery),[41] whereas the model's prediction is 61 percent for immigrants arriving in 1990–91. A possible reason for the discrepancy is the difference in age distribution between the model's sample, which only includes immigrants under the age of 56 on arrival, and the general population of immigrants arriving in 1990 since, according to the model's results, age (at the time of arrival) has a negative effect on the probability of choosing to live in the Center on arrival in Israel.[42]

The model's predictions were also compared to the data on FSU immigrants who arrived in Israel in the early 1990s and who were employed as engineers in the FSU. This group was sampled by the Brookdale Institute in 1994 (the study was unrelated to that used for the model's estimation). A total of 464 immigrants, whose characteristics are comparable to those of the model's sample (i.e., men who arrived in Israel during 1990–91 and whose age on arrival did not exceed 55), were included in this comparison. Approximately 61 percent of them chose the Center as their first place of residence, whereas the model's prediction for comparable immigrants (i.e., immigrants who worked in occupation 1 in the FSU) is 67 percent.

The model's predictions were also compared with the first choice of FSU immigrants who arrived in Israel in 2000. According to data of the Central Bureau of Statistics, approximately 43 percent of this group chose to reside in the Center upon arrival in Israel while the model's prediction for 2000 was 51 percent. The model's prediction was calculated using housing costs for 2000 and assuming that labor market conditions for new immigrants had not changed, in real terms, between 1990 and 1992 and 2000. Furthermore, in calculating the predictions for 2000, the immigrants' area of residence was normalized in order to reflect the distribution of the 2000 FSU immigrants by occupation.[43] An alternative comparison revealed that whereas, according to the data of the Central Bureau of Statistics, there was a 13 percent decrease between 1990 and 2000 in the number of immigrants who chose the Center as their first place of residence in Israel, the model predicted a slightly smaller decrease of 10 percent.

6.8 Conclusions

The data on the occupational integration of FSU immigrants indicate that they achieved only a partially successful integration in the labor market. This is particularly true for immigrants who worked in occupations 1 or 2 in the FSU.

The present study attempted to assess the influence of place of residence on immigrants' labor market outcomes. It therefore examined the first stages of the occupational integration process for a sample of male immigrants aged 25 to 55 on arrival using a dynamic model that combines job search decisions with the choice of area of residence (and employment). The model indicates that relatively cheap housing in a given area may compensate the immigrant (at least partially) for the labor market's weakness there. The estimation results also indicate that in choosing occupation and area of residence, the immigrants attributed greater weight to housing costs and labor market characteristics in each region than to nonmonetary characteristics.

In particular, it was found that the regional supply of vacant positions and the regional wage have a significant effect on the immigrant's location decision. The estimated supply of vacant positions indicates that immigrants do not have any particular difficulty in finding a job in any of the regions. However, immigrants who worked in occupation 1 in the

FSU have difficulty finding jobs in their occupation or in a similar one due to the small number of relevant job offers. This scarcity of job offers in occupation 1 is particularly noticeable in the Periphery relative to the Center. Moreover a difference of approximately 15 percent was found between wages offered in the Center relative to those offered for similar jobs in the Periphery.

The combination of labor market conditions and housing costs in the various regions, as they existed in the early 1990s, leads to the model's prediction that immigrants with an academic or technical education will tend to live in the Center and search for their first job in occupation 2. They will thus increase their probability of receiving job offers and at the same time maintain the possibility of advancing to occupation 1 in the future.

However, immigrants who do not have an academic or technical education will have a greater tendency to reside in the Periphery, where they will enjoy lower housing costs and a supply of suitable jobs at least as large as that in the Center. This prediction was strongly supported by the sample data. It should be noted that even if immigrants use optimal search strategies, such as those derived from the model, it can be expected that they will have difficulty fully realizing their wage potential in Israel due to periods of nonemployment, employment outside their occupation and residence in the Periphery where salaries are lower.

The estimation results indicate that given the housing costs and labor market conditions that existed in the early 1990s, the immigrants could expect an average wage loss of 12.3 percent relative to their potential wage. However, a simulation that tested the immigrants' expected wage loss given the housing costs that existed in 1995 indicated that it had risen to 20.5 percent. This is due to the significant increase in housing costs since the beginning of the decade, which increased the gap between housing costs in the Center and in the Periphery and therefore (according to the simulation results) enhanced the attractiveness of residence in the Periphery, which is characterized by a weaker labor market.

The simulation's prediction of an increase in the attractiveness of residence in the Periphery during the 1990s is verified by the data from the follow-up survey carried out by the Brookdale Institute in 1995 among immigrants who were included in the 1992 sample. It was also confirmed by a study performed by the Central Bureau of Statistics in 1995 among immigrants who came to Israel from the FSU in 1990 and by data on the first place of residence of immigrants who were employed as engineers in the FSU and arrived between 1990 and 1994.

The increased attractiveness of residing in the Periphery since the early 1990s can be explained by, among other things, the government's policy of subsidizing housing costs in these areas, which was adopted as the wave of immigration began. A simulation of the effect of an alternative policy that involves the full subsidization of housing costs in the Periphery indicated that it would have led to an increase of up to 30.2 percent in the mean expected wage loss.

The simulations presented here lead to the conclusion that although the policy of reducing housing costs in the Periphery does indeed induce immigrants to reside (and find employment) there, it has a negative effect on their ability to fully utilize their human capital. This may have negative effects on economic welfare (although not on the immigrants themselves, who choose the best strategy available), which should be taken into account by policy makers.

Appendix A: Supplementary Model for Estimating the Wage Premium and Rate of Promotion

Since the first Brookdale sample included immigrants who lived about two years in Israel, the data do not allow for the estimation of the probability of receiving a promotion as a result of accumulating experience (δ) or the rate of promotion (Δ). These two parameters were estimated using a supplementary model, whose estimation was based on the Income Survey conducted by the Central Bureau of Statistics. The survey included immigrants who arrived from the FSU since the establishment of the State of Israel, particularly during the 1970s, 1980s and 1990s. The estimation was based on the Income Survey of 1993, which included 501 immigrants from the FSU. The model was estimated according to the following equation:

$$\ln(w_i) = b_0 + b_1 immage_i - b_2 immage_i^2 + b_{3j} DD_j S_i - b_4\ exp^{-\delta T_i} + v_i, \qquad (6.17)$$

where DD_j is a dummy variable that takes the value 1 if the immigrant is employed in occupation j and 0 otherwise, S_i is the immigrant's number of years of schooling, b_4 is the estimated rate of wage increase as a result of the accumulation of experience in the labor market, T_i is the immigrant's number of years in Israel, and v_i is the random disturbance in observation i.

It should be noted that the structure of the Income Survey does not make it possible to directly identify the probability of receiving a promotion (δ) or the rate of promotion (Δ) since it does not include a follow-up for a given group of immigrants over time. Identification of these parameters is possible because immigrants who came to Israel at different points in time are included in the survey.[44]

Appendix B: Supplementary Tables

Table 6.A1
Distribution of immigrants who arrived from the FSU during 1990 to 1992 by occupation

Occupation	Percentage of all workers	Percentage of all employed males[a]
Occupation 1: scientific, academic, and managerial occupations	41.1%	39.7%
Academic professionals in the life and natural sciences	1.6%	1.5%
Engineers and architects	24.0%	29.8%
Physicians, dentists, and dental practitioners	5.2%	4.2%
Pharmacists and veterinarians	0.6%	0.2%
Lawyers and academic professionals in the social sciences	5.0%	3.1%
Teachers in higher, secondary, and postsecondary education	0.4%	0.2%
Managers	4.3%	0.7%
Occupation 2: technical and licensed occupations	33.8%	26.6%
Teachers in intermediary and primary schools and kindergarten	9.8%	3.2%
Authors, artists, composers, and journalists	4.8%	4.9%
Nurses and paramedical professions	4.5%	1.2%
Technicians in the natural sciences, engineering technicians, systems analysts, and programmers	11.5%	13.5%
Other professionals	3.2%	3.8%
Occupation 3: all other occupations	25.1%	33.7%
Sales workers, agents, and retail workers	2.5%	1.3%
Service workers	3.9%	2.4%
Farm workers	0.0%	0.1%
Skilled workers in industry, construction, and transportation	14.5%	24.1%
Unskilled workers	4.2%	5.8%

Source: CBS Statistical Abstract.
Note: Proportion of immigrants employed in the FSU.
a. Data on the distribution of occupations are available for all the years; data on the distribution by gender are available only for 1992.

Table 6.A2
Classification of cities by area—Center and Periphery

Center	Periphery	
Azur	Acre	Ma'ale Edomim
Bat-Yam	Afula	Ma'alot
Benei Brak	Amirim	Migdal Ha'Emek
Givataim	Ariel	Mitzpe Ramon
Haifa	Ashdod	Naharia
Herzlia	Ashkelon	Nazareth
Holon	Beer Sheba	Nazareth Ilit
Jerusalem	Beit Shemesh	Nesher
Kfar Saba	Beit Yehoshua	Netanya
Kfar Warburg	Carmiel	Netiv Ha'Lamed He
Lod	Dimona	Ofakim
Nes Ziona	Ein Hashlosha	Or Akiva
Petach Tikva	Gan Yavne	Orot
Ra'anana	Hadera	Pardes Hana
Ramat Gan	Hermesh	Rechasim
Ramla	Kfar Giladi	Rosh Ha'Ayin
Rehovot	Kiryat Arba	Shavei Zion
Rishon Le'Zion	Kiryat Ata	Tel Mond
Tel-Aviv	Kiryat Bialik	Tiberias
Yahud	Kiryat Gat	Tirat Ha'Carmel
	Kiryat Malachi	Yad Hana
	Kiryat Motzkin	Yavne
	Kiryat Tivon	Yokneam
	Kiryat Yam	Zefat
	Ma'agan Michael	

Table 6.A3
Distribution of Israeli men by occupation and their job's required years of schooling (1991)

Years of schooling[a]	Occupation 1	Occupation 2 (2 + 3)
1–4	0.0001[b]	0.0326
5–8	0.0001[b]	0.1872
9–10	0.0022	0.1606
11–12	0.0114	0.3880
13–14	0.0630	0.0994
15	0.0630	0.0497
16	0.3000	0.0330
17	0.3000	0.0330
18+	0.2602	0.0165

Source: CBS Labor Force Survey.
a. The maximal value in each cell was used in the estimation to calculate job quality (e.g., the value 4 in a cell with the values 1–4).
b. According to the data, there were no jobs in occupation 1 that require this level of education. However, in order to avoid the total absence of these types of jobs, a small positive probability was assigned to them.

Table 6.A4
Estimated parameters

Parameter	Estimate	t-Value
Wage parameters		
Constant for occupation 1 in the Center	0.6864	30.03
Constant for occupation 2 (2 + 3) in the Center	0.6950	29.07
Constant for the Periphery	0.6741	28.95
Age	0.0209	7.05
Age squared[a]	0.0004	
Fluency in English in occupation 1	−0.0320	−2.16
Fluency in English in occupation 2 (2 + 3)	0.0153	2.11
Education in occupation 1	0.0559	4.08
Education in occupation 2 (2 + 3)	0.0071	0.39
Standard deviation of the reported wage in the Center	0.3053	15.54
Standard deviation of the reported wage in the Periphery	0.2630	10.66
Job-offer probability parameters		
Occupation in the FSU and in Israel and area of residence		
1 → 1 Center	−1.6449	−4.97
1 → 1 Periphery	−2.2989	−7.70
1 → 2 + 3 Center	−1.4058	−8.59
1 → 2 + 3 Periphery	−1.6333	−5.52
2 → 1 Center	−2.3941	−5.84
2 → 1 Periphery[a]	−5.8965	
2 → 2 + 3 Center	−0.9671	−5.34
2 → 2 + 3 Periphery	−1.7082	−7.35
3 → 1 Center	−5.7235	−3.21
3 → 1 Periphery[a]	−8.4148	
3 → 2 + 3 Center	−1.2454	−7.76
3 → 2 + 3 Periphery	−0.8146	−4.48
Age in occupation 1	0.3334	0.53
Age in occupation 2 (2 + 3)	0.5045	1.71
Fluency in English in occupation 1	0.6163	1.68
Employment in the Periphery (effect on Center job-offer probability)	0.4186	3.08
Weight of the monetary component in choosing a path		
Immigrants who were employed in occupation 1 in the FSU	0.0726	2.96
Immigrants who were employed in occupation 2 in the FSU	0.1277	1.96
Immigrants who were employed in occupation 3 in the FSU	0.1185	0.50
Number of observations	328	
Value of likelihood function	−3.4378	

a. Parameters estimated outside the framework of the maximum likelihood estimation due to limitations in the data that created difficulties in identification.

7 Immigrants from the FSU after Twenty Years in Israel: Evidence and Interpretation

7.1 Introduction

The previous chapters followed the immigrants who arrived from the FSU during the period 1990 to 1995 over a relatively short period, that is, up to ten years. We now have data on these immigrants up to 2009, which can provide a longer run perspective of this dramatic event in Israel's history. This concluding chapter provides a descriptive summary of the integration process of FSU immigrants who arrived in Israel in the early wave of 1989 to 1991, which we follow for almost two decades, until 2009. We show that most of the dynamic adjustments in wages and occupation took place in the early years, while in the longer run, immigrants had higher participation rates and lower unemployment rates than comparable native Israelis. However, their wages never converged to those of comparable native Israelis. This is partly because immigrants earned less than natives in the same type of occupation and partly because some highly educated immigrants failed to find a white-collar job.[1] For instance, male immigrants who arrived from the FSU in 1990–91 aged 25 to 40 with a college degree and worked in a white-collar job in 2008 earned about 29 percent less than comparable native Israelis. However, only 56 percent of these immigrants had a white-collar job by 2008, as compared to 74 percent of native Israelis with the same age and education. Consequently, on average, the college-educated immigrants who arrived in 1990–91 aged 25 to 40 earned 42 percent less than comparable natives in 2008.

In addition to the long-term economic indicators, broader social indicators of long-term integration are presented. These include place of residence (especially with regard to the decision of whether to move into an enclave), home ownership, and marriage patterns for those who married in Israel, as well as the rate of out-migration.

Specifically, we observe a tendency among FSU immigrants to move into enclaves. This observation combined with the total absolute size of the group has made it possible for FSU immigrants to maintain their language and culture. In addition, since most of these enclaves are not located in the Center, the gradual move of immigrants to the Periphery was accompanied by a shift from rental to home ownership.

The marriage patterns of male and female immigrants who married in Israel show substantial differences between genders. While among male immigrants there is a strong tendency to marry an immigrant with only 10 percent marrying a native, about 36 percent of the female immigrants married a native. We also present data on out-migration, which reflects the long-term integration of immigrants. According to the main observation, survival rates among FSU immigrants are very high and range between 88 and 98 percent depending on age on arrival and schooling. Younger immigrants are more likely to leave the country and within the group of immigrants who were younger on arrival, better-educated immigrants have a higher propensity to out-migrate. Overall, the various indicators suggest that the large scale of this wave of immigration acted to create a relatively supportive environment for FSU immigrants in Israel, which enabled them to continue using the Russian language and to maintain cultural traditions. This made it possible for them to avoid complete assimilation and loss of identity. Furthermore the relatively higher survival rates among better-educated prime-age women and the higher rate of marriage between female immigrants and male natives is consistent with the sociological literature on the integration of FSU immigrants that documents a smoother integration among females (Remennick 2005).

7.2 Employment, Occupations, and Wages

In order to describe the integration patterns of FSU immigrants in the labor market during their first 20 years in Israel, we use two annual nationwide surveys for the period 1989 to 2009: the Labor Force Survey (LFS) and the Income Survey (IS), which are both carried out by the CBS. We define two broad occupational categories: (1) white-collar jobs (WC), which include scientific and academic occupations, managers, technical workers, and other professional occupations; and (2) blue-collar jobs (BC), which include all other occupations.[2] The data indicate that FSU immigrants entered the Israeli labor force within a short period of time and were willing to accept jobs in low-wage BC occupations. This was followed by a second phase in which highly educated immigrants upgraded to better jobs in WC occupations and their wages rose accordingly. This second phase involved a slow and gradual process that lasted about ten years. From that point on, immigrants' employment and occupational status stabilized, while their wages continued to grow at moderate rates. As will be shown, this general pattern differed in intensity and pace among the immigrants, according to level of imported schooling, age on arrival and gender.

Figure 7.1a and b plots the labor market states for male and female FSU immigrants who arrived during the period 1989 to 1991. We distinguish between three possible labor market states: employment in WC jobs, employment in BC jobs, and unemployment.[3] As mentioned in the previous chapters, immigrants entered the labor market soon after arrival. While 20 percent of the male immigrants were unemployed after two years in Israel, by the fifth year the unemployment rate had dropped to about 4.8 percent. The proportion of male immigrants employed in BC jobs reaches a peak of almost 70 percent after four years and then starts to gradually decline as immigrants move to WC jobs. Figure 7.1b presents the same information for female immigrants and shows that the employment trends of women were quite similar to those of men. The main difference between them is a more rapid decline in unemployment for men.[4] The figures show that most of the adjustment in employment occurred during the first decade, with little change in subsequent years. We can see that even after twenty years in Israel, the majority of FSU immigrants are still employed in BC jobs, although, as shown below, this outcome is mainly a characteristic of immigrants who arrived with a low level of schooling.

Figure 7.2a and b compares the rates of unemployment among male and female immigrants according to schooling and age on arrival. We distinguish between two levels of schooling: 0 to14 years and 15 years or more and between two groups for age on arrival: 25 to 40 years old and 41 to 55 years old. It can be seen in figure 7.2a that male immigrants with a high level of education are initially more likely to be unemployed than those with a lower level. This reflects two related processes: First, employers who are uncertain about the immigrants' skill levels are hesitant to offer them WC jobs and at the same time immigrants with high levels of education are reluctant to accept BC jobs. With the passage of time, however, after some sorting out has taken place, unemployment declines among higher educated workers. This in fact is the normal pattern among Israeli workers and in most other countries as well. Among female

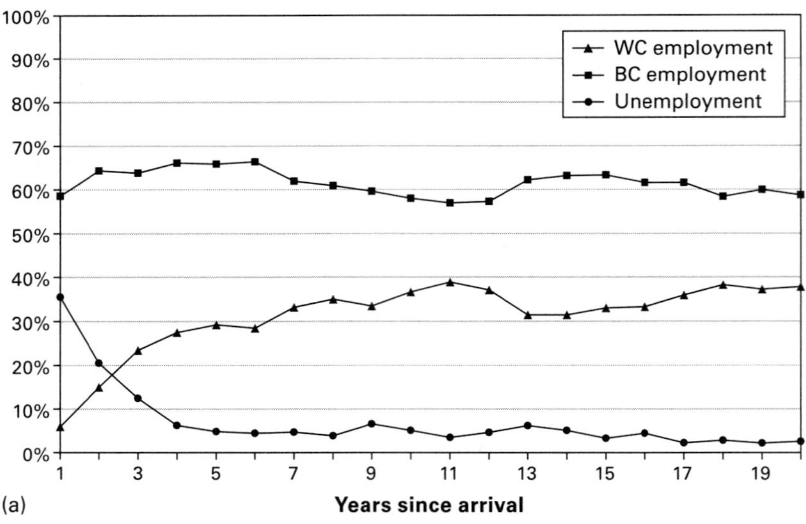

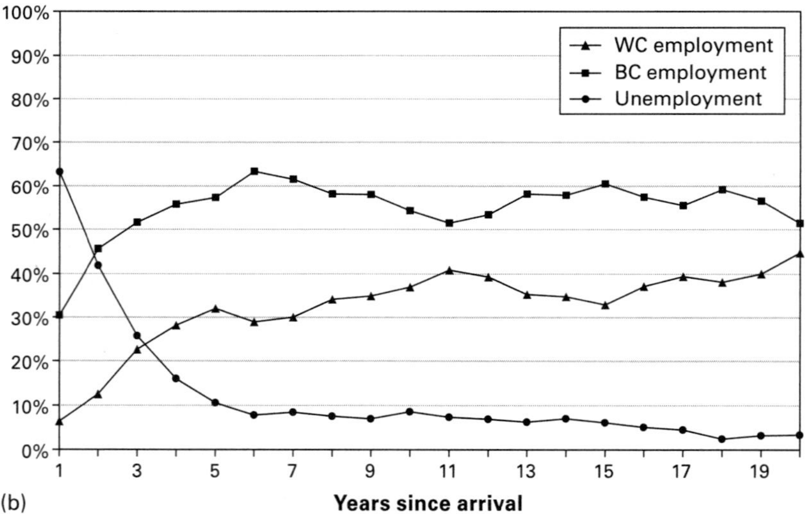

Figure 7.1
Labor market integration of immigrants, repeated cross-sectional data: (a) Males; (b) females. Immigrated during 1989 to 1991, aged 25 to 40 on arrival. Proportions of labor force participants. For details on occupation classification, see section 7.2 in the text. Source: CBS Labor Force Survey.

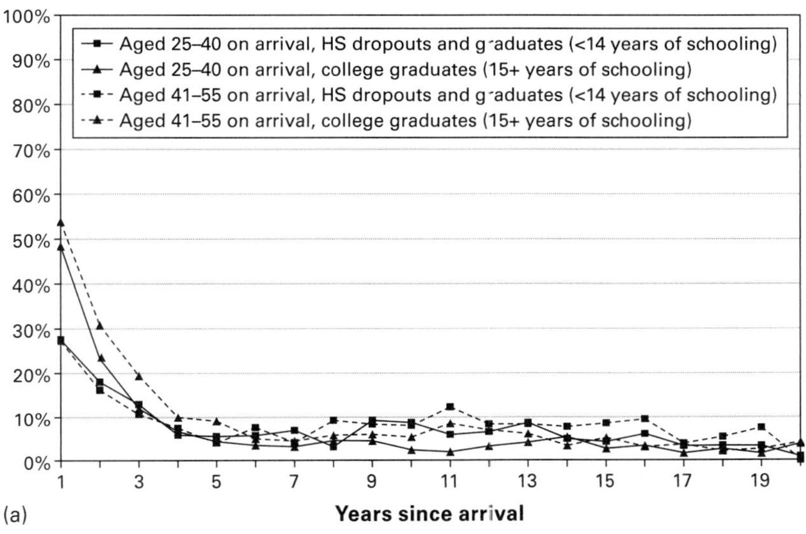

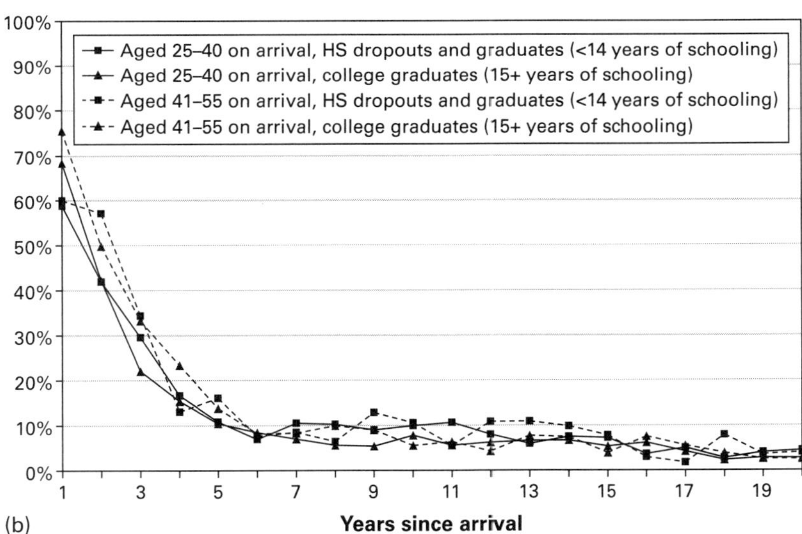

Figure 7.2
Unemployment rate of immigrants. (a) Males; (b) females. Immigrated during 1989 to 1991.
Source: CBS Labor Force Survey.

immigrants with higher levels of education (figure 7.2b) this selectivity is less pronounced than among male immigrants, probably because their chances of finding any job are much lower.

The most remarkable feature of the unemployment data is that the rates of unemployment among immigrants decline continuously with time since arrival and by 2009 they converge to within a range of only 2 to 6 percent (for immigrants who arrived aged 25 to 40 and depending on gender and education). Toward the end of the period, unemployment rates for male immigrants are the same or lower than those of comparable natives. Female immigrants generally have higher rates of unemployment and their convergence to the unemployment rates of natives occurred at a later stage (see figure 7.3a and b). In general, immigrants were willing and able to find jobs in Israel and within less than five years their unemployment rates were below the national average.

Immigrants who arrived at a later age or with less education had higher initial unemployment rates and a slower subsequent decline in unemployment. As can be seen in figure 7.2a, the unemployment rate of male immigrants who arrived at age 41 to 55 was 19 percent after three years if they had a college degree and 11 percent if they arrived with less than 14 years of education. After 11 years in Israel these rates were 9 and 12 percent, respectively, and after 19 years they were 2.5 and 7.5 percent, respectively. Among female immigrants who arrived aged 41 to 55 (figure 7.2b) initial rates of unemployment were high: 33 percent for those with a college degree and 34 percent for those without. However, the decline in unemployment was much faster than for male immigrants, reaching 6 percent after 11 years in Israel, regardless of level of education. Generally, figure 7.2a and b shows that the differences in unemployment are more pronounced according to age on arrival than according to schooling.

We now consider the process of occupational upgrading. Figure 7.4a and b displays the proportion of employed immigrants in WC jobs by schooling and age on arrival. Among immigrants who arrived in 1989 to 1991 aged 25 to 40 with a college degree, the proportion working in WC jobs in 2009 is 53 percent for men and 61 percent for women (see figure 7.5a and b). However, as can be seen, the comparable rates for native Israelis are substantially higher: 74 percent for men and 75 percent for women. Thus, in contrast to the convergence in employment, there is no convergence in occupation, conditioned on schooling and age. Immigrants who arrived at an older age display a slower rate of occupational upgrading. Among the immigrants who arrived aged 41 to 55 with a

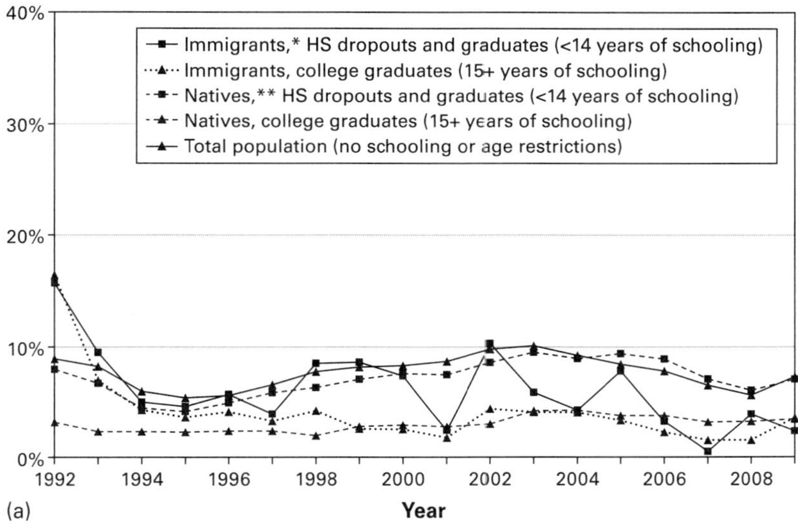

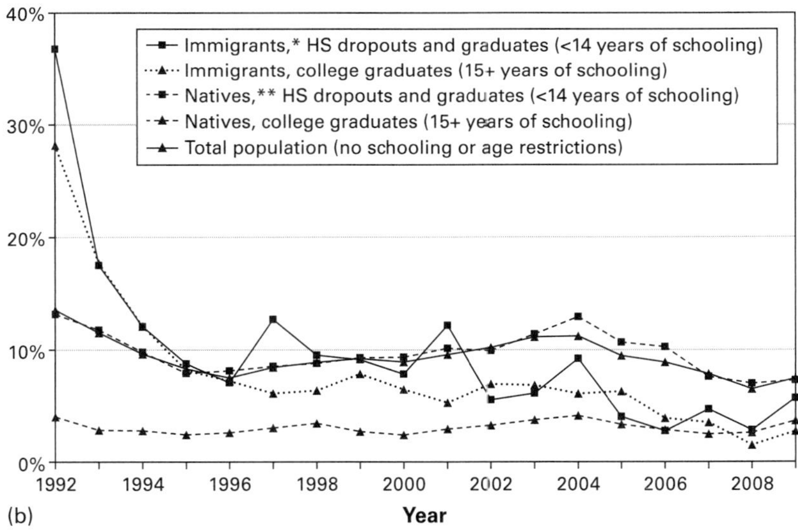

Figure 7.3
Unemployment rate by schooling. (a) Males; (b) females. *Immigrated during 1989 to 1991
and aged 25 to 40 on arrival; **born in Israel or immigrated prior to 1989, 1949–66 cohorts
(aged 25–40 in 1989–91). Source: CBS Labor Force Survey.

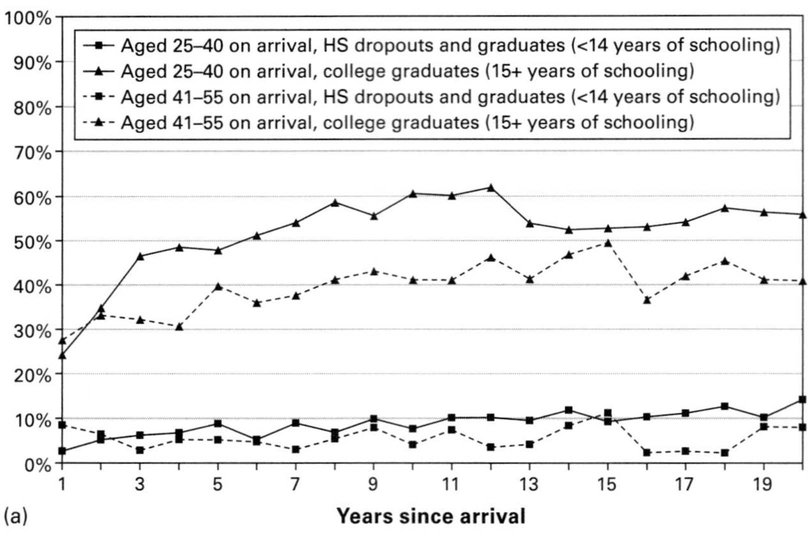

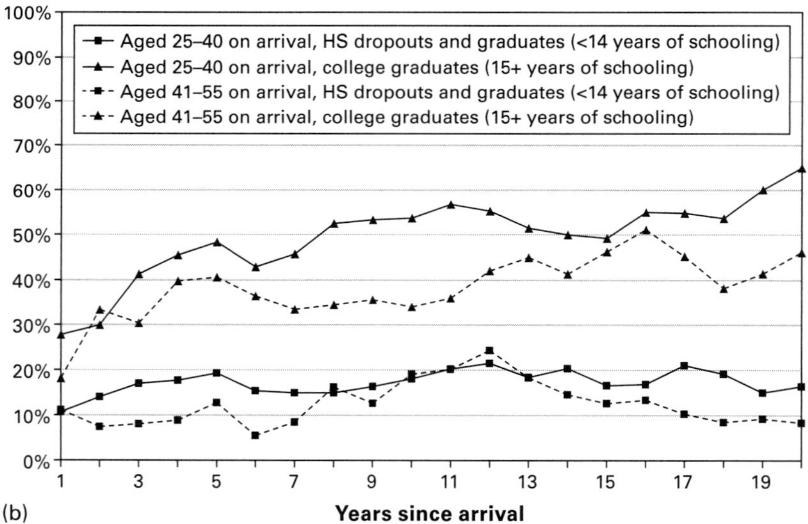

Figure 7.4
Workers in WC jobs. (a) Males; (b) females. Immigrated during 1989 to 1991. Percent of workers in each year. Source: CBS Labor Force Survey.

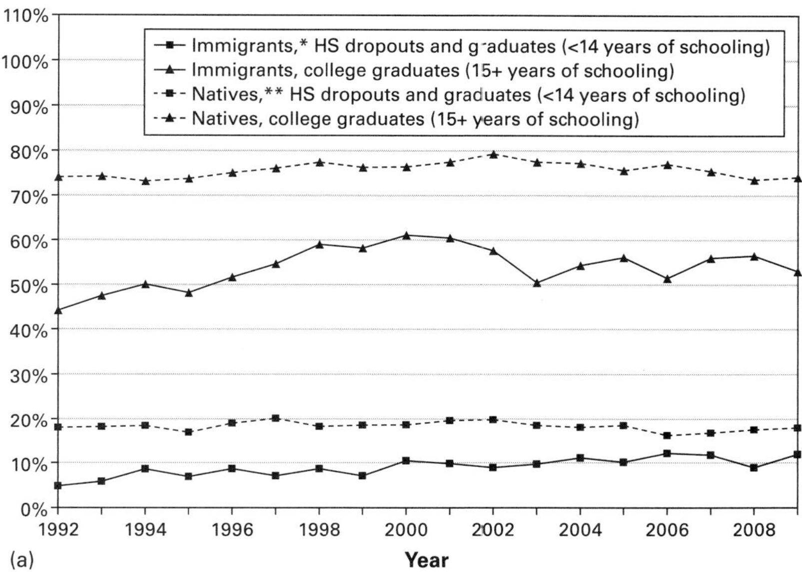

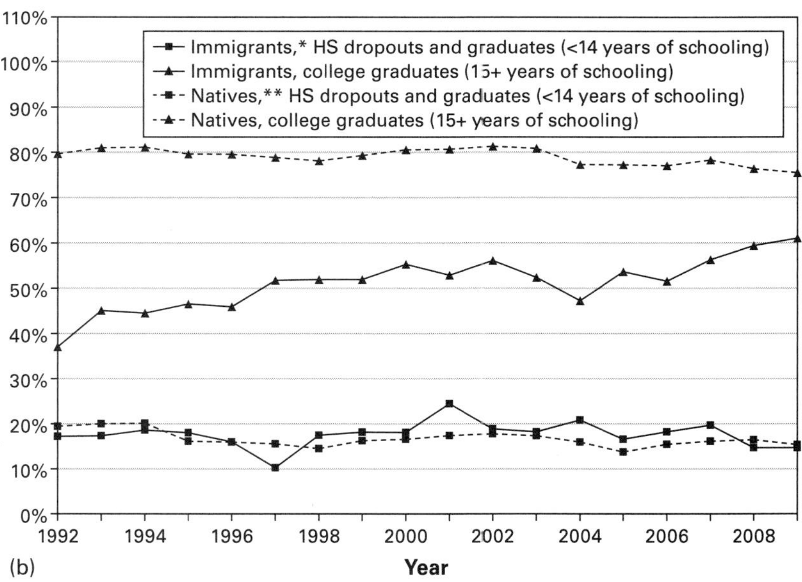

Figure 7.5
Workers in WC jobs by schooling. (a) Males; (b) females. *Immigrated during 1989 to 1991 and aged 25 to 40 on arrival; **born in Israel or immigrated prior to 1989, 1949–66 cohorts (aged 25–40 in 1989–91). Percent of workers in each year. Source: CBS Labor Force Survey.

college degree, only 41 percent of men and women were working in a WC occupation after 19 years in Israel.

There is also lack of convergence in wages. As can be seen in figure 7.6a and b, the hourly wages of both male and female immigrants remain lower than those of comparable natives throughout the period 1992 to 2008. By 2008, immigrants who arrived in 1990–91 aged 25 to 40 earned 42 percent less than comparable native Israelis if they arrived with a college degree and 22 percent less if they arrived without. The comparable figures for female immigrants are 28 and 29 percent.[5] Thus, although female immigrants earn less than male immigrants, their wage gap relative to natives is smaller than that of men, especially among the college educated. This outcome can be traced back to figure 7.5a and b, which shows that female immigrants with a college education are more likely to hold a WC job in 2008 than college-educated male immigrants. Thus, despite the higher initial rates of unemployment among female immigrants, their long-term wage and employment outcomes relative to comparable natives are better than those of male immigrants.

The lack of convergence in wages is most pronounced for male immigrants with a college degree. These immigrants enjoyed substantially higher wage growth than less-educated immigrants and college-educated native Israelis. However, because the wages of less-educated native Israelis have not risen much over time, while those of native Israelis with a college degree have risen substantially, educated immigrants had less success in catching up with natives than less-educated immigrants.

Generally, the wage dynamics differ from those of employment since the wages of immigrants, especially educated ones, continue to grow throughout the period. Following arrival, most of the immigrants worked in low-wage, blue-collar jobs and were characterized by low average wages and low variance according to schooling and experience acquired in the FSU. As can be seen in the data, the wages of both female and male immigrants who arrived during 1990–91 grew rapidly in the initial years following arrival, which was even more pronounced among better-educated male and female immigrants, whose wage growth exceeds even that of educated native Israelis. For less-educated immigrants, wage growth is only moderate and more closely resembles that of native Israelis. These patterns continue throughout the first decade, until about 2001. In subsequent years the wages of immigrants with less than 14 years of schooling stabilized, while the wages of immigrants with a college education continue to grow. During the period 1992 to 2008 the wages of men grew by 67 percent for immigrants with a college education, 40.7 percent

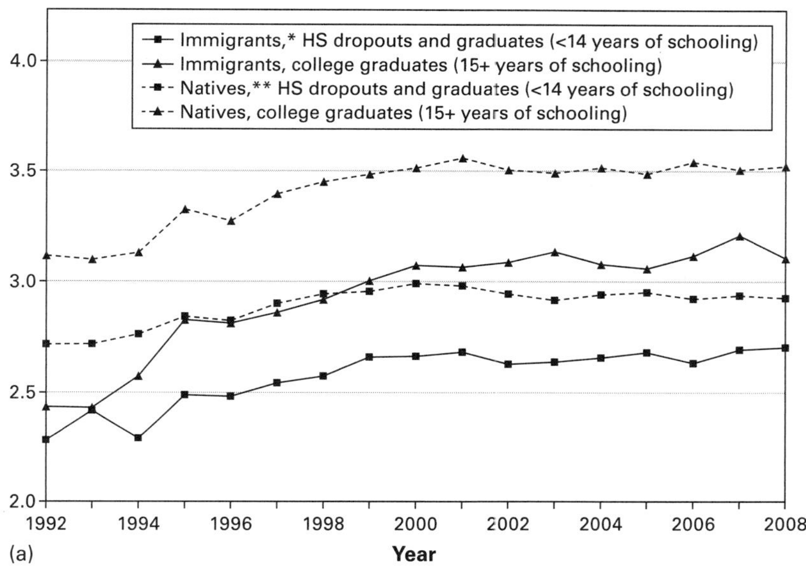

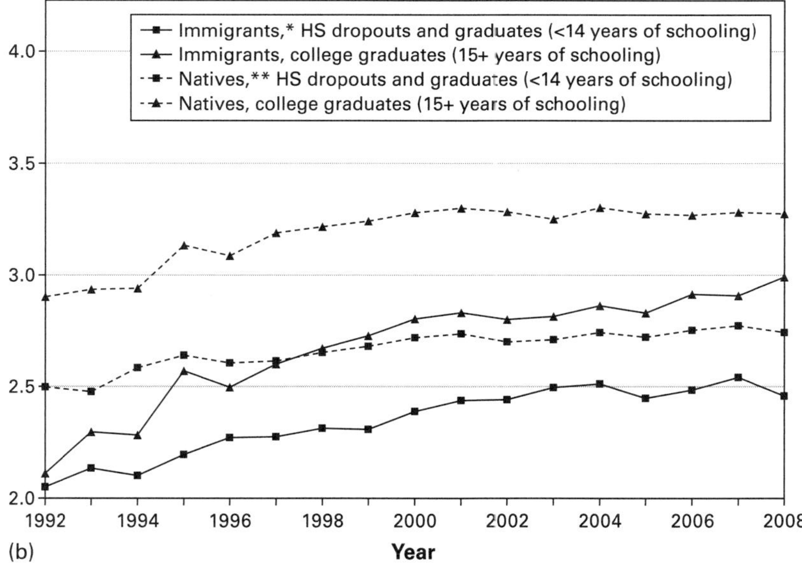

Figure 7.6
Log hourly wages by schooling. (a) Males; (b) females. *Immigrated during 1990–91; **born in Israel or immigrated prior to 1990. Wages expressed in 1992 prices; 1950 to 1966 cohorts (aged 25 to 40 in 1990–91). Source: CBS Income Survey.

for natives with a college education, 42.3 percent for immigrants without a college degree, and 20.9 percent for natives without a college degree.

In addition to the changes in average wages, there were important changes in the dispersion of immigrant wages. As time in Israel increased, the process of occupational upgrading raised both the average and the variance of wages. The explanation for these two related outcomes lies in the fact that immigrants are sorted out over time and are eventually matched with jobs that better suit their local skills. Figure 7.7a and b presents the variance of log hourly wages by schooling for men and women, respectively. It can be seen that variance increases with level of schooling and that for immigrants with 15+ years of schooling it increases with time in Israel. Sorting was more important for immigrants with a high level of imported schooling, in part because of employers' uncertainty regarding the quality of schooling in different regions of the FSU and in part because educated workers were choosier and more willing to wait for a good job offer. As can be seen, the variance of wages for highly educated immigrants increases at a faster rate than for comparable natives and at a substantially faster rate than for less-educated immigrants. In particular, the variance of the log wage for natives is almost independent of schooling, while for immigrants it increases with schooling. Finally, the variance of wages among highly educated male immigrants converges to that of comparable native men, while the variance of wages among highly educated female immigrants exceeds that of comparable native women. A similar finding regarding convergence is reported in chapter 3 (Eckstein and Weiss 2004).

The next four figures present the same analysis except by occupation rather than education. Figure 7.8a and b presents the log hourly wage profiles from 1992 to 2008 by occupation for male and female immigrants, respectively, who were aged 25 to 40 on arrival in 1990–91 and for comparable natives. Initially, immigrants in WC jobs earned the same wage as native Israelis in BC jobs. However, with time, the wages of immigrants in WC jobs became more comparable to those of natives in WC jobs. Nonetheless, even after 19 years in Israel, immigrants earn less than comparable natives. Figure 7.9a and b compares the variance of log hourly wages by occupation for men and women, respectively. The variance of wages of immigrants in WC jobs is substantially higher than that of immigrants in BC jobs, while for natives the variance of wages is quite similar in both types of occupation. Furthermore the variance of immigrants' wages in WC jobs is similar to that for comparable natives, while in the case of BC jobs it is significantly lower. The finding that the

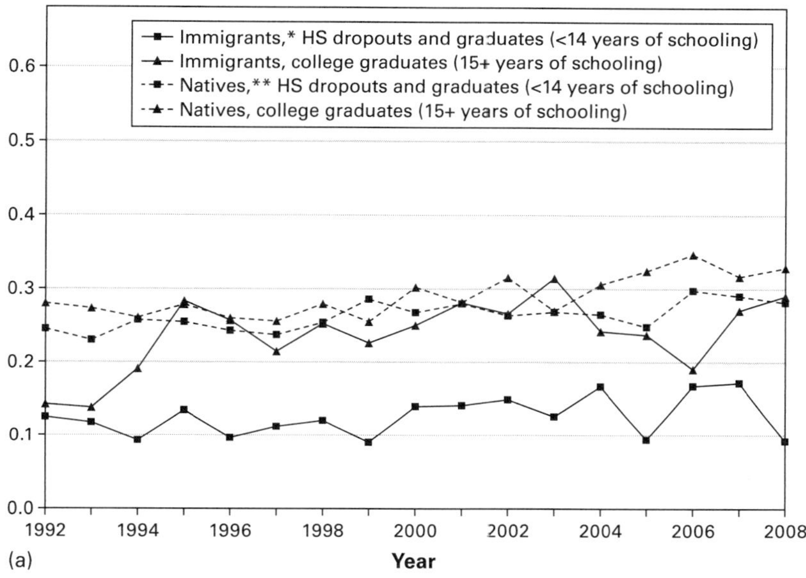

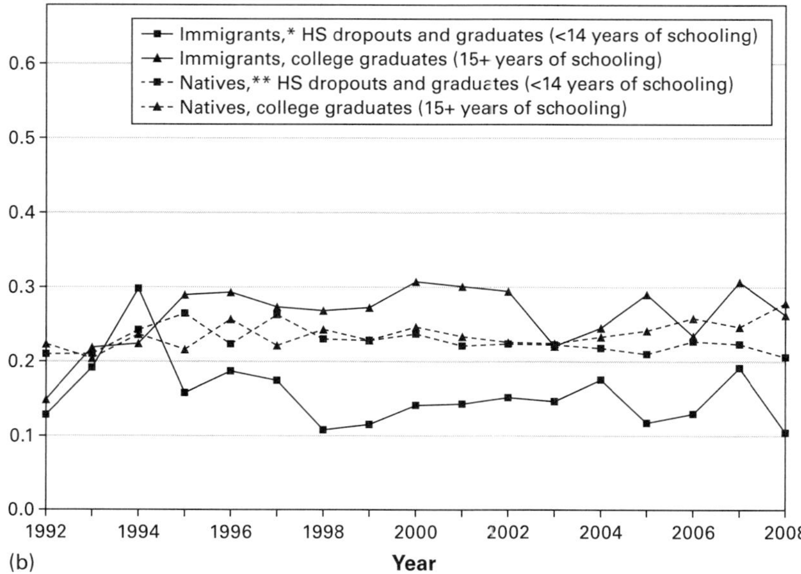

Figure 7.7
Variance of log hourly wages by schooling. (a) Males; (b) females. *Immigrated during 1990–91; **born in Israel or immigrated prior to 1990. Wages expressed in 1992 prices; 1950 to 1966 cohorts (aged 25 to 40 in 1990–91). Source: CBS Income Survey.

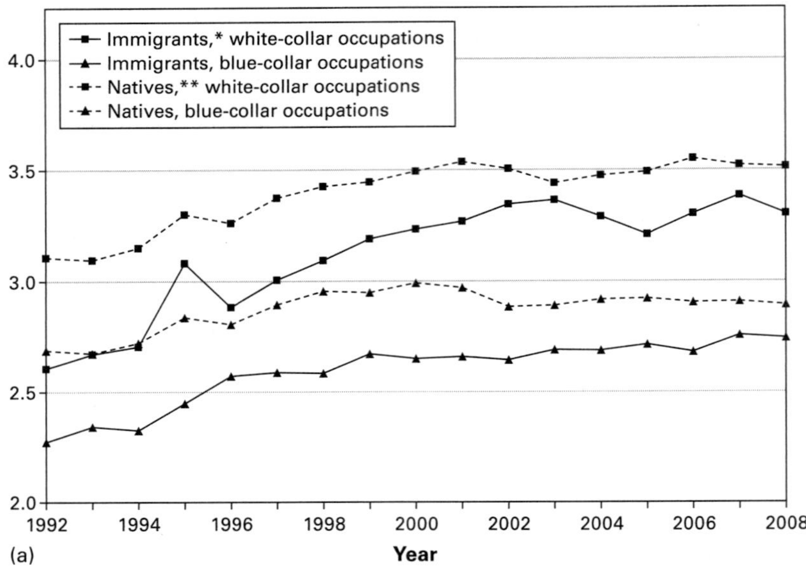

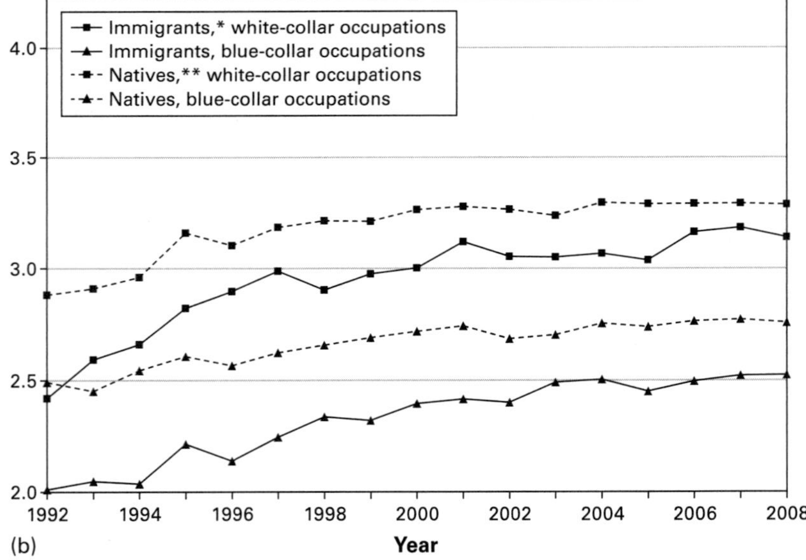

Figure 7.8
Log hourly wages by occupation. (a) Males; (b) females. *Immigrated during 1990–91;
**born in Israel or immigrated prior to 1990. Wages expressed in 1992 prices; 1950 to 1966
cohorts (aged 25 to 40 in 1990–91). Source: CBS Income Survey.

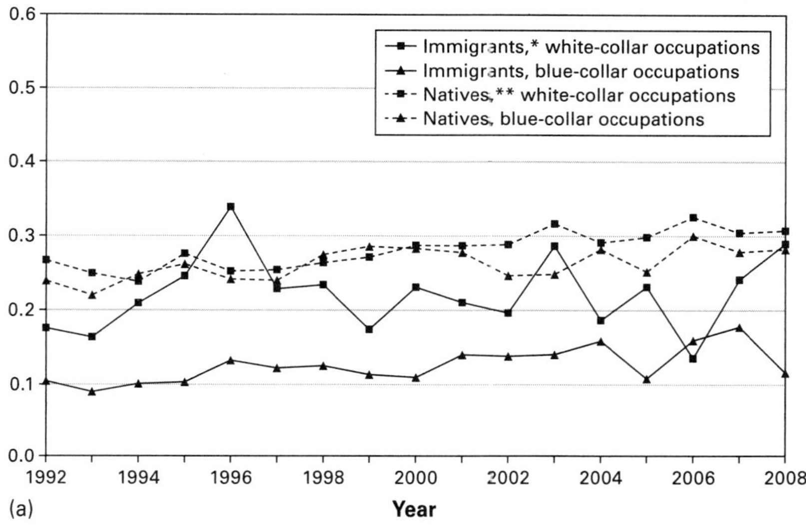

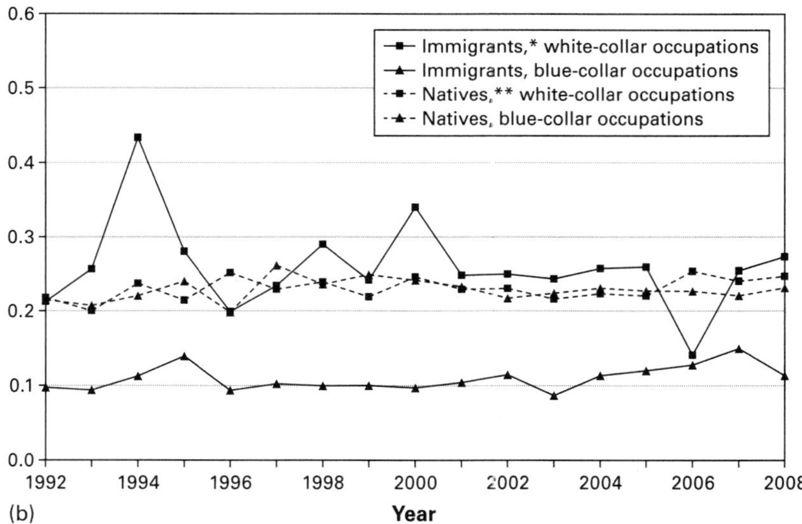

Figure 7.9
Variance of log hourly wages by occupation. (a) Males; (b) females. *Immigrated during 1990–91; **born in Israel or immigrated prior to 1990. Wages expressed in 1992 prices; 1950 to 1966 cohorts (aged 25 to 40 in 1990–91). Source: CBS Income Survey.

variance of wages rises both within a schooling category and within an occupation suggests improved matching of immigrants with jobs over time, which is associated with a rise in the return on imported education and experience.

Despite the incomplete convergence in occupation and wages, immigrants from the FSU who arrived in 1990 to 1995 and were employed in 2008 reported a high level of job satisfaction. According to the Social Survey carried out in 2008, 75.7 percent of these immigrants reported that they are satisfied or very satisfied with their job, compared to 86.3 percent of native Israelis and 66.2 percent of FSU immigrants who arrived after 1996 (see table 7.1). A remarkable feature of the integration process is that it was accomplished with relatively low average levels of fluency in Hebrew. By 2008, of those who had arrived during the period 1990 to 1995, only 48.1 percent reported being able to speak Hebrew fluently or very fluently, 38.7 percent reported being able to read Hebrew fluently or very fluently, and 35.4 percent reported being able to write Hebrew fluently or very fluently. Among those who arrived after 1996, the respective proportions are 30.7, 21.0, and 20.5 percent (see table 7.1).

7.3 Social Indicators

7.3.1 Housing

FSU immigrants tend to live in enclaves, such that in some middle-sized cities (e.g., Ashdod, Ashkelon, and Nazareth) their share of the local population had reached 30 to 40 percent by 2000 (see table 7.2). The tendency to concentrate and the absolute size of the group has made it possible for FSU immigrants to maintain their language and culture (including Russian-language newspapers, television, and theater), create social networks, and feel more at home in Israel.[6]

The establishment of enclaves was a gradual process, which accelerated over time as the total number of FSU immigrants in the country increased. Initially immigrants from the FSU settled in the larger cities and only later did they move to enclaves dispersed throughout the country, trading job opportunities for lower housing costs and improved social amenities (see chapter 6). In earlier waves of immigration to Israel, the government's policy had been to settle immigrants (who came mainly from Middle Eastern or North African countries) in the Periphery. The long-term outcome of this policy was enclaves of poverty and unemployment. During the 1990s, the government adopted a different policy,

Table 7.1

Social integration indicators in 2008

Group	FSU immigrants 1990–95	FSU immigrants 1996+	Native Israelis	Total population
Job satisfaction				
Very satisfied with current (main) job[a]	18.6%	14.1%	34.5%	31.9%
Satisfied with current (main) job[a]	57.2%	52.1%	51.8%	52.3%
Satisfied or very satisfied with current (main) job[a]	75.7%	66.2%	86.3%	84.2%
Hebrew fluency				
Speaks Hebrew very fluently	25.6%	11.2%		
Speaks Hebrew fluently	22.5%	19.6%		
Speaks Hebrew fluently or very fluently	48.1%	30.7%		
Reads Hebrew very fluently	22.5%	8.8%		
Reads Hebrew fluently	16.2%	12.1%		
Reads Hebrew fluently or very fluently	38.7%	21.0%		
Writes Hebrew very fluently	20.7%	7.9%		
Writes Hebrew fluently	14.7%	12.6%		
Writes Hebrew fluently or very fluently	35.4%	20.5%		
Home ownership and satisfaction with dwelling				
Owns their own home[b]	75.2%	43.0%	81.7%	80.6%
Very satisfied with dwelling	17.1%	12.1%	39.2%	34.0%
Satisfied with dwelling	59.4%	60.8%	46.9%	50.1%
Satisfied or very satisfied with dwelling	76.5%	72.9%	86.1%	84.1%
Marriage patterns				
Married to a native spouse[c]	6.4%	6.1%		
Social connections				
Has someone to turn to for help when in crisis or distress	91.7%	91.1%	90.6%	89.8%
Has no friends	11.9%	12.6%	9.7%	17%
Meets or speaks to friends every day or almost every day[d]	46.7%	44.7%	49.5%	46.6%
Meets or speaks to friends once or twice a week[d]	38.5%	39.7%	38.0%	39.6%
Socioeconomic status				
Ethnic origin significantly affects socioeconomic status	16.0%	15.4%	13.1%	13.4%
Ethnic origin affects socioeconomic status	54.3%	55.4%	45.3%	47.1
Ethnic origin affects or significantly affects socioeconomic status	70.3%	70.8%	58.4%	60.5%
Personal contacts significantly affect socioeconomic status	49.0%	45.5%	41.3%	41.5%
Personal contacts affect socioeconomic status	40.5%	41.0%	44.2%	44.5%
Personal contacts affect or significantly affect socioeconomic status	89.5%	86.6%	85.5%	86.0%

Source: CBS Social Survey 2008.
a. Proportion of employed individuals.
b. Among married individuals.
c. Married individuals in single-family households with only one immigrant.
d. Among those with friends.

Table 7.2
Distribution of FSU immigrants who arrived during the period 1989 to 2000, by place of residence in 2000

	FSU immigrants	Total population	Percent
Jerusalem	32,234	717,637	4.49%
Tel-Aviv–Jaffa	41,792	437,556	9.55%
Haifa	61,556	299,524	20.55%
Rishon LeZion	34,192	215,474	15.87%
Ashdod	55,090	187,568	29.37%
Holon	26,644	185,952	14.33%
Beer-Sheva	49,029	184,936	26.51%
Netanya	37,667	183,267	20.55%
Petach Tikva	32,153	181,948	17.67%
Bat-Yam	40,422	160,643	25.16%
Bnei-Brak	6,518	143,491	4.54%
Ramat-Gan	11,445	141,713	8.08%
Ashkelon	31,277	107,826	29.01%
Rechovot	14,561	106,182	13.71%
Herzlia	6,654	93,980	7.08%
Kfar-Sava	7,974	81,399	9.80%
Hadera	19,537	78,326	24.94%
Lod	15,983	72,004	22.20%
Kiryat-Gat	15,113	51,610	29.28%
Nazareth Illit	21,685	50,951	42.56%

Source: Population Registry, Ministry of the Interior.

whereby immigrants from the FSU were able to freely choose where to live. Thus settling in the Periphery was voluntary and enabled them to increase their standard of living and to find the optimal combination of job characteristics and location of residence, while maintaining close ties with fellow immigrants.

Associated with the move to the periphery was a shift from rental to home ownership. According to the Ministry of Construction and Housing, by 2003 about 90 percent of the immigrant families (not including singles and elderly couples) who had arrived from the FSU in 1989–90 owned their own home.[7] According to the CBS Social Survey in 2008, which included all married individuals, 75.2 percent of immigrants who had arrived from the FSU between 1990 and 1995 owned their own home in 2008, as compared to 81.7 percent of native Israelis, and only 43.0 percent of immigrants who arrived after 1996 (see table 7.1). The high rate of home ownership and the short time it took to achieve were made possible by the generous mortgages provided to FSU immigrants. Although this policy created a high debt–income ratio among immigrants (Benchetrit and Czamanki 2009), it strengthened the bonds of FSU immigrants to Israel and raised their general level of satisfaction. According to the Social Survey carried out in 2008, 76.5 percent of the immigrants who arrived during 1990 to 1995 are satisfied or very satisfied with their dwelling as compared to 86.1 percent of native Israelis and 72.9 percent of FSU immigrants who arrived after 1996 (see table 7.1).

7.3.2 Marriage Patterns

In this section we present data on the marriage patterns of FSU immigrants who arrived during 1989–91 and were aged 25 to 35 on arrival. For purposes of comparison, we also present data for natives in the same age group. The figures are based on the LFS during the period 1989 to 2009.

Figure 7.10a (7.10b) presents the proportions of married and nonmarried men (women) among immigrants and natives by year.[8] It is interesting that there was a higher proportion of married men among immigrants than among natives during the early and mid-1990s, although in later years the proportions converge. In contrast, the proportion of married women was similar to that of native Israelis throughout the period. The difference between male immigrants and natives in the early part of the period suggests that Jewish men in the FSU married earlier than natives in Israel and may reflect differences in the economic gains from marriage and in social norms between the FSU and Israel.[9]

Figure 7.11a (7.11b) presents the marriage patterns for male (female) immigrants by time in Israel. According to these figures, the proportion of male immigrants who were married upon arrival was about 4 percent higher than for female immigrants (85 vs. 81 percent), and in general was 3 to 14 percent higher for the same time since arrival. However, if we consider only the immigrants who married in Israel, we find that the proportion of married immigrants is an increasing function of time in Israel both for men and women and that there is much less difference between the genders. In other words, most of the difference in the proportions of married male and female immigrants can be attributed to the period prior to immigration.[10]

Table 7.3 compares the matching patterns of male and female immigrants who married in Israel and shows substantial differences between genders. Thus men have a very strong tendency to marry another immigrant, and almost 50 percent of the men married an immigrant from the same cohort (1989 to 1991) while 39 percent married an immigrant who arrived from the FSU in a later cohort. Only 10 percent of the male immigrants married a native. In contrast, 36 percent of the female immigrants married a native, and 58 percent (= 44 + 14) married an immigrant.

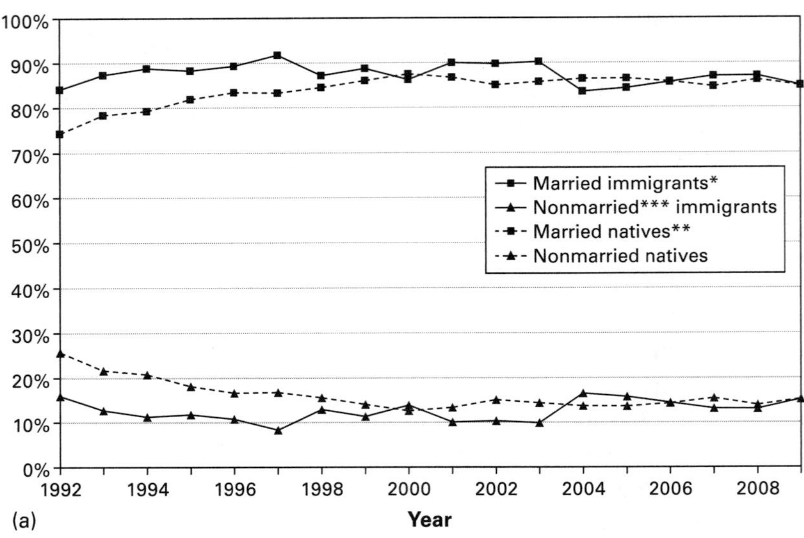

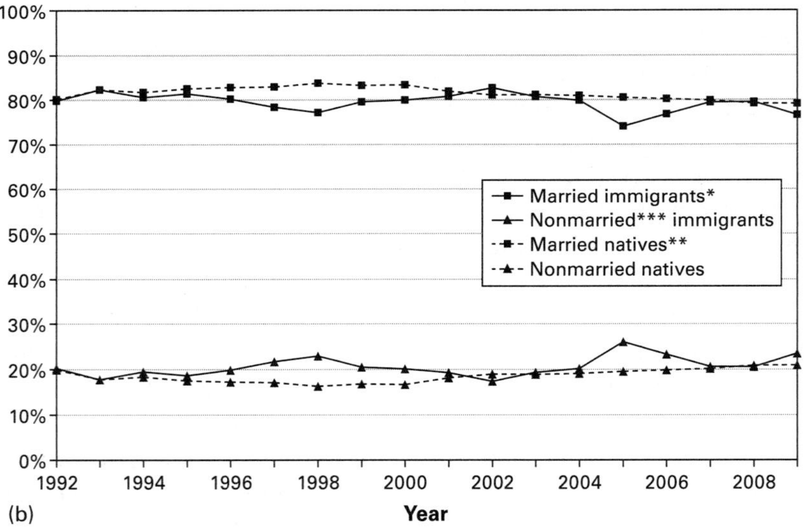

Figure 7.10
Marital status of immigrants and natives: (a) Males; (b) females. *Immigrated during 1989 to 1991 and aged 25 to 35 on arrival; **born in Israel or immigrated prior to 1989, 1954–66 cohorts (aged 25–35 in 1989–91); ***single, divorced, widowed, or living separately. Source: CBS Labor Force Survey.

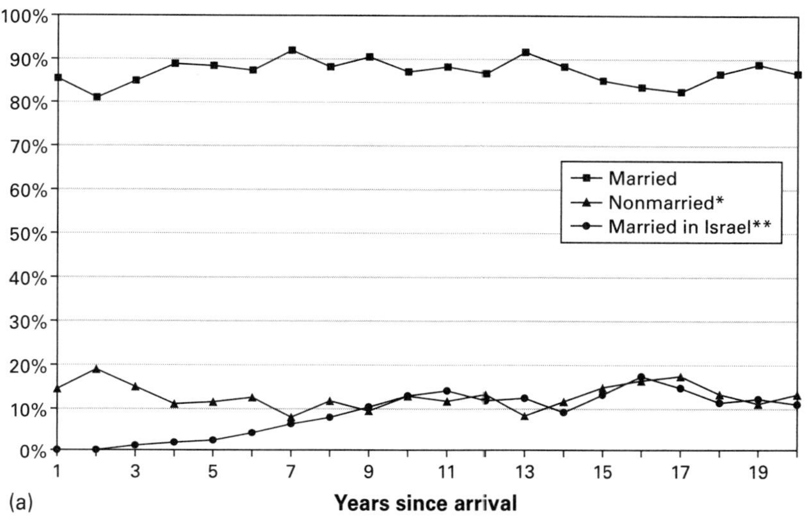

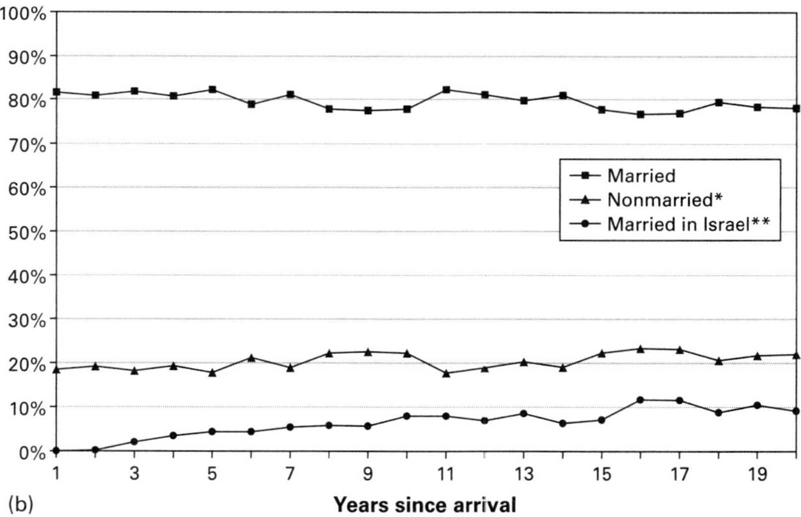

Figure 7.11

Marital status of immigrants, 1989 to 1991 cohorts. (a) Males; (b) females. *Single, divorced, widowed, or living separately; **proportion of total married immigrants. Aged 25 to 35 on arrival. Source: CBS Labor Force Survey.

Table 7.3
Spouses of immigrants who married in Israel, 1992 to 2009

	Immigrant spouse who immigrated during 1989–91	Immigrant spouse who immigrated during 1992–2009	Native spouse[a]	Other spouse[b]	Spouse unknown
Males	47.79%	39.41%	9.76%	0.75%	2.29%
Females	44.19%	14.26%	36.26%	2.09%	3.20%

Source: CBS Labor Force Survey.
Note: Immigrated during 1989 to 1991 and aged 25 to 35 on arrival.
a. Born in Israel or immigrated prior to 1989.
b. Born abroad (not in the FSU) and immigrated after 1989.

Table 7.4
Sex ratio (females/males) in 1992

	Immigrants[a]	Natives[b]
Total	1.08	0.98
Nonmarried	1.37	0.76
(single, divorced, widowed, or living separately)		

Source: CBS Labor Force Survey.
a. Immigrated during 1989 to 1991 and aged 25 to 35 on arrival.
b. Born in Israel or immigrated prior to 1989; 1954 to 1966 cohorts (aged 25–35 in 1989–91).

Explaining these patterns would require a model for spouse selection, which is beyond our present scope. Nonetheless, the beginning of an explanation can be found in table 7.4, which presents the sex ratios for immigrants and natives, and, in particular, for nonmarried immigrants and natives, which may influence spouse selection. Thus the sex ratio for all immigrants is 1.08, which increases to 1.37 if we consider only nonmarried immigrants.[11] In other words, among the immigrants who arrived from the FSU during 1989 to 1991, there were more nonmarried women aged 25 to 35 than nonmarried men in the same age group. In contrast, among natives in the same age group, there were more nonmarried men than nonmarried women (see table 7.4). These sex ratios imply that female immigrants are more likely, relative to male immigrants, to select natives who in turn are more willing to select them due to the shortage of female natives in the same age group.[12]

If we consider only female immigrants who married a native, we find that half of them married an immigrant who arrived from the FSU in earlier waves (prior to 1989) or a man born in Israel whose father immigrated from the FSU.[13] In addition about one-third of these women married a man who was himself born in either Asia or Africa (often referred to in the literature as being of "Sefardi" origin) or whose father was and about 16 percent married a man who himself was born in Europe, the Americas, or Oceania (referred to as being of "Ashkenazi" origin) or whose father was. Finally, less than 4 percent of female immigrants married a native whose father was also born in Israel.

As expected, the tendency of immigrants to marry natives whose parents are also natives rises with time in Israel. However, this is a slow process and such "mixed" marriages remain rare. Of married immigrants from the FSU who arrived during 1990 to 1995, only 6.4 percent had a nonimmigrant spouse in 2008. Among those who arrived after 1996, the proportion drops to 6.1 percent (see table 7.1).

7.4 Return Migration and Out-Migration

The arrival of the initial wave of FSU immigrants during 1989 to 1991 was sudden and unexpected, and thus exogenous to the economic conditions in Israel. At the time immigrants leaving the FSU had limited options in choosing a destination. Only Israel accepted FSU immigrants immediately and in large numbers and did not impose visa restrictions or eligibility criteria for welfare benefits. It is therefore interesting to examine the question of whether Israel was a temporary or permanent destination for these immigrants.

Table 7.5 presents the survival rates as of 2004 for FSU immigrants who arrived during 1990–91, conditional on them still being in Israel in 1995. The figures are based on the 1995 Census and border control records up to 2004. The survival rates are presented for men and for women by schooling and age on arrival.[14]

The survival rates are very high and similar for both genders, conditional on age on arrival and schooling. However, the table suggests that younger immigrants are more likely to leave the country and that within the 16 to 25 and 26 to 35 age groups better-educated immigrants have a higher propensity to out-migrate. For example, the survival rates of male immigrants who were aged 16 to 25 on arrival are 93.7 percent for high school dropouts and 88.1 percent for those with an advanced academic degree. The corresponding figures for immigrants who were aged 26 to 35 on arrival are 96.1 and 91.9 percent, respectively. The observation that within age groups there is a positive correlation between out-migration and education is confirmed by table 7.6, which presents the average years of schooling of stayers and movers by age group. The movers have 0.3 to

Table 7.5
Survival rates as of 2004: FSU immigrants who arrived during 1990–91, conditional on staying in Israel until 1995

Age on arrival	HS dropouts	HS graduates	College graduates	Advanced academic degree
Males				
16–25	93.68%	91.72%	89.97%	88.14%
	(0.71%)	(0.68%)	(1.54%)	(2.11%)
26–35	96.08%	93.82%	94.37%	91.88%
	(0.65%)	(0.72%)	(1.02%)	(0.68%)
36–45	97.98%	96.98%	96.54%	96.2%
	(0.44%)	(0.53%)	(0.73%)	(0.44%)
Females				
16–25	94.38%	93.43%	91.03%	88.78%
	(0.75%)	(0.61%)	(1.25%)	(1.56%)
26–35	95.93%	95.93%	95.33%	93.45%
	(0.66%)	(0.51%)	(0.77%)	(0.56%)
36–45	97.83%	98%	97.47%	97.06%
	(0.47%)	(0.37%)	(0.53%)	(0.36%)

Source: Calculations by Eric Gould. For a description of the data, see Gould and Moav (2008).
Note: Survivors (stayers) are individuals who did not leave the country for a full year or more. Standard errors appear in parentheses.

Table 7.6
Average schooling of stayers and movers among FSU immigrants who arrived during 1990–91, as of 2004

Age on arrival	Males		Females	
	Stayers	Movers	Stayers	Movers
16–25	12.26	12.71	12.75	13.4
	(0.04)	(0.14)	(0.04)	(0.15)
26–35	13.77	14.44	13.94	14.32
	(0.05)	(0.15)	(0.04)	(0.15)
36–45	14.04	14.53	14.14	14.43
	(0.05)	(0.27)	(0.04)	(0.22)

Source: Calculations by Eric Gould. For a description of the data, see Gould and Moav (2008).
Note: Stayers are individuals who did not leave the country for a full year or more. Standard errors appear in parentheses.

0.67 more years of schooling than the stayers and these differences are statistically significant for the age groups 16 to 25 and 26 to 35 among both men and women. Thus the proportion of WC workers after ten years in Israel (see figure 7.4a and b) is an underestimate for the true WC proportion of the 1989 to 1991 cohort. In addition such a pattern of out-migration offsets the rise in the variance of wages of stayers, as discussed in section 7.2.

The differences in emigration rates are consistent with the idea that better-educated individuals, who are able to obtain higher wages abroad, gain more from moving there. There are, however, also nonpecuniary considerations related to general satisfaction with life in Israel, such as social status, quality of education, and culture, which are probably more important to better-educated immigrants. The sociologist Larissa Remennick made an extensive study of these issues among FSU immigrants. Among other things, she found that women were less concerned about loss of occupational status in Israel than were men (Remennick 2005). These findings are consistent with the relatively higher survival rates among better-educated prime-age women, as mentioned above.[15]

7.5   Concluding Remarks

This chapter has reviewed the absorption, over a period of 18 years, of high-skilled immigrants from the FSU who arrived in Israel during the early 1990s. These immigrants found jobs in Israel rather quickly, but initially experienced a substantial occupational downgrading and earned significantly less than their native counterparts due to the difficulty in immediately exploiting imported skills in the new country.[16] Over time some of the younger and better-educated immigrants, who invested more heavily in local skills, were able to switch to jobs more closely matched to their skills and thus achieved significantly higher wages. However, this process was a gradual one and after a decade in Israel there were no substantial dynamics in the immigrants' labor market integration, and after 18 years in Israel, substantial wage differences between immigrants and natives remain.

The relatively long process of adjustment experienced by better-educated immigrants reflects several basic characteristics of the 1989–90 wave of immigration:

• Immigrants from the FSU arrived unprepared for the Israeli labor market and had to make substantial investments in local skills and occupational adjustments upon arrival in the new country.

• Better-educated immigrants from the FSU were quite heterogeneous in terms of quality of schooling, work experience, and exposure to modern Western technology. As a result Israeli employers were uncertain as to their skills and thus hesitant to hire them. Similarly immigrants' investment in the acquisition of local skills differed according to their level of imported skills, as did their rules for accepting job offers.

• The size of the wave of immigration and the fact that it was unexpected led to a relatively complex process of matching in the labor market. The gradual nature of this process meant that immigrants from the FSU had little impact on the wages and employment of native Israeli workers, despite their high level of education. Initially these immigrants competed only with less-educated Israeli workers and with foreign workers, whose supply is relatively elastic. By the time they entered white-collar jobs, the capital stock had increased (primarily due to foreign investment), which substantially diluted their effect on the wages and employment of better-educated natives. The flow of investment led to the expansion of new industries, particularly hi-tech and medical services, which absorbed a large number of immigrants.[17]

• The rates of unemployment among immigrants declined continuously with time in Israel and by 2009 converged to very low levels that were equal to or lower than those among comparable Israelis. This dispelled some of the initial prejudice against them with respect to their lack of good work habits and the inferiority of medical/technical education and work experience obtained in the FSU. In fact immigrants from the FSU did respond to economic incentives in Israel and displayed high participation rates in the labor force, as well as adapting well to unfamiliar advanced technologies.

• In contrast to the convergence to native levels in employment, convergence in wages and occupation was not achieved. This lack of convergence is most noticeable for male immigrants with a college degree, who enjoyed substantially higher wage growth than less-educated immigrants and college-educated native Israelis. However, because the wages of less-educated native Israelis have not risen substantially over time, while those of native Israelis with a college degree have, educated immigrants had less success in catching up with natives than less-educated immigrants. Even though their wages are lower than those of native Israelis, immigrants from the FSU are generally satisfied with their jobs.

• Despite the high initial rates of unemployment among female immigrants relative to male immigrants, their long-term wage and employment outcomes relative to comparable natives were superior to those of male immigrants. In this regard female immigrants adapted better to the Israeli labor market.

• Immigrants from the FSU have maintained their status as a large and distinct social group. They generally marry other immigrants and live in enclaves and report a high level of satisfaction with their dwelling. They have about the same level of social interaction as native Israelis. In some respects they have adapted quickly to Israeli attitudes and norms. They speak functional, though less-than-perfect, Hebrew while continuing to use the Russian language and enjoying Russian culture.

• The general lesson is that even a large and sudden wave of immigration can be absorbed without a negative economic impact on natives. In the case of Israel, the main factor in this process was an increase in the stock of capital, which was financed by direct foreign investment and government borrowing abroad. In addition the gradual entry of immigrants into the labor force mitigated the impact on wages and unemployment among natives. This came at some cost, however, since the skills immigrants brought with them were not put to their best use initially. It has been estimated that 14 percent of immigrants' potential lifetime earnings were lost due to nonemployment and job distribution mismatch resulting from search frictions and other costs of adjustment (chapter 5).

This research has additionally led to some methodological conclusions. The most important of them is that a search framework combined with a model for investment in human capital is the correct unified approach to analyzing immigration from the FSU. This is supported by several important features of the data:

• FSU immigrants experienced an initial occupational downgrading followed by a gradual process of upward job mobility and occupational transitions.

• The variance of wages increased with time since arrival, as high-skilled immigrants were sorted out in the labor market.

• There is an initial period of unemployment during which better-educated immigrants receive few white-collar job offers and reject blue-collar job offers.

The combination of learning by employers, accumulation of local human capital and job search by immigrants leads to a highly nonlinear assimilation process, with upward job mobility in the early years followed by slower progress subsequently. Importantly, this nonlinear process strongly depends on the immigrants' level of imported human capital. It appears that structural models with explicit modeling of search frictions, employer learning, and human capital accumulation are needed in order to capture these nonlinear effects. In the case of reduced-form models, estimation should use a flexible time pattern for the time in the host country that will interact with the initial level of imported capital. Equally important is the availability of high-frequency data, namely annual, quarterly, or even monthly, as was used here.

Can the conclusions reached here be applied to other countries and to different immigrants? First, the wave of immigration from the FSU in 1989 to 1991 can best be compared to refugee migrations. As such, a unique feature of the FSU immigrants to Israel is their high level of education. This probably slowed their entry into the labor force, but in the long run immigrants did not suffer from low participation rates, as is the case of immigrants in, for example, some of the Scandinavian countries. One obvious explanation for this is the less-generous support for the nonemployed in Israel. Second, language was not a major obstacle to entry into the labor force since the government provided free instruction in basic Hebrew (the Ulpans) and in a country where most citizens are former immigrants themselves, a basic knowledge of the language is sufficient for many jobs (Weiss 2000; Gustafsson 2000).

Notes

Chapter 2

1. The figures for 1922 to 1982 are taken from Ben-Porath (1986).

2. The main mechanism identified by Ben-Porath for this result is based on the growth in capital inflows as a result of immigration. The import of private capital was substantial during the British mandate period (1922 to 1947), and it was later replaced by government borrowing abroad during the early years of the State (1951 to 1964). During the wave of immigration from the FSU analyzed here investment from abroad played a major role in growth.

3. In the next chapter we focus on the impact of imported education on the success of immigrants in the local labor market.

4. We define three broad occupational categories: occupation 1, which includes engineers, physicians, professors, other professions requiring an academic degree and managers; occupation 2, which includes teachers, technicians, nurses, artists and other professionals; and occupation 3, which includes blue-collar and unskilled workers.

5. Chapter 3 describes in detail the wage profile of immigrants and the occupational downgrading they experienced.

6. We use the standard definition of the participation rate as the proportion of total employed and unemployed within the population of individuals aged 15 and above.

7. The unemployment rate is calculated as the proportion of unemployed individuals within labor force participants.

8. In 1993, due to political changes and reforms in the health services, the power of the main labor union in Israel (the Histadrut) weakened dramatically and union coverage declined significantly. These changes were not related to the arrival of the FSU immigrants.

9. This section is based on Eckstein and Weiss (2002).

10. Chapter 3 describes in detail the wage regressions estimated for immigrants and natives.

11. This section is based on Cohen and Hsieh (2001).

12. We lack a good measure for capital utilization. We therefore ignore it and focus only on capital accumulation. However, there is casual evidence from data on shift work and

the sharing of housing by parents and adult children, which indicates that capital utilization was a factor in smoothing the adjustment process.

13. Specifically, we assume that N_t increases by 4.67 percent in 1990, 3.56 percent in 1991, 1.48 percent in 1992, 1.45 percent in 1993, 1.47 percent in 1994, 1.36 percent in 1995, 1.21 percent in 1996, and 1.1 percent in 1997, and that it remains constant for all subsequent years.

14. We used the GAMS program for the calibration exercise.

15. Relaxing the assumption in the second method that immigrants are as productive as natives upon arrival and assuming instead that immigrants are less productive (as in the first method) would lead to smaller changes in real wages, investment in capital, and so forth.

Chapter 3

1. This chapter is based on Eckstein and Weiss (2004), On the wage growth of immigrants: Israel 1990–2000, *Journal of the European Economic Association* 2 (4): 665–95 © 2004 by the European Economic Association.

2. See the surveys by Borjas (1994, 2000) and LaLonde and Topel (1997) as well as Chiswick (1978).

3. Lalonde and Topel (1991) define the rate of convergence as the reduction in the difference between the log wages of immigrants and those of natives.

4. This result may suggest that the large government assistance for immigrants in Israel did not affect the rate of assimilation into the labor market. However, the inflow of skilled immigrants relative to the existing stocks was much smaller in the United States.

5. Since the relative prices of skills are determined by the technology of production, namely the demand side, the coefficients θ_s can also be interpreted as parameters representing quality, whether objective or perceived, and these coefficients change as the immigrant's imported skills become more applicable to local market conditions. For the analysis of individual investment decisions, the distinction between price and quality makes no difference. Following the recent literature (e.g., Juhn, Murphy, and Pierce 1993), we use the term "price." In the aggregate, the different values of θ_s together with the available number of individuals with each skill determine the supply of K and the rental rate R. Given the equilibrium value of R and the vector of θ_s, the bundle of skills that each person possesses can be evaluated in terms of the consumption good. In a more general specification, skills need not be perfect substitutes and their respective prices will depend on the aggregate stocks of the different skills (Heckman, Lochner, and Taber 1997).

6. This assumption effectively ignores the selection issues that result from endogenous occupational switches. It is substantially more difficult to analyze and estimate models in which occupational switches and investment are jointly determined. Although Weiss, Sauer, and Gotlibovski (2003) and Cohen Goldner and Eckstein (2008) estimate such structural models, here we adopt a less structural and more descriptive approach that allows us to cover a broader set of issues.

7. The two "production functions" (3.5) and (3.5′) share the crucial simplification that the value of human capital depends only on remaining working life and is thus independent of the current stock (Weiss 1986). The difference between the two specifications is that local and imported capital enter symmetrically into the production of local human capital

in (3.5), while in (3.5′) local human capital is produced by local capital and local time. Thus imported skills enter only through their effect on local earnings.

8. The time at which investment stops, t_1, is determined endogenously by the condition:.

$$\frac{\alpha}{\gamma} K_0(t_1) = \int_0^{T-t_1} e^{-(r+\delta)x} K_0(t_1 + x)dx.$$

The formal derivation of equation (3.8) is presented in the appendix of Eckstein and Weiss (2003).

9. The model above provides a simple answer to a question raised by Borjas (1994, p. 1672): "Why would immigrants accumulate more human capital than natives?" There is no need to rely on heterogeneity or self-selection to explain overtaking. The same principle applies to any group that has a lower rental rate for human capital and expects it to increase with time. Racial discrimination is a possible example.

10. The occupational classification is described in section 3.4. Occupational transitions are assumed to occur exogenously. Later in the chapter we estimate the occupational transition probability using a multinomial logit model. The occupational dummies are consistent with our assumption that the value of K_0 (or R) may differ across occupations.

11. The year effects allow for changes in the rental rate due to common aggregate shocks during the period of mass immigration and the cohort effects represent changes in the unobserved quality of the various cohorts, as well as congestion effects.

12. The NLLS is equivalent to maximum likelihood assuming that the variance of the errors is the same for immigrants and natives. The main restrictions are that the time effects are identical for natives and immigrants, as in Borjas (1985), and that immigrants obtain the same reward as natives for locally acquired experience, implying common values for the parameters b and c. In the two-stage method a standard earning function is estimated only for Israelis in the first stage and following that the nonlinear earning function for immigrants is estimated as a deviation from that of Israelis. The results for the two methods (Eckstein and Weiss 1998) turned out to be almost the same for the sample of 1990 to 1995. Moreover the results for the extended data (1990 to 2000) are also similar.

13. Eckstein and Weiss (2002) examined the wages of female immigrants and the interactions between husbands and wives. Little difference was found in the wage growth of employed immigrants by gender, although female immigrants enter the labor force at a slower rate. An interesting finding is that married male and female immigrants have higher rates of wage growth than single immigrants of the same gender.

14. The Income Survey for 1996 to 2000 reports the year of arrival only in intervals of 3 years or more. We use only those observations that can be matched with the Labor Force Survey, which does report this variable on an annual basis. The matching is based on age, schooling, occupation, hours of work, and marital status.

15. The subsamples presented in table 3.5 include only Jewish men, aged 25 to 65, who worked more than two weeks during the month prior to the survey date and for more than 25 hours per week. We also exclude all individuals with no information on age or the number of years of schooling and with more than 31 years of schooling. The wage and hours of work data are averages for the complete month prior to the survey. Wages are adjusted by the CPI and denominated in 1991 Israeli shekels.

16. When making these comparisons, however, it should be noted that most immigrants arrived before 1993, while there is a continuous inflow of young Israelis with higher educa-

tion into the Israeli sample. It is more instructive therefore to compare immigrants who arrived in 1990–91 to Israelis in 1991, as in table 3.1.

17. The descriptive statistics for this subsample are presented in the last two columns of table 3.5. The immigrants in this subsample are older by two years then those in the unrestricted 25- to 65-year-old sample of immigrants. Except for two observations, all schooling was acquired abroad.

18. The Income Survey and Labor Force Survey do not contain direct information on the schooling of immigrants in Israel. It can be inferred indirectly from age, total reported schooling and age on arrival, as with work experience. The Brookdale data, however, does report schooling acquired abroad and the distributions are quite similar when we restrict age on arrival to exceed 25.

19. The average schooling of these engineers is 16.4 years, with 36 percent having 15 years of schooling, reflecting the fact that in the FSU one could become an engineer by acquiring 10 years of elementary and high school education plus 5 years of university education.

20. Equation (3.12) is estimated directly by NLLS using STATA and based on the repeated cross-sectional data presented above. The results reported here are almost identical to those in Eckstein and Weiss (1998), who estimated this equation using data from 1991 to 1995 only and using a two-step method.

21. Under our assumptions, the difference in the prices obtained by Israelis and immigrants for skill s after $(t - t_0)$ years in Israel is

$$\theta_s - \theta_s(t - t_0) = (\theta_s - \tilde{\theta}_s) + \left[\tilde{\theta}_s - \theta_s(0)\right]\lambda e^{-\lambda(t-t_0)}.$$

22. We could not estimate equation (3.12) with different values for λ for each human capital variable since the NLLS estimators fail to converge. This is basically a multicollinearity identification problem that can be expected without additional restrictions on the adjustment terms of each human capital indicator.

23. The change in the occupational distribution of the 1990 cohort is summarized below:

	Occupation 1	Occupation 2	Occupation 3
1991	13.5	11.8	74.8
1995	22.3	11.9	65.2
2000	32.9	12.5	54.7

24. We thus abstract from the choice of jobs and occupations that are likely to be affected by the wage process. Weiss, Sauer, and Gotlibovski (2003) and Cohen Goldner and Eckstien (2008) estimate structural models that incorporate these decisions.

25. The logit equations are estimated from the Labor Force Survey for 1991 to 2000. For male Israelis, we control for schooling (set at 16+) and age. For male immigrants, we control for schooling (set at 16+), age on arrival and cohort (see appendix tables A4 and A5 in Eckstein and Weiss 2003).

26. There are two other panels that can be used for the same purpose: the CBS panel of immigrants who arrived in 1990 and were surveyed four times during 1991 to 1994 and the Brookdale Survey which in Summer 1992 interviewed a random sample of 1,200 immigrants and then re-interviewed 900 of them again in 1995. The patterns in this data, unconditioned on education, are similar to what we present here, but due to small sample size, these sources of data are not useful for the calculation of transitions conditioned on gender, schooling, and age.

27. The prediction in the graph assumes that the transition matrix is stationary. However, the structural models of Weiss, Sauer, and Gotlibovski (2003) and Cohen Goldner and Eckstein (2008), which allow transition rates to vary with time, yield similar predictions.

28. The widening gap between immigrants and Israelis with 16 years of schooling in occupation 3 suggests that immigrants who stay in this occupation for a long period of time are of increasingly lower quality compared with the Israelis who stay in this occupation.

29. Using the Kolmogorov–Smirnov (K-S) and Kruskal–Wallis (K-W) tests, the null hypothesis of equality of distribution is strongly rejected for the low-experience group (less than five years in Israel). The p-value is zero for the K-S test and 0.003 for the K-W test. For the immigrants with more than five years of experience, the p-value is 0.016 for the K-S test and 0.988 for the K-W test. It is safe to say that the results do not reject the hypothesis that the residuals distribution of immigrants converges to that of natives after five years in the country.

30. For Israelis, we use the Labor Force Survey during 1991 to 2000 to calculate the actual observed proportion of individuals with 16+ years of schooling in each occupation.

31. Note that we compare immigrants to the entire population of natives, regardless of their ethnicity, while Lalonde and Topel (1991) compare each group of immigrants to natives of the same ethnicity.

32. We use conventional specifications for these descriptive regressions for immigrants whose age on arrival is greater than 25. The regression for natives is reported in the last two columns of table 3.6. The regression for immigrants is

$$\ln y = 2.100 + 0.109 C_{<90} - 0.032 C_{92-95} + 0.047 C_{96-2000}$$
$$+ 0.022 s - 0.009 age_{arr} + 0.048 ysm$$
$$- 0.067((ysm - 5) * d_{ysm>5}) + 0.003(ysm * s),$$

where ysm is years since arrival and $d_{ysm>5}$ is a dummy variable that equals 1 if $ysm > 5$. All coefficients are significant at the 5 percent significance level. An important feature of our data, which is reflected in the descriptive regression for immigrants, is the strong positive interaction between schooling and time since arrival, with a low initial return on schooling.

33. For a more detailed discussion of these general findings, the interested reader is referred to our other publications and the summary in Weiss (2000).

Chapter 4

1. The occupational classification is described in section 4.2.

2. The main advantage of the cross-sectional sample is its size and the fact that it allows us to follow different cohorts of FSU immigrants, while the panel is small and represents only those immigrants who arrived in the first wave during 1989 to 1992.

3. The JDC-Brookdale Institute of Gerontology and Human Development in Jerusalem, Israel.

4. We focus only on immigrants who actively searched for a job in Israel following their arrival.

5. In the first survey in 1992, the immigrants were asked only about the wage in the last job they reported.

6. Codes 000–299 in the 1972 occupational classification of the Central Bureau of Statistics (CBS).

7. While in chapter 3 we distinguished between three occupational categories, in this chapter we divide occupations into only two categories, where the first category combines occupations 1 and 2 as defined in chapter 3 and the second category is equivalent to occupation 3 defined there. The reason is that here we are estimating structural search models for training and occupational choice and were forced to make the state space more compact in order to overcome computational difficulties.

8. In some experiments in the United States, dropout rates reached 40 percent of the treatment group (Heckman, Lalonde, and Smith 1999).

9. It should be noted that our definition of nonemployment is different from the standard one since it does not include individuals participating in vocational training.

10. Transition from training to training implies that the immigrant participated in a program that lasted more than one quarter.

11. All wages are in July 1995 prices.

12. Obviously these regressions do not correct for the selection biases due to the immigrant's self-selection for employment, training and occupation. Using predicted training (Heckman's correction, based on table 3 in Cohen Goldner and Eckstein 2010) does not alter the results. Note that the indicator for training equals 1 only if the wage was reported after graduation from the training program. In addition, due to the small number of wage observations, it is not possible to estimate additional parameters based on interaction terms between the included variables.

13. Note that this pattern is similar to the transition to employment among high school graduates, as described by Keane and Wolpin (1997).

14. Berman, Lang, and Siniver (2000) find similar results with respect to knowledge of Hebrew using different data on immigrants in Israel. Chiswick and Miller (1999) find that the return on English proficiency among legalized aliens in the United States is between 8 and 17 percent. Dustmann and van Soest (2001) estimate a model that controls for the endogeneity of language fluency. They find that the gain in earnings from language fluency is positive but sensitive to the specification of the model.

15. Since we observe wages only during the first five years in Israel, we did not include a quadratic element for experience. Furthermore the interaction terms for training and schooling and training and age on arrival turned out to have coefficients of zero with large standard errors. The small wage sample may explain these results.

16. WC and BC occupations are also referred to as occupations 1 and 2, respectively.

17. For notational simplicity, we omit the individual index in this section.

18. Studies that model female life-cycle marital status and labor supply decisions (Van der Klaauw 1996) or life-cycle fertility and labor supply decisions (Hotz and Miller 1988; Eckstein and Wolpin 1989) treat female labor supply as a binary decision (i.e., the women either work or are unemployed). In this chapter we focus on the various labor market activities the woman can engage in (i.e., not simply whether she works or not but in what occupation as well). We view the occupational and local human capital choices as the main decisions to be made by immigrants. Therefore, in order to maintain tractability, we do not incorporate marriage and fertility decisions into the model. Finally, note that the average age on arrival is 38.

19. No data on the husband's wage and employment status were available from the Brookdale Surveys. The assumption that the husband always works is too strong for immigrants who have just arrived in a new country and have just entered a new labor market. In order to control for family-related effects on the female immigrant's decisions (Baker and Benjamin 1997; Duleep, Reget, and Sanders 1999), we included marital status (M) and number of children (N). In the literature it is not clear that the husband's wage has a major impact on female labor supply (assortative mating).

20. The common assumption in the literature is that the return on training is independent of occupation.

21. Institutional and other considerations imply specific values for I_{at} and are explained below.

22. The CT programs last from one to three quarters. To reduce the computational burden in the estimation procedure we assume that the actual length of the program is realized only after the immigrant's decision to participate in training is made. This implies that only the expected value of participation in training matters in the decision. Allowing the length of the training program to be realized before the decision is made involves an increase of the state space by a factor of three. We also assume that programs of different length have the same impact on wages and on job-offer probabilities. This assumption is based on conversations with the administrators of the training programs. They indicated to us that the length of the program does not necessarily imply that a longer program covers more material, but rather that the same material is taught at a different pace.

23. For notational simplicity, we omit the individual index and the unobserved type index in this section.

24. Data on actual monetary transfers from the government to the immigrants was not available to us. These transfers are meant to be independent of the labor market state and hence are assumed to have no impact on choices.

25. Note that for males, we define only general experience and assume it can have a different effect on human capital in each occupation $i, j = 1, 2$. For females, we distinguish between experience accumulated in WC jobs and that accumulated in BC jobs (see equation 4.6).

26. The optimization problem (4.14) has the same format as that in Eckstein and Wolpin (1999).

27. Eligibility to participate in a training program typically expires after 18 quarters.

28. As noted above, nonemployment and BC training are always available, implying that $P_{r0t} = P_{r4t} = 1$.

29. The calculations of the probabilities that enter the likelihood function are corrected according to this additional randomness in the model. This is done through the simulations of the joint probability for the observed outcomes. These are also affected by the self-selection of the individual through the model.

30. To solve the dynamic model for periods subsequent to $t = 20$, it is internally consistent to assume that at retirement the terminal value is zero. This can be imposed by assuming that the δ's in (4.24) linearly decline to zero.

31. The smoothing function takes the standard logit form. For example, in the case of females, we use the Kernel smoothing function for the probability that the x alternative, $x \in A$, was chosen from four possible alternatives $(a = 1, \ldots, 4)$:

$$\frac{\exp[(V_x(S(t),t)) - \max(V_a(s(t),t)))/\tau]}{\sum_{a=1}^{4} \exp[(V_a(S(t),t)) - \max(V_a(s(t),t)))/\tau]},$$

where τ is a parameter. This is a standard procedure in the literature.

32. Thus for females the cost of children (g_a) and the utility from children (γ_{ac}) cannot be identified separately for $a = 1, 2, 3$. In addition, without data on unemployment benefits and earnings during training, we cannot differentiate TW from γ_{3l} nor UB from γ_{4p}.

33. If a multinomial probit model were to be specified for the transitions conditional on the earnings equation, one could estimate 3×20 separate equations with different parameters for the controlled state variables. These multinomial equations generate a larger number of parameters than we specify in the model for job-offer probabilities. Hence identification is not due to the functional forms but rather to the transition data.

34. Note that the state space increases linearly with the number of unobserved types. In this version of the model for females, we assume that there is no unobserved heterogeneity since in an earlier version of this work we used two unobserved types and the proportion of type 1 converged to 0.98, which was not significantly different from 1. For males, a previous version of the paper assumed two unobserved types; here we present the results of estimation with four unobserved types. Since the solution of the DP problem and the calculation of the likelihood function are done for each observation independently, we take advantage of the parallel processing features of supercomputers. The program runs simultaneously on 8 or 16 or 32 processors on IBM and Silicon Graphics (Origin2000) supercomputers at Tel Aviv University and on a Silicon Graphics supercomputer at Boston University.

35. The predictions in this section are based on one-step-ahead predictions. As noted in Keane and Wolpin (1994), maximum-likelihood estimation of the model under the assumption of serial independence is based on one-step-ahead forecasts of the conditional transition probabilities. These predictions are based on 50 one-step-ahead simulations of the choices of each of the 502 women in our sample.

36. The total number of quarter-to-quarter transitions is $7205 - 502 = 6703$.

37. It should be noted that there are only a few wage observations. For example, there are only six observations for WC jobs during the first year in Israel and only 41 during the fourth year. Therefore we can view the results as strong confirmation of the model.

38. It should be noted that the unconditional predictions are not used in the estimation and should be viewed as a better measure for the model's fit.

39. These predictions are based on 50 one-step-ahead simulations of the choices of each of the 419 individuals in our sample aggregated over the estimated types.

40. We also estimated the model ($M = 2$) by minimizing the sum of squared differences between the actual and predicted aggregated labor market choices, which are presented in figure 4.1b and c and figure 4.2b and c. Naturally the fit of the estimated model improved when using this procedure. However, it did not provide a good fit to the individual's choices. That is, the model succeeded in explaining the aggregate choices, but not the individual's choices, which were very different from the actual ones.

41. Note that the one-period-ahead prediction for the sample adjusts the state ($S(t)$) for each individual in the sample in each period according to the outcome in the data. Uncon-

ditional prediction is based on simulations in which the state for each individual ($S(t)$) is based on the predicted outcome.

42. Source 2 is measured by the difference between the unconditional and conditional predictions of the model. The latter is affected by the attrition of the sample at the end of the period.

43. Note that the poor fit in quarters 1 to 4 for the WC wage is a result of there being only four observations, including one major outlier.

44. Hebrew in the wage equation captures the direct wage-return conditional on employment, where Hebrew in the job-offer probability equation measures the reduction in job-offer friction.

45. These results remained unchanged when we estimated the model with unobserved heterogeneity (two types). Furthermore they are consistent with the surprisingly high return on male training in WC jobs found by Cohen Goldner and Eckstein (2008).

46. All the results in this paragraph refer to job-offer probabilities for a nonemployed immigrant who was 38 on arrival, has 14 years of schooling, and has no experience or training in Israel.

47. The contribution of an additional quarter of work experience to job-offer probabilities is not constant due to the logistic form of the probabilities and decreases with accumulated experience, other things being equal.

48. We encountered several technical difficulties in estimating the SE with four types. The SEs are larger overall than in the estimation of the model with only two types, as reported in Cohen and Eckstein (2002).

49. For the average immigrant (according to schooling and age on arrival), the probability of being of each type is reported in table 4.8B.

50. In the estimation we imposed the constraint that the return on BC (WC) training in WC (BC) jobs is zero. This restriction followed the OLS wage regression results and the estimation results obtained with two types.

51. It should be noted that all the training parameters in table 4.6B are not significantly different from zero. We had some numerical complications in generating the standard errors for the parameters reported here. However, according to the estimated specification with two types, the WC (BC) training impact for type 1 on wages in WC (BC) jobs is significant (Cohen and Eckstein 2002). In this case we also conducted several Wald tests for the various outcomes of training. The null hypothesis that training does not affect wages (four zero restrictions) is rejected at a marginal probability level of 10 percent. We also tested for three additional zero effects of training on: (1) wages and job-offer probabilities (six restrictions); (2) wages, job-offer probabilities, and terminal value (ten restrictions); and (3) wages, job-offer probabilities, terminal value, and utility values of training equal to utility in nonemployment (14 restrictions). All restrictions were rejected at a marginal probability value of less than 1 percent. We conclude that the small number of wage observations with additional types (four) increased the estimated standard errors of the wage regression coefficients.

52. Note that the indexes of fluency in English and Hebrew vary from one to four, where one indicates no language skills. The average index is 1.76 for English and 2.7 for Hebrew.

53. The result in Eckstein and Weiss (2004) is based on a nonlinear interaction between schooling, age on arrival, and time in the host country.

54. An alternative way to estimate the indirect effect of imported human capital on local accumulated human capital in the model would involve additional interaction parameters. However, given the number of wage observations in the data these interactions cannot be precisely estimated.

55. The average attributes for age on arrival, English fluency index, and Hebrew fluency index are 38, 1.76, and 2.7, respectively. For the WC job-offer calculation, we consider an immigrant who worked in a WC job in the FSU.

56. This result is consistent with the standard assumption regarding arrival rates of offers in search models, in which on-the-job search is allowed for (Eckstein and van den Berg 2008).

57. The consistency of the estimated terminal value is a complicated problem that is not considered here.

58. The transitions here are based on the same simulations used to calculate the weighted transitions in table 4.4B.

59. This does not hold during the first two quarters in Israel when only immigrants with prior knowledge of Hebrew are permitted into the training programs, which is the standard prerequisite.

60. For example, consider a nonemployed immigrant with the following characteristics: no prior training, worked in a WC job in the FSU, 38 years of age on arrival, 14 years of schooling, and Hebrew fluency index of three. The probability of a WC job offer in Israel will increase from 3.3 to 6.6 percent in this case (see 6 rows from the bottom in table 4.7A).

61. In fact the offered wage during the first year for a WC job is $w_{1t} = \exp\{\alpha_{01} + \alpha_{11}SC + \alpha_{21}EX_{1t}^{-}1 + \alpha_{31}EX_{2t-1} + \alpha_{41}DT_t + \alpha_{51}AGE + \alpha_{61}Heb_t + \varepsilon_{1t}\} + 6$. During the second year, the 6 is replaced by a 3.

62. This assumption is necessary in order to avoid sample selection based on the time between arrival in Israel and the interview.

63. The present value of annual earnings is calculated as $\dfrac{4}{502 x 5}\sum_{i=1}^{502}\sum_{t=1}^{20}\beta^t(w_{i1t} + w_{i2t})500$ and is reported in table 4.12.

64. The cost of unemployment benefits provides an upper bound since not all nonemployed individuals are eligible for unemployment benefits.

65. We assume that this policy would not affect native Israeli workers in WC jobs. In other words, employers would not replace natives with immigrants but rather would increase the total number of employees in WC jobs. This assumption is consistent with a CRS production function, the existence of which is supported by various papers on recent immigration to Israel (Cohen and Hsieh 2001; Eckstein and Weiss 2002, 2004; Cohen Goldner and Paserman 2006).

66. We also calculated the annual present value of *earnings* (of only employed immigrants). In this case an always-available training policy leads to a 3.9 percent increase in annual earnings while a no-training policy leads to a 4.2 percent decrease in annual earnings. Hence the gain from the implementation of always-available training in comparison to no training is only 8.1 percent (as compared to 34 percent in table 4.13). This implies that the main source for the large social gain reported above is the effect of training on nonemployment (table 4.11) and not, as conventionally assumed, its effect on wages.

67. The implicit assumption is that the average wage is a measure of average productivity. The net return to the economy should include the costs and benefits of the programs (both

social and individual), which are not taken into account here. These wage changes are used in the government decision process to compare the outcome of the training program to those of other public investments. The actual costs of training programs are relatively small and can be easily calculated.

68. Here we present the results only for females in order to save space. In addition the results for males are not as convincing and the marginal contribution is limited.

69. Studies of labor market performance and mobility among immigrants in the United States usually use two (or more) consecutive censuses. This way one can observe the labor market choices of a particular cohort after ten years in the new country; however, it is not possible to study the transitions between these two points in time, nor can any conclusions be drawn regarding the assimilation path between these points.

70. Specifically, if the estimated coefficient of a particular attribute (see table 4.8A) is v for the effect of a particular state variable after 21 quarters (five years) in the terminal value equation, this coefficient "depreciates" over time, and its value for individual i after ten years in Israel is given by $v - [v/(65 - (AGE_i + 5))] \times 5$, where AGE_i is age on arrival for immigrant i. For example, in the estimated model, training incremented the terminal value by 1,400 NIS ($\delta_4 = 1,400$; see table 4.8A). Consider an immigrant who was 40 years old on arrival, after 21 quarters (five years) in Israel. The estimated δ_4 reflects the contribution of her training over the next 20 years, from age 45 until retirement (at age 65). Assuming that this contribution depreciates linearly, it will decrease by 70 NIS ($=1,400/[65-(40 + 5)]$) for every year closer to retirement. Therefore the (future) contribution of training after 41 quarters (ten years) in Israel and 15 years prior to retirement is 1,050 NIS ($= 1,400 - 70 \times 5$).

71. The unconditional prediction is based only on the state variables at the time of arrival in Israel.

72. In 1995 the LFS changed its definitions of unemployment and participation, which might also have affected our comparison.

73. The data on training among engineers was only collected in the 2001–2 survey. Thus, we suspect that participation in a training course is underreported due to the ten-year lag in collecting the data. This could be one important reason for the overprediction of participation in a training course.

74. Specifically, the measure of utility may also include nonlabor income such as government support for new immigrants.

75. We do not have figures on earnings by level of education for the FSU. The figures used here are based on Katz (1997), and we assume quarterly wage growth of 0.5 percent. All figures in this section are expressed in July 1995 prices for females and June 1995 prices for males.

Chapter 5

1. A downgrading of skills was also observed among immigrants who arrived from the FSU during the period 1970 to 1980. The skills and occupational profile of these immigrants were similar to those of the current wave, though their number (about 150,000) was smaller (Flug, Kasir, and Ofer 1992).

2. The approach was suggested by Reder (1957, 291–95). In his view, jobs are arranged in a "job hierarchy," such that workers search for the best jobs for which they are qualified but may end up in a less preferable job if their search fails. In a favorable labor market

(for workers), job seekers find it relatively easy to move up the job hierarchy toward better jobs since fewer workers are competing for the good jobs and firms have relaxed their hiring standards.

3. The model does, however, include an explicit adjustment for differences in the quality of schooling between the two countries.

4. Several recent studies analyzed the unemployment spells and wage losses following displacement due to plant closure. See, for instance, Jacobson, LaLonde and Sullivan (1993), Carrington and Zaman (1994), and Neal (1995), which find a substantial and long-lasting loss of wages.

5. Sicherman (1991) noted a prevalence of overeducation in a sample of American workers (surveyed in the Panel Study of Income Dynamics). When asked "How much formal education is required to get a job like yours?" about 40 percent of the respondents reported a number which was lower than their own schooling attainment (only 16 percent of the respondents reported a higher number). The author ascribes this discrepancy to a variety of reasons, including temporary mismatching and career mobility.

6. The questions in each survey differed slightly. Consequently 26 percent of the reported wages in the engineers' sample are net of taxes, while in the representative sample the figure is 61 percent.

7. Immigrants reported whether they can understand, speak, write, and read professional material. The possible answers were: fluently, with some difficulty, with a great deal of difficulty, and not at all. A respondent is considered to know Hebrew if he answered "fluently" or "with some difficulty" in all four categories. Knowledge of Hebrew is reported at the time of the survey in both samples. The representative sample also reports speaking ability upon *arrival*. There is *no* effect of such ability on wage outcomes.

8. The immigrants do not vary significantly with respect to knowledge of Hebrew due to the availability of publicly provided language courses. About 85 percent of the sample finished a 6-month program in a language school and, at the time of the survey, 75 percent reported having knowledge of Hebrew.

9. $\lambda_{jkt} * P_k(s)$ can be collapsed into one term, say $\lambda_{sjs'kt}$. For reasons of computational tractability, parsimony and identification, the original specification is adopted.

10. Traditional models of search assume stationarity and an infinite horizon. See Mortensen (1986), Burdett (1978), and the application by Flinn and Heckman (1982). Recent applications of search models in a nonstationary environment include Miller (1984), Wolpin (1992), and Sauer (1998).

11. The occupational classification is described in section 5.2.

12. These cohort effects capture potential congestion effects, the learning process of employers regarding immigrants' quality and differences in quality between early and late entrants. In addition to cohort effects, there may be year effects, which are not discussed here, but see Beenstock, Chiswick, and Paltial (2005).

13. We attempted to estimate the model without assigning an empirically defined minimum schooling requirement to the immigrant's two-digit occupation. However, this introduces a form of serial correlation which, in the presence of a high number of job transitions in the data, necessitates high-dimensional integrations.

14. It is not possible to identify $P_j(s)$ jointly with the other two components of the job-offer probability, though it is also reasonable to assume that the proportion of jobs that require

s in occupation j is correlated with the arrival rate of job offers. The empirically defined $P_j(s)$ distributions are described in appendix table 5.A2.

15. For analytical simplicity, employers are assumed not to update their beliefs regarding true schooling levels.

16. The intercepts of the linear translations were restricted to be equal across occupations for purposes of identification.

17. The subsample indicator and the net wage indicator thus appear in the density of the measurement error, rather than in the wage-offer functions.

18. Type 0 is used as a benchmark and we estimate the effects of being type 1 or type 2 relative to it.

19. 580 NIS is the average level of nonemployment benefits received by the immigrants during the sample period.

20. Cohen Goldner and Eckstein (2008) focus on the decision to participate in immigrant training programs and estimate its effect on wages and offer probabilities.

21. We attempted to estimate the interest rate along with the other parameters of the model but were unsuccessful since the interest rate could not be separated from the arrival rates of job offers.

22. The state space is small enough to enable a full solution to the dynamic program. The incorporation of endogenously accumulated job and/or occupation-specific work experience in the model would increase the size of the state space to an extent that would require approximate solution techniques (see Keane and Wolpin 1994 for further discussion).

23. Standard errors are calculated by using numerical derivatives and the outer product approximation to the Hessian.

24. This is due to its correlation with the terminal value parameters, which also influence the value of a job within the sample period. The terminal value parameters, however, are highly significant.

25. Approximately 40 percent of skilled male immigrants (i.e., who worked in occupations 1 or 2 in the FSU) participate in job training programs for 6 months on average. Job training is provided by the government and is conditioned on a prior course in Hebrew language proficiency, which lasts an average of 4 months (Cohen Goldner and Eckstein 2008).

26. The predicted values in this section are also calculated by simulating 10,000 choice histories for each individual in the sample.

27. The chi-square statistics are not adjusted for the fact that the parameters of the model are estimated. Rejection of the null hypothesis is at the 5 percent level of significance.

28. The OLS regression is similar, but not identical, to the wage functions estimated in the model. For example, the regression is not estimated separately for each occupation and does not include controls for unobserved heterogeneity. The corresponding measure of fit is 0.592 in terms of logs.

29. The data on wages in the sample is very sparse and there are no observations of wage changes among stayers or movers in *adjacent* months. Therefore it is not possible to present the corresponding actual wage changes.

30. Since s^* is occupation-specific, there is a counterfactual job distribution and corresponding mean wage for each occupation. The potential wage is thus defined as the *maximum*

over the mean wages in each occupation. In order not to overstate this maximum, restrictions were imposed according to the occupation of the immigrant in the FSU. Specifically, if the immigrant worked in occupation 3 in the FSU, then the potential wage is defined as the mean wage in occupation 3 in Israel. If the immigrant worked in occupation 2 in the FSU, then the potential wage is defined as the maximum over the mean wages in occupations 2 and 3 in Israel. If the immigrant worked in occupation 1 in the FSU, then the potential wage is defined as the maximum over the mean wages in occupations 1, 2, and 3 in Israel.

31. The regression parameters are estimated by nonlinear least squares using data on 8,178 *Israeli* workers (selected from the CBS Income Survey for 1991–94). The regression specification is described in appendix table 5.A4.

32. The regression specification, which is similar to that in Eckstein and Weiss (1998), is described in appendix table 5.A4. The out-of-sample predictions show no pure time effects. The growth in wages is attributed to the accumulation of experience and the rising prices of imported skills.

33. It is interesting to note that connecting the monthly and annual models by a full backward recursion starting from age 65 does not substantially change the simulation results. The terminal value functions estimated in the model are thus consistent with the value functions generated using the imported wage functions.

34. Estimated monthly job-offer probabilities are also transformed into their annual equivalents. Let q be the probability of meeting an employer in a particular month, where $q = 1 - \lambda_{j1t} - \lambda_{j2t} - \lambda_{j3t}$. The probability that the immigrant will meet an employer in occupation k *once* during the year (i.e., in one of the n months) is

$$\lambda_{jkt}\left[1 + q + q^2 + \cdots + q^{n-1}\right] = \lambda_{jkt}\left[(1 - q^n)/(1 - q)\right].$$

The probability that the immigrant will not receive an offer is q^n. Clearly,

$$\lambda_{j1t}\left[(1 - q^n)/(1 - q)\right] + \lambda_{j2t}\left[(1 - q^n)/(1 - q)\right] + \lambda_{j3t}\left[(1 - q^n)/(1 - q)\right] + q^n = 1$$

since $q = 1 - \lambda_{j1t} - \lambda_{j2t} - \lambda_{j3t}$. The other two components of the job-offer probability, $P_j(s)$ and $\Phi_j(s* \geq s)$, are not dependent on the length of the period.

35. Zeros are used in the calculation of discounted lifetime earnings when the immigrant is simulated to be in nonemployment.

36. Other studies have also found a higher rate of return on locally acquired schooling (Eckstein and Weiss 1998; Friedberg 2001).

37. The mass immigration from the FSU led to a significant expansion of the national health system.

38. It should be noted that the loss we estimate is that resulting from frictions and the implied mismatches of immigrants in the Israeli labor market. We are thus comparing actual outcomes to an ideal frictionless world. We focus only on the loss experienced by immigrants since it is shown in other studies (Cohen Goldner and Paserman 2011; Friedberg 2001) that, despite its scope, natives were not affected by the wave of immigration from the FSU.

Chapter 6

1. In light of the crude division of areas of residence adopted in the empirical analysis below into Center and Periphery, it is assumed that all immigrants work in their area of

residence. The infinite horizon assumption is reasonable as long as it is applied to young immigrants. The sample was therefore restricted to immigrants up to the age of 55 on arrival.

2. The model assumes that when there are two spouses in the family, the choice of place of residence is made according to the man's employment preferences, since he is the "main provider."

3. It is assumed that an immigrant's utility from housing services is identical whether he owns or rents his apartment.

4. A list of the occupations included in each category is presented in appendix table 6. A1.

5. The model was estimated using data for a relatively short period, 1989 to 1992.

6. It is assumed that an immigrant can search for his first job only in his area of residence and that, due to travel costs, living in an area different from the one in which his job is located is not worthwhile.

7. This value can be calculated recursively under the model's assumptions that the numbers of areas of residence, of occupations and of wage promotions are finite.

8. The model is based on the assumption that immigrants do not acquire any formal education in Israel. The estimation was therefore restricted to immigrants whose age on arrival was at least 25.

9. This variable, which is based on self-evaluation, is composed of four measures of fluency in English at the time of the survey: understanding, speaking, reading and writing. The values taken by this variable range from 0 to 12, where 0 indicates complete fluency in all measures and 12 indicates total lack of fluency in all measures. It is assumed that an immigrant's fluency in English does not change following arrival (and is not expected to do so in the future).

10. The parameter a_2 is estimated from a regression on salary only and is assumed to be constant in the full model.

11. Since the Brookdale Survey included immigrants who had been no more than two years in Israel, δ and Δ were estimated using a supplementary model (see appendix A).

12. Since the quality of the immigrant's job is not known, the salary range predicted by the model for each immigrant lies between the salary paid by a job with quality equal to the immigrant's threshold level and that paid by a job with quality S_i. In order to avoid cases in which the actual wage does not fall within the predicted range, it is assumed that the wage in the sample is reported with measurement error that has an expectation of zero and whose variance was estimated within the framework of the full model.

13. In other words, occupations 2 and 3 were combined for occupation in Israel.

14. It is assumed that immigrants live and work in the same area, an assumption that is supported by the data on the immigrants' first place of residence and the location of their first job. Since the estimation used only the immigrants' first place of residence in Israel (except for cases in which the immigrants stayed there only a few weeks), this assumption is not unrealistic.

15. All immigrants included in the subsample used for estimation had been employed in the FSU.

16. These assumptions are necessary in order to explain the high proportion of immigrants who worked in occupation 1 or 2 in the FSU and chose to begin their careers in Israel in occupation 2.

17. We assume that a nonemployed immigrant will search for a job only in his area of residence.

18. The random component in the individual's preferences can also represent an error in maximization made by the immigrant when calculating the value of each situation.

19. The period of nonemployment is calculated from the beginning of the job search, as reported by the immigrant, until he found a job of at least 25 weekly hours.

20. The salary of each immigrant in the sample is expressed in terms of a 45-hour work week.

21. For a detailed description of the Brookdale Survey, see chapter 4, section 4.2.

22. Only three of the immigrants included in the subsample immigrated in 1989. This group was meant to represent those immigrants with the best prospects for occupational absorption. The data for this population therefore may not necessarily reflect the situation of all immigrants.

23. The estimation only includes immigrants who were resurveyed in 1995 since the second survey included several questions on behavior during the first sample period that were not included in the first survey and that were used in the estimation (e.g., first place of residence following immigration).

24. Allowing for the possibility that returns on human capital characteristics are dependent on the occupation and the quality of the specific job is critical due to the downgrading of immigrants on the occupational ladder (e.g., an engineer employed as a cleaner). In these cases traditional empirical methods, in which an individual's salary is only a function of his characteristics and not those of his job, are inappropriate.

25. It should be noted that our definition of nonemployment differs from the standard notion since it includes immigrants who did not find a full-time job (25 or more weekly hours) since their arrival.

26. The wage and period of time that appear in the table do not represent the employment opportunities in each area in an unbiased manner since they are affected by the immigrants' endogenous decisions and since some of the immigrants had not yet found a job at the time of the survey.

27. Because of the relatively small number of observations for occupation 1 in the Periphery, it was assumed in the estimation that the constant is identical for occupations 1 and 2 in the Periphery. However, the estimation does allow for a different rate of return on each utilized year of schooling in each occupation.

28. This parameter was estimated within the framework of a regression on the wage only and was taken to be constant in the structural model.

29. As captured by a dummy variable that takes a value of 1 if the immigrant's age at the time of arrival is higher than 40 and 0 otherwise.

30. Weiss and Gotlibovski (1995) found that the mean effective monthly probability of receiving a job offer in occupation 1 is 0.1 and in occupation 2 is 0.2. These estimates are almost identical to those obtained in the current study, namely 0.095 and 0.19. In the present study the probability of receiving a job offer in each of the occupations was calculated by

weighting the probability of receiving a job offer in each occupation and in each area by the probability of choosing that area.

31. Weiss and Gotlibovski (1995) found that age has a significant but small negative effect on the probability of receiving a job offer in occupation 1 and a positive but not significant effect in occupation 2.

32. The model's fit was tested using $Q_{R_J} = \sum_{d=1}^{2} \sum_{j=0}^{3} \left[\left(predicted_{dj} - actual_{dj} \right)^2 / predicted_{dj} \right]$, where Q_{RJ} is the test value for the group of immigrants who were employed in occupation j in the FSU, lived in area of residence d (which takes a value of 1 or 2), and worked in occupation j in Israel (which takes a value of 0, 1, or 2, where 0 represents the situation in which the immigrant did not find a full-time job in Israel prior to the date of the survey). The critical value for the test is $\chi^2_{0.95}(5) = 11.1$, namely the model is rejected in each line if and only if the test value is greater than 11.1.

33. First full-time job, namely of at least 25 weekly hours.

34. For a detailed description of the Engineers' Survey, see chapter 5, section 5.2.

35. Due to the stationary nature of the model, it is assumed that immigrants do not change area of residence if they have not found a job in the new area. However, the moves between areas of residence calculated from the data of the follow-up survey do not depend on the point in time at which the immigrant found employment prior to the move. Still, this difference cannot explain the deviation of the model's prediction since most of the immigrants whose first place of residence was in the Periphery were employed soon after their arrival in occupation 2.

36. This figure is obtained by weighting the data in table 6.8 by the number of immigrants in each initial situation.

37. The simulation does not accurately reflect the conditions faced by the immigrants in the current sample since within the framework of the empirical model housing costs cannot be changed during the period in which the immigrants lived in the country. Instead, it represents a situation in which high housing costs already existed when the immigrants arrived in the country. Nonetheless, the simulation does reflect the immigrants' preferred permanent area of residence in light of the new housing costs.

38. Based on a similar definition, Weiss and Gotlibovski (1995) estimated the immigrants' average expected wage loss in Israel at 9.5 percent.

39. Note that it was assumed that an immigrant who chooses to search for his first job in Israel in occupation 1 in the Periphery does not later move to the Center.

40. The wage loss derived from choosing occupation 1 in the Center or in the Periphery is not dependent on housing costs since it is assumed that immigrants who chose this occupation did not search for a job after finding employment.

41. In contrast to the Brookdale Survey in which the data on place of residence were reported according to city, the data for the 1990 immigrants published by the Central Bureau of Statistics were divided into seven regions. As a result there may a discrepancy in the classification into Center/Periphery between the two sets of data.

42. Another reason for this difference may be that the model was estimated only for families that included a male spouse. Furthermore, at the time of the model's estimation, the first area of residence was defined as the one in which the immigrant resided for longer than a few weeks after immigrating, in order to eliminate temporary residence with relatives, in a hotel, and so forth.

43. From the early 1990s until 2000 there was a major decline in the occupational levels of the immigrants arriving in Israel, including a decrease of approximately 50 percent in the proportion of immigrants who were employed in occupation 1 in the FSU.

44. Since the data from the Income Survey are in annual terms, the estimated probability of promotion is as well. The value of this parameter was then translated into monthly terms in order to integrate it within the search model, which is expressed in monthly terms.

Chapter 7

1. The occupational classification is described in section 7.2.

2. The first category combines occupations 1 and 2 as defined in the previous chapters, while the second category is equivalent to occupation 3 as defined there.

3. These rates are calculated as a proportion of labor force participants.

4. As shown in chapter 4, women initially acquire more training than men. Since a participant in a training course is counted as unemployed in the LFS, the higher unemployment rate among women can be attributed, at least partially, to training.

5. These gaps are somewhat larger than those predicted by Eckstein and Weiss (2002, 2004) for out-of-sample years, as reported in chapter 3. Since they did not have data on the 1990–91 cohort after twenty years in Israel, they used the predicted occupational outcomes of immigrants who arrived from the FSU in the 1970s and 1980s. In retrospect, we can see that the occupational achievements of immigrants who arrived in the 1990–91 wave fall short of those who arrived earlier. This discrepancy may reflect a cohort size effect or differential time effects for immigrants and native workers.

6. According to Kheimets and Epstein (2001), most Russian immigrants believe their language and culture to be superior to those of Israel and see no reason to shed their cultural identity. They also found that good knowledge of English is crucial for the successful social and economic integration of immigrant scientists.

7. Ministry of Construction and Housing, *Monthly Bulletin*, April 2008 (Hebrew).

8. Nonmarried includes singles, divorced, widowed, and separated.

9. The average age at marriage for Israeli Jews in 1990 was 26.7 for men and 23.9 for women. According to the 1989 Census of the Soviet Union, the corresponding figures for Jews in the USSR were 25 and 22.2 (Tolts 2009).

10. Single motherhood is a widespread and well-documented phenomenon among female FSU immigrants.

11. Tolts (2009) reports that by 1989 there were more Jewish men than women in the FSU. However, more Jewish women than men chose to emigrate, which demonstrates a certain amount of selection by gender.

12. The higher rate of marriage between female immigrants and male natives is consistent with the idea that female immigrants integrated more successfully into Israeli society than male immigrants (Remennick 2005).

13. Recall that according to our definitions a native is someone who was born in Israel or was born abroad and immigrated to Israel prior to 1989.

14. We thank Eric Gould for providing this data. For details, see Gould and Moav (2008).

15. According to Remennick (2005), "Women proved to be more ready than men to trade their higher occupational status for pragmatic benefits of employment and some financial security. Driven by their responsibility for the family, women were ready at the outset to undergo occupational change in any direction that would bring a steady income. By converting to white-, pink-, or blue-collar occupations demanded on the Israeli marker, these women revealed flexibility, ability to learn rapidly, and successful social networking with their new milieu . . . . Additional social benefits women get from their greater economic activity during initial resettlement years include faster improvement of their Hebrew skills and broadening circles of informal communication with both co-ethnics and Hebrew speakers."

16. The occupational downgrading of immigrants is not unique to the Israeli case and has also been found in Britain (Dustmann, Frattini, and Preston 2008).

17. See Cohen Goldner (2006) for a discussion of immigrants in the hi-tech industries and Kugler and Sauer (2005) for a detailed analysis of immigrant physicians.

References

Baker, M., and D. Benjamin. 1997. The role of the family in immigrants' labor market activity: An evaluation of alternative explanations. *American Economic Review* 87 (4): 705–27.

Bank of Israel. 2000–2002. *Annual Report.* Jerusalem.

Becker, G. 1975. *Human Capital,* 2nd ed. New York: Columbia University Press.

Beenstock, M., B. R. Chiswick, and A. Paltial. 2005. Endogenous assimilation and immigrant adjustment in longitudinal data. Discussion paper 1840. Institute for the Study of Labor (IZA).

Bellman, R. 1957. *Dynamic Programming.* Princeton: Princeton University Press.

Benchetrit, G., and D. Czamanki. 2009. Immigration and home ownership: Government subsidies and wealth distribution effects in Israel. *Housing Theory and Society* 26 (3): 210–30.

Ben-Porath, Y. 1967. The production of human capital and the life cycle earnings. *Journal of Political Economy* 75 (4): 352–65.

Ben-Porath, Y. 1986. The entwined growth of population and product, 1922–1982. In Y. Ben-Porath, ed., *The Israeli Economy: Maturing through Crisis.* Cambridge: Harvard University Press, 27–41.

Berman, E., K. Lang, and E. Siniver. 2000. Language skill complementarity: Returns to immigrant language acquisition. Working paper 7737. National Bureau of Economic Research.

Blanchard, O., C. Rhee, and L. Summers. 1993. The stock market, profit, and investment. *Quarterly Journal of Economics* 108 (1): 115–36.

Blinder, A. S., and Y. Weiss. 1976. Human capital and labor supply: A synthesis. *Journal of Political Economy* 84 (3): 449–72.

Borjas, G. J. 1985. Assimilation, changes in cohort quality, and the earnings of immigrants. *Journal of Labor Economics* 3 (4): 463–89.

Borjas, G. J. 1994. The economics of immigration. *Journal of Economic Literature* 32 (4): 1667–1717.

Borjas, G. J. 1999. The economic analysis of immigration. In A. Ashenfelter and D. Card, eds., *Handbook of Labor Economics,* vol. 3A. Amsterdam: North Holland, 1697–1760.

Borjas, G. J. 2000. The economic progress of immigrants. In G. J. Borjas, ed., *Issues in the Economics of Immigration.* Chicago: University of Chicago Press, 15–49.

JDC—Brookdale Institute of Gerontology and Human Development, Jerusalem, Israel, and the Public Opinion Research of Israel survey company (PORI). Brookdale Survey.

JDC–Brookdale Institute of Gerontology and Human Development, Jerusalem, and the Public Opinion Research of Israel survey company (PORI). Engineers' Survey.

Burdett, K. 1978. A theory of employee job search and quit rates. *American Economic Review* 68 (1): 212–20.

Carrington, W., and A. Zaman. 1994. Interindustry variation in the costs of job displacement. *Journal of Labor Economics* 12 (2): 243–75.

Central Bureau of Statistics (CBS). 1980–2008. Income Survey. Israel Social Science Data Center (ISDC) at the Hebrew University of Jerusalem.

Central Bureau of Statistics (CBS). 1982–2003. Statistical Abstract of Israel.

Central Bureau of Statistics (CBS). 1989–2009. Labor Force Survey. Israel Social Science Data Center (ISDC) at the Hebrew University of Jerusalem.

Central Bureau of Statistics (CBS). 2008. Social Survey.

Central Bureau of Statistics (CBS). Time Series–DataBank.

Chiswick, B. R. 1978. The effect of Americanization on the earnings of foreign-born men. *Journal of Political Economy* 86 (5): 897–921.

Chiswick, B. R. 1992. The performance of immigrants in the labor market: A review essay. Unpublished manuscript.

Chiswick, B. R., and P. W. Miller. 1999. Language skills and earnings among legalized aliens. *Journal of Population Economics* 12 (1): 63–89.

Cohen, S., and Z. Eckstein. 2002. Labour mobility of immigrants: Training, experience, language and opportunities. Discussion paper 3412. Centre for Economic Policy Research.

Cohen, S., and C. T. Hsieh. 2001. Macroeconomic and labor market impact of Russian immigration in Israel. Working paper 11–01. Bar Ilan University.

Cohen Goldner, S. 2006. Immigrants in the Israeli hi-tech industry: Comparison to natives and the effect of training. *Research in Labor Economics* 24: 265–92.

Cohen Goldner, S., and Z. Eckstein. 2008. Labor mobility of immigrants: Training, experience, language, and opportunities. *International Economic Review* 49 (3): 837–72. doi:10.1111/j.1468-2354.2008.00499.x.

Cohen Goldner, S., and Z. Eckstein. 2010. Estimating the return to training and occupational experience: The case of female immigrants. *Journal of Econometrics* 156 (1): 86–105.

Cohen Goldner, S., and M. D. Paserman. 2006. Mass migration to Israel and natives' employment transitions. *Industrial and Labor Relations Review* 59 (4): 630–52.

Cohen Goldner, S., and M. D. Paserman. 2011. The dynamic impact of immigration on natives' labor market outcomes: Evidence from Israel. *European Economic Review* 55 (8): 1027–45.

Duleep, H., M. Reget, and S. Sanders. 1999. *A New Look at Human Capital Investment: A Study of Asian Immigrants and Their Family Ties*. Kalmazzo, MI: Upjohn Institute of Economic Research.

Dustmann, C., T. Frattini, and I. Preston. 2008. The effect of immigration along the distribution of wages. Discussion paper 03/08. Centre for Research and Analysis of Migration.

Dustmann, C., and A. van Soest. 2001. Language fluency and earnings: Estimation with misclassified language indicators. *Review of Economics and Statistics* 83 (4): 663–74.

Eckstein, Z., and G. J. van den Berg. 2008. Empirical labor search: A survey. *Journal of Econometrics* 136 (2): 531–64.

Eckstein, Z., and Y. Weiss. 1998. The absorption of highly-skilled immigrants: Israel, 1990–1995. Discussion paper 1853. Centre for Economic Policy Research.

Eckstein, Z., and Y. Weiss. 1999. The integration of immigrants from the former Soviet Union in the Israeli labor market. Working paper 33–99. The Foerder Institute for Economic Research.

Eckstein, Z., and Y. Weiss. 2002. The integration of immigrants from the former Soviet Union in the Israeli labor market. In A. Ben-Bassat, ed., *The Israeli Economy, 1985–1998: From Government Intervention to Market Economics, Essays in Memory of Prof. Michael Bruno*. Cambridge: MIT Press, 349–77.

Eckstein, Z., and Y. Weiss. 2003. On the wage growth of immigrants: Israel 1990–2000. Discussion paper 3770. Centre for Economic Policy Research.

Eckstein, Z., and Y. Weiss. 2004. On the wage growth of immigrants: Israel 1990–2000. *Journal of the European Economic Association* 2 (4): 665–95.

Eckstein, Z., and K. I. Wolpin. 1989. Dynamic labour force participation of married women and endogenous work experience. *Review of Economic Studies* 56 (3): 375–90.

Eckstein, Z., and K. I. Wolpin. 1999. Why youth drop out of high school: The impact of preferences, opportunities and abilities. *Econometrica* 67 (6): 1295–1339.

Eyal, Y. 2005. Capsules of information possessed by individuals: Their value in estimating the effect of public intervention programs. Mimeo. Hebrew University.

Farber, H. S., and R. Gibbons. 1996. Learning and wage dynamics. *Quarterly Journal of Economics* 111 (4): 1007–47.

Fertig, M., and C. Schmidt. 2002. Mobility within Europe: What do we (still not) know? Discussion paper 447. Institute for the Study of Labor (IZA).

Flinn, C., and J. J. Heckman. 1982. New methods for analyzing structural models of labor force dynamics. *Journal of Econometrics* 18 (1): 115–68.

Flug, K., N. Kasir, and G. Ofer. 1992. The absorption of Soviet immigrants into the labor market from 1990 onwards: Aspects of occupational substitution and retention. Discussion paper 9213. Bank of Israel.

Friedberg, R. M. 2000. You can't take it with you? Immigrant assimilation and the portability of human capital. *Journal of Labor Economics* 18 (2): 221–51.

Friedberg, R. M. 2001. The impact of mass migration on the Israeli labor market. *Quarterly Journal of Economics* 116 (4): 1373–1408.

Gandal, N., G. Hanson, and M. J. Slaughter. 2004. Technology, trade, and adjustment to immigration in Israel. *European Economic Review* 48 (2): 403–28.

Gotlibovski, M. 1997. Absorption of 1990–92 immigrants in Israel: Interaction between housing and labor markets. PhD dissertation. Tel Aviv University (Hebrew).

Gould, E. D., and O. Moav. 2008. When is "too much" inequality not enough? The selection of Israeli emigrants. Discussion paper 6955. Centre for Economic Policy Research.

Gustafsson, B. 2000. Comments on high skill immigration: Some lessons from Israel. *Swedish Economic Policy Review* 7 (2): 157–61.

Heckman, J. J., R. J. LaLonde, and J. A. Smith. 1999. The economics and econometrics of active labor market programs. In A. Ashenfelter and D. Card, eds., *Handbook of Labor Economics*, vol. 3A. Amsterdam: North Holland, 1865–2097.

Heckman, J. J., L. Lochner, and C. Taber. 1997. Explaining rising wage inequality: Explanations with a dynamic equilibrium model of labor earnings with heterogeneous agents. Unpublished manuscript.

Heckman, J. J., and B. Singer. 1984. A method for minimizing the impact of distributional assumptions in econometric models for duration data. *Econometrica* 52 (2): 271–320.

Helpman, E. 2004. *The Mystery of Economic Growth*. Cambridge: Belknap Press of Harvard University Press.

Hercowitz, Z., and E. Yashiv. 2002. A macroeconomic experiment in mass immigration. Discussion paper 475. Institute for the Study of Labor (IZA).

Hotz, V. J., and R. A. Miller. 1988. An empirical analysis of life cycle fertility and female labor supply. *Econometrica* 56 (1): 91–118.

Israel Social Science Data Center (ISDC) at the Hebrew University of Jerusalem. Economic Time Series for Israel, 1982–2001.

Jacobson, L., R. J. LaLonde, and D. Sullivan. 1993. Earning losses of displaced workers. *American Economic Review* 83 (4): 685–709.

Jorgenson, D., and Z. Griliches. 1967. The explanation of productivity change. *Review of Economic Studies* 34 (3): 249–83.

Juhn, C., K. M. Murphy, and B. Pierce. 1993. Wage inequality and the rise in returns to skill. *Journal of Political Economy* 101 (3): 410–42.

Katz, K. 1997. Gender, wages and discrimination in the USSR: A study of a Russian industrial town. *Cambridge Journal of Economics* 21 (4): 431–52.

Keane, M. P., and K. I. Wolpin. 1994. The solution and estimation of discrete choice dynamic programming models by simulation and interpolation: Monte Carlo evidence. *Review of Economics and Statistics* 76 (4): 648–72.

Keane, M. P., and K. I. Wolpin. 1997. The career decisions of young men. *Journal of Political Economy* 105 (3): 473–522.

Kheimets, N. G., and A. D. Epstein. 2001. The role of English as a central component of success in the professional and social integration of immigrant scientists from the former Soviet Union in Israel. *Language in Society* 30 (2): 187–215.

Kugler, A., and R. M. Sauer. 2005. Doctors without borders: The returns to an occupational license for Soviet immigrant physicians in Israel. *Journal of Labor Economics* 23 (3): 437–66.

LaLonde, R. J., and R. H. Topel. 1991. Immigrants in the American labor market: Quality, assimilation and distributional effects. *American Economic Review* 81 (2): 297–302.

LaLonde, R. J., and R. H. Topel. 1997. Economic impact of international migration and the economic performance of migrants. In M. R. Rosenzweig and O. Stark, eds., *Handbook of Population and Family Economics*, vol. 1B. Amsterdam: North Holland, 799–847.

McFadden, D. 1989. A method of simulated moments for estimation of discrete response models without numerical integration. *Econometrica* 57 (5): 995–1026.

Miller, R. A. 1984. Job matching and occupational choice. *Journal of Political Economy* 92 (6): 1086–1120.

Mincer, J. 1974. *Schooling, Experience and Earnings.* New York: Columbia University Press.

Ministry of the Interior. Population Registry, 2000.

Mortensen, D. 1986. Job search and labor market analysis. In O. Ashenfelter and R. Layard, eds., *Handbook of Labor Economics*, vol. 2. Amsterdam: North Holland, 849–919.

Neal, D. 1995. Industry-specific human capital: Evidence from displaced workers. *Journal of Labor Economics* 13 (4): 653–77.

Razin, A., and E. Sadka. 1993. *The Economy of Modern Israel: Malaise and Promise.* Chicago: University of Chicago Press.

Reder, M. 1957. *Labor in a Growing Economy*. New York: Wiley.

Remennick, L. 2005. Immigration, gender, and psychosocial adjustment: A study of 150 immigrant couples in Israel. *Sex Roles* 53 (11–12): 847–63.

Rust, J. 1994. Structural estimation of Markov decision problems. In R. Engle and D. McFadden, eds., *Handbook of Econometrics*, vol. 4. Amsterdam: North Holland, 3081–3143.

Sauer, R. M. 1998. Job mobility and the market for lawyers. *Journal of Political Economy* 106 (1): 147–71.

Sicherman, N. 1991. Over education in the labor market. *Journal of Labor Economics* 9 (2): 101–22.

Solow, R. M. 1956. A contribution to the theory of economic growth. *Quarterly Journal of Economics* 70 (1): 65–94.

Sussman, Z. 1998. Impact of the immigration on the economic situation of the veteran population. In M. Sikron and E. Leshem, eds., *Profile of an Immigration Wave: The Absorption Process of Immigrants from the Former Soviet Union, 1990–1995*. Jerusalem: Magness Press, Hebrew University.

Todd, P., and K. I. Wolpin. 2006. Assessing the impact of a school subsidy program in Mexico: Using a social experiment to validate a dynamic behavioral model of child schooling and fertility. *American Economic Review* 96 (5): 1384–1417.

Tolts, M. 2009. Demography: Soviet Union, the Russian Federation and other successor states. In *Jewish Women: A Comprehensive Historical Encyclopedia*. Jewish Women's Archive. http://jwa.org/encyclopedia/article/demography-soviet-union-russian-federation-and-other-successor-states.

Van der Klaauw, W. 1996. Female labour supply and marital status decisions: A life-cycle model. *Review of Economic Studies* 63 (2): 199–235.

Weiss, Y. 1986. The determination of life-time earnings: A survey. In O. Ashenfelter and R. Layard, eds., *Handbook of Labor Economics*, vol. 1. Amsterdam: North Holland, 603–40.

Weiss, Y. 2000. High skill immigration: Some lessons from Israel. *Swedish Economic Policy Review* 7 (2): 127–55.

Weiss, Y., and M. Gotlibovski. 1995. Immigration, search and loss of skill. Working Paper 34-95. Sackler Institute for Economic Studies.

Weiss, Y., R. M. Sauer, and M. Gotlibovski. 2003. Immigration, search and loss of skill. *Journal of Labor Economics* 21 (3): 557–92.

Welch, F. 1969. Linear synthesis of skill distribution. *Journal of Human Resources* 4 (3): 311–27.

Wolpin, K. I. 1992. The determinants of black-white differences in early employment careers: Search, layoffs, quits and endogenous wage growth. *Journal of Political Economy* 100 (3): 535–60.

Young, A. 1995. The tyranny of numbers: Confronting the statistical realities of East Asian growth experience. *Quarterly Journal of Economics* 110 (3): 641–80.

Index